KEYGUIDE TO INFORMATION SOURCES IN

Animal Rights

Charles R. Magel

MANSELL

McFARLAND

First published 1989 by
Mansell Publishing Limited, *A Cassell Imprint*
Artillery House, Artillery Row, London SW1P 1RT, England

Published in the United States of America by
McFarland & Company, Inc., Publishers
Box 611, Jefferson NC 28640.

British Library Cataloguing in Publication Data

Magel, Charles R.
  Keyguide to information sources in animal rights.
  1. Animals. Treatment by man. Ethical aspects. Information
sources
  I. Title
  179'.3'07

  ISBN 0-7201-1984-7

Library of Congress Cataloging-in-Publication Data

Magel, Charles R.
  Keyguide to information sources in animal rights/Charles
  R. Magel.
      p.   cm.
  Bibliography: p.
  Includes index.
  ISBN 0-89950-405-1
  1. Animals, Treatment of—Bibliography.   2. Animal
experimentation—Bibliography.   3. Vegetarianism—Moral and
ethical aspects—Bibliography.   4. Animals, Treatment of—
Societies, etc.—Directories.   II. Title.
  Z7164.C45M36   1988
  [HV4708]
  016.179'3—dc19   88-21574
                                               CIP

This book has been printed and bound in Great Britain:
typeset in 10/12 pt Compugraphic Baskerville by Colset Private Limited, Singapore
and printed and bound at the University Press, Cambridge.

KEYGUIDE TO INFORMATION SOURCES IN
Animal Rights

I dedicate this work to Henry S. Salt.

Contents

Introduction

The animal rights movement began in the early 1970s. As early as 1964 Ruth Harrison's *Animal machines: The new factory farming industry* [87] had aroused public indignation in Great Britain. It wasn't until 1971, however, with the publication of a collection of essays edited by Stanley and Roslind Godlovitch and John Harris [97] that the movement had a manifesto. Richard D. Ryder, in his seminal *Victims of science* [114] published in 1975, used the term "speciesism" to refer to discrimination against other species and criticized experiments on animals which were not intended to benefit the individual animal serving as subject of the experiment. By 1975, Peter Singer's *Animal liberation* [103] [115] had argued that all animals are equal, and Tom Regan's "The moral basis of vegetarianism" [112] had developed a theory of moral rights for animals. Since 1975, there has been an avalanche of animal rights literature, not only in philosophy but also in the life sciences, medicine, law, education, religion, the social sciences, literature, and other fields. On the subject of the moral status of animals, it is possible that more has been written during the past eighteen years than in all years prior.

Like all movements, the animal rights movement has its precursors. In the sixth century BC Pythagoras, the Greek philosopher and mathematician, argued for vegetarianism [1]. Plutarch, in the first and second centuries, argued that animals should be treated with justice [2]. In the third century the Neoplatonist Porphyry [3] concluded that consistency requires that we apply justice to both humans and animals. Thomas Tryon, in the seventeenth century, using a Christian theological framework, was perhaps the first English writer to use the term "rights" in relation to animals [4]-[6]. James Granger's 1773 sermon, *An apology for the brute creation* [11], profoundly influenced Arthur Broome, one of the founders of the Society for the Prevention of Cruelty to Animals (later, the RSPCA). Lewis Gompertz, another founder of the SPCA, found it necessary to serve as publisher of his own abstract, tightly-reasoned *Moral inquiries on the situation of man and brutes* [24], arguing for the equality of all sentient beings. Jeremy Bentham and John Stuart Mill emphasized that animals were to be included in the utilitarian calculus; however, most of their discussions about animals were restricted to footnotes. Essays by Frances Power Cobbe [48] and Anna Kingsford [37] [38] were historically important for the nineteenth-century anti-vivisection movement. Henry S. Salt's important *Animals' rights* [49], published in 1892, was largely ignored, as were most of Salt's other works on animals. Zoologist J. Howard Moore's *The universal kinship* [65] and *The new ethics* [66], arguing for the rights of animals on the basis of evolutionary kinship, continue as little known today as they were when published in 1906 and 1907. Albert Schweitzer's reverence-for-life principle [74] has profoundly inspired many but has received little attention from philosophers, until recently.

The British and American anti-vivisection movements of the nineteenth century and the first half of the twentieth century were motivated by deep concern for the welfare of animal subjects, but in the absence of philosophical underpinning they were unable to rebut, effectively, the charges of "sentimentality," "anti-science," "ignorance of science," and "fear of science" brought by proponents of the rapidly-growing biological and medical sciences. To the extent that prevention-of-cruelty societies and humane societies and other animal protection organizations have been based on the following imperatives, they have not been able to sustain a strong stand in defense of animals: (1) Do not be cruel to animals! (2) Be kind to animals! (3) Treat animals humanely! (4) Do not cause animals unnecessary suffering!

The term "animal" in the title of this *Keyguide* is used in the biological sense to include all human and nonhuman animals. A working definition of "animal" as "organism possessing sensory and spontaneous-movement capacities" is probably sufficient to identify the intended referents of the term. Included are birds, fish, humans, bees, squirrels, lobsters, porpoises, snakes, and turtles, etc. However, it must be kept in mind that the term "animal" is ambiguous in ordinary usage. It is often used to mean "nonhuman animal." It is sometimes popularly used to mean "mammal," excluding birds and fish. These ambiguities pervade the animal rights literature, and also this *Keyguide*. The reader should be able to tell from contexts the intended meanings.

The expression "animal rights" is fundamentally an ethical term; consequently the issue of animal rights is essentially a philosophical issue. It is impossible, in a paragraph, to give a precise statement of the animal rights position. However, it is helpful to isolate several themes recurrent in the literature:

(1) The lives of animals – human and nonhuman – have significant value.
(2) Animals – nonhuman and human – have sentience (the capacity to enjoy and suffer, to experience pleasure and pain), desires, and interests.
(3) To obstruct an animal – human or nonhuman – in the pursuit of its interests is to harm that animal. To cause pain or distress or suffering or misery or terror

in an animal, unless to benefit that animal, is to harm that animal. To mutilate an animal, unless to benefit that animal, is to harm that animal. To kill an animal, unless to benefit that animal, is to harm that animal.

(4) We have a duty not to harm animals – nonhuman and human.

(5) Animals – human and nonhuman – have a right not to be harmed by us.

Each of these categorical statements is subject to interpretation. Some animal rightists may not maintain all five or may vary the emphases among them. These statements are suggested as a ''litmus test'' to determine the meaning and strength of any animal rights view under consideration.

Given the recency of the animal rights movement and the voluminous flow of its controversial literature, extending into many disciplines, the bibliographer must resort to unorthodox methods. Standard types of sources (bibliographies, encyclopedias, dictionaries, abstracts, indexes, catalogues, atlases, directories, data bases, etc.) are either non-existent or in early stages of development or too diffuse to be of much value. For example, the United States Library of Congress does not use the heading ''Animal rights''; the most relevant heading is ''Animals, Treatment of.'' Following the author's intensive, three-year study of the animal rights literature, this *Keyguide* took over the task of organizing itself.

It is important to clarify what this *Keyguide* is not. It is not a guide to the complete animal rights literature; it is selective. It does not cover the non-English-language literature (except for several items discovered in the course of studying the English-language literature). As a result, the literature published in the United States, the United Kingdom, Canada, and Australia and New Zealand predominates. It does not cover all topics embraced by the animal rights issue. It does not significantly cover recreational uses of animals, conservation, use of animals for labor, and literary or artistic works on animals.

Part I presents an overview of the literature, arranged by disciplines: philosophy, science and medicine, education, law, and religion; also the topic of vegetarianism. Within each discipline the arrangement is roughly chronological. Included are not only many of the annotated items from Part II but also publications less directly related to animal rights, also works opposed to animal rights. All non-annotated items referred to in Part I are listed in Literature Cited (following Part III). Numbers within square brackets (for example ''[232]'') refer the reader to entries in Part II or Part III. Author–date citations (for example ''J. Hick (1978)'') refer the user to items listed in Literature Cited. The notation ''⟨   ⟩'' is used to indicate either when a work was written or when it was first published (for example ''I. Kant (⟨1785⟩ 1962)'').

Part II is an annotated bibliography arranged chronologically. It contains major works in defense of, or tending toward, or consistent with, or historically important for animal rights. The reader should be able to trace the historical flow of ideas preceding the animal rights movement (entries [1]–[95]) as well as those after 1970 (entries [96]–[335]). The annotations are intended both to describe the works and also, indirectly, to provide a conceptual guide to animal rights issues.

The last twelve entries ([324]–[335]) are not in strict chronological order; they were discovered after the numerical sequence was established.

Part III contains a selected list of organizations of two types: (1) international and regional, and (2) national. Included are not only those which adopt a strong animal rights position but those which from various perspectives are concerned with animal welfare. Detailed information is provided for a number of organizations in English-speaking nations. Little information is given on organizations in other countries. The omission of an organization from this list should not be interpreted as an indication that it is any less important than organizations selected.

Acknowledgements

For inspiration, I would like to thank Henry Salt, Albert Schweitzer, and the animals.

For philosophical enlightenment, I would like to thank Tom Regan and Peter Singer. My students in Animal Rights classes at Moorhead State University, Moorhead, Minnesota, were honored by their visits. If a student interested in animal rights were to ask what to study, my advice would be: first, read all the works by Regan and Singer; then read all the responses to their works; and then read whatever you wish.

For editorial advice and assistance, I would like to thank Colin Hutchens, Commissioning Editor at Mansell Publishing Limited, and Mary Struck.

Librarians in the London Library and the British Library were most helpful in my study of nineteenth-century British publications. I am deeply indebted to the library staff – especially Jim Moore – at the University of California San Diego for professional informational assistance during my two-year "residence" in the architectural jewel housing the Central Library collection; also my gratitude to the librarians at the Biomedical Library. Other libraries utilized were: University of California Los Angeles, University of California Berkeley, University of California Davis, and the University of Minnesota (especially the Owen H. Wangensteen Historical Library under the curatorship of Judith Overmier). The services of the San Diego Public Library, especially the Inter-Library Loan Department and the Pacific Beach Branch, were invaluable.

I would like to thank those who so generously kept me well-informed about their publications and the writings of others: Alan Bowd, Silvana Castignone, Stephen Clark, Daniel Dombrowski, Michael A. Fox, Michael W. Fox, Ruth Friedman, Michael Giannelli, Clive Hollands, Andrew Linzey, Randall Lockwood, Tom Regan, Bernard Rollin, Andrew Rowan, Richard Ryder, Steve Sapontzis,

Robert Sharpe, Peter Singer, Henry Spira, Kim Stallwood, John Stockwell, Bernard Unti, and Peter Wenz.

Assistance in translations was kindly given by Elli Sorensen, Otto Sorensen and Hannelore Wierschin.

Had it not been for Bruce Gilden, the computer no doubt would have mastered me rather than I it. Betty and Ernest Boldrick were most gracious in maintaining electronic backup copies of the manuscript to insure against California earthquake or fire or flood.

PART I

Overview of the animal rights literature

Note

The United States *Library of Congress subject headings* does not contain the headings "Animal rights" or "Animal welfare." The heading most directly related to animal rights is "Animals, Treatment of" which includes subheadings: "Hunting," "Pets," "Trapping," "Vivisection," "Animals, Cruelty to," "Animals, Protection of," "Humane treatment of animals," "Kindness to animals," "Mistreatment of animals," "Neglect of animals," "Prevention of cruelty to animals," "Ethics." Other relevant headings: "Animal behavior," "Animal intelligence," "Laboratory animals," "Vegetarianism."

The *Subject guide to books in print* (also BIPS database), published by R. R. Bowker, New York, is a useful source of books in print in the United States. Relevant headings: "Animal communication," "Animal ecology," "Animal industry," "Animal intelligence," "Animals," "Animals and civilization," "Animals – Juvenile literature," "Animals – Poetry," "Domestic animals," "Laboratory animals," "Animals, Treatment of," "Vivisection," "Animals in art," "Animals in literature."

1 Philosophy and Animals

The *Philosopher's Index* (also DIALOG database), issued quarterly, covers English-language journals and books, also major philosophy journals in other languages. Relevant headings: "Animals," "Animal rights," "Animal experimentation," "Environmental ethics," "Vegetarianism."

Through 1970

There are no extant writings by Pythagoras (6th cent. BC) who argues for vegetarianism on the basis of transmigration of souls among humans and animals. About Pythagoras: W. K. C. Guthrie (1962, 181–95), D. A. Dombrowski [214, pp. 35–53], D. Laertius (⟨3rd cent.⟩ 1958, bk. 8). Poetic versions of Pythagorean philosophy: Ovid [1] and J. Dryden (⟨1700⟩ 1958). Empedocles (5th cent. BC) is committed to reincarnation and vegetarianism (K. Freeman 1962, Empedocles' fragments 127–39 from Diels) (W. K. C. Guthrie 1965, 244–65). Herodotus (⟨5th cent. BC⟩ 1961, vol. 2, chaps. 65–76) provides an interesting account of the Egyptian veneration for animals.

Plato draws sharp distinction between the rational soul of humans and appetitive soul of animals (Plato ⟨5th–4th cents. BC⟩ 1961, *Republic*, bk. 4, 435a–42e), claims superior rational humans naturally rule over inferior appetitive animals (*Statesman*, 271e), and characterizes animal existence as "beastly," sexually wanton, lawless, murderous, warlike (*Republic*, bk. 9, 571a–77e). D. A. Dombrowski (1984a) argues Plato is sympathetic to vegetarianism as an ideal.

Aristotle claims animals with the lower type sensitive soul are to serve the purposes of humans with the higher type rational soul, heavily influencing the Western anthropocentric view of animals (Aristotle ⟨4th cent. BC⟩ 1908–52, *De partibus animalium*, bk. 1, chap. 1, 641a 35–641b 10; *De anima*, bk. 2 chap. 3, 414a

28–415a 10). He defends property in human slaves and animal slaves on grounds that both types lack rationality (*Politica*, bk. 1, chaps. 4–5). Aristotle discusses extensively physiology, psychology, the principle of continuity in the scale of organisms (*De partibus animalium* and *De generatione animalium*).

The Stoics (3rd cent. BC–2nd cent. AD) conclude that since animals have no reason they exist for the use of humans and have no rights. On the Stoics: M. T. Cicero (⟨1st cent. BC⟩ 1887, *The nature of the gods*, bk. 2, chap. 14) and E. V. Arnold (1958, 274). In *Moralia* [2] Plutarch, in the first or second century, argues for rationality of animals and vegetarianism. Porphyry's third-century *On abstinence from animal food* [3] is important, providing his and others' views of the nature of animals and vegetarianism. On Porphyry: D. A. Dombroski [214] (1984b) and A. Preus (1983).

E. Martinengo-Cesaresco (1904a) (1904b) (1909) explores views and treatment of animals in ancient Greece, Rome, and in the major world religions. L. Bodson (1983) examines attitudes toward animals in Greco-Roman antiquity. J. Passmore (1974, chaps. 1–2) (1975a) (1975b) is very informative on Western philosophical and religious attitudes from Greek antiquity to K. Marx; also a bit on Eastern traditions. R. S. Brumbaugh [130, pp. 6–25] gives brief history of Greek, Roman, Christian, Cartesian, Lockean, Kantian, utilitarian, evolutionist views.

A. O. Lovejoy and G. Boas (⟨1935⟩ 1965) explore early Greek and Roman themes of superiority of animals to humans, considering Plutarch, Seneca, Pliny, Ovid, Cicero, Philo, Menander, Philemon, Diogenes, Democritus, Cynics, Aristotle, Anaximander, Anaxagoras, Xenophon, Diodorus Siculus. U. Dierauer (1977), in a detailed study of animals and humans in the thought of Greek and Roman antiquity, covers Hesiod, Plato and the Academy, Aristotle and the Peripatetics, Theophrastus, Porphyry, Cynics, Epicurus, Stoics, Philo, Plutarch, Celsus, Anaxagoras, Anaximander, Chrysippus, Cicero, Democritus, Diogenes, Galen, Heraclitus, Homer, Neoplatonism, Ovid, Plutarch, Protagoras, Pythagoras, Sextus Empiricus, Sophists, Xenophanes, Xenophon, Zeno.

J. Haussleiter (1935) provides a detailed study of vegetarianism in Greco-Roman antiquity, including discussions of Orphics, Pythagoras, Empedocles, Socrates, Cynics, Diogenes, Plato, Xenocrates, Heraclitus, Carneades, Plutarch, Celsus, Porphyry, Aristotle, Theophrastus, Stoics, Seneca, Epictetus, Marcus Aurelius, Epicurus, Polystratos, Neoplatonism, Julian. W. E. H. Lecky (⟨1859⟩ 1869, vol. 2, 170–88) discusses early Roman and Greek views of animals (Pythagoras, Xenocrates, Plutarch, Empedocles, Porphyry) as well as legends of Christian saints about animals.

A. Augustine shows little sensitivity to animal pain (⟨4th or 5th cent.⟩ 1966, 102, 105), relying upon interpretation of the New Testament and upon the Stoic emphasis on rationality of humans. J. Hick (1978, 84–7) critiques Augustine's (1964, 141–2) theodicy in which he attempts to justify animal pain by its spiritual benefit to humans, and also by the pain of animals fitting into the harmonized beauty of the cosmological process.

T. Aquinas, synthesizing Aristotelianism and Christianity, argues irrational animals are instruments for any use humans choose to make of them (⟨13th cent.⟩ 1947, pt. 2 of pt. 2, question 64, art. 1, reply to objection 2). Proscriptions against cruelty to animals are intended to minimize cruelty to humans (1956, bk. 3, chap. 112, pars. 12–13). Rational humans exist for the sake of individual well-being but animals exist only for the sake of the species (1956, bk. 3, chap. 113, par. 1). On Aquinas: R. J. McLaughlin (1985) and J. Barad (1988).

M. Montaigne in the essay "Apology for Raymond Sebond" asserts humans are absurdly arrogant in their attitude toward nature, that humans are no better than the animals (⟨16th cent.⟩ 1958, 331), that animals are much more self-controlled than we (346). In "Of cruelty" (1958, 318): ". . . There is a certain respect, and a general duty of humanity, that attaches us not only to animals, who have life and feeling, but even to trees and plants." G. Boas (1933) discusses theriophily (view that animals are superior to and/or happier than humans) in Montaigne and other French thinkers of the 17th century.

L. C. Rosenfield (⟨1941⟩ 1968) examines the themes of beast-machine and animal soul in French literature from Descartes to La Mettrie; appendices and notes are bibliographic gold mines. G. Boas (1933) studies theriophily in French thought of the 17th century, including Montaigne, Charron, Cureau de la Chambre, La Fontaine, and the satirists: Fontenelle, Cyrano de Bergerac, Boileau, Deshoulières. Boas (1973) gives a short account of theriophily in antiquity, and in Montaigne, G. B. Gelli's *Circe*, Condillac, W. Whitman, J. E. Gill (1969) supplements the accounts of theriophily by A. O. Lovejoy and G. Boas. H. Hastings (1936) continues the study of French thought about animals where G. Boas' book ends, covering the debate for and against human essential superiority to animals, tracing the development of the feeling of compassion for animals in France, and including attacks on hunting, harmful experiments on animals; also discusses vegetarianism.

F. Bacon, emphasizing domination of nature for human benefit, describes animal experiments and safety testing in the utopian "New Atlantis" (⟨1627⟩) 1907, 323–4). On Bacon: B. Klug (1983a) and M. W. Fox (1988). T. Hobbes views animals and humans as interacting collections of minute bodies in motion or at rest, governed by necessary laws of physics; consciousness, pleasure and pain are caused by bodily motions but have no effect on body (epiphenomenalism) (⟨17th cent.⟩ 1962, 1: pt. 4; 3: 1–17). Humans have no more freedom of willing than do animals (1: 408–9). Animals (unlike humans) live in peace by natural inclination and natural consent (2: 66–7; 4: 120–1; 3: 44–5).

R. Descartes views animals as God-created machines (automatons) without consciousness, pleasure or pain, similar in principle to, but much more complicated than, clocks; hence humans are absolved from any suspicion of crime in eating or dissecting or killing animals (⟨17th cent.⟩ 1911–12, *Discourse on the method* 117). See Descartes' letters to Marquess of Newcastle, Henry More, and Plempius for Fromondus (Descartes ⟨17th cent.⟩ 1970). N. Fontaine gives an account of 17th-century experiments on dogs by monks at Port-Royal, utilizing Descartes' automaton theory: "They administered beatings to dogs with perfect indifference. . . . They said that the animals were clocks. . . . They nailed poor animals up on boards by their four paws to vivisect them . . ." (quoted by L. C. Rosenfield ⟨1941⟩ 1968, 54). On Descartes: L. D. Cohen (1936), J. Cottingham (1978), L. C. Rosenfield (1968), K. Gunderson (1964), A. M. Ritchie (1963–64), K. Squadrito (1980), H. Hastings (1936), W. Shugg (1968), N. Malcolm (1977), A. G. A. Balz (1951), G. A. Lindeboom (1978), T. Regan [208, chap. 1], Z. Vendler (1972), G. B. Matthews [128], R. Boakes (1984, 84–92).

B. Spinoza's philosophy, which regards animals and humans as modifications of the one eternal substance, seems to imply a non-anthropocentric view of animals and nature; however, Spinoza condones human use of animals "as much as we wish and treat them as we will, since they do not agree with us in nature" (⟨17th cent.⟩ 1910 *Ethics*, pt. 4, prop. 37, note 1). On Spinoza: A. Naess (1977) (1980), G. Lloyd (1980), and S. R. L. Clark (1987a).

P. Bayle's dictionary (⟨1697⟩ 1734–8) contains three critical discussions on the nature of animals; regards the machine view to be absurd; see "Rorarius," "Sennertus," and "Pereira."

J. Locke argues animals are capable of perceptions, memory and concrete ideas, but not general ideas or reason (⟨1706⟩ 1975, Bk. 2, chap. 1, par. 19; chap. 10, par. 10; chap. 11, pars. 5, 7, 10, 11; chap. 27, par. 5. Bk. 4, chap. 17, par. 1). Humans have God-given dominion over, and property in, animals (⟨1690⟩ 1966, Treatise 1, chap. 4, pars. 21–43. Treatise 2, chap. 2, par. 4; chap. 5, pars. 25–51). See K. M. Squadrito's essays on Locke's view of dominion (1979), on Locke and Descartes on the soul of animals (1980), on why Locke's theory of property cannot be used to substantiate animal property rights (1981).

G. W. Leibniz holds there is no absolute, qualitative difference between animals and humans; the difference is one of degree of perception (⟨1714⟩ 1965, pars. 19–28, 66–84). Animals have sentiency and immortal souls, have particular but not abstract ideas (⟨1716⟩ 1949, 62–3, 68, 145–6, 178, 244–7, 552–3). M. Kulstad (1981) explores Leibniz's views.

D. Hume argues animals are endowed with thought and reason (⟨1740⟩ 1888, bk. 1, pt. 3, sec. 16); discusses pride and humility of animals (bk. 2, pt. 1, sec. 12), love and hatred in animals (bk. 2, pt. 2, sec. 12), superiority of humans to animals mainly due to reason (bk. 3, pt. 3, sec. 4), animals and personal identity (bk. 1, pt. 4, sec. 6), social nature of animals (bk. 2, pt. 2, sec. 5), will and passion of animals (bk. 2, pt. 3, sec. 9), animals and morality (bk.3, pt. 1, sec. 1). Hume (⟨1751⟩ 1946, sec. 3, pt. 1) urges "gentle usage" to animals but denies equality and justice applicable to them. On Hume: S. Mendus (1980) on personal identity; S. R. L. Clark (1985a) on animals and morals; M. J. Seidler (1977) on nature of animals; K. E. Tranöy (1959) on morals, animals and humans.

Descartes' automaton view of animals is sharply attacked by Voltaire: "Answer me, machinist, has nature arranged all the springs of sentiment in this animal that he should not feel?'' (⟨18th cent.⟩ 1962, ''Beasts'' entry; also see ''Viands'' and ''Love''). H. Hastings (1936) and L. C. Rosenfield (⟨1941⟩ 1968) are valuable sources on Voltaire and animals. R. Giraud (1984–85) discusses Voltaire and animal rights.

J. J. Rousseau: Since animals share sensibility with humans ''they ought to partake of natural right; so that mankind is subjected to a kind of obligation even toward the brutes. . . . If I am bound to do no injury to my fellow-creatures, this is less because they are rational than because they are sentient beings'' (⟨1772⟩ 1973, 41–2). R. Giraud (1984–85) discusses Rousseau and animal rights. H. Hastings (1936) makes many references to Rousseau.

I. Kant argues humans, as free rational beings, are never to be treated as mere means but that animals are ''things'' to be used as mere means (⟨1785⟩ 1962, 95–108). Animals have no moral status; we have no direct duties to them; our duty not to be cruel to animals is really a duty to humans (animal cruelty leads to human cruelty; Kant interprets W. Hogarth's famous four engravings ''The four stages of cruelty'' as supporting his view) (⟨1780⟩ 1978, 239–41). On Kant: A. Broadie and E. M. Pybus (1974); T. Regan (1976a); E. M. Pybus and A. Broadie (1978); J. G. Murphy (1972); T. Regan [208, pp. 174–94]; C. Hoff (1983).

W. Paley, finding it difficult to justify a right to the flesh of animals by reason, resorts to God's intention as revealed in scriptures (⟨1785⟩ 1803, 100–8).

D. Harwood (1928) is primarily concerned with the attitude of humans toward animals as expressed in English 18th-century literature. K. Thomas [212] presents a detailed history of human (mainly British) views and attitudes toward animals and nature during the period 1500–1800, providing thousands of references.

J. Bentham, applying hedonistic utilitarianism to all sentient beings, is much concerned about suffering of animals, less concerned about killing. Strongest statement appears in footnote to par. 4, chap. 19 of *Introduction to the principles of morals and legislation* (⟨18th and 19th cents.⟩ 1962, 1: 142–3): ''The day has been . . . in which . . . slaves have been treated by the law exactly upon the same footing as . . . animals are still. The day *may* come, when the rest of the animal creation may acquire those rights which never could have been withholden from them but by the hand of tyranny. . . . A full-grown horse or dog is beyond comparison a more rational . . . animal than an infant. . . . The question is not, Can they *reason*? nor, Can they *talk*? but, *Can they suffer*?'' In *Principles of the civil code*, Pt. 2, chap. 1, par. 4 (1962, 1: 328) Bentham discusses origin of animals as property of humans. Bentham's opposition to animal baiting, hunting, fishing is evident in his discussion of cruelty to animals and humane treatment of animals in pt. 3, chap. 16 of *Principles of penal law* (1962, 1: 562). Bentham's humanity to animals is noted in chap. 1 of *Memoirs of Bentham* (1962, 10: 17). His letter of 4 March 1825 to the *Morning Chronicle* asserts adult dogs and horses and other quadrupeds have much more intelligence and morality than human infants (1962, 10: 549–50). Bentham's fondness of animals (cats, mice, asses) is revealed in chap. 26 of *Memoirs of Bentham* (1962, 11: 80-1). Other comments by Bentham on animals: (1891, 66, 425, 428-9), (1970, 48-50, 35 (note), 138), (1962, 10: 550). W. Whewell (1852, 223-5) attempts to reduce to absurdity Bentham's utilitarianism which "would make it our duty to increase the pleasure of pigs or of geese rather than that of men, if we were sure that the pleasures we could give them were greater than the pleasures of men."

G. W. F. Hegel argues animals have no right to their life because they cannot think and therefore cannot will (⟨1821⟩ 1958, 43, 47, 227, 236-7; ⟨1807⟩ 1978, 229; ⟨1830⟩ 1970, chap. 3, 102-213).

A. Schopenhauer, who views animals and humans as essentially of the same nature – will objectifying itself as body – discusses similarities and differences between humans and animals (⟨1819⟩ 1958, 1: 35-50, 83-5, 114-19, 130-3, 150-2, 296-301, 372 note; 2: 59-62, 203-7, 342-3, 482-3), (⟨1813⟩ 1974, 70-4, 110-11, 145-47, 252-3). Denounces Kant's view of animals as things revolting and abominable; regards the failure of the Western world to acknowledge duties to animals morally barbaric (⟨1841⟩ 1965, 80-3, 94-7, 150-2, 175-82), (⟨1850⟩ 1974, 2: 297-8, 370-7), (⟨1839⟩ 1985, 32-41). S. Walker (1983, chap. 1) discusses views of animals held by Descartes, Locke, Hume, Kant, Hegel, Schopenhauer.

J. S. Mill applies utilitarianism (actions are right in proportion as they tend to promote happiness/pleasure, wrong as they tend to produce the reverse) to the whole sentient creation (⟨19th cent.⟩ 1963-1986, 3: 952; 10: 167-89, 209-14, 398-9; 24: 925, 952-4; 25: 1172-3). On J. Bentham and J. S. Mill: H. B. Acton (1961) and W. E. H. Lecky (⟨1859⟩ 1869, 1: 47-50).

The role of animals in 19th-century English life, how they serve as metaphors for human psychological needs and sociopolitical aspirations, are studied in H. Ritvo's (1987) work, with topics including the nature of animals as perceived by the British, cattle, pets, natural history, rabies control, compassion for animals, protection of animals, animal experimentation, humane movement (especially RSPCA), zoos, big game hunting.

F. Nietzsche has few comments specifically on animals (⟨19th cent.⟩ 1964, 5: 149-55; 7: 225-7; 9: 258; 10: 105, 200). Nietzsche's use of animal imagery is explored by T. J. Reed (1978).

F. H. Bradley (⟨1876⟩ 1927, 32) suggests "a time would seem coming when we shall hear of the 'rights of the beast.' Why not, in Heaven's name? Why is the beast not a subject of right, civil, at least, if not political?" T. H. Green (⟨1885⟩ 1960, 45-6, 207) claims animals cannot have rights because they have no capacity of free action, no conception of a common good. Admitting animals to be sentient, conscious, capable of enjoying or suffering, intelligent, J. B. Austin (1887, 445-71) argues against cruelty and for kindness to animals so they will best serve humans in God's established order.

J. Rickaby (⟨1888⟩ 1918) claims animals are things, chattels; we have no duties of any kind to animals "as neither to sticks and stones"; they exist for us, not for themselves (see [121, pp. 179-80]). Animals cannot have rights because they have no rational will (1902, 134). F. P. Cobbe (1895) attacks the views of Rickaby and G. Tyrrell; Tyrrell replies (1895). The controversy between Cobbe and Rickaby–Tyrrell is discussed in relation to modern animal rights theory by D. A. Dombroski (1985).

S. Butler (⟨1890⟩ 1967, 209–44): "... Animals not only know what's what themselves, but can impart to one another any new what's-whatness that they may have acquired." In *Erewhon*, Butler (⟨1872⟩ 1970, chaps. 26, 27) satirically and humorously considers the rights of animals and the rights of vegetables; it is not obvious what interpretation Butler intends.

W. James (⟨1890⟩ 1981, 2: 973–83) agrees with G. J. Romanes that animals have "recepts" – general ideas which are not analyzed or defined but only imagined, formed spontaneously, without any intentional comparing or sifting or combining. James' (⟨1891⟩ 1948, 73) language suggests a direct duty to animals: "Take any demand, however slight, which any creature, however weak, may make. Ought it not, for it own sake, to be satisfied? If not, prove why not."

P. Carus attacks vegetarianism (1898), attacks "the immorality of the anti-vivisection movement," claims "vivisection . . . is a moral obligation" and that "truth is more than life. . . . Truth is more even than liberty" (1897). R. N. Foster (1897) replies: Humans "may not justify any means whatever of acquiring knowledge. One can acquire knowledge by torturing his neighbor, or his own wife or child, but he is not at liberty morally so to do."

H. S. Salt, although not a professional philosopher, in 1900 was probably the first to publish an essay on animal rights in a philosophical journal [55], such essay based on his important book *Animals' rights* [49]. D. G. Ritchie's (⟨1894⟩ 1952, 107–11) (1900) criticism is answered by Salt (1900). Ritchie argues our duty to animals is a duty to human society. Although heavily ignored by his contemporaries, Salt's works are amazingly modern in concept and argument, and are historically of great importance: [45] [47] [51] [54] [55] [58] [59] [61] [67]–[69] [77] [78] (1930).

L. T. Hobhouse, British philosopher and sociologist, theorizes mind may be the essential driving force in all evolutionary change; extensively discusses mental capacities of humans and animals (1901).

His life an inspiring exemplar of "der Ehrfurcht vor dem Leben," A. Schweitzer discusses reverence for life in *The philosophy of civilization*, first published in 1923 [74, pp. 307–44]. Schweitzer's (1949) autobiography is informative. Five collections of writings by Schweitzer (1950) (1965) (1961, chap. 7) (1980) (1982) are illuminating on reverence for life. J. Brabazon (1975, chap. 16) and A. Linzey [175, pp. 117–25] explain reverence for life. P. Shepard (1974) critiques Schweitzer's reverence-for-life view from an ecological perspective.

J. Dewey (1926) argues experimenters have not only moral right but duty to promote human welfare by experiments on animals, and not on humans, that agitation for legal restriction is mainly an expression of opposition to scientific inquiry due to misunderstanding, envy, dread of science. Claims much more suffering in slaughter houses than in laboratories.

L. Nelson's lecture "Duties to animals" [75], written prior to 1927, arguing for animal rights on basis of animal interests, is probably the first systematic essay by a professional philosopher defending animal rights. Nelson's argument is sympathetically discussed by W. Brockhaus [333] and critically analyzed by R. G. Frey (1979) (1980).

W. D. Ross (1930, 48-54) argues we have duties to animals (and human infants) but seems to deny animals have rights against us because of his apparent acceptance of correlativity of rights and duties. J. P. Plamenatz (1938, 92-3), defining a right as a power which a creature ought to have and which rational creatures ought to secure for it, claims it incontestable that animals can have rights. The use of anthropomorphism in psychology is discussed by M. Mandelbaum (1943).

R. G. Collingwood (1946, 227): "The idea that man, apart from his self-conscious historical life, is different from the rest of creation in being a rational animal is a mere superstition." Among humans, rationality is a matter of degree. A flickering rationality cannot be denied to animals. "There are even among non-human animals the beginnings of historical life: for example, among cats . . . taught by their mothers."

P. Weiss (1947, 119, 127-8, 239, 252-62, 267), agreeing with C. Darwin that reason does not radically distinguish humans from animals, argues that being a self (which is constant, active, concerned, unique, beneficial to the body, responsible, sensitive to values) is what distinguishes all humans (including idiots and infants) from animals – a self which is concerned with the good of all beings.

B. A. G. Fuller (1949) notes the tendency of Western philosophical traditions to ignore the existence and nature of animals. According to H. B. Acton (1950, 108-10) there is hesitation to recognize legal rights for animals because to do so would imply animals are persons, which would raise serious questions about our hunting and eating animals.

L. Wittgenstein makes several cryptic comments on the nature of animals (1953, pt. 1, sects. 25, 495, 647; pt. 2, pp. 174e, 184e, 223e, 229e). Wittgenstein's thesis that thinking is impossible without language would imply that languageless animals cannot think (Malcolm 1967). H. L. A. Hart (1955) asserts that talk of rights of animals or babies makes idle use of the expression "right" since the wrongness of ill-treating animals can adequately be handled in terms of violating our duty. R. J. Pumphrey (1954) asserts the evidence is decisive that animals think in the way that we do, and that in both animals and ourselves, thinking depends on the ability to accept experience in the form of rules, by which expectation is usually fulfilled.

B. Russell (1956, chaps. 2, 3, 12) accepts the hypothesis of mental continuity throughout organic evolution. Animals "*may* have minds in which all sorts of things take place, but we can know nothing about their minds except by inferences from their actions. . . . Actions alone must be the test of the desires of animals" (62); satisfactory explanation of desires in animals and in humans is fundamentally the same. Entertains possibility of animals having image-propositions, belief-feelings, bare assent to propositions not expressed in words (241–51).

According to P. Geach (1957, 17) it is misleading to say animals have concepts like us or to call the noises made by animals "language." Critiques of Geach: J. King-Farlow and E. A. Hall (1965) and J. King-Farlow (1978). G. E. M. Anscombe (1958, 5) admits animals may have intentions but they cannot express them for lack of language or other suitable conventional devices. S. Hampshire (1959, 96–100) argues it is senseless to attribute intentions to animals because animals have no concepts, no concept of order, no memory that distinguishes the order of events in the past, no expectation of an order of events in the future. Critiques of Hampshire: T. A. Long (1963) and J. Bennett (1976, 29–31).

R. B. Brandt's (1959, 439–40) definition of "right" implies animals have rights if we have obligations to them. "But why have animals no rights? Of course, they cannot *claim* rights; but inability to claim does not destroy the right. It seems not unnatural to say that animals have rights, for example, the right not be be hurt without some good reason."

J. Rawls (1963, 284), claiming that capability of a sense of justice is a necessary condition for being owed duties of justice, would not recognize rights for animals and probably not for marginal humans.

R. M. Hare (1963, 222–4) argues for universalization of our prescriptions: "Am I prepared to accept a maxim which would allow this to be done to me, were I in the position of this man or animal, and capable of having only the experiences, desires, etc. of him or it?" Applies to bear-baiting. Critiques of Hare: H. S. Silverstein (1974) and T. Goodrich (1969, 129).

J. Bennett (1964) argues language is necessary for rationality; bees' dances are not language; bees not rational since their behavior not rule-guided. Critiques of Bennett: J. King-Farlow and E. A. Hall (1965) and A. W. Collins (1968). As a result of R. Kirk's (1967) critique, Bennett (1976, 28, 109) seems to admit the possibility of rationality without language, and also beliefs without language.

H. J. McCloskey (1965): Animals cannot have rights because they cannot possess things, and because they can have no interests (because having an interest requires possessor to care or be concerned about that in which there is an interest). McCloskey (1969, 235): ". . . It is persons and not animals who merit respect. . . . We cannot without absurdity speak of a duty to respect animals."

U. T. Place (1966, 101–2) argues it makes sense to attribute consciousness to animals and there are no good reasons for supposing that consciousness is a process that cannot be described in physical terms.

M. J. Adler (1967, chap. 17), concerned that if C. Darwin be correct in holding that humans and animals differ only in degree then we have no principled moral reason for treating animals differently from humans, claims humans are radically, qualitatively different in that they alone possess an immaterial power of freedom of choice associated with rationality – a freedom independent of causal laws. Animal intelligence is entirely sensory, not conceptual. This human difference, along with the normative principle "*an inferior kind ought to be ordered to a superior kind as a means to an end*" (266), justifies "the almost universal moral conviction that there is nothing reprehensible in the killing and exploitation of animals" (267). M. W. Fox (1985) regards Adler's view "bio-fascist."

By 1975 P. Singer and T. Regan will have taken exception to S. I. Benn's (1967a, 40) claims: "No one claims equal consideration for all mammals – human beings count, mice do not, though it would not be easy to say *why* not. . . . Although we hesitate to inflict unnecessary pain on sentient creatures, such as mice or dogs, we are quite sure that we do not need to show good reasons for putting human interests before theirs . . . Not to possess human shape *is* a disqualifying condition. However faithful or intelligent a dog may be, it would be monstrous sentimentality to attribute to him interests that could be weighed in an equal balance with those of human beings." Because of the characteristically human enterprise of freely choosing, responsibly, among ways of life open to one, making of oneself something worthy of one's own respect, it seems reasonable to treat humans as more important than dogs. Since rationality is normal for the human species it is unfair to exploit the deficiencies of the imbecile who falls short of the norm, but it is not unfair to exploit the dog since irrationality is normal for dogs. Benn (1967b) additionally comments on animals.

The Nature of Animals

The factual question *What are the basic characteristics (especially mental qualities) of animals?* needs to be answered before tackling the question *Do animals have rights, and if so what rights?* For scientists' views on the nature of animals see chapter 2. See bibliography by C. R. Magel [176, entries 51–196, 453–988].

D. Gustafson (1971) explores the natural expressions of intention by animals in response to the question raised by L. Wittgenstein (1953, pt. 1, sect. 647). Z. Vendler (1972, 160–4) argues animals do not really think or have thoughts since real thought is propositional in a speech–act sense.

N. Malcolm (⟨1972–73⟩ 1977) argues nonlinguistic animals can think but cannot have thoughts; see critiques of Malcolm by D. D. Weiss (1975), G. B. Matthews [128], D. Davidson (1985), and J. King-Farlow (1978), who criticizes philosophical psychology for supporting in an a priori fashion an "unbridgeable chasm between man and the animal kingdom."

M. Midgley analyzes the misuse of the concept "beast" which results in distortion of our view of the nature of animals and humans [102]; emphasizes we are not just rather like animals but we *are* animals; demonstrates there is far more order in the animal kingdom than previously imagined, and we are a part of that order [129]; investigates how both sentimentality and brutality play a role in distortions of accurate characterization of animals' feelings and emotions (1979); examines the question: Are animals persons? [246, pp. 52–62].

D. M. Armstrong (1973, 31) argues animals have concepts as well as beliefs. B. Williams (1973, 138) asserts animals have beliefs in a "somewhat impoverished sense" without effective concepts. T. Nagel (1974) raises the question of what it is like to be an experiencing bat; L-M. Russow (1982) responds. J. Margolis (1975)

(1978) asserts we ascribe beliefs to animals in a way that depends on a heuristic use of a model of linguistic utterances.

P. Singer discusses the following topics in relation to the nature of animals: sentience, the capacity for pleasure and pain [115, chap. 1], consciousness, self-consciousness, intentions, personhood in animals [170]; types of animal lives: non-conscious, conscious but not self-conscious; self-conscious (persons) [148, chaps. 3-5].

Anthropomorphism is discussed by J. Benson (1975). R. Rorty (1979, 190-1) considers pre-linguistic awareness in pigs, claiming that we send pigs to the slaughter house with equanimity because the pig's face is the wrong shape for us to imagine it talking to us, claiming moral prohibitions against hurting human babies and better-looking animals are not based on their possession of feelings but on our imagined possibility of their talking to us, of their asking for help. D. A. Dombrowski (1983) responds.

S. P. Stich (1979) argues animals have beliefs but without expressible content; T. Regan [208, pp. 35-8, 49-61] responds. C. Kagan (1979) examines the notion of the rationality of animals.

R. G. Frey (1980) argues animals have no desires because they have no beliefs because they they have no propositions because they have no linguistic capacity. T. Regan (1982) attacks Frey's claim that animals cannot have simple desires. Regan [208, pp. 37-49, 67-73] critiques Frey on animal beliefs and desires. Another critique of Frey is by S. F. Sapontzis [303, pp. 115-29].

L. S. Carrier (1980) argues for the intelligibility of ascribing beliefs to language-lacking animals. R. Routley (1981) criticizes a wide range of recent arguments against attributing beliefs and intentionality to animals, including those of S. P. Stich, B. Williams, Descartes, Z. Vendler, N. Malcolm, D. Davidson (1975). J. Bishop (1980) also critiques Davidson. R. Jeffrey (1985) critiques Davidson, and argues for the intelligibility of preference in nonlinguistic, unreflective animals.

B. E. Rollin discusses animal life, awareness, interests, rationality, language, pleasure, pain, concepts, the *telos* of living things [181, pp. 19-42] and extensively considers animal consciousness and pain [241] [270] [298] [318].

S. R. L. Clark finds tendencies in animals to behave in ways suggestive of what we would judge to be moral (or immoral) behavior [189]; recognizes virtues of character in animals which prefer the path of friendship and fidelity to those of war [246, pp. 41-51]; and discusses the description and evaluation of animal emotion (1987a). S. F. Sapontzis [169] concludes animals act virtuously.

P. Smith (1982), criticizing arguments used by D. Davidson and S. P. Stich, concludes languageless animals can legitimately be attributed beliefs. R. C. Solomon (1982) observes that psychologists once dismissed out of hand the idea that animal consciousness might be a reality, but now consciousness is the starting point for much of their work.

T. Regan [208, pp. 1-81] provides extensive discussion of mental capacities in animals: awareness, consciousness, beliefs, desires, concepts, perception, intentions, memory, self-consciousness, sense of future, emotions, sentience; also analyzes anthropomorphism.

T. L. Benson [207, pp. 79–89] explains how conflicting stereotypes prevent us from understanding the nature of animals. D. C. Dennett (1983) defends the use of intentional system theory, the "intentional stance" in comparative psychology and ethology: ". . . Adopting . . . the Panglossian assumption of rationality in our fellow cognizers can be an immensely fruitful strategy in science . . ." (354). J. O. Nelson (1983) concludes animals do not propositionally believe but they do propositionally know.

L. E. Johnson argues that some animals can sometimes act as moral agents [204] and that animals have an interest in continuing to live [205]. R. Crisp (1985b) studies the minds of nonhuman animals.

According to M. J. Adler (1985), C. Darwin to the contrary, humans differ radically in kind from other animals; we are totally bereft of instincts; animal intelligence is entirely sensory; animals have no concepts. M. W. Fox (1985) regards Adler's view as "bio-fascist."

P. G. Muscari (1986) concludes human self-awareness is different enough from animal self-awareness to legitimize a claim to human uniqueness. J. Griffin (1986, 315, note 19) argues animals are capable of informed desire. E. Pluhar [315] argues many animals are agents capable of action, controlling their own behavior, and having goals or purposes.

J. Bennett (1988), in his 1987 presidential address to the Eastern Division of the American Philosophical Association, reports and evaluates recent work by psychologists and cognitive ethologists aimed at finding out whether animals can think about themselves, can think about the minds of others, can think about the past, can use language. "Despite recent sceptical literature tending the other way, I unashamedly conjecture that many animals of other species have beliefs and wants, and that this is not anthropomorphism . . ."

Tom Regan and Animal Rights

T. Regan, who argues for equal moral rights of experiencing subjects of lives (human and animal), is the most prolific writer and editor of works on animal rights: [112] [120] [121] [143] [144] [165]–[167] [179] [191] [193] [208] [218] [246] [263]–[269] [287] [293]–[296] [311]–[313] [317] [328] [335] (1976a) (1976b) (1977a) (1977b) (1978) (1980a) (1980b) (1981a) (1981b) (1981c) (1982) (1984); also T. Regan and D. Jamieson (1978); also D. Jamieson and T. Regan (1985).

R. G. Frey, an opponent of moral rights theory for humans or animals, argues Regan fails to establish that animals have interests (1977a); Regan responds (1977a). Frey attacks one version of the argument from marginal cases used to support animal rights (1977b); Regan and D. Jamieson (1978) respond; S. R. L. Clark (1978) also replies to Frey. Frey argues animals cannot have rights because they have no interests, no desires, no beliefs, no propositions, no linguistic capacity (1980); B. Smart refutes Frey's scepticism about attributing desires to non-self-conscious beings (1981); Regan attacks Frey's claim that animals cannot have simple desires (1982); S. F. Sapontzis attacks Frey's claim that having an interest requires language use (1983) [303, chap. 7]. Regan critiques Frey on animal beliefs and desires [208, pp. 37–49, 67–73]. Frey attacks moral rights theory for both humans and animals [207, pp. 285–306] (1983b) and critiques Regan on preference autonomy in animals and the value of animal life (1987) [317].

J. Narveson (1977) (1983) (1987), favoring contractarian rational egoism allowing no moral status for animals, criticizes Regan's rights view. Regan (1977b) [208, pp. 156–63] responds. D. Jamieson (1981) attacks rational egoism, concluding this theory implies marginal humans are no better off than animals. G. P. Cave (1985) attacks Narveson, Regan and Jamieson on topic of rational egoism.

H. J. McCloskey (1965) (1969, 234–5) (1975) (1979) (1987), defining rights as entitlements possessed by autonomous moral agents, argues animals (with possible exception of very intelligent animals such as whales and dolphins) cannot have rights; Regan (1976b) [208, pp. 281–2] replies; R. Elliot (1987) defends Regan's rights view against McCloskey's attack.

R. Nozick (1974, 35–42), regarding rights as moral side constraints, raises significant questions about the moral status of animals, conjectures the possibility of "utilitarianism for animals, Kantianism for people," and seems to leave animals dangling in an intermediate stage between rocks and persons. Nozick (1983), reviewing Regan's *The case for animal rights* [208], accuses him of going too far in attributing equal rights to animals, and opts for speciesism but without providing a justification. H. Cohen (1983a) replies: "If this is the best that the chairman of the Harvard philosophy department can do, then the case for animal rights must be strong indeed." J. Rachels (1986, 74–7) attacks Nozick's speciesism.

D. VanDeVeer (1980) argues Regan, in his "The Moral basis of vegetarianism" [112], does not provide a criterion for what is to count as gratuitous suffering. Regan (1980b) responds.

A. Rowan and J. Tannenbaum (1986), arguing against Regan's rights theory, favor "limited" rights for animals; for example, animals when used in biomedical research have the right to be treated humanely, not to be caused unnecessary suffering. S. R. L. Clark (1987b) critiques Regan's abstract theory of rights and argues for a synthesis of deep ecology, libertarianism and zoophily. L-M. Russow (1988) critiques Regan's theory of inherent value and develops her own doctrine of inherent value based on being a subject with a personality, with the result there are degrees of inherent value. S. Finsen [335, pp. 197–212] argues that Regan's claim that it may be necessary in a lifeboat situation to sacrifice a dog in order to save human life is consistent with calling for the abolition of animal experimentation.

Although J. Rawls has not published on the topic of animal rights, his works on justice have important implications and have generated significant discussion. Rawls (1963, 284), claiming that capability of a sense of justice is a necessary condition for being owed duties of justice, would not recognize rights for animals and probably not for marginal humans. Later he (1971, 512) weakens his claim: "It does *seem* that we are not required to give strict justice to creatures lacking this capacity [the sense of justice]," again precluding rights for animals. Regan (1981b) discusses Rawl's dilemma in regard to duties to animals; A. E. Fuchs (1981) argues Regan misinterprets Rawls, and that there is no dilemma. Regan [208, pp. 163–74] criticizes Rawls' contractarianism and concludes that his exclusion of animals from principles of justice is arbitrary. E. Johnson [141, chap. 4] critiques Rawls' view on animals, argues that contractors in the original position would choose to extend justice to animals. D. VanDeVeer (1979) [207, pp. 147–67] explores the implications of extending Rawls' principles of justice to include all sentient beings (humans and animals). Additional critiques of Rawls: M. S. Pritchard and W. L. Robinson (1981), R. Elliot (1984), B. F. Blackwelder [109], P. S. Wenz [320, chap. 12]. M. Midgley (1985) argues against Rawls' and G. R. Grice's (1967) contract theories of justice and rights, and argues for many kinds of human duties in different contexts to humans, animals, plants, the environment.

Although Regan and P. Singer are in close agreement on practical conclusions in regard to the treatment of animals, they disagree in theoretical foundations, Regan using moral rights theory and Singer using a type of utilitarianism. Regan (1980a) disputes Singer's attempt to base the obligatoriness of vegetarianism on utilitarianism; Singer (1980a) responds; Regan (1981a) [208, pp. 200–28] replies. Singer (1985a) criticizes Regan's reasoning by which he comes to the conclusion that if there be four humans and one dog in a lifeboat and one must be thrown overboard, the dog must go; Regan (1985) responds; Singer (1985b) replies. Singer [304] argues against Regan's moral rights theory, defends animal liberation based on equal consideration of interests as recognizing the inherent value of individuals. Regan (1987) states his theoretical difference from Singer; Singer [305] responds.

M. A. Fox (1978a) argues it makes no sense to ascribe rights to animals; Regan (1978) responds; Fox (1978b) replies. Other critiques of Regan: W. Aiken (1980), L. D. Willard (1982), T. Young (1984), G. Liddell (1985), D. E. Ost (1986), P. W. Taylor (1987), M. A. Warren (1986).

R. Elliot (1987) defends Regan's moral rights theory from attacks by P. Montague (1980) and H. J. McCloskey (1979). E. Pluhar [315] critiques part of Regan's moral rights theory and develops her own equally strong theory of animal rights adapting principles from A. Gewirth (1978). P. S. Wenz [320, chaps. 8, 13, 14] attempts to incorporate many of Regan's insights into a broader, pluralistic, concentric-circle theory of environmental justice.

D. Jamieson and T. Regan (1985) argue whales have the right to be treated with respect; our moral task is to let whales alone. G. Namkoong and Regan [335, pp. 213–21] argue that linguistic ability is not a necessary condition for possession of rights by animals.

Although not directed specifically to Regan's theory, the following tend to be favorable to moral rights for animals: J. W. Lowry (1975), B. F. Blackwelder

[109], L. Haworth [123], E. B. Pluhar (1981).

Denials of moral rights (in the strict theoretical sense) for animals: J. Passmore (1974) (1975a), J. Margolis (1975), S. I. Benn (1977), R. W. Burch (1977), M. A. Fox (1978c), L. B. Cebic (1981), R. E. Moseley (1984), B. J. Singer (1986), A. White [317], R. Cigman (1981). Cigman is critiqued by S. F. Sapontzis [196].

Peter Singer and Animal Liberation

P. Singer, who argues for the equality principle (equal interests of sentient beings – human and animal – should be given equal consideration) in the context of utilitarianism, and who develops analogies between speciesism (a concept originated by R. Ryder [114] [182], meaning discrimination on the basis of species membership), racism and sexism, writes extensively on animal liberation: [103] [106] [115] [121] [134] [146]–[150] [163] [170] [184] [245]–[247] [273] [282] [304] [305] [317] [328] (1977) (1978) (1980a) (1980b) (1983) (1985a) (1985b).

J. Margolis (1974) and K. Donaghy (1974) are early critics of Singer's first publications on the equality of animals [103] [106]. Singer's important *Animal liberation* [115] is reviewed by A. Townsend (1979).

M. E. Levin (1977a) misinterprets Singer to hold a rights theory; Singer (1977) responds with clarification of his utilitarian view; Levin (1977b) again attacks rather futilely. J. Rodman (1977), arguing from an ecological perspective, attacks Singer's animal liberation view based on sentience as an "enlightened, humane form of speciesism." J. Narveson (1977), arguing from a contractarian perspective, attacks Singer's use of utilitarianism as basis for moral status of animals. M. A. Fox (1978a) mistakenly interprets Singer as holding an animal rights view; Singer (1978) replies; Fox (1978b) responds, claiming Singer's misleading use of "rights language" invites misinterpretation.

J. Benson (1978) in his review of *Animal liberation* [115] criticizes Singer's thesis of equality of animals as not very useful in practice and unsound in theory. R. Norman and L. P. Francis (1978) criticize Singer's use of the principle of equal consideration of the interests of all animals as a moral basis for vegetarianism.

B. Steinbock (1978) argues against Singer's equality principle. K. E. Goodpaster (1978) argues for *being alive* instead of *sentience* as the criterion for moral considerability. C. Pierce (1979) argues against the analogy between the liberation of animals and the liberation of women and blacks. P. S. Wenz (1979) argues act-utilitarianism is an unsatisfactory basis for vegetarianism.

M. Lockwood (1979) critiques Singer's [146] [148, pp. 99–103] [170] analysis of the replaceability argument in regard to animals. (The replaceability argument holds that utilitarianism is committed to the conclusion that it would be morally permissible to kill sentient animals painlessly (including humans?) living pleasant lives given that their lives be replaced by an equal number of equally pleasant lives.) H. L. A. Hart's (1980) review of Singer's *Practical ethics* [148] results in Singer's (1980b) response.

Singer and T. Regan are in close agreement on practical conclusions but they disagree in theory, Singer using utilitarianism and Regan using moral rights theory (see preceding section). Their interchanges: Regan (1980a), Singer (1980a), Regan (1981a) [208, pp. 200–28], Singer (1985a), Regan (1985), Singer (1985b), Singer [304], Regan (1987), Singer [305].

R. G. Frey (1980) attacks Singer's commitment to the interests of animals, and also the equality of interests principle. J. B. Callicott (1980) (1985a) [317] argues for a Leopoldian environmental ethic in opposition to animal liberation. Critiques of Callicott are by E. Johnson (1981) and S. F. Sapontzis (1984). Callicott (1984b) sharply responds to Sapontzis.

Attacking E. O. Wilson's (1975) sociobiological denial of non-reciprocal altruism toward strangers, Singer (1981) argues we need not be the slaves of our genes: our capacity to reason can be used to expand the circle of ethical concern (altruism) to all sentient beings.

S. F. Sapontzis (1982a) [303, chap. 10] critiques Singer on the replaceability argument. E. B. Pluhar (1982) argues Singer's replaceability argument would apply to normal humans as well as to animals, and should be rejected. G. P. Cave (1982) argues the replaceability argument is inconsistent with utilitarianism and our ordinary moral intuitions. D. Lamb (1982) argues Singer meets the criterion for a reform movement but not a liberation movement.

As late as 1982, Singer is mistakenly regarded as holding a moral rights view: C. Perry and G. E. Jones (1982); G. E. Jones (1983); R. W. Loftin (1983); C. Perry and G. E. Jones (1983); response by Singer (1983). J. Narveson (1983) argues utilitarianism does not necessarily lead to vegetarianism.

R. G. Frey (1983b), who seems sympathetic to utilitarianism, criticizes Singer's attempt to base vegetarianism on utilitarianism, and claims that the utilitarian goal could be achieved by reforms within factory farming of animals while humans continue to eat meat. Singer responds (1985a). J. A. Nelson (1986) presents a critical review of Frey's (1983b) *Rights, killing, and suffering.*

L. C. Becker (1983) argues for a type of speciesism. T. Young (1984) argues Singer's preference utilitarianism does not entail that killing self-conscious beings is usually wrong. Singer [147] applies the equality principle to environmental ethics. M. Sagoff (1984) claims environmentalism and animal liberation are inconsistent. A. F. Holland (1984) argues for a moderate speciesism. R. Crisp (1985a) critiques Holland.

A sympathetic study of Singer's philosophical argument for vegetarianism is made by H. F. Kaplan (1988).

Other Philosophers and the Moral Status of Animals

Bibliographies on the moral status of animals: C. R. Magel [176, entries 220–42, 1107–303]; Magel and T. Regan (1979); Magel [49, pp. 170–218]. J. A. Nelson (1985) reviews recent studies in animal ethics.

G. J. Warnock (1971, 151) recognizes the moral status of animals based on their capacity to suffer. S. B. Armstrong (1976) makes a Whiteheadian study of the rights of nonhuman beings.

S. R. L. Clark draws from several traditions (Aristotelianism, Neoplatonism, Christianity, Leopoldian ecological ethic), arguing for the immediate rejection of all flesh-foods and most animal experimentation: [122] [126] [138] [157] [189] [213] [229] (1976) (1978) (1983a) (1983b) (1985a) (1985b) (1986) (1987a) (1987b). J. Benson (1978) and A. Townsend (1979) review Clark's *The moral status of animals* [122].

B. E. Rollin, who writes extensively on the moral issues inherent in animal experimentation and veterinary medical education, and who argues for the ideal of animal rights but practically adopts a utilitarian approach given that the ideal is not now attainable, is in close dialogue with scientists: [131] [132] [181] [209] [210] [219] [241]–[243] [270] [298] [299] [318] (1977) (1979) (1983) (1986a) (1986b) (1986c) (1986d). Rollin's *Animal rights and human morality* [181] receives a favorable review by D. Jamieson (1983) and a negative review by a physiologist who charges Rollin guilty of "sentimentalist philosophy" and "simplistic pseudologic" (M. B. Visscher 1982). Rollin's (1979) essay on the nature of illness is indirectly important for animal rights in that it stresses the heavy value (non-scientific) component in the concepts "disease," "health," "welfare," "illfare," leading to the conclusion that it is impossible to have a value-free science of animal welfare.

C. Hartshorne (1979) gives an aesthetic interpretation of the intrinsic and instrumental values of animals. D. A. Dombroski [214, pp. 133–9] [307] (1988) analyzes Hartshorne's philosophy especially in relation to vegetarianism; D. N. James (1988) comments.

S. F. Sapontzis emphasizes animal liberation rather than moral rights for animals, drawing upon well-accepted moral standards of fairness, minimizing suffering and maximizing enjoyment, and virtue: [169] [195] [196] [222] [223] [244] [301]–[303] [335] (1982a) (1982b) (1983) (1984) (1987) (1988). Sapontzis' writings are reviewed by J. A. Nelson (1982).

P. W. Taylor holds a theory of biocentric egalitarianism, the view that all living organisms have equal inherent worth: [186] [274] (1983) (1984) (1987). Critiques by G. Spitler (1982) and L. G. Lombardi (1983) are answered by Taylor (1983) (1984). P. S. Wenz [320, chap. 14] evaluates Taylor's biocentrism.

R. L. Fern (1981), influenced by D. VanDeVeer's [152] two-factor egalitarianism, provides a guide to resolving conflicts between animal and human interests. G. P. Cave [188] finds M. Heidegger's concept of *care* superior to utilitarianism in regard to animals' right to life. A. S. Gunn (1983) argues individualistic utilitarianism and rights theory are unsuitable for the moral status of animals, and opts for stewardship or trusteeship based on the intrinsic value of nonhuman life and nature. L. W. Sumner [335, pp. 159–76] argues for a moderation of the gap between the utilitarian moral approach and the animal rights approach to animal liberation.

M. Wreen (1984) defends speciesism, claiming that membership in the human species is sufficient for ascribing a right to life. E. B. Pluhar (1984) contends Wreen fails to make his case; Wreen (1986a) replies; Pluhar (1986a) again attacks Wreen; Wreen (1986b) again replies. Pluhar (1987) explores the challenge of the argument from marginal cases to the view that personhood is the basis for rights possession. Pluhar (1988a) takes seriously the argument from marginal cases, criticizes defenses of speciesism (by M. Wreen, M. A. Fox, T. Young), and concludes speciesism is a form of bigotry. S. F. Sapontzis (1988) responds, regarding the argument from marginal cases as no more than an "excellent rhetorical device." Pluhar (1988b) responds to Sapontzis.

See two essays by S. Castignone (1983) (1987) on the rights of animals.

Animal Experimentation

Bibliographies on animal experimentation and safety testing: C. R. Magel [176, entries 271-400, 1353-1650, 1934-43]; R. Friedman's [280] bibliography on animal experimentation and animal rights, 245 entries; F. P. Gluckstein (United States 1984-87); L. Walters and T. J. Kahn (1975-86).

T. Regan, on the basis of the moral right of animals not to be harmed, calls for the total elimination of the use of animals in toxicity tests and the total elimination of harmful use of animals in research: [179] [193, chap. 3] [208, pp. 363-94] [296, chaps. 4, 5] [295].

P. Singer, on the basis of the equality principle in the context of utilitarianism, concludes the best way to advance the interests of animals and humans would be to stop all harmful research on animals and use the money thereby saved in other more productive ways: [115, chap. 2] [134] [148, pp. 57-9] [282, pp. 65-95] [305].

B. E. Rollin argues for a theoretical ideal of moral rights for animals; but given that in practice animal experimentation is imbedded so heavily in our culture, it is impossible at present to put the ideal into effect, we should apply the utilitarian principle to animal experimentation; any justified research on an animal should be conducted in such a way as to maximize the animal's potential for living its life according to its nature (telos), and certain fundamental rights should be preserved as far as possible, given the logic of the research, regardless of cost: [181, pp. 89-148] [241] [298] [318].

S. F. Sapontzis [223] [303, pp. 209-28] [335, pp. 177-96] argues the consent requirement can meaningfully be applied to animal experimentation and that animal experimentation should be governed by the same moral principles which govern experiments on humans. T. L. S. Sprigge [151] [211] argues harmful experiments should be totally prohibited since the result would be preferable to current experimentation practice.

S. R. L. Clark [122] argues for the immediate rejection of most animal experimentation; takes a strong stand (1976) against animal experimentation in response to W. Lane-Petter (1976). D. G. Mayo [207, pp. 339-59] critiques animal experimentation on the basis of irrelevance, invalidity; justifications for experiments on animals can be used to justify experiments on humans. D. Jamieson and T. Regan [191]: the burden of proof must always be on those scientists who cause harm to innocent animals. Jamieson (1985) lays out three basic scientific views on animal experimentation in contrast to the animal liberation view.

M. A. Fox [308] [309], dismayed at his previous defenses of animal experimentation, now concludes animal experiments cannot be morally justified. His earlier works defending animal experimentation: (1979–80) (1984) (1986a). Two critical reviews of Fox's *The case for animal experimentation* (1986a): M. Cartmill (1986) and J. Tannenbaum (1986a). Fox (1986b) agrees with some of Tannenbaum's criticisms, and now finds himself in radical disagreement with several of the major theses of his own book. An extended critical review of Fox's book is by L. Finsen and S. Finsen (1988).

A. L. Kaplan [201] (1983) clearly explains the moral issues in animal experimentation, concluding animals which are sentient and purposive have prima facie rights to live and to be left alone, and that the burden of proof is always on the experimenter to give good reasons for overriding these prima facie rights. At the CFN symposium on the ethics of animal experimentation, Caplan (M. Thelestam and A. Gunnarsson 1986, 78–91) recommends animal husbandry as the ideal concept to be used by scientists in the laboratory; scientists have the duty to care for the helpless and powerless, to act as stewards of animals.

R. G. Frey (1983a) (1983b, 111–16) argues for experiments on animals because of benefits gained, and accepts the consequence that the benefits argument will justify experiments on both animals and humans. W. Paton (1983) either does not understand Frey's argument or chooses not to respond to it.

M. Midgley [185, pp. 319–36] and C. R. Magel [162] explore the dilemma of performing harmful psychological experiments on animals: to the extent the animals are emotionally similar to humans, the experiments are morally unjustified; to the extent the animals are not similar to humans, the results of the experiments cannot provide reliable information about humans; knowledge for its own sake must be considered in the context of the cost to the animals. C. Diamond [185, pp. 337–62] explores two sides of the dispute over the ethics of animal experimentation.

S. Gendin [269, pp. 15–60] analyzes the use of animals in science (for what purposes they are used, under what conditions, with what legal protection). C. Cohen (1986) denies animal rights and encourages increased animal experiments for human benefits: "I am a speciesist. Speciesism is not merely plausible; it is essential for right conduct. . . . The analogy between speciesism and racism is insidious" (867). E. C. Hettinger [317] regards Cohen's defense a showcase of the most common mistakes made by those who seek to defend the human use of animals and suggests that only if researchers would be willing to experiment on severely retarded humans at comparable levels of psychological sophistication are their experiments on animals morally justified. Cohen (1987) responds to criticism by B. Truett (1987).

H. J. McCloskey (1987), criticizing T. Regan's animal rights view, defends experiments on animals on the basis of goods to be realized, evils to be avoided, duty to respect persons and secure them in their natural rights.

The genetic manipulation of animals raises ethical questions. E. Pluhar (1985) argues that although much current research in this area is ethically questionable, genetic manipulation *in itself* is not wrong. M. W. Fox (1986a), in response to Pluhar, argues against genetic manipulation on the basis of harms to both animals and humans. B. Rollin (1986a) (1986c) concludes it is prima facie wrong to infringe upon an animal's *telos* but it may not be wrong to change the *telos* of the animal if such change does not result in greater suffering or unhappiness. E. B. Pluhar (1986b) responds to M. W. Fox (1986a). Fox (1987) warns that genetic engineering, rather than fulfilling nature's cornucopia, may become a terrifying Pandora's box. L. Finsen [335, pp. 145–58] explores advantages and disadvantages of relying on institutional animal care and use committees to subject research proposals to ethical scrutiny.

Vegetarianism and Animals

Bibliographies: C. R. Magel [176, entries 401–36, 1651–800] and J. C. Dyer [190].

P. Singer criticizes intensive methods of raising animals for food and argues for vegetarianism on moral (the equality principle and utilitarianism) and world-food-supply (efficient use of resources) grounds: [115, chaps. 3, 4] [163] [282, pp. 95–127] [148, pp. 54–7] [247] (1980a). H. F. Kaplan (1988) makes a sympathetic study of Singer's philosophical argument for vegetarianism. Three philosophers question utilitarianism as an adequate basis for vegetarianism: R. G. Frey (1983b); T. Regan (1980a) (1981a) [208, pp. 218–26, 349–51]; P. S. Wenz (1979). B. Gruzalski [207, pp. 251–65] argues for vegetarianism on the basis of utilitarianism.

T. Regan argues for vegetarianism on the basis of animals' moral rights: [112] [208, pp. 330–53] [218] [296, pp. 64–82] (1980a) (1981a). Two philosophers reject the theory of moral rights (for humans or animals) and therefore also its use as a basis for vegetarianism: R. G. Frey (1983b) and P. Singer [247] [304] [305] (1978) (1980a) (1985b). T. Auxter [137] argues animals have a right not to be eaten.

S. R. L. Clark [122] argues for the immediate rejection of all flesh-foods. Vegetarianism is argued for by C. Diamond [127] on the basis of the sense of fellow creaturehood, by P. W. Taylor [274] on the basis of biocentric egalitarianism, by P. S. Wenz [227] on the basis of ecology, by S. F. Sapontzis [303, pp. 199–207] on the basis of generally accepted moral principles, by J. Rachels [124] on the bases of the animals' interests and the reduction of world hunger. C. Perry (1981) claims Rachels' arguments lead to conclusion that it is immoral not to eat human carrion during periods of food scarcity.

J. Harris critiques fallacious arguments often used to try to defend eating animals [97, pp. 97–110] and discusses economic and moral prospects for vegetarianism [143, pp. 117–21]. W. H. Davis [116] asks: What moral appeals could we use to try to persuade powerful, intelligent aliens from outer space not to eat us?

D. VanDeVeer [207, pp. 147–67] applies J. Rawls' device of rational contractors behind a veil of ignorance to the question of animal slaughter for food. P. E. Devine (1978), who rejects utilitarianism as well as non-utilitarian theories in regard to animals, opts for ''the overflow principle'' but gives little practical guidance how we should treat animals. M. Martin (1976) (1979) argues vegetarianism is not a moral duty but it may be a supererogatory policy.

F. Ferré (1986) argues for moderate meat-eating on the basis of due respect for beings with different degrees of intrinsic value within the framework of an organicist ethic. D. A. Dombrowski [214] finds it illuminating to compare ancient philosophical vegetarianism in Greece and Rome with contemporary views held by S. R. L. Clark, P. Singer, T. Regan, C. Hartshorne. Dombrowski [307] uses Hartshorne's process metaphysics to defend philosophic vegetarianism.

B. Klug (1982) (1983b) attacks the attempt of the Council for Agricultural Science and Technology (1981) to defend confinement methods of raising animals for food by identifying animal welfare with productivity and profitability.

Animal Rights and Environmental Ethics

Bibliographies on environmental ethics: C. R. Magel [176, entries 2026–171] and S. R. Kellert and J. K. Berry [235]. The journal *Environmental Ethics* is a valuable source.

Animal rights and animal liberation views tend to emphasize the moral status of individuals. Holistic, ecological theories of ethics give priority to species and ecosystems and the biosphere. Intermediate positions attempt to accommodate the rights or values of both individual organisms and ecosystems. Extreme individualistic and holistic theories tend to conflict.

J. Passmore (1974) argues only humans have rights but that there are already within the Western tradition basic attitudes and metaphysics adequate to serve as a basis for our solving environmental problems. However, Passmore (1975b): ''. . . We do need a 'new metaphysics' which is genuinely not anthropomorphic. . . . The working out of such a metaphysics is, in my judgement, the most important task which lies ahead in philosophy.''

W. T. Blackstone (1980) discusses the search for an environmental ethic. A. Naess (1979) places emphasis on community-type coexistence of humans and animals as respected members. The basic principles of deep ecology recognize the well-being of human and nonhuman lives having value in themselves (G. Sessions and A. Naess 1986).

R. and V. Routley (1979) (1980) argue against the inevitability of human chauvinism and explore the question: Is there a need for a new – an environmental – ethic? Apparently in the Hartshornian tradition, C. Birch and J. B.

Cobb (1981) argue against anthropocentrism and for an ethics of the biosphere incorporating the basic principle of enhancing the total richness of experience as an evolutionary goal.

Individualistic views are held by T. Regan [208, pp. 361–3] (1981c) (1984), P. Singer [147], W. K. Frankena (1979), P. W. Taylor [186] [274], K. E. Goodpaster (1978), S. F. Sapontzis [303, chap. 14], R. M. Hare [283], B. E. Rollin [299].

Ecoholistic theories are favored by the ecologist A. Leopold (1949) (''A thing is right when it tends to preserve the integrity, stability, and beauty of the biotic community. It is wrong when it tends otherwise.''); by K. E. Goodpaster (1979); by J. B. Callicott [317] (1979) (1980) (1984a) (1985a); by R. Loftin (1985); by H. Rolston III (1986) (1988). T. Regan's [208, p. 362] dubbing Leopoldian ecoholism ''environmental fascism'' invites controversy. E. Johnson (1981) and S. F. Sapontzis (1984) [303, chap. 14] attack Callicott; Callicott (1984b) replies.

J. Rodman (1977) uses an ecological perspective in criticizing P. Singer. S. F. Sapontzis (1982b) [303, pp. 249–72] attacks T. Regan's conception of environmental ethics. S. R. L. Clark (1983a) uses the Gaia hypothesis in sympathetically interpreting the ecoholism of A. Leopold (1949). R. Attfield (1983b), arguing for the moral standing of living organisms (but with varying moral significance), finds the ancient and continuous Jewish and Christian tradition of stewardship suitable for an adequate environmental ethic; no new ethic is required.

H. J. McCloskey (1983) argues animal rights (if there were such, but there are none) would not complement but would be in conflict with conservation and preservation. M. A. Warren (1983) argues a harmonious marriage between the Leopoldian land ethic and animal liberation is possible. E. B. Pluhar (1983) analyzes two rival conceptions of an environmental ethic – individualism (Singer, Regan) and holism (Leopold, Callicott) – and concludes a plausible environmental ethic must contain both individualistic and holistic elements. R. Attfield (1983a) defends the individualistic methods of J. Feinberg, P. Singer, T. Regan, the early K. E. Goodpaster against the holistic methods of J. Rodman, the later Goodpaster, S. R. L. Clark, J. B. Callicott, J. King-Farlow.

E. Partridge (1984) criticizes T. Regan's attempt to articulate an environmental ethic on an individualistic foundation and sketches a synthesis of individualism and holism in environmental ethics. M. Sagoff (1984) critiques Regan and Singer from an environmental perspective. J. B. Callicott (1985b) critically reviews Regan's *The case for animal rights* [208] from an ecological perspective.

Philosophical issues involved in the preservation of species are explored by J. B. Callicott (1986), E. Sober (1986), D. H. Regan (1986). S. Armstrong-Buck (1986) uses A. N. Whitehead's metaphysical system as a basis for environmental ethics; claims to solve problems in the views of T. Regan, P. Singer, A. Leopold, B. Spinoza.

Animal rights theory and practice are critiqued from an environmental perspective by A. Herscovici (1985). Although D. Foreman (1987), radical environmental activist in Earth First!, does not evidence complete understanding of philosophic theory, his views based on deep ecology reveal both tensions and commonalities between animal liberationists and ecological activists. P. S. Wenz [320] discusses environmental issues in relation to biocentric individualism (P. W. Taylor) and ecocentric holism, and develops his own pluralistic theory of environmental justice, using a concentric-circle perspective.

R. Sylvan (1987) critiques T. Regan's rights theory and develops a broad theory of human and animal rights in the context of valuable ecosystems which sometimes ought to overpower individual rights. S. Finsen (1988) argues that animal rights individualism (Regan) and ecoholism (Leopold, Callicott) are entirely complementary if viewed from an evolutionary perspective, and that the "environmental fascist dilemma" can be resolved; in response S. Gendin (1988) argues that animal rights and ecoholism (Leopold, Loftin, Callicott) are not compatible, and sides with the animal rights views; E. Katz (1988) also comments on Finsen.

D. Dombrowski (1988) provides a Hartshornian, panpsychist view of our moral and aesthetic relations to animals, animal species, ecosystems and the biosphere. D. N. James (1988) and E. Katz (1988) reply.

J. B. Callicott ("Animal liberation and environmental ethics: Back together again," *Between the species*, 4 Summer 1988, pp. 163–9) attempts an alliance between individualistic theories (à la P. Singer and T. Regan) and ecocentric environmental ethics (A. Leopold's land ethic) by incorporating insights from the theories of D. Hume, C. Darwin, E. Pluhar and M. Midgley. H. B. Miller responds (pp. 170–3). Callicott replies (pp. 174–5).

G. Comstock ("How not to attack animal rights from an environmental perspective," *Between the species*, 4 Summer 1988, pp. 177–8) argues that M. Sagoff and B. Callicott, in their attempt at a *reductio* argument against animal rights on the basis of A. Leopold's land ethic, are attacking a straw man.

R. Kalechofsky ("Metaphors of nature: Vivisection and pornography – The Manichean machine," *Between the species*, 4 Summer 1988, pp. 179–85) explores the implications of the Cartesian mechanistic view of nature for animals in experimentation and for women in pornography. L. Westra responds (pp. 186–90). R. G. Frey ("Moral standing, the value of lives, and speciesism," *Between the species*, 4 Summer 1988, pp. 191–201): animals have moral standing; the value of lives depends on the richness, the quality of lives; since lives vary in richness and quality (due to variations in capacities, complexity, role of agency (autonomy), etc.) they vary in value; human lives vary in value; animal lives vary in value; animals have no agency (autonomy); since the value of some animal lives is greater than the value of some human lives, if we are to continue to use animals for research and if we are to avoid speciesism (and we should), we must envisage the use of some humans for similar research. P. Singer responds (pp. 202–3). (Note: This paragraph logically belongs in an earlier section of this chapter, but the lateness of publications made insertion there impossible.)

2 Science and Medicine and Animals

The Nature of Animals

Bibliography: C. R. Magel [176, entries 51–196, 453–988]. An answer to the factual question *What is the nature of animals?* would require a complete inventory of characteristics possessed by animals; however, psychological and mental qualities and capacities are most relevant to animal rights. For philosophers' views on the nature of animals, see Chapter 1.

In Greek–Roman antiquity three writers are major sources on the nature of animals: (1) Aristotle (⟨4th cent. BC⟩ 1908–52, vols. 4, 5): *Historia animalium, De partibus animalium, De generatione animalium, De motu animalium, De incessu animalium.* (2) Pliny (⟨1st cent.⟩ 1967–80, vol. 3, bks. 8–11). (3) Aelian (⟨3rd cent.⟩ 1958–59).

Two major medieval sources blend animal facts, legend and allegory for moral and spiritual guidance: (1) *Physiologus* (⟨between 2nd and 5th cents.⟩ 1979); extremely popular; translated into many languages over many centuries. (2) *The bestiary* (⟨12th cent.⟩ 1960); one of many expanded versions in the 12th and 13th centuries; heavily based on the *Physiologus.*

C. Linnaeus, 18th-century founder of taxonomy: "I demand of you, and of the whole world, that you show me a generic character . . . by which to distinguish between Man and Ape. I myself most assuredly know of none. . . . But, if I had called man an ape, or vice versa, I would have fallen under the ban of all the ecclesiastics. It may be that as a naturalist I ought to have done so" (quoted by C. Sagan, 1977, 106).

C. Darwin's [28] [30] [31] theory of evolution based on natural selection, implying physiological and psychological continuity in the development of life forms and entailing the kinship of humans and animals, launches a revolution still to be assimilated by the Western mind. R. Boakes (1984, 1-22) discusses mental evolution as viewed by Darwin, and reactions of others.

M. Twain's (⟨1896⟩ 1973) comparative study of the traits and dispositions of animals and humans "obliges me to renounce my allegiance to the Darwinian theory of the Ascent of Man from the Lower Animals . . . in favor of a new and truer one, this new and truer one to be named the Descent of Man from the Higher Animals" (81).

G. J. Romanes [41] [42], Darwin's intellectual descendant, breaks new ground in comparative psychology, emphasizing consciousness and continuity of mental capacities in animals and humans. Useful discussions of Romanes by: B. E. Rollin [270] [318], E. A. Wasserman (1984), G. M. Burghardt (1985), R. Boakes (1984, 23-32).

T. H. Huxley (1893), scientific colleague of Darwin, argues animals are conscious automata. Huxley (1897) agrees with Hume on the similarity of mental operations in humans and animals, concluding animals have generic ideas, beliefs and inferences. See discussion by R. Boakes (1984, 16-22).

W. James (⟨1890⟩ 1981, 2: 970-2; 3: 1470 note) claims human reasoning is based on association by similarity, and that animals, without propositions, expect immediate consequences through sensible associations by contiguity.

C. L. Morgan (⟨1894⟩ 1977) suggests "Morgan's canon": ". . . In no case is an animal activity to be interpreted as the outcome of the exercise of a higher psychical faculty, if it can be fairly interpreted as the outcome of the exercise of one which stands lower in the psychological scale" (59). Morgan, Romanes' intellectual descendant, recognizes animal consciousness, feelings, pleasure, pain, emotions (anger, fear, antipathy, affection, sympathy), perceptual inferences without concepts, but denies concepts, reason, self-awareness. Other works by Morgan: (1886) (1890) (1896a) (1896b). See discussions of Morgan by R. Boakes (1984, 32-44) and S. Walker (1983, 56-60).

W. Wundt (1894) asserts that the mental processes of animals must be estimated by comparison with human introspections. W. Mills (1898, 15) claims some animals capable of some degree of reasoning, imagining, abstraction, generalizing, grief, moral sense of right and wrong: "He who would understand animals thoroughly must live among them, endeavour to think as they think, and feel as they feel, and this at every stage of their development."

M. F. Washburn (1908) and J. A. Bierens de Haan [80] write in the Darwin-Romanes tradition, stressing consciousness in animals and psychological continuity with humans. The naturalist J. Muir, who refers to animals as his "horizontal brothers," emphasizes their kinship with humans, their intelligence and individuality; criticizes the doctrine "that animals have neither mind nor soul, have no rights that we are bound to respect, and were made only for man, to be petted, spoiled, slaughtered or enslaved" (quoted by L. Mighetto 1986, in preface).

I. Pavlov (1906) (⟨1917⟩ 1962) introduces physiological experimentation into the study of animal behavior; develops the theory of conditioned reflexes; imposes in his laboratory fines for use of psychological expressions (wishes, desires, fears, etc.); concludes the use of mentalistic terms in psychology is unscientific. On Pavlov: R. Boakes (1984, 111–35), S. Walker (1983, 65–73), G. B. Shaw (1933).

E. L. Thorndike (1911), student of W. James, criticizes Romanes' methodology; introduces laboratory experiments into animal psychology and develops stimulus–response theory of learning. W. Mills (1899) accuses Thorndike of coming close to regarding animals as automata. Thorndike (1899) responds, emphasizing his recognition of animal consciousness, pleasure, mental processes, representations (which "are the beginning of the rich life of ideas in man"). On Thorndike: R. Boakes (1984, 68–78) and S. Walker (1983, 61–5).

J. B. Watson (1913) (1914) wonders whether he be psychologist or physiologist; claims questions about an animal's consciousness are unanswerable; argues psychology should study behavior without use of mentalistic terms; claims thinking is really sub-vocal speech, implying animals cannot think, claims the time has come when human and animal psychology must discard all references to consciousness and that the findings of psychology lend themselves to explanation in physico-chemical terms. On Watson: R. Boakes (1984, 136–75).

D. O. Hebb (1946) finds anthropomorphic language provides a more intelligible and practical guide to chimpanzee behavior than does non-anthropomorphic description. Neurologist W. R. Brain is quoted by W. H. Thorpe [91, p. 79]: "I personally can see no reason for conceding mind to my fellow men and denying it to animals. . . . Since the diencephalon is well developed in animals and birds, I at least cannot doubt that the interests and activities of animals are correlated with awareness and feelings in the same way as my own, and which may be, for ought I know, just as vivid."

K. Lorenz (1952) (1954) (1978) and N. Tinbergen (1953) (1972–73) are generally regarded as founders of modern ethology, emphasizing observation of animals in their natural environment. Lorenz (1971), asserting he would have to solve the mind–body problem in order to determine whether animals undergo subjective experience, accepts the general belief that animals experience things, experience pleasure and sorrow, and quotes O. Heinroth: ". . . Animals are emotional people with very little ability to reason." K. von Frisch's (1967) study of the dance language of bees is a classic. A condensed history of ethology is given by K. Heinroth and G. M. Burghardt (1977).

Ethologist W. H. Thorpe, especially interested in birds, assesses pain and distress in animals [91] and concludes there are animals who learn, conceptualize and reason, have some form of language, court, make use of tools, have an aesthetic sense, have an ethical sense (1974).

Cognitive ethologist D. R. Griffin [117] (1978) (1982) (1984) criticizes behaviorists for ignoring or denying consciousness in animals; argues it is no more anthropomorphic to postulate mental experience in animals than to compare their bony structure, nervous system, or antibodies, with our own. Griffin (ed.) (1982) edits papers presented at the important Dahlem Conference in Berlin to explore the nature of the animal mind and develop new approaches to its understanding; biologists, psychologists, ethologists discuss questions of animal intelligence, thinking, intentionality, problem solving, knowledge, cognitive processes, language, communication, awareness, consciousness, self-consciousness, feeling, suffering. C. M. Heyes (1987) contrasts and evaluates the approaches of ethologist Griffin and philosopher D. C. Dennett to the legitimation of intentional language within comparative psychology.

N. K. Humphrey (1976) (1980) (1982) (1983) argues that consciousness has evolved in animals to enable them, in a social context, to be natural psychologists with the ability to model the behavior of other members of the group; consciousness gives the natural psychologist direct access to psychological concepts: feeling, pain, contentment, etc. M. W. Fox (1976) is informative on similarities between animals and humans in needs, emotions, consciousness.

C. Sagan (1977) discusses the abstractions of cetaceans and primates: "If chimpanzees have consciousness, if they are capable of abstractions, do they not have what until now has been described as 'human rights'? How smart does a chimpanzee have to be before killing him constitutes murder?" (120). E. Hilgard (1980) delineates the re-entry of consciousness into American psychology in the last two decades.

M. S. Dawkins [159] studies methods and criteria for determining the occurrence and extent of animal suffering. Dawkins (1987) defines animals' suffering as an unpleasant emotional state which they will work hard to get out of. We can ask animals whether and how much they suffer, how much suffering matters to them, by observing how hard they work ("voting with their feet") to avoid a suffering situation. Argues it is probable that all animals which suffer are clever enough to do something about it.

E. A. Wasserman (1981) (1984) reviews the nature and history of comparative psychology, discussing G. J. Romanes, H. S. Jennings, C. L. Morgan, E. A. Thorndike, M. F. Washburn, C. J. Warden, E. C. Tolman, B. F. Skinner, J. A. Bierens de Haan, D. R. Griffin. Wasserman (1983) argues that cognitive psychology is behavioral: "I, for one, have tried to steer clear of the possibility of subjective experience in my animal subjects . . ." (10).

H. L. Roiblat (1982) explores the meaning of representation in animal memory. H. S. Terrace (1982): "What is news is that animals can encode stimuli and relationships between stimuli that are not immediately present. . . . In short, it appears as if psychologists have, for the first time, shown that animals can think." G. G. Gallup Jr. (1983) argues for a resurrection of mind in the context of comparative psychology; claims anthropomorphism still has a legitimate place in psychology; concludes chimpanzees and orangutans, and perhaps cetaceans and elephants, are self-aware.

P. S. Silverman (1983, 244) draws a dichotomy between empirical science and ethics: ". . . For ethical purposes, a chimpanzee may be as aware and intentional as we are (or close to it), but in the context of purely empirical judgments, the most that can be offered is that its behavior reflects mind-like or belief-like states."

C. A. Ristau (1983) discusses evidence for awareness, cognition, language in animals through analysis of honey bee dances, animal deception, ape language experiments.

H. S. Terrace (1984): Animal cognition is not the study of animal consciousness; neither human cognition nor animal cognition requires reference to consciousness; in both human and animal cognition it is assumed that the normal state of affairs is unconscious activity and thought; animals form representations; animals can think without language, but how? Terrace (1985) argues that animals (including apes) lack linguistic ability but that animals (pigeons included) can represent features of their environment, can think. Terrace [226] (1987) explores the question: How can animals think without language? R. J. Herrnstein (1985) discusses the riddles of natural categorization, the remarkable powers of classification by animals (pigeons, for example) which we usually do not regard as intelligent.

G. M. Burghardt (1985) reviews literature of 19th and early 20th century comparative psychologists (G. J. Romanes, C. L. Morgan) in relation to current cognitive psychology and ethology (D. Griffin); favors critical anthropomorphism as an aid in formulating testable hypotheses; extensive references.

A. Jolly (1985) informally describes cognitive ethology as viewed by C. Ristau (do plovers intend to lead predators away?), D. Griffin (can bees think?), J. Goodall (can chimpanzees deceive?), S. Savage-Rumbaugh (can apes lie to apes?). F. Wemelsfelder (1985a) (1985b) explores the scientific study of the subjective experiences of animals, concluding boredom is a serious problem in present husbandry systems. Self-awareness in animals, including birds and mammals (rats, chimpanzees, dogs), is explored by D. G. M. Wood-Gush and others [187]. R. Lockwood (1985a) analyzes types of anthropomorphism; opts for projective anthropomorphism.

E. Macphail (1987) adopts the hypothesis that there are no qualitative or quantitative differences among the intellectual capacities of nonhuman vertebrates; concludes comparative research shows "not only that fish and rats possess comparable intellects, but that their common cognitive capacities are such that we may sensibly speak of their being decision-making creatures which form, on the basis of their past experience, expectancies concerning future events, and base their decisions on those expectancies" (193). N. Mackintosh (1987) concludes that conditioning experiments show that rats have beliefs about the world, learn about the relations in time between events, can predict one event from the occurrence of another, have knowledge about the world.

D. A. Oakley (1985a) (1985b) explores theories of cognition, imagery, awareness, consciousness and self-consciousness in animals. "If we are prepared to accept the validity of a cognitive approach for human psychology then we must be prepared also to do the same when talking of other animals" (128). ". . . Self-awareness has high biological adaptiveness and is present to some degree whenever representational systems have been developed. . . . All animals which display consciousness will also display self-awareness . . ." (141).

R. J. Hoage and L. Goldman (1986) edit a set of non-technical essays on animal intelligence, including: B. B. Beck, "Tools and intelligence"; J. L. Gould and C. G. Gould, "Invertebrate intelligence" (bees); C. A. Ristau, "Do animals think?"; D. M. Rumbaugh and S. Savage-Rumbaugh, "Reasoning and language in chimpanzees"; S. J. Vicchio, "From Aristotle to Descartes: Making animals anthropomorphic." V. Hearne (1986) explores the conflict between mechanistic, academic theories of animals and the views of those who work with and live with and train them.

C. A. Ristau and D. Robbins (1982) critically review ape-language projects until 1981, providing extensive references. E. S. Savage-Rumbaugh (1986) makes a detailed study of the intelligence and symbolic competence of Sherman and Austin, chimpanzees, concludes these chimpanzees have the ability to use arbitrary symbols representationally, to represent things and events not present. Chapters 16 and 17 are illuminating on ape-language research; see references, pp. 411-21. A more popular account of ape-language experiments can be found in the works of E. Linden (1974) (1986). J. Goodall's (1986) heavily illustrated study gives insight into the mind of the chimpanzees; many references, pp. 627-46.

L. M. Herman (1980) explores the cognitive capacities of dolphins. L. M. Herman et al. (1984) study the ability of bottlenosed dolphins to understand sentences expressed in artificial languages, concluding there is convincing evidence the animals are capable of processing both semantic and syntactic features of sentences.

Animal Experimentation through 1970

Bibliographies: C. R. Magel [176, entries 271-400, 1353-650, 1934-43]; R. Friedman [280]; F. P. Gluckstein (United States 1984-87); L. Walters and T. J. Kahn (1975-86). For views of philosophers on animal experimentation, see Chapter 1. For religious perspectives, see [269].

Histories of animal experimentation and controversy generated by it: E. Westacott (1949); H. Bretschneider (1962); S. Benison (1970); R. D. Ryder [114, pp. 167-77]; R. D. French (1975) (1978); J. E. Hampson (1978); W. G. Roberts (1979); J. A. Sechzer (1983); H. Ritvo (1984); S. E. Lederer (1987); N. A. Rupke (1987); S. Benison et al. (1987).

On F. Magendie, French physiologist in first half of 19th century: J. M. D. Olmsted (1944); R. D. French (1978); J. A. Sechzer (1983). French physiologist C. Bernard (⟨1865⟩ 1949) sets the tone for experimental physiology: "A physiologist is . . . absorbed by the scientific idea which he pursues: he no longer hears the cry of animals, he no longer sees the blood that flows, he sees only his idea and perceives only organisms concealing problems which he intends to solve" (103). "Experiments must be made either on man or on animals. . . . If it is immoral, then, to make an experiment on man when it is dangerous to him, even though the result may be useful to others, it is essentially moral to make experiments on an animal, even though painful and dangerous to him, if they may be useful to man'' (102).

L. Pasteur, 19th-century French chemist: ''I feel the sufferings of animals keenly enough never to have taken up hunting or shooting. The cry of an injured lark would stab me to the heart. But when we are to probe the mysteries of life and acquire new truth, the sovereignty of the end in view carries all before it'' (quoted by H. Cuny 1966, 144-7).

Reports of student surgical operations (sometimes 200 distinct procedures on the same immobilized, unanesthetized horse on the same day until death results) at the Veterinary College, Alfort, France generates public concern in Great Britain (Alfort 1895). The first English handbook (illustrated) for the physiological laboratory (J. Burdon-Sanderson 1873) stirs public concern. E. Magnan, French colleague of F. Magendie, performs experiment on live dog before British Medical Association; RSPCA brings cruelty charges under Martin's Act (R. D. French 1975, 55-60).

Queen Victoria appeals to J. Lister to use his influence to put a stop to animal experiments (letter quoted by E. G. Fairholme and W. Pain 1924, 378); Lister refuses (letter quoted by R. J. Godlee 1918, 378-81). A. Kingsford sharply attacks experimental use of animals in medical school in Paris (letter by E. Maitland in *Examiner*, 17 June 1876; reproduced by Maitland 1896, vol. 1, 79-87 and by E. Westacott 1949, 160-4).

The 1876 Royal Commission on Vivisection (Great Britain 1876-77) holds hearings: 49 of the 53 testifiers are from the medical-scientific community; four are from animal protection organizations; there is no participation by intellectuals other than scientists. E. Klein provides ammunition for critics of animal experimentation when he testifies he never uses anesthetics except for his own convenience and that he has no regard at all for the sufferings of the animals (Great Britain 1876-77, questions 3538-44). C. Darwin testifies briefly, defending experiments because of expected benefits to humans but urging use of anesthetics (questions 4669-72). R. D. French (1975, chaps. 3-4) and E. Westacott (1949, 34-109) are informative on the 1876 Royal Commission. Political compromises leading to probably the first legislation specifically dealing with animal experimentation - the Cruelty to Animals Act 1876 - are described in detail by R. D. French (1975, chap. 5).

C. Darwin, torn between deep concern for the suffering of animals and a deep respect for science, is reluctant to make public statements, even when urged by scientific colleagues. One of Darwin's sons writes: ''The two subjects which moved my father perhaps more strongly than any others were cruelty to animals and slavery. His detestation of both was intense, and his indignation was overpowering in case of any levity or want of feeling on these matters'' (quoted by R. W. Clark 1984, 76). ''You ask my opinion on vivisection. I quite agree that it is justifiable for real investigations on physiology; but not for mere damnable and detestable curiosity. It is a subject which makes me sick with horror . . .'' (letter quoted by F. Darwin 1887, vol. 3, 200). ''. . . Everyone has heard of the dog suffering under vivisection, who licked the hand of the operator; this man, unless the operator was fully justified by an increase of our knowledge, or unless he had a heart of stone, must have felt remorse to the last hour of his life'' [30, p. 100]. In a letter of 14 April 1881 (which he allowed to be published in *The Times*, 18 April 1881) to P. Holmgren, Darwin, emphasizing his lifelong advocacy for "humanity to animals," states his support of animal experimentation in physiology (C. Darwin ⟨19th cent.⟩ 1977, vol. 2, 226). F. P. Cobbe [48, pp. 103–8] reproduces letters (appearing in *The Times*, 19 and 23 April 1881) by Cobbe and Lord Shaftesbury on Darwin and animal experimentation.

J. Ruskin, in 1885, resigns his professorship at Oxford University when Oxford establishes an animal laboratory: "I meant to die in my harness there, and my resignation was placed in the Vice-chancellor's hands on the Monday following the endowing vivisection in the University . . ." (letter of 24 April 1885, *Pall Mall Gazette*). "I cannot lecture in the next room to a shrieking cat nor address myself to the men who have been – there's no word for it" (unpublished letter quoted by J. Abse 1980, 311). Ruskin organizes the Guild of St. George which adopts as part of its moral code: "I will not kill nor hurt any living creature needlessly, nor destroy any beautiful thing, but will strive to save and comfort all gentle life, and guard and perfect all natural beauty, upon the earth" (quoted by D. Leon 1949, 459).

W. James (1909) attacks the view "that it is no one's business what happens to an animal, so long as the individual who is handling it can plead that to increase science is his aim. . . . The rights of the helpless, even though they be brutes, must be protected by those who have superior power." Physiologists should give up "the preposterous claim that every 'scientist' has an unlimited right to dissect . . . " The public demand for regulation rests on a perfectly sound ethical principle. ". . . The sufferings of his [scientist's] animals are somebody else's business as well as his own . . ."

Animal experimentation is defended by scientists, surgeons and physicians: G. F. Etherington (1842); C. Bernard (⟨1865⟩ 1949); J. C. Dalton (1867) (⟨1875⟩ 1980); J. Lister (1875 letter quoted by R. J. Godlee 1918, 378–81); C. Darwin (⟨19th cent.⟩ 1977, vol. 2, 226); J. Paget (1881); R. Owen (1881) (1882); S. Wilks (1881); Philanthropos (1883); E. D. Girdlestone (1884): ". . . There is more sacredness, surely, about one human being than about all the other animal species put together!''; H. P. Bowditch (1896); W. H. Welch (1898) (1900) (accounts of Welch's defense, in the political context, of animal experiments, given by D. Fleming 1954 and P. P. Gossel 1985; also by T. A. Woolsey et al. 1987); S. Paget (1900); H. C. Ernst (1902); C. Richet (1908); W. B. Cannon (1908) (American Medical Association 1923) (Cannon's role described by S. Benison 1970, W. G. Roberts 1979, S. Benison et al. 1987); C. W. Eliot (American Medical Association 1923); W. W. Keen (1914); F. A. Tondorf (1920); J. B. S. Haldane (1928); M. B. Visscher (1967).

Animal experiments are defended by non-scientists: F. Bacon (⟨1627⟩ 1907, 323–4); R. Descartes (⟨17th cent.⟩ 1911–12, *Discourse on method*, 117); P. Carus (1897); J. Dewey (1926); H. G. Wells (1927).

Animal experiments are opposed by scientists, physicians and surgeons: A. J. Leffingwell (1880) (1907) [70]; L. Tait (1882); H. J. Bigelow [57]; E. Berdoe (1903a) (1903b); W. R. Hadwen (1914) (1926).

Animal experiments are opposed by non-scientists: J. Lawrence [16]; L. Gompertz [24] [27]; W. Youatt [25]; Queen Victoria (1875 letter quoted by E. G. Fairholme and W. Pain 1924, 378); L. Carroll [33] [34]; R. Browning [35]; R. Wagner (⟨1879⟩ 1966) (M. R. L. Freshel 1933); E. von Weber (1880); F. P. Cobbe [39] [48]; J. D. Coleridge [40]; Ouida [43] [50]; J. Ruskin (letter of 24 April 1885, *Pall Mall Gazette*); A. Kingsford [46]; H. S. Salt [49] [55] [58] [77]; E. Carpenter [51] [63]; E. Maitland [51]; G. B. Shaw [60] [76] [84] (1927) (1911, 1v: "Once grant the ethics of the vivisectionist and you not only sanction the experiment on the human subject, but make it the first duty of the vivisector. If a guinea pig may be sacrificed for the sake of the very little that can be learnt from it, shall not a man be sacrificed for the sake of the great deal that can be learnt from him?"); M. Twain (1901: "I believe I am not interested to know whether vivisection produces results that are profitable to the human race or doesn't. To know that the results are profitable to the race would not remove any hostility to it. The pain which it inflicts upon unconsenting animals is the basis of my enmity toward it, and it is to me sufficient justification of the enmity without looking further."); E. Bell [62]; L. Lind af Hageby and L. K. Schartau (1903); J. H. Moore [66]; S. Coleridge [71]; C. S. Lewis [82]; B. Brophy [93]; J. Vyvyan [94] [98].

The 1965 Littlewood report [92] studies control over animal experimentation and recommends tighter legislation.

The animal-experimentation theme appears in several fictional works: M. Twain (1904), E. Robinson (1906), F. R. Nolan (1929), H. G. Wells (1934), J. C. Powys (1937), B. Brophy (1964).

Animal Experimentation after 1970

Index Medicus (also MEDLINE database), published by the United States National Library of Medicine, providing access to the worldwide biomedical literature, is the best source on animal experimentation and animal rights from the scientific viewpoint; relevant headings: "Animal rights," "Animal welfare," "Speciesism," "Vivisection," "Animal testing alternatives," "Animal care committees." The United States National Library of Medicine *Current Catalog* (also CATLINE database), published quarterly and cumulated annually, contains citations to all printed monographs and serials cataloged by the national Library of Medicine; relevant headings: "Animal communication," "Animal husbandry," "Animal testing alternatives," "Animals," "Animals, Domestic," "Animals, Laboratory."

Psychological Abstracts (also PsycINFO database), published by the American Psychological Association, is informative on psychological experiments on animals and on psychologists' perspectives on animal experimentation.

Government publications are an important source: (1) In the United States, *Monthly Catalog of Government Publications*. A convenient microfilm reader, *Government Publications Index*, produced by Information Access Co., Belmont, CA, lists publications within the last eight years. (2) In Great Britain the subject index of the *Government Publications Annual Catalogue* issued by HMSO is useful.

Descriptions of animal experiments, heavily based on reports by experimenters, are given by R. D. Ryder [114, chaps. 2–5]; P. Singer [115, chap. 2]; N. Wade (1976); L. R. Aronson and M. L. Cooper (1976); D. Pratt (1980); Animal Welfare Institute (1985); A. Pacheko (United States 1982) [239]; J. Diner (1979) (1985) (1986) (1987); S. Gendin [269, chap. 2]; G. Langley (1987); B. Gunn (1987); B. Kuker-Reines (1982) (1984) (1985); B. Reines (1986); M. L. Stephens (1986a) (1987).

Three collections of essays mainly by scientists provide scientific views on animal experimentation: (1) Universities Federation for Animal Welfare (1977–1987): *The rational use of living systems in biomedical research*, 1972. (2) D. Sperlinger [185]. (3) M. Thelestam and A. Gunnarsson (1986).

Government hearings are informative: (1) Great Britain (1980): position statements by many scientific and animal protection organizations. (2) United States (1982): Alex Pacheko's slide presentation on E. Taub's deafferentation experiments on monkeys at Institute for Behavioral Research, Silver Springs, Maryland, sets the tone for position statements by many scientific organizations and animal protection groups. (3) United States (1984a): nearly 40 presentations on benefits of animal research, and on moral responsibilities of scientists. (4) United States (1984b): hearing on improved standards for laboratory animals.

G. M. Burghardt and H. A. Herzog Jr. [155] appreciate the ethical problems in animal experimentation implied by the Darwinian continuity of human and other animal life. Harvard University (1982), on the basis of research by P. W. D. Martin, prepares a report on the potential impact of the animal rights movement on scientific research at Harvard University and other institutions. A. N. Rowan [220], concerned about the ethical costs to animals, recommends legislative regulation of animal experimentation, and stresses development of alternatives. J. C. Zola et al. (1984) explore issues for the 1980s in regard to animal experimentation. T. H. Moss (1984) discusses the modern politics of laboratory animal use.

M. Rothschild (1986): "Looking back at the first half of my life as a zoologist I am particularly impressed by one fact: none of my teachers, lecturers, or professors with whom I came into contact . . . none of the directors of laboratories where I worked, and none of my co-workers, ever discussed with me, or each other in my presence, *the ethics of zoology.* . . . I know several zoologists who have admitted that they suffered from the fear of being dubbed 'unmanly' and struggled to overcome their dislike of causing animals pain, or killing them" (50).

A major biomedical spokesman for animal experimentation is physiologist M. B. Visscher (1967) (1972) (1975) (1979) (1982). R. J. White (1971), an advisor to Pope John Paul II on medical ethics: ". . . It would appear that this preoccupation with the alleged pain and suffering of the animals . . . may well represent . . . true psychiatric abberations'' (504). ''. . . The inclusion of lower animals in our ethical system is philosophically meaningless and operationally impossible and . . ., consequently, antivivisection theory and practice have no moral or ethical basis'' (507). O. Fallaci (1967) describes and C. Roberts (1971) criticizes White's head-transplant experiments on monkeys. White (1988) opposes animal-care-and-use committees to pass on animal research proposals; presents a glowing picture of possibilities within the next 25 years in regard to leukemia, Alzheimer's, AIDS, diabetes, high blood pressure, better vaccines, coronary-artery disease, strokes. ''But they can't be accomplished if we surrender to the mindless emotionalism and intimidation of the animal-rights fanatics.''

A. D. Macdonald (1972) defends animal experimentation on basis of benefits. True, animals cannot give consent to be experimented upon, but neither can they give consent to be eaten. ''. . . Science is more concerned with evidence and logic than with emotion; let us keep our heads and remember the facts!''

W. Lane-Petter (1972) regards animal rights talk a contradiction of reality since animals have no direct power to exercise any rights; animals will be used rationally if both science and ethics correctly answer the same question: Is this animal the best experimental system for the job? Lane-Petter (1976) comments on the ethics of animal experimentation in the context of discussing the report of the Littlewood Committee [92]; responses by S. R. L. Clark (1976), R. D. Ryder (1976), T. W. Hegarty (1976).

S. Shuster (1978) charges his opponents guilty of ''wet sentimentality.'' Ethics and morals are nothing but the rules of current expediency. There is no intrinsic right or wrong. The current revulsion against animal experimentation has been manufactured by the media on the basis of false allegation that animal experiments are not for medical research but mostly for cosmetics and trivia. R. D. Ryder (1978) replies.

F. L. Marcuse and J. J. Pear (1979): ''. . . Animal research is not only desirable but is ethically mandatory. . . . If animal research has even the vaguest possibility of contributing to the human field, it should be done.'' Critics of animal experimentation are woefully ignorant, use emotionalism.

W. A. Mason's (1979) personal response to the conflict between the value of the scientific approach and ''the inherent value of the animals I work with and their right to a free and independent existence . . . is to muddle through'' (13).

D. J. Barnes, a psychologist who conducted radiation experiments on primates, changes his mind and becomes an activist against experimentation (D. Dunheim 1981).

According to B. J. Cohen (1981) present laws, standards, and policies provide adequate protection for animals against abuse in laboratories. M. W. Ross (1981), exploring the ethics of experiments on higher animals, concludes that in the majority of cases ethical treatment and scientific approach are synonymous. W. Paton (1983) either does not understand R. G. Frey's (1983a) argument that justifying animal experiments on the basis of benefits also justifies human experiments or chooses not to respond to it. Paton (1984) argues animals have no rights because they have no duties, cannot make claims, are not participants in society; we must responsibly strike a balance between suffering in animal experiments and benefits received; dismisses P. Singer's equality principle. M. E. DeBakey (1985) defends animal experimentation on the basis of resulting medical advances.

T. D. Overcast and B. D. Sales (1985) discuss the conflict between scientists and animal rightists; critique proposed legislative solutions; suggest a conceptual framework for dealing with the issues; conclude regulation is neither necessary nor desirable; extensive references. R. W. Leader and D. Stark (1987), using the conceptual framework suggested by Overcast and Sales, stress the benefits of animals in biomedical research. J. Will (1986) presents a case for the use of animals in science, and G. F. Merrill (1986) argues for the use of animals in medicine.

P. Bateson (1986), arguing animal behavioral experiments should flourish in the interests of humans and animals, sets up a graphic representation of the "cost/benefit equation" for determining when to experiment, considering three factors: quality of research, certainty of medical benefits, amount of animal suffering. D. M. Feeney (1987) argues for animal experimentation on basis of benefits, especially to handicapped or crippled persons with incurable diseases.

There is disagreement on animal experimentation in psychology. Several scientific perspectives on the ethics of psychological research on animals are provided in essays edited by J. D. Keehn (1982). R. E. Ulrich [136] concludes that the results of his earlier research on aggression in animals do not justify its continuance. G. G. Gallup and S. D. Suarez (1980) argue there is no moral problem in animal experimentation. C. R. Gallistel (1981) critiques the proposed "Research Modernization Act" by applying its provisions to experiments by C. Bell and F. Magendie: "I can scarcely comprehend how it can be right to use animals to provide food for our bodies but wrong to use them to provide food for thought."

N. E. Miller (1983) argues for animal experiments on basis of benefits; our opponents should not eat animals; pet animals suffer more, totally, than do animals in experiments, does not mention the moral cost to animals. Miller (1985), using photos, presents evidence for the value of behavioral research on animals; attacks radical animal activists who mislead humane people by repeatedly asserting such research is completely without value; such false statements are a disservice to animal welfare by deflecting funds from worthy activities. Miller (1986) uses the biblical situation of Abraham being told by God to spare Isaac and sacrifice a ram instead to conclude that Christians, Jews and Muslims clearly affirm that animal suffering is to be chosen over human suffering; also claims that "the answer of biology to our moral issue is like that of the Bible, Torah and Koran: 'Save your child'."

F. A. King (1984) (1986) makes a case for animal experimentation by appealing to moderates who have confidence in scientists as compassionate humans and in the benefits of research, attacks extremists within animal rights movement who "take the position that animals have rights equal to or greater than humans." Argues for speciesism and hierarchical variation in values of species; claims animals have no rights and we are justified in using them for human self-interest.

D. C. Coile and N. E. Miller (1984), surveying psychological journals of 1979 through 1983, accuse radical animal activists of trying to mislead humane people in regard to the amount of suffering in animal experiments and thus diverting energy and funds from areas where animal abuse is common (pet abandonment, for example). G. G. Gallup Jr. and S. D. Suarez (1985) accuse opponents of using different terminology to describe similar actions by pet owners and scientists: "For example, many localities have 'leash laws' that require dog owners to maintain control of their pets to prevent them from running at large. Yet when scientists place dogs in harnesses or monkeys in restraint chairs, this merits a cover photo on an anti-vivisection newsletter."

J. A. Gray (1987) defends psychological experiments on animals on basis of benefits to humans. Attacks "animal liberationists": if they have a coherent moral case they keep it well hid; instead of following the rules of democratic debate they, politically motivated, resort to violence and lies and distortion. Suggests we "let the animals vote with their feet, and they often do. It is common in even the best run laboratory for a rat to escape from its cage. Finding the escapee is not difficult: it is usually sitting two or three feet from the cage. The security that surrounds animal laboratories is to keep liberationists out, not rats in" (223-4). "In arguments concerning moral doctrines . . . the choice between rivals doctrines is in the end an act of arbitrary . . . preference" (219).

R. D. Ryder [114] [182] opposes psychological, as well as other types of, experiments on animals. R. F. Drewett (1977) sharply attacks animal experiments in psychology. A. Heim [174] (1979) criticizes animal experimentation in psychology on basis of triviality, intrinsically objectionable means, and the desensitization of teachers and students. A. D. Bowd [154] (1980) (1986) (1987) has ethical reservations about psychological research with animals; claims there is a denial of ethics by defenders of exploitation of animals, provides extensive references documenting the debate within psychology. M. A. Giannelli [234] responding to N. E. Miller (1985) and F. A. King (1984), attacks psychological experiments: ". . . I am grieved to see my beloved profession glorify and engage in behavior so unbecoming of *civilized* humanity." Extensive references. J. A. Kelly (1986) disagrees with N. E. Miller on psychological research and the rights of animals.

Psychologists for the Ethical Treatment of Animals [504], with membership of 300 psychologists, develop position papers [240], concluding psychologists must develop principles and techniques protecting the rights and welfare of research animals. Also publish *Humane innovations and alternatives in animal experimentation* and *PsyETA Bulletin*.

The Humane Society of the United States [259] condemns all use of animals in psychological experimentation. J. McArdle (1984) attacks psychological animal experiments as not necessary, not valid. B. Kuker-Reines (1982) critiques animal models of human psychopathology; M. L. Stephens (1986a) critiques maternal deprivation experiments including those of H. Harlow and S. Suomi (extensive bibliography); Stephens (1987) critiques animal experiments on cocaine abuse. J. Diner (1985) provides a non-technical summary of criticisms of animal use in psychological research; Diner (1987) gives detailed descriptions of psychological experiments on animals based on reports of experimenters in technical journals.

Various aspects of animal experiments and/or use of live animals in education are opposed by: C. Roberts (1971) (1974) (1980); G. K. Russell [100] [168] (1978); B. Brophy [99]; R. Ryder [101] [114] [182] [246, pp. 77–88] [319]; A. Heim [178, pp. 37–45]; W. J. Jordan (1975); H. and M. Stiller (n.d.); R. F. Drewett (1977); A. D. Bowd [154] (1980) (1986) (1987); H. Ruesch [133] [194]; J. D. Whittall (1981); B. Kuker-Reines (1982) (1984) (1985); M. A. Giannelli [233] [234]; D. J. Barnes [246, pp. 157–67] [252]; A. M. Droeven (1985); B. Reines (1986) (1987); J. Diner (1985) (1987); J. McArdle [288] [289] [314] (1984) (1986); M. W. Fox (1981) (1986b); R. Sharpe [272] [329]; M. L. Stephens (1986a) (1987); B. Carlsson [253]; C. R. Boylan and A. D. Bowd (1985); L. Gruen [282]; V. Moran [291]; N. D. Barnard (1987).

The veterinarian's oath is anthropocentric, viewing the protection of animal health and the relief of animal suffering as means to the benefit of humans: "Being admitted to the profession of veterinary medicine, I solemnly swear to use my scientific knowledge and skills for the benefit of society through the protection of animal health, the relief of animal suffering, the conservation of livestock resources, the promotion of public health, and the advancement of medical knowledge" (adopted by the American Veterinary Medical Association in 1969). M. J. McCulloch (1978) confirms the anthropocentric view of veterinary medicine: "I would argue that although the object is different, the ultimate goal in both professions [human medicine, veterinary medicine] is the same – the promotion and maintenance of human health" (53).

J. Tannenbaum (1985) (1986b) claims the animal rights movement is not in the interests of the veterinary profession, and attacks some of the views of B. E. Rollin. Rollin (1986d) replies. Tannenbaum (1986c) responds. Other works by Rollin relevant: (1977) (1983) [132]. T. Regan (1983) criticizes the anthropocentric veterinarian's oath. F. M. Loew (1987), documenting the remarkable inactivity and disinterest of organized veterinary medicine in animal welfare issues, urges the profession "to temper its science with the compassion and commitment to study issues such as pain and suffering, animal behavior, and the ethical treatment of animals."

The Association of Veterinarians for Animal Rights [473], with members primarily veterinarians in the United States but also from other countries, is establishing student chapters at veterinary schools, publishes bimonthly newsletter, publishes carefully prepared *Position Statements* [306] recognizing animals' interests and the inherent value of their lives.

The Physicians Committee for Responsible Medicine. P.O. Box 6322,

Washington, DC 20015, is a nation-wide group of physicians which supports students' rights to do no harm to animals, promotes alternative methods not using animals, publishes bimonthly *PCRM Update* and *Alternatives in medical education* (Physicians Committee for Responsible Medicine 1987).

The Medical Research Modernization Committee [494], with nearly 700 members from medicine and science, has the primary function of scientifically critiqueing irrelevant, outdated animal models, and promoting alternatives to live animal use. Will publish quarterly newsletter, first issue to be sent to thousands of medical students. Will sponsor summer research fellowships for medical and veterinary students, to evaluate animal models.

The Universities Federation for Animal Welfare [454] is a British scientific society with principal aim to promote humane behavior toward animals so as to reduce the sum total of pain inflicted on animals by humans. Does not engage in controversy relating to legitimacy of scientific experiments on animals; cooperates in a practical way with those who work with experimental animals. See partial list of publications (Universities Federation for Animal Welfare 1977–1987).

The Scientists Center for Animal Welfare [506] promotes animal welfare through various educational activities, including newsletter, workshops, seminars, publications. Proceedings of the 1981 conference on scientific perspectives on animal welfare are published (W. J. Dodds and F. B. Orlans 1982). Effective animal-care-and-use committees in accordance with new regulations by the US Department of Agriculture and the Public Health Service are discussed by F. B. Orlans et al. (1987).

The Canadian Council on Animal Care, 1000–151 Slater St, Ottawa, Ontario K1P 5H3, is an autonomous advisory and supervisory body operating on a voluntary basis, emphasizing control exercised by the scientists themselves from within the institution. Details are provided by F. H. Flowers (1983). Publishes detailed guide to the care and use of experimental animals (Canadian Council on Animal Care 1980–84). Views of the Executive Director expressed by H. C. Rowsell (1977) (1978–79).

The Research Defence Society, Grosvenor Gardens House, Grosvenor Gardens, London SW1W 0BS, consisting of scientists, physicians and others, has as its purpose "to make generally known the value and necessity of experiments on animals." Publishes *Conquest* periodically. Sponsors annual Stephen Paget Memorial Lectures, beginning in 1927, emphasizing benefits of animal experiments; nine recent lectures are representative (Research Defence Society 1927–85).

In cooperation with the Association of American Medical Colleges, the Foundation for Biomedical Research, 818 Connecticut Ave NW, Suite 303, Washington, DC 20006, with the purpose of providing the media and the public with information on animal research and its benefits, and of counteracting what it perceives to be a threat to biomedical research by the animal rights movement, publishes a variety of materials (Foundation for Biomedical Research 1987a, 1987b). F. L. Trull (1987) discusses the animal rights movement and the Foundation for Biomedical Research.

The Federation of American Societies for Experimental Biology (1986) symposium, dealing with the practical problem of how scientists and universities can most effectively work with the government and the media in defending animal experimentation, reveals strong concern over the negative publicity resulting from the media coverage of the baboon head injury experiments conducted by T. Gennarelli at the University of Pennsylvania. C. Grunewald and J. Mason (1985) provides details of the head injury laboratory break-in. Also see [239].

The American Association for the Advancement of Science (1986), in its Media Outreach Program Roundtable, exploring the effects of new regulations on the use of animals in biomedical research, evidences concern over increased costs, role of institutional animal-care-and-use committees, and bafflement over interpretation of and compliance with the requirement of an environment "to promote the psychological well-being of primates."

Lab-Animal (65 Bleecker St, NY, NY 10012) published monthly, the biomedical community's semi-official commercial organ, devotes space to news and articles on tactics and strategies designed to "contain" pro-animal advances. A new publication, *The Animal Rights Reporter* (Perception Press, Suite 9, 1000 Connecticut Ave NW, Washington, DC 20036), is a monthly newspaper tracking the growing animal rights movement, protests, boycotts, legislative pressures, etc. Other biomedical publications with articles defending animal experimentation, and news items on the animal rights movement, are described by P. Greanville (1988a).

Fictional works involving themes of animal experimentation by: R. C. O'Brien (1972), M. Duffy (1973), P. White (1973), W. Kotzwinkle (1976), J. Tiptree (1977), R. Adams (1978), M. W. Tuttle (1978), I. Hamilton (1980), R. Roy (1985), J. L. Conly (1986).

Alternatives to Animal Experimentation and Testing

Bibliographies: R. Friedman [280, entries 203–45] and A. N. Rowan [220, pp. 287–312].

W. M. S. Russell and R. L. Burch (1959) discuss three ways of diminishing animal distress in experiments: replacement (substitution of insentient material for conscious, living animals), reduction (in the number of animals used), refinement (decrease in distress through refined procedures). Authoritative information, technical and general, on alternatives (especially to toxicity testing) is found in the writings of A. N. Rowan: (1977) (1979) (1980) [185, pp. 257–83], (1981a) (1983) [220, pp. 261–73] (1987). Perspectives on alternatives to current animal toxicity testing are given by A. N. Rowan and A. M. Goldberg (1985). Goldberg (1986) discusses problems and opportunities for alternatives in toxicology.

Alternatives are emphasized in a symposium sponsored by the Institute of Laboratory Animal Resources (1977). A conference on alternatives is sponsored by the International Association Against Painful Experiments on Animals (National Anti-Vivisection Society, London 1977). G. K. Russell (1978) provides a series of experiments in basic physiology making use of the students themselves as experimental subjects in lieu of animals. D. H. Smyth (1978) addresses the questions: What is meant by alternatives? What alternatives are there? What actions, policies are possible using alternatives?

D. Pratt (1980) describes painful experiments on animals matched with possible alternatives where available. Interesting interchanges between scientists and animal welfarists and rightists permeate the symposium on alternatives organized by the National Institutes of Health (United States 1981). Proceedings of a 1982 Royal Society conference provide a rather technical study of alternatives in toxicity testing (M. Balls et al. 1983). Proceedings of a Humane Research Trust symposium on alternatives are edited by P. Turner (1983). Descriptions and critical evaluations of, and alternatives to, the LD-50 test constitute the subject of a CFN symposium in Sweden (P. Lindgren et al. 1983).

A. M. Goldberg (ed.) (1984) (1987) and J. M. Frazier et al. (1987) provide technical information on alternative methods in toxicology. Proceedings of University of Liverpool symposium on alternatives are edited by N. Marsh and S. Haywood (1985). Alternatives to animal uses in research, toxicity testing and education are discussed by Office of Technology Assessment (United States 1986a). Useful treatments of alternatives for the lay reader are by M. L. Stephens (1986b) and J. Diner (n.d.). S. M. Niemi and W. J. Dodds (1986) discuss alternatives to animal experimentation, and the "new dialogue" between animal researchers and animal-welfare advocates in the context of animal-care-and-use committees.

M. Stephens (1986c) studies the significance of alternatives through an analysis of Nobel Prize awards. R. Sharpe [272] [329] summarizes methods used to advance medical research without the use of animals, and discusses ethical issues: "The alternative to many . . . animal experiments is . . . simply not to do the research." S. R. Kaufmann (1987): "In medical practice there is little if any use for the classical LD-50. . . . Extrapolating its results from animals to man is inaccurate and misleading. . . . The needs of the physician would be better served by the abandonment of the classical LD-50 . . ." A series of volumes, *Alternative methods in toxicology*, is published by Mary Ann Liebert, Inc., New York. A new journal *In Vitro Toxicology* is published by Pergamon Press, Elmsford, New York.

Organizations researching and promoting alternatives include: (1) FRAME (Fund for the Replacement of Animals in Medical Experiments) [444]. (2) American Fund for Alternatives to Animal Research [460]. (3) Johns Hopkins Center for Alternatives to Animal Testing, 615 No. Wolfe St, Baltimore, MD 21205.

H. Spira [224] [248] (1984) coordinates the Coalition to Abolish the LD-50 [477] and the Coalition to Stop Draize Rabbit Blinding Tests [478].

The consumer can practice an effective alternative by purchasing only cosmetics and other products from manufacturers which do not test products on animals and which do not use animal components. See Appendix E for sources of animal-free products.

Welfare/Illfare of Animals used for Food

Bibliographies and abstracts: (1) C. R. Magel [176, entries 401–3, 1651–719]. (2) The annual *Bibliography of Agriculture* (also AGRICOLA database), issued by the United States National Agricultural Library; relevant headings: "Animal research," "Animal welfare," "Animal health," "Animal husbandry," "Animal experiments," "Animal behavior," "Laboratory animals." (3) *Animal Science and Production Abstracts* (covering the world literature on animal breeding production, dairy science, research on pigs, pig news, nutrition, poultry, small animals), published by CAB International, Slough, United Kingdom (also CAB ABSTRACTS database).

Descriptions of methods of production, transportation and slaughter of animals: R. Harrison [87] [97, pp. 11–24] [143, pp. 122–30]; F. W. Brambell [90], P. Singer [115, chap. 3]; J. Mason and P. Singer [163]; M. Gold [203]; M. W. Fox (1980a) (1984); L. Gruen et al. [282].

Given that "health," "disease," "welfare," "illfare," "well-being," "ill-being" are value-laden terms (Rollin 1979), expressing what should or should not be, so-called scientific discussions of animal welfare/illfare tend to be empty and/or not scientific. Motivated by public concern generated by R. Harrison's important *Animal machines* [87], the Brambell report [90] contains one of the best discussions of animal welfare, and recommends changes in rearing of animals; considers both physical and mental well-being of animals; denies growth rate or productivity to be adequate criteria for well-being; recognizes the complexity of animal emotions and needs. The appended essay by W. H. Thorpe [91] assesses pain and distress in animals.

R. Harrison (1970, 3–16) considers steps toward legislation regulating the raising of animals for food. Various views on pain and farm efficiency are given in a series of articles in *New Scientist*: R. Ewbank (1973), I. Duncan (1973), G. Perry (1973), T. Ewer (1973), C. Tudge (1973). Animal welfare in modern agriculture is discussed by D. G. M. Wood-Gush (1973). M. Kiley-Worthington (1977) deals with behavioral problems of farm animals. Essays edited by D. W. Fölsch (1978) cover the ethology and ethics of farm animal production. Universities Federation for Animal Welfare (1979) (1981) assesses developments in the livestock industry and publishes proceedings of a symposium on alternatives to intensive husbandry systems.

The Council for Agricultural Science and Technology (1981), stating that animal welfare cannot yet be measured objectively or expressed quantitatively, restricts itself to traditional criteria: rate of growth or production, efficiency of feed use, efficiency of reproduction, mortality, morbidity; claims "the goal of maximum profitability pursued by animal producers (and others) leads automatically to improved welfare of both animals and humans." B. Klug (1982) (1983b) sharply criticizes, accusing CAST of propagandizing rather than presenting scientific study.

I. J. H. Duncan (1981) presents a useful overview of approaches to animal welfare. The House of Commons Select Committee on Agriculture (Great Britain 1981) condemns factory farming of pigs and veal calves, and recommends a phase out of battery cages for hens; but their suggestions rejected by the government.

The Working Party convened by E. Carpenter [156] concludes the dignity of animals requires respect for seven of their basic needs, and precludes intensive systems of raising animals. M. S. Dawkins [159] studies criteria for determining suffering in animals. J. F. Hurnik (1980), critical of some intensive systems, concludes human creativity has the potential to achieve efficiency in production of animals without compromising animal welfare. J. F. Hurnik and H. Lehman (1982) analyze the definition of and evidence for unnecessary suffering.

M. W. Fox writes extensively on factory farming, farm animal welfare and husbandry: (1980a) (1980b) (1983) (1984) [231] [256]. M. W. Fox and L. D. Mickley (1986) present the case against intensive farming of food animals. M. Gold [203] critiques factory farming of animals in the British context. Indicators relevant to farm animal welfare are discussed in essays edited by D. Smidt (1983). S. E. Curtis (1980) (1982) (1986) (1987) defends intensive farming of food animals. E. R. Bennett (1985) argues P. Singer has a romanticized view of animals in his analysis of factory farming. J. L. Albright (1986), emphasizing "the animal welfare issue is not going away," discusses strategies for animal producers to use in facing the animal rights movement.

D. M. Broom (1986), first professor in animal welfare (Cambridge School of Veterinary Medicine), isolates indicators of poor animal welfare. A recent work on farm animal welfare (cattle, pigs, poultry) is by D. Sainsbury (1986). Proceedings of a British workshop on the teaching of animal welfare are edited by P. M. Ray (1987); useful reading list. The Animal Welfare Institute (1987) argues factory farming of animals is an experiment that fails the animals, family farmers, the environment, and the consumer; the beneficiaries are those who profit from "farming the tax code."

The American Veterinary Medical Association (n.d.) approves of: confinement rearing of livestock and poultry; individual tethers and stalls for sows; castration, ear notching and tail docking of piglets; caging of layer hens; beak trimming of chickens and turkeys; inducing moulting of layer birds through reduced light and low sodium/calcium diets. A sharply different view is held by the Association of Veterinarians for Animal Rights [306]. The Animal Welfare Foundation of the British Veterinary Association (n.d.) adopts "a natural charter" of animals' rights to five types of freedom: from hunger or malnutrition, from thermal or physical discomfort, from pain or injury or disease, from fear and distress, to indulge in patterns of behavior normal for the species.

K. Davis (1988) discusses similarities between the situations of women/ minorities and farm animals; criticizes the "macho ecology" of A. Leopold, J. B. Callicott and P. Shepard; claims we should put farm animals at the forefront of global ethics. A campaign to end sow and hen suffering is launched by the Humane Society of the United States [284].

P. Greanville (1988b) discusses eleven agrijournals which promote the "animal food industry'' and which frequently contain reactions to the animal rights movement.

D. Stewart (1972) gives a fictional account of the Troogs who conquer the earth and factory-farm humans for food. P. Curtis [158, pp. 73–89], in fiction based on fact, tells the story of the veterinarian who becomes involved in the campaign for legislation to reform the factory-farming system.

Fiction by C. Redman (1986–87): Gail, 20, candidate for Nebraska Beef Queen, becomes enlightened about the meat industry (a visit to the kill floor part of her education). At the announcement of winning, Gail collapses on the stage in her own vomit, and is rescued by her sympathetic friend Randy.

3 Education and Animals

Bibliographies and Sources of Educational Materials

(1) C. R. Magel's bibliography [176, entries 1840–53]. (2) W. DeRosa's (1984) annotated bibliography on research relevant to humane education. (3) S. R. Kellert and J. K. Berry [235, "Education"]. (4) National Association for the Advancement of Humane Education curriculum guide [177]. (5) T. Threadingham (1986): directory of resources on animals in education (mainly British), on companion animals, wild animals, birds, endangered species, farm animals, animal experimentation, using animals in sport and entertainment. (6) R. Lockwood [260]: annotated bibliography for higher education. (7) D. Pratt (1986); 136 annotated and evaluated animal films for humane education under categories: attitudes toward animals, fights, food and commercial uses, hunting, performing animals, pets, research and testing, riding, service animals, transportation, trapping, veterinary medicine, wildlife, zoos. (8) Universities Federation for Animal Welfare (1983): list of audio-visuals on animals in scientific research for use in higher education. (9) Focus on Animals [484]: *Educators' Newsletter* and annotated catalog of films and videotapes available for rent with teachers' guides. See Appendix C for list of 16 films available. (10) The Fund for Animals [487] *Animal rights resources catalog*, edited by V. Handley, n.d., non-paginated: a wealth of films, books, literature, lesson plans, organizations. (11) National Association for the Advancement of Humane Education [500] publishes *Children and Animals* (formerly *Humane Education*): teachers' quarterly magazine containing activities, games, worksheets, mini-posters, teaching units. Also *Kind News*, issued five times yearly with teaching guide: four-page newspaper motivating students to read, to care, to write. (12) References are provided by participants in two

symposia on animals and education: [178] and H. McGiffin and N. Brownley (1980). (13) The Royal Society for the Prevention of Cruelty to Animals [451], through its education department, offers a wide variety of materials for teachers and students, in four areas: companion animals, animal experimentation, farming, wildlife. (14) The Humane Society of the United States [489] offers a wide variety of pamphlets, audio-visuals, literature for students and teachers. (15) The American Humane Association [461] offers classroom kits, teachers' guides, pamphlets, periodicals, posters, audio-visuals. (16) The International Society for Animal Rights [344] issues "Educational materials for animal rights," listing folders, brochures, booklets, books, video tapes available for rent (see Appendix C). (17) The Athene Trust [435], an educational charity, produces slide sets, videos, monographs, etc., with emphasis on the welfare of animals used for food.

Through 1970

J. Locke (⟨17th cent.⟩ 1968, par. 117) urges that children should be taught not to be cruel "for the custom of tormenting and killing of beasts will, by degrees, harden their minds even toward men, and they who delight in the suffering and destruction of inferior creatures will not be apt to be very compassionate or benign to those of their own kind."

J. J. Rousseau, in *Émile*, discusses importance of development of the sentiment of pity in education of children: "How do we let ourselves be moved by pity if not by transporting outside of ourselves and identifying with the suffering animal?" (⟨1762⟩ 1979, 222–3).

S. Trimmer's (⟨1786⟩ 1977) "fabulous histories designed for the instruction of children respecting their treatment of animals," emphasizing kindness to animals, becomes very popular and is published in many editions.

H. J. Bigelow (⟨1871⟩ 1977), horrified by the surgical practicing on live horses without anesthetics by students at the Veterinary College, Alfort, France (Alfort 1895), urges: "Nobody should do it. Watch the students at a vivisection. It is the blood and suffering, not the science, that rivet their breathless attention. . . . Vivisection deadens their humanity, and begets indifference to it" (310). The first English handbook (illustrated) for the physiological laboratory (J. Burdon-Sanderson et al. 1873), using C. Bernard's techniques, intended for beginners and to encourage students to practice experiments themselves, arouses protest in Great Britain.

H. S. Salt in 1896 [51, vol. 3], in a 32-page essay "Literae humaniories" appeals to teachers on the need of humane education (pets, collecting insects, hunting, use of animals for food). L. Lind af Hageby and L. K. Schartau (1903), medical students at University College in London, record details of demonstrations on dogs in physiological classes, resulting in litigation and the erection of the Brown Dog statue in London (E. K. Ford 1908) and the Brown Dog riots (C. Lansbury 1985).

A bulletin issued by the State Normal School of San Diego (1906) expresses an anthropocentric rationale for humane education: "The general purpose of humane education . . . is to contribute to the highest and most enduring happiness of the human race. The temporary desires and pleasures of the inferior animals are to be taken into consideration, rather in view of the effect of their recognition upon human character, than from the standpoint of the positive rights of the animals themselves. . . . The only right anything possesses is the right to be useful. . . . Man, standing at the head of the hierarchy of animal species, rightfully claims sovereignty over this great kingdom and demands that the brute creation . . . should, in the long run, subserve his ends" (4). ". . . Unnecessary and wanton injury or destruction of either plants or animals is uneconomical, positively injurious to society, and reacts detrimentally upon the character of the offender" (5).

J. R. Bronars (1970) describes various science program units in the elementary school on plant and animal life, instructing students to enclose insects in jars to cut off air supply, chloroform and mount insects, drop acid on worms, induce malnutrition in mice through deficient diet, put frogs in ice water, dissect fish and frogs. Bronars isolates and criticizes fundamental anthropocentric assumptions underlying these practices, finding them in conflict with the attempt to teach respect for life.

Pre-college

For a comprehensive curriculum guide to humane education, pre-school through sixth grade, see [177]. *PETA Kids*, published by People for Ethical Treatment of Animals [503], is especially for elementary students and their teachers. Children's books featuring animals are analyzed by M. Blount (1974). M. Banton's (1987) illustrated *Animal rights* is intended for grades 7-9. Three books for teenagers on animal rights: [158] [217] [332]. The National Association for the Advancement of Humane Education [500] offers for students the brochure *Does the idea of dissecting or experimenting on animals in biology class disturb you?* and for teachers the brochure *The living science: A humane approach to the study of animals in elementary and secondary school biology. Humane biology projects* is published by the Animal Welfare Institute [471].

K. Frucht (1979, 259): "Humane education far too often preaches more than it teaches. . . . Much of today's illustrated juvenile literature dealing with animals has very little in common with zoological reality. . . . Rather than trying to teach kindness to animals, the mere conveyance of facts about them will prepare the young mind far better to accept kinship with animals." H. N. Christensen (1986) pleads for biological realism in children's books, claiming that sentimental portrayals of animals are partially responsible for later negative attitudes against animal research and science.

A. R. Felthous and S. R. Kellert (1987), reviewing controlled studies, conclude: ". . . Studies using direct interviews to examine subjects with multiple acts of violence point to an association between a pattern of childhood animal cruelty and later serious, recurrent aggression against people'' (710). Felthous and Kellert (1986) explore the question: Is aggression against living creatures generalized? See also study by A. R. Felthous (1980). Kellert and Felthous (1985) study childhood cruelty toward animals among criminals and noncriminals.

G. K. Russell [100] [168] (1978) criticizes the harmful use of animals at the high school and college levels, and develops alternatives. E. S. Leavitt and B. Beary [125, pp. 146–55] give a short history of humane education in America and reproduce public school laws from 20 states requiring teaching of humane education. A Canadian perspective on high school science fairs and experiments using live animals in the classroom is given by H. C. Rowsell (1980). B. Orlans (1980) argues against invasive experiments on animals at the high school level and describes alternatives; gives examples of unacceptable and acceptable science fair projects. M. W. Fox and H. McGiffin criticize the use of animals in biology classrooms and science fairs [185, pp. 239–54]. A. N. Rowan (1981b) discusses animals in education.

The speciesist use of live animals for dissection by students can lead to trauma, "hardening," sadism, according to R. Ryder [182]. The use of animals in British schools is discussed by D. Paterson [143, pp. 143–6] [185, pp. 225–38]. B. E. Rollin [181, pp. 105–7] critiques the use of animals in teaching: ''. . . There is no reason that high school and grade school children need to experiment on living creatures.'' S. R. Westerlund [198] edits a collection of readings on humane education and realms of humaneness.

C. R. Boylan and A. D. Bowd (1985) explore problems in enhancing students' respect for animal life through the teaching of science, and suggest alternative procedures; valuable list of references. V. Moran [291], J. McArdle [289] and T. Regan [296, pp. 136–51] emphasize students' right not to violate the rights of animals in the course of their education.

College and University

R. F. Drewett (1977) sharply attacks two books (B. L. Hart 1976 and J. Bures et al. 1976) used for practical work by psychology students as involving cruelty of an order impossible to justify (food and water deprivation, swimming to exhaustion, paralysis with curare-like drug followed by electric shocks), seemingly indicating an absolute lack of concern with the suffering of animals; hopes students will protest forcibly; hopes that Elsevier and W. H. Freeman will in due course come to be deeply ashamed of what they have published. J. Bures et al. (1978) respond, arguing that since students will be forced in their future jobs to perform exactly similar experiments, it is important that they now be taught how to perform them ''humanely.'' Using examples from experimental psychology, A. Heim discusses the blunting of sensibilities in schools with respect to the suffering of animals [178, pp. 37–45]. G. Langley [178, pp. 25–35] considers the use of animals in British universities.

A dialogue on philosophical vegetarianism, for use by teachers in generating discussions on the moral issues of eating meat, is presented by R. M. Feezell and D. A. Dombrowski (1984). R. Lockwood (1985b) develops a model syllabus for a course in human–animal relationships. Topics considered: our place in nature; philosophical perspectives on our relationship to animals; cruelty and kindness; animals and the law; hunting; endangered species; scientific and educational use of animals; animals in captivity; animals in entertainment; contemporary activism; origin of domestic animals, our relationship with companion animals.

Many courses at the college and university level – especially in philosophy, ethics, environmental ethics, medical ethics, ecology, humanities, animal welfare, veterinary ethics, interdisciplinary courses – contain segments on various aspects of animal rights. The anthology *Animal rights and human obligations* [121] [317 forthcoming revised], edited by T. Regan and P. Singer, is designed for use in such courses. *Animals and Christianity: A book of readings* [311], edited by A. Linzey and T. Regan, is intended for use in courses at Christian colleges, universities and seminaries.

Medical School

Bill Davidson, entering medical school, worries intelligently about laboratory animal experimentation and plans a strategy for getting a medical degree without performing harmful experiments: fiction, but based on fact [158, pp. 1–19]. Alternatives to the use of animals in education at the college and graduate levels (especially medical education) are discussed by M. L. Stephens (1986b, 53–6). Alternatives are also emphasized by the Physicians Committee for Responsible Medicine (1987), covering animal labs in medical school, teaching methods for surgery and manual skills, teaching methods for physiology and pharmacology, videos and films, computer simulations and state-of-the-art simulators. The National Coalition to Protect Our Pets [501] provides an educational packet: "Sacrificing Pound or Shelter Animals for Medical or Veterinary School Training: A Needless Waste of Lives."

B. E. Rollin [181, p. 106]: "In Great Britain, veterinarians are trained without ever laying hands on an animal, save for therapeutic purposes." Rollin [210] argues moral reasoning and moral philosophy are desperately needed in biomedicine and biomedical education. T. Regan (1983) raises the question whether veterinary students are being taught to serve animals or to serve humans; criticizes the veterinarian's oath.

Proceedings of a British workshop on the teaching of animal welfare are edited by P. M. Ray (1987); useful reading list. D. M. Broom, professor of animal welfare, reports (by letter to the author of this *Keyguide*) that his animal welfare course is required for all veterinary students at the University of Cambridge, and that all veterinary and agricultural courses in the United Kingdom now include some lectures on animal welfare.

4 Law and Animals

Bibliographies: C. R. Magel [176, entries 2236–321] and S. R. Kellert and J. K. Berry [235, "Law-Regulation"]. Indexes and databases: (1) The *Index to Legal Periodicals* (also ILP database), produced by H. W. Wilson Co., New York, covers nearly 500 journals published in United States, United Kingdom, Canada, Australia, New Zealand. (2) The *Current Law Index*, in microfilm reader form, issued by Information Access Co., Belmont, CA, is a convenient source for items published during the past eight years.

Jurisprudence

H. Grotius (⟨1625⟩ 1901, 23) maintains animals cannot possess rights because they cannot form general maxims; J. Rodman (1979) finds an incoherence in Grotius' interpretation of natural right and law which excludes animals from the sphere of justice. O. W. Holmes (1881, 7–27) explores the rationale of the liability of animals, plants and inanimate objects in ancient Greek and Roman law; traces influence of such law on early German and English laws with some tendency to regard slaves, children and animals in similar categories. The rationale for criminal prosecution and punishment of animals from the Middle Ages until the 19th century is covered by E. P. Evans (⟨1906⟩ 1987) and W. W. Hyde (1916).

J. C. Gray (⟨1909⟩ 1963, 42–5), emphasizing that animals in modern jurisprudence have no legal rights or duties, notes there may have been, indeed may still be, systems of law in which animals have legal rights – for instance, cats in ancient Egypt or white elephants in Siam. H. L. A. Hart (1963, 34) maintains the intelligibility of regarding protection laws as concerned with the suffering of animals and not merely with the immorality of torturing them. C. Morris [88] argues for conferring legal rights on nature ("beasts and trees"), rights that can be enforced in the courts by nature's friends. L. H. Tribe (1974) critiques the homocentric view of nature underlying present environmental policy and law which are concerned only with the satisfaction of human interests, and explores the possibility of new foundations wherein rights for animals and natural objects are recognized.

C. E. Friend (1974) makes the case for reform in animal cruelty laws in the United States, the basic problem being that animals are considered personal property: ". . . The field of animal protection law is in a sorry state." Problems in estate planning for animals are considered by B. W. Schwartz (1974). S. I. Burr [110] argues for revision of our legal system enabling legal guardians to represent animals' interests in courts. C. D. Stone [107] (1976) argues for legal standing of natural objects. It is not clear whether Stone (1984) (1985) (1987a), in urging legal considerateness for natural objects, rejects his former position or is clarifying and expanding it in the context of moral pluralism. G. E. Varner (1987) argues Stone's retreat is both unnecessary and undesirable. Stone (1987b) clarifies his position.

J. S. Tischler (1977) explores the question of legal rights for animals and proposes a guardianship model for dogs and cats, removing them from the property category, and extending legal rights to them. According to R. B. Edwards and F. H. Marsh (1978), since our murder laws are designed to afford protection to "reasonable creatures in being," and since the higher apes and porpoises are reasonable creatures in being, consistency requires our murder laws apply to them. J Feinberg [130, pp. 45–69] asserts that legal theory and practice should change to recognize animals' legal standing and legal rights.

M. A. Fox (1978c) advocates animals be given legal rights. A. Dichter (1978) argues for legal rights and standing for animals: "The possession of legal rights is meaningless unless one has standing to vindicate these rights in court." Arguments for animals' legal rights are by B. E. Rollin [181, pp. 67–86] and T. Regan [193, pp. 148–64] [296, pp. 164–73] [294]. V. P. McCarthy [192]: ". . . Inevitably, some owner or animal group will eventually introduce a breakthrough case, on behalf of an animal, in which a court will award damages for the loss to the animal himself." S. M. Wise (1983) (1986) discusses using courts for animals. H. Cohen (1983b) explores the idea of extending common law rights of action to animals, animals recovering for personal injury and wrongful death.

R. W. Galvin [232] urges recognition of three basic legal rights for all sentient beings. R. Dresser (1985) proposes a model for legal reform to integrate interests of laboratory animals and interests of humans, using a risk–benefit basis, arguing her model deals only with method of experiments, not content, hence eliminating conflict with the first amendment. Dresser (1988) analyzes recently revised policy of the Public Health Service and the recently amended Animal Welfare Act in the context of her model. G. L. Francione (1988) critiques Dresser's model, arguing the method–content distinction collapses; presents arguments against interpreting animal experimentation as "expression" or "expressive conduct" protected by the first amendment.

D. Favre [254] proposes a federal Laboratory Animal Act regulating painful research on animals, with special protection for primates. J. O. Nelson (1987) claims there is an intrinsic incoherence in the concept of legal rights for animals since they can have no idea of rights and duties. P. Wenz (1988) finds that current anti-cruelty state laws do no more than prohibit what the majority find most distasteful, hence violate people's civil liberties, and fail to substantially ameliorate the suffering of animals.

United Kingdom

Early unsuccessful attempts by W. Pulteney (1800 bill against bear baiting) and by Lord Erskine (1809 bill to prohibit cruelty to animals; see [21]), and R. Martin's successful attempt (1822 passage of Martin's Act for preventing cruelty to animals; additional bills to extend Martin's Act) are described by W. Pain (1925) and A. W. Moss (1961, 14–19). The Cruelty to Animals Act 1876, controlling experiments upon living vertebrates, is analyzed, criticized and reproduced by R. D. Ryder [114, pp. 116–33, 265–8]. This Act is also studied in the Littlewood report [92], which recommends changes. The Protection of Animals Act 1911 (with amendments) is the basic legislation protecting domestic or captive animals. T. G. Field-Fisher (1964) covers animals and the law. A more recent survey of animal law in England and Wales is provided by G. Sandys-Winsch [221].

P. M. Ray and W. N. Scott (1976) summarize United Kingdom legislation relevant to the keeping of laboratory animals. Notes on the law relating to experiments on animals in Great Britain are provided by Research Defence Society (1979).

Two White Papers (Great Britain 1983, 1985) precede passage of the Animals (Scientific Procedures) Act 1986, replacing the Cruelty to Animals Act 1876. Under the new Act the Home Secretary, advised by a statutory Animal Procedures Committee, has the responsibility of making judgments on the scientific merit of experiments authorized. C. Hollands (1986) (1987) provides background and detailed provisions of the 1986 Act.

M. E. Cooper [334] provides a current guide to animal law, primarily in the United Kingdom but also in the United States and other countries, and international. The analysis of the British Animals (Scientific Procedures) Act 1986 is detailed (44–79).

United States

R. Bennon (1984) provides a legal research guide for animal welfare and animal rights, covering sources within past 15 years; includes federal statutes, cases, books, journal articles, legal newspapers, loose-leaf services, databases. *Animal Law Report*, containing editorials, animal-related laws, case decisions and articles, is published by American Bar Association, Young Lawyers Division, Animal Protection Committee (begun in 1984; scheduled for twice yearly but the March 1987 issue is the fifth).

The Animal Welfare Institute [125, will be revised 1988] provides an informative survey of American laws from 1641 to 1978; also deals with local, state, federal and international laws. Federal and state laws affecting animals are discussed by C. Stevens (1979). E. S. Leavitt and B. Beary [125, pp. 146–55] reproduce laws from 20 states requiring teaching humane education. D. S. Favre and M. Loring (1983) cover United States laws (national and eight representative state), emphasizing animals as property, without legal rights. D. S. Favre (1979) discusses wildlife rights.

M. J. Bean (1983) explores the evolution of national wildlife law. A detailed guide to United States wildlife laws is by C. Estes and K. W. Sessions (1983–84). D. S. Moretti (1984) gives a brief account of state anti-cruelty laws and several federal laws on laboratory animals, slaughter, etc. Brief treatments make the book more valuable for the public than for lawyers. Title is misleading in that animal rights are not discussed.

There are no federal laws regulating intensive production of animals for food. And it is questionable what application state anti-cruelty laws have to procedures used in factory farming of animals for food. R. F. McCarthy and R. E. Bennett (1986) analyze and summarize federal and state statutes pertaining to the protection of animals used in agriculture.

Human animals are well protected by federal law (United States 1978) from physical or psychological or social harm resulting from experiments; informed consent is required from adult subjects; vulnerable persons (children, the mentally infirm, terminally ill, comatose, etc.) are given rigorous protection. Not so in the case of the other animals. The major federal law regarding laboratory animals is the Animal Welfare Act (United States 1966–1985) applying only to animals in experiments funded by the federal government, including dogs, cats, nonhuman primates, guinea pigs, hamsters, rabbits, but excluding birds, rats, mice, horses, other farm animals, poultry, all cold-blooded animals. The Act covers transportation, purchase, sale, housing, handling and care of animals, but it does not control what can be done to the animal during an experiment. C. Stevens [125, pp. 46–68] provides a history of events leading to enactment. A *Life* magazine article (S. Wayman 1966) with powerful photos of "dognaped" dogs sold to laboratories and medical schools is historically important in generating support for the Animal Welfare Act.

Congressional hearings provide insight into various views (United States 1966, 1970, 1974, 1975, 1976, 1982). H. Spira (United States 1976, 42) testifies: "The Animal Welfare Act [is] Orwellian travesty on the English language. It protects not laboratory animals but live animal researchers by lulling and reassuring the citizenry that there is a law, numbing concerned people with the calming thought that our government is looking after the voiceless and helpless. In fact, animal researchers have the power of absolute tyrants within the laboratory."

The 1985 amendment (Public Law 99–198, Subtitle F, sects. 1751–9) to the Animal Welfare Act (known as "The Improved Standards for Laboratory Animals Act") includes provision for (1) exercise of dogs; (2) physical environment adequate to promote the psychological well-being of primates; (3) requirement for animal care, treatment, and practices in experimental procedures to ensure that animal pain and distress are minimized, including adequate veterinary care; (4) establishment of institutional animal care and use committees, at least one member representing community interests. A philosophical critique of institutional animal care and use committees is given by L. Finsen [335, pp. 145–58]. The National Institute of Health (United States 1986b) provides policy and detail on establishment of institutional animal care and use committees, and also reproduces the nine provisions of the "U.S. government principles for the utilization and care of vertebrate animals used in testing, research and training." The *Guide for the care and use of laboratory animals* (United States 1985) is coordinated with these nine principles. Regulations proposed by the Secretary of Agriculture for compliance with Public Law 99–198: United States (1987). An up-to-date analysis of United States federal laws and regulations governing animal experiments and tests (Animal Welfare Act as amended effective 23 December 1986; Health Research Extension Act of 1985; regulations of the Public Health Service, the Food and Drug Administration and the Environmental Protection Agency) is made by Foundation for Biomedical Research (1987a, 45–65).

E. F. Dukes (1987), recognizing that the Improved Standards for Laboratory Animals Act encourages the use of alternatives in research, and reduction or elimination of animal pain and distress, has little confidence in significant improvement in practice unless there is added a statute giving concerned citizens standing to bring suit to compel the Department of Agriculture to prosecute violations. H. Cohen (1987) questions the legality of the Agriculture Department's exclusion of rats and mice from coverage under the Animal Welfare Act.

R. Slade and L. Shultz (1986) make a case against certain kinds of animal experiments (E. Taub case, baboon head injury experiments at University of Pennsylvania). H. Metz (1986) discusses legal issues in relation to animal experimentation. Various aspects (legal, historical, political, scientific, economic, ethical) of the pound animal controversy are analyzed by K. Vetri (1987). Articles by R. Dresser (1985) (1988) and G. L. Francione (1988) use the Animal Welfare Act (as amended) as an example in discussing the constitutional status (first amendment) of restrictions on animal experiments.

The Animal Legal Defense Fund (1987) provides a guide for the animals' advocate in investigating animal abuse: federal and state laws, investigation, how to use Federal Freedom of Information Act, suggestions for working with legislators and the press, reading list. See [464].

Most state and local anti-cruelty laws proscribe wanton cruelty or torture or abuse or neglect, committed maliciously or willfully, knowingly and intentionally. Michigan animal cruelty law, studied by S. LaRene (1987), is typical. Many state laws are so vague and ambiguous it is uncertain whether they apply to experiments; and if they do, prosecution is extremely difficult. The Association for Biomedical Research (1984) analyzes state laws on the use of animals in research.

E. Taub is convicted in 1982 under Maryland anti-cruelty law for failing to provide adequate veterinary care for monkeys, but such conviction is overturned by the Court of Appeals ruling that Maryland's law not intended to cover federally supported animal experiments. Using the example of *Taub* v. *State*, L. Falkin (1985) explores whether state anti-cruelty statutes are sleeping giants waiting to be used by animal rights advocates or are usable only to prevent wanton sadism.

G. Daws [207, pp. 361-73] gives details of the Hawaii dolphin case: in 1977 two employees of University of Hawaii release two dolphins from experimental situation to the ocean. The defense argues (unsuccessfully) that dolphins are persons and therefore cannot be stolen property, and therefore their liberation justified.

State laws on the use of live animals in elementary and secondary schools are few and weak. Laws of six states are reproduced in anthology edited by H. McGiffin and N. Brownley (1980, 141-4).

Other Nations; and Regional and International Law

M. E. Cooper's [334] introduction to animal law provides the most recent survey of national and international laws. J. Hampson (1985) summarizes laboratory animal protection laws in Europe and North America (United States, Canada, Austria, Cyprus, Belgium, Denmark, Eire, Federal Republic of Germany, France, Greece, Iceland, Italy, Luxembourg, Lichtenstein, Malta, Netherlands, Norway, Portugal, Spain, Sweden, Switzerland, Turkey, United Kingdom).

Universities Federation for Animal Welfare (1986) summarizes in tabular form laws in 42 nations relating to the use of animals in experiments: Argentina, Australia, Austria, Belgium, Bulgaria, Canada, Cyprus, Czechoslovakia, Denmark, East Germany, Egypt, Eire, Finland, France, Greece, Holland, Hong Kong, Hungary, Iceland, India, Iran, Italy, Japan, Kenya, Luxembourg, Malaysia, Mexico, New Zealand, Nigeria, Norway, Poland, Portugal, South Africa, Spain, Sweden, Switzerland, Thailand, Uganda, United Kingdom, United States, USSR, West Germany.

G. B. Taylor's (1977) article on animal welfare legislation in Europe is dated. A rather general treatment of legislation on laboratory animals (mainly United Kingdom, Western European countries, United States, Australia) is in the latest edition of *The UFAW handbook on the care and management of laboratory animals* (T. B. Poole 1987, 99-106). H. Weber (1986) discusses a Swiss plebiscite in 1985 rejecting the initiative "For the abolition of animal vivisection"; also explains Swiss law on animal experimentation.

The Council of the European Communities (1978) approves on behalf of the European Economic Community the European Convention for the Protection of Animals Kept for Farming Purposes; several member countries have ratified. The Council of the European Communities (1986a) adopts a directive in regard to the protection of animals used for experimental and other scientific purposes (covers only animals used in the production and testing of products). The Council

of Europe Convention for the Protection of Vertebrate Animals Used for Experimental and Other Scientific Purposes is signed by six member states on 18 March
1986; when at least four members deposit instruments of ratification the Convention will become effective six months later. The Council of the European Communities (1986b) adopts a directive laying down minimum standards for the
protection of laying hens kept in battery cages. See M. E. Cooper's [334] coverage of legislation by the Council of Europe and the European community.

There seem to be no comprehensive sources on national laws (where they exist)
applicable to raising animals for food. The Humane Society of the United States
[284] reports that Switzerland is outlawing the use of battery cages for hens
effective 1991, that the Netherlands has begun such a phase-out, that there is a
movement underway to ban the cage for hens throughout the European Economic
Community, that the use of tethers for restraining breeding sows is outlawed in
Sweden and Switzerland. It is reported in the April 1988 *Animals' Agenda* (30) that
it is practically certain that proposed legislation in Sweden will be enacted; cows
will enjoy the right to spend some time outdoors; permanent ban on the tethering
of pigs; reforms in chicken-farming methods, etc.

Compassion in World Farming (1987) reports the European Parliament on
20 January 1987 passes a report on animal welfare which would ban keeping veal
calves in individual crates, phase-out poultry battery cages within ten years,
discontinue close confinement of pregnant sows, ban routine tail-docking and
castration of piglets.

S. Lyster (1985) studies the basic principles of international wildlife law; covers
international law on whales, seals, polar bears, birds, vicuna; deals with treaties
and conventions. D. W. Allen (1983) concludes it is quite possible that a declaration similar to the Universal Declaration of the Rights of Animals (see Appendix B
to this *Keyguide*) could be adopted by the world's nation-states within the next
generation.

5   Religion and Animals

Bibliography: C. R. Magel [176, entries 205-19, 1043-99].

Christianity

Several older but historically important works published in Great Britain are written in the context of Christianity. J. Hildrop [9], a chaplain, writes in 1742 that it is a breach of natural justice wantonly or without necessity to torment or take the life of any creature. H. Primatt [12], an English Doctor of Divinity, in 1776 argues mercy to animals to be a duty, and cruelty a sin. J. Granger's [11] 1772 book, censuring animal abuse, has a profound influence on A. Broome, a founder of the RSPCA. R. Dean [10], a curate, in 1768 attacks the notion that animals were created only for human purposes as a "groundless conceit" and argues for the immortality of animal souls. The Quaker J. Woolman (⟨1774⟩ 1922), who refuses to take stage coaches because of the ill-treatment of horses and drivers, is "early convinced in my mind that true Religion consisted in an inward life, wherein the Heart doth Love and Reverence God the Creator, and learn to Exercise true Justice and Goodness, not only toward all men, but also toward the Brute Creatures. That as the mind was moved by an inward Principle to Love God as an invisible, Incomprehensible Being, by the same principle it was moved to love him in all his manifestations in the Visible world. That as by his breath the flame of life was kindled in all Animal and Sensible creatures, to say we Love God as unseen, and at the same time Exercise cruelty toward the least creature moving by his life, or by life derived from Him, was a Contradiction in itself" (156-7).

J. Wesley (⟨1782⟩ 1985) recognizes self-motion, understanding and liberty in animals; but only humans are "capable of God"; argues for a general deliverance of both humans and animals. S. Jenyns [13], using a theological context, argues animals have an equal right to enjoy life. W. Youatt [25], a veterinary surgeon, in 1839 claims the Creator wills the greatest possible happiness for all creatures. Drawing heavily on anecdotal evidence, J. G. Wood [32], a minister, argues in 1875 that animals share with humans many mental capacities, and hence will also share in immortality. J. Macauley (1875) takes prevention-of-cruelty and promotion-of-kindness-and-mercy to animals approaches, based on the dominion theme of the Bible.

P. Austin (1885) interprets Christian philosophy in a sharply different manner: if animals have rights (as claimed by the "animalists") then it follows, absurdly, that plants and natural objects have rights. "Animals should be treated with perfect indifference; they should not be petted, they should not be ill-treated. . . . They are our slaves, not our equals, and for this reason it is well to keep up such practices as hunting and fishing, driving and riding, merely to demonstrate in a practical way man's domination over the brutes" (32). Attacks the "effeminacy of the 19th century."

C. S. Lewis [82, p. 185]: "Once the old Christian idea of total difference in kind between man and beast has been abandoned, then no argument for experiments on animals can be found which is not also an argument for experiments on inferior men." L. G. Stevenson (1956) traces the religious elements in the background of the British anti-vivisection movement. J. G. Lawler (1965) attacks the Scholastic doctrine that animals are treatable as things; argues animals are a symbol of what creation was in its state of innocence: "The vivisector should in his own conscience refuse to inflict any pain that he would not himself be willing to undergo" (189).

There is disagreement on Christianity's view of nature, environment and animals. E. A. Westermarck (1939), C. W. Hume (1957) and J. A. Rimbach (1982) explore the status of animals in the Christian religion. The meaning of human dominion over nature and animals is discussed by C. J. Glacken (1967), J. N. Black (1970) and J. Limburg (1971). L. White (1967) argues that the dominion doctrine is the major source of human arrogance and exploitation of nature. White's influential essay leads to responses in essays edited by I. G. Barbour (1973) and additional papers edited by D. and E. Spring (1974). An environmental ethic and theology are developed in a set of essays edited by I. G. Barbour (1972). The studies of a working group within the Church of England "to investigate the relevance of Christian doctrine to the problems of man in his environment" are edited by H. Montefiore (1975). The Fellows of the Calvin Center for Christian Scholarship, Calvin College (L. Wilkinson 1980) combine careful thought, sensitive concern, humor, hope and detailed practical suggestions for "earthkeeping" – Christian stewardship of natural resources; provide illuminating treatment of Greek views of nature (Platonists, Aristotelians, Stoics, Epicureans), also the medieval view of nature; discuss dominion theme in detail; claim stewardship is dominion as service; broaden the concept of justice to include all creation. R. Attfield (1983c), defending the suitability of the Christian attitude to nature, critiques L. White (1967) and J. Passmore (1975a) (1975b).

Theodicy is concerned with the problem of reconciling the facts of pain and suffering in humans and animals with the existence of a perfect God. This knotty problem is discussed by C. S. Lewis (1943), and is debated by C. E. M. Joad and C. S. Lewis (⟨1950⟩ 1970). Theodicy and animal neglect are dealt with by A. R. Kingston (1967). J. Hick (1978, 309–17) ignores the problem of pain in animals and focuses on the reason animals exist at all, suggesting they contribute to the "epistemic distance" by which humans are enabled to exist as free and responsible creatures in the presence of God. G. B. Wall's (1983) free-will defense of suffering is attacked by F. Ferré [255] as trivializing animal suffering. P. Geach (1977) critiques C. S. Lewis' theodicean analysis of animal pain, and claims God cannot have the virtue of sympathy with physical suffering of animals because God's nature has no animal ingredient: "Only anthropomorphic imagination allows us to accuse God of cruelty in this regard" (80). R. W. K. Paterson (1984) critiques Geach's view.

E. Turnbull [143, pp. 43–7] discusses animals and moral theology. A. Linzey [118] [236] [286] argues for a strong animal rights view within Christianity. He discusses the place of animals in creation [269, pp. 115–48], and animals and moral theology [143, pp. 34–41]. His (1986) condensed entry "Animals" in *The Westminster dictionary of Christian ethics* is informative. For ages 11–14, Linzey (1985) explains Christian attitudes to animals. A. Linzey and T. Regan: audio cassette discussions on the rights of animals [287]; book of readings on animals and Christian theology [311]; anthology of religious readings, poetry, prayers [312]; poetry in celebration of animals [313]. The promise and challenge of religion is presented by T. Regan [296, pp. 152–63]; in the film *We are all Noah* [268] he explores the ethical teachings of Christianity and Judaism in human–animal relationships.

R. Griffiths (1982) argues that the Christian doctrines of creation, of the image of God in humans, and of human dominion over the world, are superior as a basis for animal welfare to any secular theory of animal rights. S. R. L. Clark's (1983b) entry "Nature, Theology and" in *A New Dictionary of Christian Theology* analyzes several interpretations of nature. Clark [213] explores the possibility of animal rights and the peaceable kingdom. Clark (1986) discusses Christian responsibility for the environment.

J. B. Clair (1987) describes a memorial service in a traditional place of worship for Wind-of-Fire (a deceased animal companion) and for all unmourned and suffering animals; also gives reactions by ministers. Ministries for Animals [496] publishes *Anima/l: A Magazine of Religion and Animal Rights*. S. Arnold [322] gives a sermon in celebration of animals. S. Rosen [300, pp. 15–39] and C. A. Skriver (1987) discuss Christianity and vegetarianism. In addition to considering how Christianity has viewed animals, D. A. Dombrowski [307, chap. 1] briefly analyzes Judaism, Islam, Hinduism, Jainism, Confucianism.

The position of the Catholic Church on animals, based on the doctrines of T. Aquinas, is clearly stated in the *Catholic Dictionary* (W. E. Addis and T. Arnold 1957, 29). J. H. Newman (1858, 106–7): "We have no duties towards the brute creation; there is no relation of justice between them and us. . . . They can claim nothing at our hands; into our hands they are absolutely delivered. We may use them, we may destroy them at our pleasure, not our wanton pleasure, but still for our ends . . . provided we can give a rational account of what we do.'' D. A. Dombrowski (1985) analyzes the speciesist views of the Jesuits J. Rickaby (⟨1888⟩ 1918) and G. Tyrrell (1895). J. S. Vaughn (1903–04) provides a clear statement of the Catholic view of the denial of animal rights in the context of experimentation. A compendium of Roman Catholic sources on animals and their treatment is given by A. Agius (1970). R. J. McLaughlin (1985) identifies various arguments developed by T. Aquinas in support of humans' privileged moral status. The relevance of animal experimentation to Roman Catholic ethical methodology is explained by J. Gaffney [269, pp. 149–70].

The Church of England (Board for Social Responsibility of the Church of England 1970) ethically assesses the relationship of humans and animals. Also see essays edited by H. Montefiore (1975).

Quaker Concern for Animal Welfare (1985) reflects views of some Quakers on treatment of animals. Quakers and animals are discussed by H. H. Brinton (1960). Also see J. Woolman's (⟨1774⟩ 1922) journal.

G. E. Jones' (1972) dissertation considers concern for animals as manifest in five American churches: Bible Christian, Shaker, Latter-day Saint, Christian Scientist, Seventh-day Adventist.

Other Religions

J. D. Bleich [269, pp. 61–114] analyzes the views of Judaism: concern for the welfare of animals. R. H. Schwartz [197] and S. Rosen [300, pp. 41–55] discuss Judaism and vegetarianism. L. A. Berman (1982), motivated by his teenage son's quiet announcement of a decision to eat no more meat, produces an interesting study of vegetarianism and the Jewish tradition; discusses Hebrew Bible, Talmud, dietary laws, slaughter as a mode of worship; draws significantly from A. I. Kook's ''A vision of vegetarianism and peace,'' an essay not generally available (copy at Yeshiva University Library). The concept of tsa'ar ba'ale hayim is discussed by N. J. Cohen (1976). Animal life in the Jewish tradition, based on Hebrew scriptures and the Talmud, is explored by E. J. Schochet (1984). R. Kalechofsky (1985) presents a Haggadah which seeks to reawaken atrophied sensibility and provide a ritual for a seder that is both traditional and vegetarian.

F. S. C. Northrop [130, pp. 173–204] favors Buddha's view of compassion for suffering fellowship of humans and animals, in contrast with Western metaphysical views. The principle of ahimsa (non-harming) is discussed by J. Austin [143, pp. 25–33]. The Buddhist case for vegetarianism is given by P. Kapleau (1982). C. Chapple [269, pp. 218–35] discusses the Buddhist principle of noninjury to animals in relation to experiments. Buddhism and vegetarianism are dealt with by S. Rosen [300, pp. 77–87].

Hindu perspectives on the use of animals in science are presented by B. K. Lal

[269, pp. 199–212]; discusses Vedic sacrifice of animals, attitudes toward pets, veneration of the cow, affinity of humans with animals and nature, *ahimsa*; Hinduism recognizes duties *regarding* animals but not duties *to* animals; therefore animals have no rights; *ahimsa* toward animals is practiced for the purpose of the agent's spiritual development toward salvation (*moksa*); theoretically and ideally, Hinduism does not permit medical or exploratory or cosmetic use of animals; popularly and practically, Hinduism supports medical and exploratory use of animals on basis of sacrificing lesser goods for greater goods, but does not support cosmetic use of animals. Hinduism and vegetarianism are discussed by S. Rosen [300, pp. 89–101].

Islamic concern for animals is explored by Al-Hafiz B. A. Masri [290]. The Muslim view of animals and animal experimentation is provided by Masri [269, pp. 171–97]. Vegetarianism and Islam is discussed by S. Rosen [300, pp. 57–69].

The path of purification in Jainism, discussed by P. S. Jaini (1979), requires strict vegetarianism: killing animals, involving passions and attachments, inhibits the soul's ability to attain *moksa* (spiritual liberation). Jainism in regard to animal experiments is covered by C. Chapple [269, pp. 213–18].

R. L. Taylor [269, pp. 237–63] discusses classical Confucianism (Confucius, Mencius and Hsün Tzu) and Neo-Confucianism in regard to animals and animal experiments.

6 Vegetarianism and Animals

Vegetarianism is the obvious alternative to harming animals by eating them. J. C. Dyer [190] provides an annotated bibliography on vegetarianism, 1412 entries. See entries 404–36, 1720–800 in C. R. Magel's bibliography [176]. Philosophers' views on vegetarianism are in Chapter 1 of this *Keyguide*. Scientific sources on vegetarianism: (1) *Bibliography of Agriculture* (also AGRICOLA database), published by the United States National Agricultural Library; relevant headings: "Nutrition," "Vegetarian diets," "Vegetarians." (2) *Food Science and Technology Abstracts* and *Nutrition Abstracts and Reviews* (also CAB ABSTRACTS database), published by CAB International, Slough, United Kingdom.

Vegetarian cookbooks are listed and sold by: (1) Vegetarian Times Bookshelf, P.O. Box 570, Oak Park, IL 60303. (2) American Vegan Society, 501 Old Harding Highway, Malaga, NJ 08328. (3) Vegetarian Centre and Bookshop, 53 Marloes Road, Kensington, London W8 6LA. Vegetarian associations and organizations may be found in *International Vegetarian Health Food Handbook* available from North American Vegetarian Society [345] or Vegetarian Society of the United Kingdom [456]; also in the directory of Data Notes (1983).

Through 1970

Early views favorable to vegetarianism are presented by Ovid [1], Plutarch [2] [121, pp. 111–17] [317, sect. 1], and Porphyry [3]. J. Dryden (⟨1700⟩ 1958) gives an English version of Ovid's [1] poetic rendition of the views of Pythagoras. J. Haussleiter (1935) provides a detailed study of philosophical vegetarianism in Greco-Roman antiquity. Ancient philosophical vegetarianism in Greece and Rome is discussed by D. A. Dombrowski [214]. D. Giehl [139] gives accounts of several prominent vegetarians from the time of Porphyry to the present. J. Barkas

[108] considers Porphyry, Pythagoras, Plutarch, and mainly 19th-century vegetarians.

L. da Vinci: "I have from an early age abjured the use of meat, and the time will come when men such as I will look upon the murder of animals as they now look upon the murder of men: (quoted in [249, p. 65]). T. Tryon [4] [6] influences B. Franklin (〈18th cent.〉 1875, 111–12, 142–3) to become a vegetarian and spend the money saved on books; but later tempted by the smell of frying fish, and seeing smaller fish taken from the stomachs of bigger fish, he rationalizes: "If you eat one another, I don't see why we mayn't eat you."

J. Swift (〈1730〉 1979) satirically argues that roast pork is no more defensible than roast children (reproduced in [121, pp. 234–7]). In the 18th century J. Oswald [14] and G. Nicholson [17] argue for vegetarianism. O. Goldsmith (〈1760〉 1934, letter 15) writes as a Chinese philosopher, residing in London, to his friends in the Orient, conveying attitudes of Londoners: "Strange contrariety of conduct; they pity and they eat the objects of their compassion" (38). Tells story of Kabul who surfeits himself on animal flesh all his life; at death his soul is carried off to judgment court; the judges are the souls of the animals he ate on earth.

J. J. Rousseau comments favorably on vegetarianism, emphasizing nutritional benefits; argues children's preferences prove the taste for meat is not natural to man; claims eaters of meat are generally more cruel, that hunting hardens the heart as well as the body (〈1762〉 1979, 57–9, 153–5, 320). J. Ritson (1802), compiling heavily from works of predecessors, stresses abstinence from animal food as a moral duty. P. B. Shelley (1813) vindicates vegetarianism, arguing it is biologically natural, more efficient in labor and land, resulting in tranquility, happiness and longevity.

L. Gompertz [24], first secretary of the SPCA (later RSPCA), disapproves of eating animals unless they die of natural causes or accidentally. Vegetarians arguing for vegetarianism on the basis of physiology during the period 1830–1860 are discussed by J. C. Whorton (1977); included are R. Trall, S. Graham, W. Alcott, R. Mussey, E. G. White; many references. W. A. Alcott (1838) presents seven arguments defending vegetarianism. J. Smith (1845) attempts to prove from history, anatomy, physiology and chemistry that the original, natural and best diet is derived from the vegetable kingdom.

H. D. Thoreau (〈1854〉 1939), candidly admitting that he does not completely follow the "higher laws," has "no doubt that it is a part of the destiny of the human race, in its gradual improvement, to leave off eating animals, as surely as the savage tribes have left off eating each other when they come in contact with the more civilized" (220). J. Jones (1957) accuses Thoreau of self-contradiction. According to R. Epstein (1985), Thoreau is a prophet of the meatless ideal, and his "Higher laws" deserves a place among the sacred writings of vegetarianism. D. A. Dombrowski (1986a) argues that Thoreau's approach to vegetarianism exemplifies a type of sainthood that forces all moral agents to at least consider the possibility that meat-eating is morally reprehensible, and that Thoreau's writings evidence an understanding (in literary form) of the argument from sentiency and the argument from marginal cases.

H. Williams [44] writes a scholarly biographical history of the literature of vegetarianism from Hesiod to Schopenhauer. L. Tolstoy (⟨1892⟩ 1968), in a preface to the Russian edition of Williams' *The ethics of diet*, characterizes vegetarianism as the first step toward moral perfection. In a French publication, Tolstoy (1895) discusses the cruelties in hunting and killing animals for food, and claims the growth of vegetarianism indicates moral and spiritual progress. A. Kingsford [37], and A. Kingsford and E. Maitland [38] argue for vegetarianism on the bases of physiology, economic efficiency, morality, health, aesthetics and spiritual development.

H. S. Salt writes extensively at the end of the 19th century, defending vegetarianism: [45] [47] [49, chap. 4] [51, vol. 3] [54]. The views of two anti-vegetarian sages – G. K. Chesterton and W. R. Inge – are attacked by Salt (1930). L. Stephen (1896) attacks vegetarianism: "The pig has a stronger interest than any one in the demand for bacon. If all the world were Jewish, there would be no pigs at all. He has to pay for his privileges by an early death. . . . He gets a superior race of beings to attend to his comforts" (vol. 1, 236). H. Thompson (1898) promotes flesh-eating, arguing meat-eaters are promoting the existence and happiness of animals which otherwise would not exist; J. Oldfield (1898) replies.

G. B. Shaw (1898) is asked why he is a vegetarian: "Oh, come! That boot is on the other leg. Why should you call *me* to account for eating decently? If I battened on the scorched corpses of animals, you might well ask me why I did that" (quoted in [153, p. 330]). B. Brophy (1979) describes Shaw's way of no flesh.

C. W. Forward (1898) gives a history of the vegetarian movement in England, including consideration of J. Oswald, G. Nicholson, J. Ritson, W. Cowherd, W. Lambe, R. Phillips, J. F. Newton, and P. B. Shelley. Forward (1904) summarizes the arguments in favor of a non-flesh diet. E. Bell [62] and J. H. Moore [66], holding a strong animal rights position, argue for vegetarianism. L. B. Mendel (1903–04) provides historical aspects of vegetarianism, mainly in England and America. E. Crosby [64] attacks flesh-eating as a "fetish that makes us continue such savage customs, just as slavery and the stake and instruments of torture survived long after men should have known better" (214).

F. Wood (1916), arguing the Judaic–Christian tradition is too anthropocentric to generate reform of the wrongful use of animals for food, suggests a new religion of immanence. J. H. Kellogg (1923), fifty years a vegetarian, defends a non-flesh diet as natural for humans, explodes twenty popular delusions about flesh foods, presents scientific objections to the use of meat, describes diseases due to flesh-eating, and gives ethical arguments for vegetarianism.

M. K. Gandhi (1949) expresses "My faith in vegetarianism" (3–8) and addresses the London Vegetarian Society in 1931 on "The moral basis of vegetarianism" (8–12). In his autobiography, Gandhi (1927) describes his experiments in dietetics, defends vegetarianism on bases of ethics, health, and economics. Cow protection and "how we may save the cow" are major concerns of Gandhi (1954). At times Gandhi interprets "cow" as symbolizing all life which serves humans.

The Gandhian symbol of the cow as a model of human–animal ethics is analyzed by M. Juergensmeyer (1984–85).

After 1970

Several general works on vegetarianism: [108] [111] [135] [139] [172] [199] [238] [333]. The 1976 anthology [121] includes items by Plutarch, H. S. Salt and J. Swift; the forthcoming 1988 revised and enlarged edition [317] tentatively will include articles on vegetarianism by Plutarch, B. Gruzalski, R. G. Frey, and J. Narveson.

H. and S. Nearing (1970) (1979) vividly describe living the good (vegetarian) life. J. Wynne-Tyson [153] presents a complete case for vegetarianism as the diet of the future. A self-defense manual for vegetarians is provided by R. Bargen (1979). R. Berry Jr. (1979) interviews thirteen vegetarians, including D. Gregory, S. Satchidananda, and H. and S. Nearing.

H. V. McLachlan (1980) presents the moral case of a carnivore. J. C. and N. J. Hartbarger [173] guide the reader through vegetarian nutrition, arguing the vegetarian diet is healthier. F. M. Lappé's revised edition (1982) of her important study of a diet for a small planet, originally published in 1971, provides useful information on protein sources other than meat; emphasizes eating low on the food chain as a means of efficient use of land.

P. Kapleau (1982) presents the Buddhist case for vegetarianism. R. H. Schwartz [197] relies on Jewish ideals in arguing for vegetarianism. A guide for teenagers going vegetarian is by S. Fretz [202]. J. A. Scharffenberg (1982), MD and nutritionist, claims that next to tobacco and alcohol "the use of meat is probably the greatest single cause of mortality in the United States" and that "it is *more difficult* to have a good diet *with* meat than without it" (11); discusses meat diet in relation to atherosclerosis, cancer, longevity, kidney disorders, salmonellosis, osteoporosis, trichinosis, and nutritional problems. P. Cox (1986) explains why we don't need meat.

H. Schleifer [246, pp. 63–73] critiques the meat industry; presents ethical, ecological and world-food-supply arguments for vegetarianism. Detailed factual accounts of vegetarianism and veganism are given by N. Altman [251]. L. Gruen et al. [282] include a graphic guide to maltreatment of animals raised for food, and argue for vegetarianism.

Vegetarianism for children is covered by S. K. Yntema (1987), and by J. Gross and K. Freifeld (1983). Children under twelve are the intended readers for J. Inglis' illustrated book [285]. G. Null's (1987) vegetarian handbook is designed for total health. J. Robbins [297] takes on the "Great American Food Machine" (meat–egg–dairy industry) in the course of his defense of a vegetarian life style. World religions on vegetarianism are studied by S. Rosen [300]. C. A. Skriver (1987) argues Christianity has forgotten its essentially vegetarian roots. Jewish defenses of vegetarianism: R. H. Schwartz [197], L. A. Berman (1982), N. J. Cohen (1976) and R. Kalechofsky (1985).

Nobel laureate I. B. Singer, a vegetarian, expresses concern for animals in his fiction:

> As often as Herman had witnessed the slaughter of animals and fish, he always had the same thought: in their behavior toward creatures, all men were Nazis. The smugness with which man could do with other species as he pleased exemplified the most extreme racist theories, the principle that "might is right." (1972, 157)

> They have convinced themselves that man, the worst transgressor of all the species, is the crown of creation. All other creatures were created merely to provide him with food, pelts, to be tormented, exterminated. In relation to them, all people are Nazis; for the animals it is an eternal Treblinka. (1968, 270)

For a discussion of Singer on vegetarianism see [139, pp. 141–5].

J. Hurwitz (1978) tells the story of a boy who becomes a vegetarian, having been exposed to the issues of vegetarianism in the course of a school research project (fiction).

PART II

Annotated bibliography
arranged chronologically

Annotated Bibliography
Arranged Chronologically

1 Ovid (43 BC–AD 17). "The doctrines of Pythagoras." In *Metamorphoses*, XV, lines 60–478. Trans. by A. D. Melville. Oxford: Oxford University Press, 1986.
A Roman poet puts into verse the Pythagorean philosophy of vegetarianism:

> Abstain! Preserve your bodies unabused,
> Mortals, with food of sin.
> ....
> Abstain! Be warned! I beg you! Understand
> The ox whose meat you savour, whom you slew,
> Worked, your own farmhand, in your fields for you.
> ....
> Abstain! Never by slaughter dispossess
> Souls that are kin and nourish blood with blood!
> ....
>   These creatures might have housed
> Souls of our parents, brothers, other kin,
> Or men at least, and we must keep them safe,
> Respected, honoured, lest we gorge ourselves
> On such a banquet as Thyestes ate.

John Dryden (⟨1700⟩ 1958), in his English version of Ovid's poem on Pythagoras, uses the language of equal rights:

> Take not away the Life you cannot give:
> For all Things have an equal right to live.
>   (p. 1736)

2 Plutarch (46?–120?). *Plutarch's Moralia.* Trans. by H. Cherniss and W. C. Hembold. London: William Heinemann, 1968; Cambridge: Harvard University Press, 1968.
Vol. XII contains three essays. (1) "Whether land or sea animals are cleverer," 309–479. Discusses intelligence of animals, followed by debate whether land or sea animals most intelligent. Argues animals' sense experience would be meaningless unless they have the ability to remember, anticipate, plan, fear, desire. Animals vary in intelligence and in sense of fellowship. They should be treated with justice; we must not harm them or be cruel to them. Dolphins the most intelligent animal. (2) "Beasts are rational," 487–533. Gryllus, once a Greek, was turned into a pig by Circe. Gryllus, who can still speak Greek, is questioned in dialogue: Which mode of existence would be chosen by one who has experienced both human life and pig life? Gryllus argues animals' virtues (courage, temperance, intelligence) are natural, genuine, sincere whereas human virtues are products of convention, self-interest. "I do not believe there is such difference between beast and beast in reason and understanding and memory, as between man and man."(3) "On the eating of flesh," 535–79. Instead of asking why vegetarians (Pythagoras, for example) abstain from flesh we should ask why the flesh-eaters eat animals. Argues flesh-eating unnatural, unnecessary for humans, leading to spiritual coarseness, lack of compassion for other humans. ". . . For the sake of a little flesh we deprive them of sun, of light, of the duration of life to which they are entitled by birth and being."

3 Porphyry (234?–305?). *On abstinence from animal food.* Trans. by T. Taylor. Ed. by E. Wynne-Tyson. London: Centaur Press, 1965. 196 pp. New York: Barnes and Noble, 1965.
Porphyry was a Neoplatonist student of Plotinus. Book written on occasion of one of Plotinus' students becoming non-vegetarian. Critiques popular arguments against vegetarianism. Argues practice of sacrificing animals to gods does not justify eating animals. Justice is owed to rational beings. Many animals are rational and therefore are owed just treatment. In answer to the critic who claims that humans are more rational than animals, Porphyry emphasizes that there is much variation in the rationality of both humans and animals; given that justice is owed to all humans (in spite of different degrees of rationality), to be consistent we must admit that justice is owed to animals (in spite of different degrees of rationality). Given that many humans live at the level of sensation (without reason) and justice is owed to them, it is irrational to hold that animals living at the level of sensation (without reason) not be owed just treatment. Vegetarian diet healthier; whole nations have lived very well as vegetarians. D. A. Dombrowski (1984b) argues Porphyry anticipates the 20th-century "argument from marginal cases."

4 Tryon, Thomas (1634–1703). *The way to health, long life and happiness.* London: Andrew Sowle, 1683. 669 pp. Ann Arbor, MI: University Microfilms, 1972 (English Books 1641–1700, reel 440:18, microfilm of original in Huntington Library).
Perhaps the first publication in English language using the term "rights" in regard to animals. "It should be considered that flesh and fish cannot be eaten without violence, and *doing that which a man would not be done unto*, and making

destruction of God's creatures'' (343). ''. . . Man was not made to be a tyrant unto the rest of God's creatures . . . but in love and meekness to have dominion over all things for their good, and to maintain unity and concord . . .'' (143–4). ''The Complaint of the cows'' (496–503): ''Thus all of us live in great slavery most part of our lives, far below that generous liberty wherein our great and good Creator had estated us by his grand charter of nature . . .'' (502). ''Have we not then just reason, O man! to complain of thy injustice?'' (502). ''The sheep's complaint'' (503–9). ''The horses' complaint'' (509–15): ''Do we not proceed from the very same earth man did? Are we not the sons of the stars and elements, even as man himself?'' (514). Man ''would fain be an absolute monarch or arbitrary tyrant, making nothing at his pleasure to break the laws of God, and invade and destroy all the rights and privileges of the inferiour creatures'' (515).

5 **Tryon, Thomas** (1634–1703). *The country-man's companion.* London: Andrew Sowle, 1688. 173 pp. Ann Arbor, MI: University Microfilms, 1976 (English Books 1641–1700, reel 583:16, microfilm of original in Bodleian Library).
''The complaints of the birds and fowls of heaven to their Creator'' (141–73): ''But tell us, O men! We pray you to tell us what injuries have we committed to forfeit? What laws have we broken, or what cause given you, whereby you can pretend a right to invade and violate our part, and natural rights, and to assault and destroy us, as if we were the aggressors, and no better than thieves, robbers and murderers, fit to be extirpated out of creation?'' (146). ''From whence did thou derive thy authority for killing thy inferiors, merely because they are such, or for destroying their natural rights and privileges?'' (165–6).

6 **Tryon, Thomas** (1634–1703). *Wisdom's dictates; or, aphorisms and rules, physical, moral, and divine; for preserving the health of the body, and the peace of the mind.* London: Tho. Salusbury, 1691. 153 pp. Ann Arbor, MI: University Microfilms, 1980 (English Books 1641–1700, reel 1076:15, microfilm of original in Huntington Library).
''Refrain at all times such foods as cannot be procured without violence and oppression''(6). ''Refrain hunting, hawking, shooting, and all violent oppressive exercises, and instead, spend your spare time in gardening, planting, and cultivating the earth''(7). Warns of the danger of fat foods such as flesh, fish, butter, eggs, cheese. ''A bill of fare'' (139–53): A vegetarian ''banquet I present to the sons of wisdom, and to all such as shall obtain that happy condition, as to decline that depraved custom of killing and eating their fellow creatures, and whose desire is to live according to the innocent law of nature, and do unto all creatures as they would be done unto . . .'' (139). Argues superiority, for body and mind, of vegetarian diet.

7 **[Mandeville, Bernard de** (1670?–1713).] *The fable of the bees or, private vices publick benefits.* London: J. Roberts, 1714. 228 pp. Published anonymously.
Mandeville, from Holland, had a medical degree but spent much time writing in England. Is sometimes (but mistakenly?) credited as author of theory of animal rights. Ideally, humans would not eat flesh of animals. Tyranny, luxury, and custom play large role in human consumption of animals. ''It is only man . . . that can make death a sport. Nature taught your stomach to crave nothing but

vegetables; but your violent fondness to change, and great eagerness after novelties, have prompted you to the destruction of animals, without justice or necessity . . .'' Critical of slaughter houses and of Cartesian view of animals as machines without feeling.

8 Pope, Alexander (1688–1744). *An essay on man.* (Originally published in 1733–1734.) Ed. by M. Mack. London: Methuen, 1950. 186 pp.
A poetic critique of anthropocentrism:

> One all-extending, all-preserving Soul
> Connects each being, greatest with the least;
> Made beast in aid of Man, and Man of Beast;
> All serv'd, all serving! Nothing stands alone;
> The chain holds on, and where it ends, unknown.
> Has God, thou fool! worked solely for thy good,
> Thy joy, thy pastime, thy attire, thy food?
>   . . .
>   Know, Nature's children all divide her care;
> The fur that warms a monarch, warm'd a bear.
> While Man exclaims, "See all things for my use!"
> "See man for mine!" replies a pampered goose;
> And just as short of Reason he must fall,
> Who thinks all made for one, not one for all.
>   (Epistle III, lines 22–48, pp. 94–7)

9 Hildrop, John (?–1756). *Free thoughts upon the brute creation: or, an examination of Father Bougeant's "Philosophical amusement upon the language of beasts."* London: R. Minors, 1742. (In the form of two letters to a lady: 64 pp. and 88 pp.)
Hildrop was Rector of Wath, near Ripon in Yorkshire. Argues animals immortal. Misery of animals due to fall of Adam and humans. It is a breach of natural justice, wantonly and without necessity, to torment, take away the life of any creature, except for the preservation and happiness of our own being, which is sometimes unavoidable. Attacks John Locke's hypothesis that God could make matter think.

10 Dean, Richard (1727?–1778). *An essay on the future life of brutes, introduced with observations upon evil, its nature and origin.* 2d ed. London: G. Kearsley, 1768. Vol. I, 111 pp.; vol. II, 115 pp.
Dean was curate of Middleton. Animals somehow contracted demerit in the fall of humans. Scriptural evidence for immortality of animals. Is a mistake to hold animals exist only for the use of humans. Animals are not machines; they have an intelligent principle, the source of their actions; are capable of pain, perhaps even more so than humans. They must not be treated as stocks or stones or things. They are under human government to be protected, not to be tormented. Humans must account for every act of barbarity to animals on judgment day.

11 Granger, James (1723–1776). *An apology for the brute creation, or abuse of animals censured.* 2d ed. London: T. Davies, 1773. 25 pp.

Sermon on Proverbs 12:10, preached in Parish Church of Shiplake, Oxfordshire, 18 October 1772. There is a 3-page dedication to T. B. Drayman ("neighbour Tom") whom Granger accuses of excessive cruelty, when drunk, to his horses. A 2-page postscript notes the sermon "gave almost universal disgust to two·considerable congregations" and was regarded as proof of the author's growing insanity. This historically important work heavily influenced Arthur Broome, a founder of the RSPCA. Characterizes England as "the hell of horses." Dominion does not mean tyranny. "The righteous and merciful man considers that the meanest creature was pronounced by the great Creator to be very good; and that if it is in no respect hurtful to him, it has an equal right with himself to live, and to enjoy the benefits of life . . . To deprive the meanest insect of life, without a good reason for so doing, is certainly criminal."

12 Primatt, Humphrey. *A dissertation on the duty of mercy and sin of cruelty to brute animals*. London: T. Cadell, 1776. 326 pp.
Primatt was an English Doctor of Divinity. Justice, a rule of universal extent and invariable obligation, applies to humans and animals. Argues in context of natural religion and revealed theology. Domestic animals have undoubted right to food, rest, tender usage. Principle of strict justice requires non-cruelty. Principle of mercy is the basis of duty to increase welfare of animals. "Do you that *are* a man so treat your horse, as you would be willing to be treated by your master, *in case that you were a horse?*" (21). Duty of humans to wild animals: *"Let them alone."* "No creature is so insignificant, but whilst it has life, it has a right to happiness"(269).

13 Jenyns, Soame (1704–1787). "On cruelty to animals." Chap. 2, pp. 19–34, in *Disquisitions on several subjects*. London: J. Dodsley, 1782.
Vivid account of many types of cruelty. Animals have an equal right to enjoy life. Humans should show gratitude, follow laws of justice, practice tenderness and mercy. Theological context.

14 Oswald, John (1730–1793). *The cry of nature; or, an appeal to mercy and to justice on behalf of the persecuted animals*. London: J. Johnson, 1791. 156 pp.
Argues for vegetarianism. Attacks sophistic argument that canine teeth show that humans are intended by nature to be carnivores. "Respect in other animals that principle of life which they have received, no less than man himself, at the hand of nature." If we had to kill animals ourselves we would become vegetarians. Vegetarianism is healthier, more aesthetic. Plant agriculture softens the human heart, promotes love of peace, justice, nature; hunting does the opposite. Cruelty to animals harms us as much as harms them.

15 [Taylor, Thomas (1758–1835)]. *A vindication of the rights of brutes*. London: Edward Jeffery, 1792. 103 pp. Published anonymously.
Taylor was a Platonist. Ridiculing Thomas Paine's *The rights of man* and Mary Wollstonecraft's *A vindication of the rights of women*, he attempts a *reductio ad absurdum* argument which reveals the structure of an argument for animal rights: once you allow that the least rational of men, and even women, have rights, you must

conclude animals have rights – that animals are equal to men in intrinsic dignity and worth.

16 Lawrence, John (1753–1839). *A philosophical treatise on horses, and on the moral duties of man towards the brute creation.* London: T. N. Longman, 1796–1798. Vol. I, chap. 3: "On the rights of beasts." Vol. II, chap. 1: "The philosophy of sports."
Lawrence, a "literary farmer" and authority on horses, was consulted by Richard Martin on the Ill-treatment of Cattle Bill 1822. Life, intelligence, and feeling necessarily imply rights. "Can there be one kind of justice for men and another for brutes?" The *jus animalium* ought to form a part of the jurisprudence of government. "I . . . propose that the rights of beasts be formally acknowledged by the state . . ." Attacks animal baiting, torturing, experiments on live animals. Does not recognize a right to life, "but every act that bears the semblance of torture shocks me to the marrow."

17 Nicholson, George (1760–1825). *On the conduct of man to inferior animals.* Manchester: G. Nicholson, 1797. 134 pp.
Compilation of passages illustrative of human cruelty to animals. Arguments for vegetarianism. ". . . Treat the animal which is in your power, in such a manner as you would willingly be treated, were you such an animal."

18 Coleridge, Samuel Taylor (1772–1834). *The rime of the ancient mariner.* (Originally published in 1798.) New York: Reynal and Hitchcock, 1946.
Six lines by a profound poet can express deeper spirituality than tomes by theologians:

> He prayeth well, who loveth well
> Both man and bird and beast.

> He prayeth best, who loveth best
> All things great and small;
> For the dear God who loveth us,
> He made and loveth all.
>
> (Part VII, p. 58)

D. A. Dombroski (1986b) argues that this is the greatest poem written dealing largely with nonhuman animals.

19 Young, Thomas (1772–1835). *An essay on humanity to animals.* London: T. Cadell, 1798. 202 pp.
Bases "the *rights* of animals" on the light of nature: animals are capable of pleasure, pain; the Creator wills their happiness; therefore, cruelty is against God's will and humanity is in accordance with God's will. Regrets killing animals for food; agonizes over killing bees in taking honey; against animal experimentation "only to gratify curiosity." The morally sensitive person would probably abstain from oysters and lobster, not send boys out to rob plover nest eggs, not walk on worms or snails, would help flies in distress, always try to increase

pleasure and diminish pain, and will "feel for everything that is capable of feeling."

20 Blake, William (1757–1827). "Auguries of innocence." (1803?) In *The poetry and prose of William Blake*, ed. by D. V. Erdman, 481–4. Garden City, NY: Doubleday, 1965.
Poetic genius often compresses more profundity into two lines than others do in chapters:

A Robin Redbreast in a Cage
Puts all Heaven in a Rage.

21 Erskine, Thomas (1750–1823). *The speech of Lord Erskine in the House of Peers on the second reading of the bill for preventing malicious and wanton cruelty to animals* (15 May 1809). London: Richard Phillips, 1809. 27 pp.
Erskine's unsuccessful argument attempting to pass the first British law (it passed in the House of Lords but was defeated in the Commons mainly due to opposition by W. Windham) is historically, conceptually and legally important. "Animals are considered *as property only. . . . The animals themselves are without protection. . . . They have no RIGHTS.*" Human dominion is a moral trust; abuse of the dominion by cruel treatment of animals is unjust, immoral, tending to harden the heart against the natural feelings of humanity. The bill applied to horses, mares, mules, asses, oxen, cows, sheep, swine.

22 Shelley, Percy Bysshe (1792–1822). "Queen Mab." (1813) In *The complete poetical works of Percy Bysshe Shelley*, ed. by N. Rogers, vol. I, 231–95. Oxford: Clarendon Press, 1972.
The poet envisions a future suggestive of the equality endorsed by animal libera-tionists and animal rightists. The developments of science will be consistent with the happiness of humans and animals:

No longer now
He slays the lamb that looks him in the face,
And horribly devours his mangled flesh.
. . . .
All things are void of terror: Man has lost
His terrible prerogative, and stands
An equal amidst equals: happiness
And science dawn though late upon the earth.
(VIII, lines 212–28)

23 Crowe, Henry (1778–1851). *Zoophilos; or, considerations on the moral treatment of inferior animals*. London: Henry Crowe, 1819. 120 pp.
Critical of maltreatment of horses, asses, dogs. Attacks bull-baiting, cock fight-ing, cock throwing, bear and badger baiting (enjoyed by Queen Elizabeth), plucking live geese, mole-catching. Criticizes methods of slaughter for food and some types of animal experimentation and testing.

24 Gompertz, Lewis (?–1861). *Moral inquiries on the situation of man and brutes. On the crime of committing cruelty on brutes, and of sacrificing them to the purposes of man.* London: Lewis Gompertz, 1824. 165 pp.

Gompertz, a brilliant inventor, first secretary of the Society for the Prevention of Cruelty to Animals (later became RSPCA), rescued it from financial disaster; resigned because his views attacked as being Pythagorean and non-Christian; founded the Animals' Friend Society. A strict vegetarian who would never ride in a coach due to maltreatment of horses. Abstractly attempts to lay out definitions, axioms, theorems (in the style of Spinoza?) to provide a rational morality for our treatment of humans and animals. Axiom 5: We should never admit of the propriety of the will or volition of one animal being the agent of another, unless we should perceive its own good to result from it, or that justice should require it. The constant pursuit of a moralist is to render all beings equally happy, to increase the stock of happiness, and to lessen the stock of pain, as far as it is in his power. Disapproves of eating animals (unless died of natural causes or accidentally), of drinking milk (unless calf died by accident), of eating eggs, using leather (unless animal died naturally), using animals for labor, using silk, tallow for soap, experiments on animals. ''. . . Every animal has more right to the use of its own body than others have to use it.'' This little known work deserves careful analysis and perhaps republication.

25 Youatt, William (1777–1847). *The obligation and extent of humanity to brutes, principally considered with reference to domesticated animals.* London: Longman, 1839. 218 pp.

A veterinarian and member of the Society for the Prevention of Cruelty to Animals. Animals have as much right to protection from ill-usage as the best of their masters have. Because animals cannot remonstrate or defend their rights, theologians and philosophers have not pled their cause.

26 Fletcher, Ralph. *A few notes on cruelty to animals: on the inadequacy of penal law: on general hospitals for animals.* London: Longman, 1846. 105 pp.

A surgeon and member of Gloucester branch of RSPCA. Vivid account, sensitively written, of almost unbelievable cruelties to animals in the Gloucester area in the early 1840s: badgers (baiting), cats (mutilation, torturing), calves (beating, carting, bleeding for white veal), cocks (shooting at tied), dogs (overloaded dog-carts, fights), donkeys (overloading, mutilation, use for towing), horses (over-working, beating, collar wounds, starving), lambs (pre-slaughter mutilation and bleeding), deer (carting and stag-hunting of tame), pigs (starvation). Inadequacy of Martin's Act: provisions and enforcement. Recommends general hospitals for animals similar to human hospitals.

27 Gompertz, Lewis (?–1861). "On the causes of cruelty to animals." In *Fragments in defence of animals, and essays on morals, soul, and future state*, 19–29. London: W. Horsell, 1852.

Fallacious doctrines from which cruelty springs: that every animal was created for the use of humans; that only humans have reason, animals having instinct only; that man alone has an immortal soul. ''. . . We . . . condemn all surgical experiments on animals, which are not done for their good, as morally criminal and sacrilegious in the highest degree. . . .''

28 Darwin, Charles (1809–1882). *The origin of species by means of natural selection or, the preservation of favored races in the struggle for life.* Reprint from 6th ed. (1st ed. 1859). New York: A. L. Burt, 1910. 538 pp.
Although Darwin's theory of evolution is completely a scientific theory, containing nothing about morals in relation to animals, the implications of the kinship of all life have enormous significance for animal rights.

29 Cobbe, Frances P. (1822–1904). "The rights of man and the claims of brutes.'' In *Studies new and old of ethical and social subjects*, 209–57. London: Trübner, 1865.
Originally published in *Fraser's Magazine*, November 1863. This early essay presents a weaker view on human obligations to animals than later developed by Cobbe. Uses Bishop Butler's principle that if any creature be sentient (capable of pain or pleasure) that is sufficient reason we should refrain from inflicting pain, and we should bestow on it pleasure when we can. Approves of painless taking of animal lives but criticizes wanton, needless infliction of pain.

30 Darwin, Charles (1809–1882). *The descent of man and selection in relation to sex.* (First published 1871) 2d ed. New York: P. F. Collier, 1902. 868 pp.
Argues for biological and psychological continuity of animal and human life, based on theory of natural selection. Chap. 2, "Comparison of the mental powers of man and the lower animals,'' 94–171, important. ". . . There is no fundamental difference between man and the higher mammals in their mental faculties.'' Applies wide range of terms to various animals: pleasure, pain, happiness, misery, play, terror, suspicion, intentional deceit, timidity, ill-temper, sulkiness, good temper, rage, revenge, love, maternal affection, jealousy, desire to be loved, feel emulation, love praise, pride, excitement, boredom, wonder, curiosity, imitation, attention, memory, judge intervals of time, imagination, dreaming, reason, learning from past experience, deliberate, resolve, association of ideas, subject to insanity, capable of progressive improvement, use of tools, idea of property, fashioning of tools, abstraction, self-consciousness, language, communication, anger, joy, sense of beauty, love of novelty for its own sake, sociability, sympathy, regard for feelings of others, possess something like conscience, shame, modesty, magnanimity, dislike being laughed at, sense of humor. Agrees with T. H. Huxley that in every visible character humans differ less from the higher apes than these do from the lower members of the same order of primates. ". . . Everyone has heard of the dog suffering under vivisection, who licked the hand of the operator; this man, unless the operation was fully justified by an increase of our knowledge, or unless he had a heart of stone, must have felt remorse to the last hour of his life.''

31 Darwin, Charles (1809–1882). *The expression of the emotions in man and animals.* (First published 1872) Reprint from authorized edition of D. Appleton and Co. Chicago: University of Chicago Press, 1965. 372 pp.
Compares methods of expressing emotions in humans and animals. Animal emotions and activities include affection, pain, pleasure, grinning, attention, terror,

playing, weeping, joy, anger, sulkiness, frowning, caressing, purring, fighting, grief, fear, laughter, astonishment, humility, hostility, disappointment, snarling. Claims movements and gestures of dogs, monkeys are almost as expressive as those of humans. Conclusion: similarity of expression gives some evidence for descent of humans from lower forms of life.

32 Wood, J. G. (1827–1889). *Man and beast: here and hereafter illustrated by more than three hundred original anecdotes*. London: Daldy, Isbister, 1874.
A naturalist and minister, Wood attempts to carry out the train of thought in Joseph Butler's *Analogy of religion*: animals are capable of a future life. Argues Scriptures do not deny a future life for animals. Animals share with humans reason, language, memory, sense of moral responsibility, unselfishness, love. Since humans expect to retain these qualities after death, why not animals likewise? Anecdotal evidence.

33 Carroll, Lewis [C. L. Dodgson] (1832–1898). "Vivisection as a sign of the times." (Letter in *Pall Mall Gazette*, 12 February 1875) In *The works of Lewis Carroll*, ed. by R. L. Green, 1089–92. London: Hamlyn, 1965.
Rather than resulting in higher moral character and civilization the increase of knowledge from animal experimentation, divorced from religious or moral training, results in unmitigated selfishness.

34 Carroll, Lewis [C. L. Dodgson] (1832–1898). "Some popular fallacies about vivisection." (Originally in *Fortnightly Review*, 1 June 1875) In *The complete Works of Lewis Carroll*, 1189–201. London: Nonesuch Press, 1939.
Critiques twelve fallacies used by animal-experimentation advocates who argue animal experimentation is justified because: (1) Infliction of pain on animals is a right of humans, needing no justification. (2) The right to inflict pain on animals is co-extensive with our right to kill animals. (3) Humans are infinitely more important than animals. (4) It is fair to compare aggregates of pain. (5) Pain inflicted is not greater than in hunting, fishing. (6) The charge against animal experimentation consists chiefly in the pain inflicted on animals (and not the effect on the experimenter). (7) It has no demoralizing effect on the experimenter. (8) It does not demoralize character more than sport does. (9) The motive is essentially unselfish, while the motive in sport is essentially selfish. (10) Toleration of one evil necessitates toleration of all others. (11) Legislation against it would only increase the evil. (12) It will never be extended so as to include humans.

35 Browning, Robert (1812–1889). "Tray." In *The poems and plays of Robert Browning*, 1064–5. New York: Modern Library, 1934.
Powerful poem against animal experimentation, written in 1879, resulting from the testimony of E. Schafer before the 1876 Royal Commission on Vivisection in which Schafer attempts to justify drowning over 50 dogs in order to discover a method of resuscitating drowned humans. Tray not only rescues the child from drowning, but also plunges into the stream to save her doll. Impressed by such feats, a scientist reasons:

Why he dived,
His brain would show us, I should say.

John, go and catch – or if needs be,
Purchase – that animal for me!
By vivisection, at expense
Of half-an-hour and eighteenpence,
How brain secretes dog's soul, we'll see!''

Browning: ''I would rather submit to the worst of deaths, so far as pain goes, than have a single dog or cat tortured on the pretence of sparing me a twinge or two.'' (Quoted on p. 1064)

36 Nicholson, Edward W. B. (1849–1912). *The rights of an animal: A new essay in ethics.* London: C. Kegan Paul, 1879. 124 pp.
Argues abstractly for animals' rights to life and liberty on the basis of sentience (feeling pleasure and pain). Critiques arguments against animal rights. However, author claims that in practice the abstract theory of animals' rights is unworkable, and that there are limits on application, mainly because (so the author believes) many animals are dangerous to humans, in competition for food resources, and if allowed their rights they would overpopulate and crowd humans out of existence. Seems to defend many violations of animal rights on basis of ''self-defense'' by humans against animals. Example of a very strong theoretical animal rights view with a very weak practical animal rights position. Modern ecology and ethology probably show some of Nicholson's factual presuppositions to be false.

37 Kingsford, Anna (1846–1888). *The perfect way in diet: A treatise advocating a return to the natural and ancient food of our race.* London: Kegan Paul, Trench, 1881. 121 pp.
A translation of Kingsford's thesis for Doctor of Medicine, Faculty of Medicine, Paris, 1880. Argues for superiority of vegetarianism on the basis of comparative anatomy and physiology (humans are naturally frugivorous), chemistry, history, political and social economy (more efficient use of land and resources). Also on basis of moral duties to animals.

38 Kingsford, Anna (1846–1888) and **Maitland, Edward** (1824–1897). *Addresses and essays on vegetarianism, 1881–1893,* ed. by S. H. Hart. London: John M. Watkins, 1912. 227 pp.
Biographies of Kingsford and Maitland given, 1–60. Favorably discuss vegetarianism in relation to economics, health, aesthetics, physiology, social and moral progress, and especially spiritual development.

39 Cobbe, Frances P. (1822–1904). ''Zoophily.'' *Cornhill Magazine* 45 (1882): 279–88.
Argues for a human duty to animals based upon the principles of J. Bentham (''The question is not, Can they reason? or Can they speak? but Can they suffer?'') and Bishop Butler (if a creature is sentient we have a responsibility to save it pain or give it pleasure). Since we cause the existence of domestic animals, they

are rightful claimants of justice that they should on the whole be happy and not miserable. Argues for ''an absolute stop to vivisection'' (287).

40 Coleridge, John Duke (1820–1894). ''The Nineteenth Century defenders of vivisection.'' *Fortnightly Review* 37 (1882): 225–36.
Morally shocked by the growing indifference of scientists to animal sufferings, their ''open scoffing at laws of mercy which not so long ago were honoured,'' and their claim that in pursuit of knowledge any cruelty may be inflicted on animals, Lord Coleridge argues for complete abolition of animal experimentation and testing. It is inconsistent to claim all pursuit of knowledge is lawful where animals are concerned but that moral restrictions apply where humans are concerned. Critiques argument that animal experimentation is justified because it is no more painful or no less useful than hunting, trapping.

41 Romanes, George J. (1848–1894). *Animal intelligence.* London: Kegan Paul, Trench, 1882. 520 pp. Reprint: Brookfield, VT: Gregg International. Also Washington, DC: University Publications of America, 1978.
A founding work in comparative psychology exploring the limits of animal intelligence with comparison to human intelligence. Defining reason or intelligence as intentional adaptation of means to end based on learning from past experience, presents factual material based on reports of observers (including Charles Darwin) on limits of intelligence in various species (mollusca, ants, bees, wasps, termites, spiders, scorpions, fish, reptiles, birds, mammals, rodents, elephants, cats, foxes, wolves, jackals, monkeys, apes, baboons) with intent of fitting this data into the theory of evolution. Preface (v–xii) and Introduction (1–17) are important theoretically. Activities of animals viewed as ambassadors of mind. Mental operations in animals inferred on basis of observed activities and analogy from human mental operations. Consciousness and choice emphasized as distinctive characteristics of mind. Discussion of distinctions between reflex action, instinctive activity, and reason or intelligence.

42 Romanes, George J. (1848–1894). *Mental evolution in animals.* London: Kegan Paul, Trench, 1883. 411 pp. Reprint: Brookfield, VT: Gregg International.
The appendix contains a posthumous essay on instinct by Charles Darwin (355–84). Romanes was a younger personal and intellectual associate of Darwin. Darwin gave to Romanes all his manuscripts relating to psychological subjects, requesting that he publish any parts of them as desired. Using Darwin's theory of evolution as an hypothesis, and drawing upon observation and anecdotal evidence, Romanes attempts to trace the evolution of mental capacities (emotions, will, intellect) in animals, in continuity with human mental evolution. His views are summarized in a detailed, complex diagram showing fifty levels of mental capacities. Attributes to various animals the following emotions, in probable order of historical development: surprise, fear, sexual and parental affection, social feelings, pugnacity, industry, curiosity, jealousy, anger, play, affection, sympathy, emulation, pride, resentment, aesthetic love of ornament, terror, grief, hate, cruelty, benevolence, revenge, rage, shame, remorse, deceit, the ludicrous. Attributes intellectual capacities to various animals in probable

historical order: consciousness, pleasure and pain, memory, primary instincts, association by contiguity, recognition of offspring, secondary instincts, association by similarity, reason (intentional adaptation of means to ends), recognition of persons, communication of ideas, recognition of pictures, understanding of words, dreaming, understanding of mechanisms, use of tools, and indefinite morality.

43 Ouida [Louise de la Ramée] (1839–1908). "The future of vivisection." *Gentleman's Magazine* 252 (1882): 412–23.
Movement against animal experimentation is really human self-defense. "There is not a single argument used by the advocates of vivisection which will not apply in as complete an entity to human as to animal subjects." Physiologists, instead of meeting argument logically, shout "squeamishness," "sentimentality." That they do not resort to human experiments is due only to their timidity of public opinion. ". . . The superstitious awe of science has succeeded to the supersititious awe of religion."

44 Williams, Howard. *The ethics of diet: A catena of authorities deprecatory of the practice of flesh-eating*. London: F. Pitman, 1883. 336 pp.
A classical scholar and a founder of the Humanitarian League, Williams was a close intellectual associate of Henry Salt's. The preface, iv–xii, discusses fallacies and subterfuges used by flesh-eaters. Scholarly, extremely informative, well-documented, with copious quotations and notes, conveying views favorable to vegetarianism of over 60 important thinkers, from Hesiod to Schopenhauer. Leo Tolstoy, sufficiently impressed to have it published in Russian, added a long introduction: "The first step" (L. Tolstoy ⟨1892⟩ 1968). Almost encyclopedic, this rich source of information should be republished for the modern reader. Persons covered: Hesiod, Buddha, Pythagoras, Plato, Ovid, Seneca, Musonius, Plutarch, Tertullian, Clement of Alexandria, Porphyry, Chrysostom, Cornaro, Thomas More, Montaigne, Lessio, Gassendi, Ray, Cowley, Evelyn, Mandeville, Gay, Tryon, Cheyne, Pope, Jenyns, Thomson, Hartley, Chesterfield, Voltaire, Haller, Cocchi, Bentham, Rousseau, Linne, Buffon, Hawkesworth, Paley, St. Pierre, Oswald, Hufeland, Ritson, Nicholson, Abernethy, Lambe, Newton, Gleizes, Shelley, Phillips, Michelet, Cowherd, Metcalfe, Graham, Lamartine, Struve, Daumer, Schopenhauer.

45 Salt, Henry S. (1851–1939). *A plea for vegetarianism and other essays*. Manchester: Vegetarian Society, 1886. 115 pp.
Nine essays giving insight into reactions to vegetarians, with suggestions how vegetarians should respond. (1) "A plea for vegetarianism," 7–20. This essay, picked up by Gandhi in a vegetarian restaurant in London, had a profound influence on him. (See Gandhi's letter to Salt, 12 October 1929, in *The selected works of Mahatma Gandhi*, vol. 5, 180. Ahmedabad: Navajivan Publishing, 1968.) (2) "Morality in diet," 21–3. (3) "Good taste in diet," 31–9. (4) "Some results of food reform," 40–7. (5) "Medical men and food reform," 48–55. (6) "Sir Henry Thompson on diet," 56–72. (7) "On certain fallacies," 73–91. (8) "The philosophy of cannibalism," 102–10. (9) "Vegetarianism and social reform," 111–15.

46 Kingsford, Anna (1846–1888). "Unscientific science: Moral aspects of vivisection." In *Spiritual therapeutics*, ed. by W. W. Colville, 292–308. Chicago: Educator Publishing, 1888.

Sharp critique of animal experimentation. Harming of animals by scientists compared to actions of inquisitors and slaveholders. Desire for knowledge has its moral limits, in science as in art. Kingsford relates the example of the artist who crucified an unfortunate youth in order to secure a faithful model for an altarpiece portraying the expiring Christ. Science based on harming animals is neither legitimate nor civilized, with results ending in obliteration of true science and true civilization. "We have no right to inflict upon innocent animals torments to which pity forbids us to subject guilty men." How can children be taught duties of humanity toward animals when at school they learn what horrors are perpetrated in the work-rooms of science by the teachers they are expected to revere and imitate? Experimental scientists have shown themselves incapable of recognizing the obligations of public morality. Society is right in refusing to admit the assumption of infallibility on the part of a caste exclusively scientific in matters affecting the public conscience.

47 Salt, Henry S. (1851–1939). *Flesh or fruit? An essay on food reform.* London: William Reeves, 1888. 48 pp.

Discusses the literature of vegetarianism, including that by Seneca, Plutarch, Porphyry, Wesley, Montaigne, Sylvester Graham, Anna Kingsford. The vegetarian diet is advantageous in that it is necessary in order to be consistently humane, is aesthetically in good taste, is healthful, is economic. Criticizes objectors to vegetarianism who use the argument from physiology (humans' canine teeth), who claim vegetarianism violates the laws of nature (predator and prey), who say some people who have tried vegetarianism have failed to stick with it, who ask what will we do for leather, soap, candles, who claim that eating animals is in the animals' interests.

48 Cobbe, Frances P. (1822–1904). *The modern rack.* London: Sonnenschein, 1889. 267 pp.

Collection of Cobbe's major addresses and essays in opposition to animal experimentation. In "The moral aspects of vivisection" (1–17) she attacks arguments used by scientists to defend experiments. Does the good of man justify the torture of animals? What is there in man which should make his trifling pain so inexpressibly solemn a matter, and the agony of another animal, no less physically sensitive, insignificant by comparison? "The higher expediency" (31–48) argues against animal experimentation on the basis of disutility to the higher life of humans (the effect on human character, the higher interests of the community). Other essays are: "The right of tormenting" (49–60), "What is cruelty?" (61–4), "A reply to Sir James Paget on vivisection" (91–102), "Light in dark places" (181–212), "Four reasons for total prohibition of vivisection" (221–6), "Darwin and vivisection" (103–8).

49 Salt, Henry S. (1851–1939). *Animals' rights, considered in relation to social progress.* (Reprint of first edition: London: Macmillan, 1892) Clarks Summit, PA: Society for Animal Rights, 1980. 232 pp.

Preface by Peter Singer, v–x. Appendix includes Salt's discussion of the term "rights" (133–5), a valuable annotated bibliography by Salt (136–69), an updated bibliography by C. R. Magel (170–218), a list of works by Salt (219–25), and a short biography of Salt (226–30). An important work anticipating many of the issues and arguments in the contemporary debate over animal rights. Bases animal rights and human rights on the kinship of sentient beings implicit in Darwin's theory of evolution. Animals have individuality, moral purpose (moral standing); they are not tools for human use. Justice requires that all animals (human and nonhuman) have the right to freedom in natural development of individuality. Avoidable infliction of pain or suffering is morally unjustified. Discusses implications for domestic and wild animals, human diet, hunting, fishing, use of animal products, experimentation on animals. Rigorous argument for vegetarianism, and for the cessation of all experiments harmful to animals. Emphasizes education, legislation. Argues human social progress – the achievement of human rights, individual fulfillment, civilization, genuine happiness – is intimately linked with the fulfillment of animals' rights. "I know my belief in the creed of kinship will be accepted one day. Man will have to accept it or perish."

50 Ouida [Louise de la Ramée] (1839–1908). "The new priesthood." *New Review* 8 (1893): 151–64.
Contrasts animal experimenters (physiologists) with medieval inquisitors. ". . . the motive of the inquisitor was a higher one, for he sincerely believed that he saved souls and benefited his victims themselves; the physiologist . . . only expects to save bodies, and those not the bodies of his victims." The rationale of pursuit of knowledge has the logical consequence of justifying experiments on "the idiot, the cripple, the mute." The priesthood of physiology is a gang, operating behind closed doors, whose members are sworn to mutual support when mistakes are made. Physiologists, as interested in money and reputation as anyone else, should be subjected to public scrutiny like everyone else.

51 Salt, Henry S. (1851–1939), ed. *Cruelties of civilization: A program of humane reform.* 3 vols. London: William Reeves, 1896–1897.
Reprints of Humanitarian League publications, each essay separately paginated. Salt defines humanitarianism as the study and practice of compassion, love, gentleness, justice, and universal benevolence applicable to all sentient beings, human and nonhuman. Draws a sharp distinction between humanitarianism and a "sentimentality view" or a 'be kind to humans and animals" view. Volume I applies to humans: punishment and prison reform, economic discrimination against women, humanizing the poor laws, protection of children, aged, sick, insane. Volume II is on animals. Two essays against harmful experiments on animals ("Medical science: The true method and the false" by Edward Carpenter; "An appeal to hearts and heads" by Edward Maitland). "The horrors of sport" (hunting) by Florence Dixie (who once was an avid hunter). "Royal sport" (vivid description of and sharp attack on the Queen's Buckhounds and stag hunting – the hunting (?) of tame deer from Windsor Park) by J. Stratton. "Rabbit coursing" by R. H. Jude. "The extermination of birds" (use of feathers in millinery, hunting, robbing birds' nests, caging) by Edith Carrington. "The horse" (service to civilization, abuses, disposal of) by B. Coulson. "Cattle ships"

(imports from Ireland and America, abuses in loading and transporting, lack of food and water, injuries) by Isabella M. Greg and S. H. Towers. "Behind the scenes in slaughter-houses" by H. F. Lester. Volume III contains two important essays by Salt: (1) "The humanities of diet," 22 pp. Principle and purpose of vegetarianism, misconceptions of vegetarianism, slaughter-house horrors, aesthetic considerations. (2) "Literae humaniores: An appeal to teachers," 32 pp. The need for humane education; pets, collecting insects, blood-sports, flesh-food; what teachers can do.

52 Seton, Ernest Thompson (1860–1946). *Wild animals I have known*. New York: Charles Scribner's, ⟨1898⟩ 1926. 298 pp. Also Berkeley, CA: Creative Arts, 1987 or 1988.
A naturalist writes personal histories of eight individual wild animals and birds (wolf, crow, rabbit, 2 dogs, fox, mustang, partridge), emphasizing a theme common to much of the animal rights literature: "We and the beasts are kin. Man has nothing that the animals have not at least a vestige of, the animals have nothing that man does not in some degree share. Since, then, the animals are creatures with wants and feelings differing in degree only from our own, they surely have their rights" (11–12).

53 Moore, J. Howard (1862–1916). *Better-world philosophy: A sociological synthesis*. Chicago: Ward Waugh, 1899. 275 pp.
Argues for evolutionary development of altruism as an ideal overcoming egoism. In the "better world", anthropocentrism will be dethroned by zoocentrism in which the entire sentient universe should be contemplated through universal consideration and love. Moore's interpretation of the Golden Rule: "The ideal relation of the inhabitants of the universe to each other is that relation which will aid most actively in the satisfaction of the desires of the universe."

54 Salt, Henry S. (1851–1939). *The logic of vegetarianism: Essays and dialogues*. (First published 1899) 2d ed. rev. London: George Bell, 1906. 116 pp.
Arguments for vegetarianism: moral, scientific, economic, health, social, and aesthetic. Amazingly comprehensive, devastating critique of 31 anti-vegetarian arguments (some so silly they are humorous, but many of these arguments still in use). The arguments or claims made by opponents of vegetarianism: (1) Consuming eggs and dairy products contradicts the meaning of "vegetarian." (2) There is no difference between roasting an ox and boiling an egg. (3) Vegetarians who do not immediately and completely shun all animal products are hypocrites. (4) No great empires (Roman, British) were ever founded by vegetarians. (5) Human canine teeth prove the necessity of flesh-eating. (6) The human stomach is much different than that of true herbivora. (7) History shows that humans are omnivorous. (8) Vegetarianism is contrary to the laws of nature, red in tooth and claw; to kill is natural. (9) It is necessary to destroy life in order to live. (10) Raising food animals in pleasant conditions and killing them painlessly are not cruel. (11) Eating animals is no worse than using them for labor. (12) The rapid death of food animals is preferable to the agonizing death of humans. (13) Food animals, free of the fears and dangers experienced by wild animals, are happier. (14) It is better for animals that we use them for food than that they not exist at all.

(15) Vegetarians who eat eggs and dairy products are inconsistent. (16) Consistent vegetarians could never kill lice or germs. (17) Flesh-eating is just as aesthetic as vegetarianism. (18) Vegetarians are sentimentalists. (19) Meat is necessary for strength. (20) Flesh-food is easier digested than vegetarian food. (21) Flesh diet is necessary in cold climates ("What would become of the Eskimoes if all became vegetarians?"). (22) What difference does it make whether we eat flesh or non-flesh, so long as the spirit in which we eat be a proper one? (23) Vegetarianism is economically impractical. (24) Vegetarianism is an inconvenient diet. (25) Eating flesh is necessary for developing a manly spirit. (26) How could we exist without leather? Soap? Candles? (27) How could the land be fertilized without manure from food animals? (28) If the life of animals be regarded as sacred as human life, civilization will revert to a primitive condition. (29) If we turn loose all the food animals they will over-populate, overrun the land, starve, lie dead on highways and in the suburbs. (30) We were given permission by God to eat animals. (31) Vegetarians do not give sufficient priority to more important social reforms (war, poverty, etc.).

55 Salt, Henry S. (1851-1939). "The rights of animals." *Ethics* 10 (1899): 206-22.
Argues for the right of animals to live their own lives as individuals with own purposes and value. Emphasizes direct duties of humans to animals. The kinship of humans and animals as evidenced by evolution is basic to ethics. A matter of justice: treat an animal in such a manner as you would willingly be treated, were you the animal. Discusses implications for animals used for labor, food, experimentation, sports. Argues against D. G. Ritchie's (〈1894〉 1952) denial of animal rights.

56 Trine, Ralph Waldo (1866-1958). *Every living creature or heart-training through the animal world*. New York: Thomas Y. Crowell, 1899. 85 pp.
The title suggests main emphasis: teaching moral and spiritual development through being compassionate to animals. Criticizes hunting, animal experimentation, docking, furs, eating animals. "We [humans and animals] are all different forms of the manifestation of the Spirit of Infinite Life, Love, and Power that is back of all, working in and through all, the life of all. . . . The Golden Rule must be applied in our relations with the animal world, just as it must be applied in our relations with our fellow men, and no-one can be a Christian until this finds embodiment in his or her life."

57 Bigelow, Henry J. (1818-1890). "Vivisection." In *Surgical anaesthesia: Addresses and other papers*, 363-74. (Republication of edition of 1900) Boston: Longwood Press, 1977.
Bigelow was a professor of medicine at Harvard Medical School. Sharply attacks painful animal experimentation and demonstrations; argues for regulation by law. The public should not rely on the discretion of scientists. "The right to vivisect a dog for the benefit of mankind inevitably involves the right, apart from human legislation, to dissect alive a living idiot or the lowest grade of savage." If superior beings were to arrive from outer space, experimenters would rightfully expect the human community to protect the experimenters from being

experimented upon by the superior visitors. Why then has not the dog a right to the active defense by the human community? "There is no objection to vivisection except the physical pain it inflicts." "In order that painful vivisection may be as nearly as possible suppressed, not only by public opinion, but by law, it is essential that public opinion should be frequently informed of what it is and may be. It is an arbitrary and conventional line which separates the intellect of animals from that of humans, and it is an equally arbitrary line that places animals in the power of humans; such a line needs frequent supervision."

58 Salt, Henry S. (1851–1939). *A lover of animals.* (Reprint of a play performed in London, 1900.) Rochester, NY: Lion's Den Press, 1984. Also in *Henry Salt: Humanitarian reformer and man of letters*, by G. Hendrick, 174–95. Urbana: University of Illinois Press, 1977.
Humorous, short play portraying different interpretations of "lover of animals" through interaction of surgeon, hunter, pet owner, vegetarian, and butcher. A critique of animal experimentation implicit.

59 Salt, Henry S. (1851–1939). "Restrictionists and abolitionists." *Humanity* 4 (November 1900): 85–6. Reprinted in *Animals' Agenda* 7 (November 1987): 42–3.
In regard to animal experimentation, using animals for food, and hunting, a plea for restrictionism *and* abolitionism as the wiser policy, rather than restrictionism *or* abolitionism. ". . . The acceptance or refusal of compromise . . . is a matter of policy, not principle . . ." Restrictionists and abolitionists should regard each other not as rivals but as allies. One and the same individual, one and the same organization can advocate both restriction *and* abolition. Take all the good we can get, while forever aspiring to something more. It is sometimes more noble and difficult to be willing to accept the humblest installment of reform.

60 Shaw, George Bernard (1856–1950). *The dynamitards of science.* London: London Anti-Vivisection Society, 1900. 8 pp.
Compares scientists' attempt to justify animal experimentation on basis of results with the fictional situation of person using dynamite in an attempt to reform society. Since it is impossible to prove the uselessness of anything, warns against attacking animal experimentation on the basis of its being useless. The logic of utility would result in experimenting on humans. No person whose life is worth living will have anything to do with animal experimentation.

61 Salt, Henry S. (1851–1939), ed. *Kith and kin: Poems of animal life.* London: George Bell, 1901. 95 pp.
Selection of 85 poems, some abridged, reflecting kinship of humans and animals. 56 writers, including W. Blake, E. B. Browning, R. Burns, Lord Byron, S. T. Coleridge, W. Cowper, O. Goldsmith, L. Hunt, J. Keats, H. W. Longfellow, A. Pope, P. B. Shelley, R. Southey, H. D. Thoreau, W. Whitman, W. Wordsworth. "Where the non-human races are concerned – birds perhaps excepted – the treatment of animals in verse has been almost as bad as their treatment in actual life."

62 Bell, Ernest (1851–1933). "The rights of animals." *Humane Review* (Journal of the Humanitarian League) 2 (1901–1902): 324–35.
Clear statement of a strong animal rights position, comparing recognition of animals' right to life and right to freedom with earlier recognition of rights for slaves, women, children. Emphasizes feeling of sympathy combined with sense of justice as a basis for ascribing rights. Animals cannot be denied rights if we admit them for humans. Argues against eating animal flesh (except where died from natural causes), harmful experiments on animals. If we admit the right to sacrifice one being for the benefit of another there is no crime on earth which might not be so justified. Against the harming of animals for amusement; also against caging zoo animals, birds, or pets.

63 Carpenter, Edward (1844–1929). "Vivisection." *Humane Review* 4 (1903–1904): 289–300.
Critiques two defenses often made for animal experimentation: curing of disease and general advance of knowledge. Argues S. Paget (1900) in his *Experiments on animals* overstates both of these defenses. There is no doom of disease except what we bring on ourselves. To thrust on animals the consequences of our foolish, idiotic living is evil and futile. Health is in our own hands. Fear of disease and callousness to animal suffering are themselves diseases, producing more diseases in society than animal experimentation has ever succeeded in curing. To pursue knowledge in this way is to blind ourselves to the most health-giving of all knowledge – the sense of our common life and unity with all creatures. Suggests feverish energy now directed to animal experimentation be devoted to best methods of health, diet, exercise, etc. Apart from benefiting animals, stopping animal experimentation will compel humans onto the road of sanity, deliver them from darkness and losing their way on a false trail.

64 Crosby, Ernest (1856–1907) "The meat fetish." *Humane Review* 5 (1904–1905): 199–216.
Criticizes flesh diet as unclean, unwholesome, unatural, non-economic, non-aesthetic, and harmful to animals. Raising animals for food is "to raise corpses." Argues for vegetarianism as a reassertion of the obligation to love one's neighbor. Answers superficial objections to vegetarianism often made by flesh-eaters: What will become of us if we do not kill animals? Will they crowd us out of existence? What will we do for boots and shoes? Should domestic animals be exterminated?

65 Moore, J. Howard (1862–1916). *The universal kinship*. Chicago: C. H. Kerr, 1906. 329 pp.
Henry Salt's judgement: the best book ever written in the humanitarian cause. Evolution serves as background for the physical, mental, and ethical kinship between all animals, human and nonhuman. Animals "are not conveniences, but cousins." "*All* beings are *ends*; *no* creatures are *means*. . . . *All have rights*. . . . Act toward others [all animals, human and nonhuman] as you would act toward a part of your own self."

66 Moore, J. Howard (1862–1916). *The new ethics*. London: Ernest Bell, 1907. 216 pp.

Both book and author (brother-in-law of Clarence Darrow and friend of Henry Salt) are little known. Applies Golden Rule and utilitarianism impartially to all sentient beings in universal kinship as evidenced by evolution. Animals should be treated as associates, as "somebodies," not as slaves or machines. Simple justice requires we avoid for others that which we do not like ourselves. Regards biologists "blind as bats" to the underlying psychological and moral relationships. Argues for vegetarianism; against animal experimentation, hunting, trapping, leather clothing and shoes. All animals (human and nonhuman) should have right to live, be free, and enjoy their legitimate share of world.

67 Salt, Henry S. (1851–1939). "Have animals rights?" *Humane Review* 8 (1907–1908): 219–36.
This essay shows "Humanitarian" as author, but surely it is Salt. We should use the expression "man and the *other* animals"instead of "man and the animals." An animal has its own individuality and life to live as surely as a human has. We claim for animals and humans a measure of individuality and freedom, a space in which to live their own lives – rights. If humans have rights, animals have them also. Treat the animal in such a manner as you would willingly be treated, were you such an animal. Simple justice is required.

68 Salt, Henry S. (1851–1939). "What is humanitarianism?" *Humane Review* 8 (1907–1908): 178–88.
Discusses what humanitarianism is and what it is not. Emphasizes rights of both humans and animals. It is iniquitous to inflict avoidable suffering on any sentient being. Humanitarianism is not a "be kind to sentient beings" view or a sentimental view.

69 Salt, Henry S. (1851–1939), ed. *Killing for sport: Essays by various writers.* London: G. Bell, 1915. 186 pp.
Preface by G. B. Shaw, xi–xxxiv. Covers hunting, including hunting of carted deer, rabbit coursing, pigeon shooting, trapping, and fishing, in relation to cruelty (G. Greenwood, 1–33), agriculture (E. Carpenter, 34–44), cost (M. Adams, 45–59), game laws (J. Connell, 69–84), economics (W. H. S. Monck, 60–8), destruction of wildlife (E. B. Lloyd, 85–94), fox hunting (H. B. M. Watson, 95–100), big-game hunting (E. Bell, 101–15), blood sports at schools ("by an old Etonian," apparently H. S. Salt), 116–29. In H. S. Salt's important essay "Sportsmen's fallacies," 130–46, he analyzes and critiques 13 sophisms used by hunters who claim that hunting is justified because: (1) hunters have a God-given instinct to hunt; (2) animals hunt other animals; (3) it is necessary to control animal populations; (4) it adds to the national food supply; (5) it helps the economy; (6) it develops courage, manliness, virility; (7) hunters enjoy it; (8) the hunted enjoy it; (9) the animals would rather live a happy life and be shot rather than not exist at all; (10) hunters save species from extinction; (11) hunters, because of extensive hunting experience, are specialists who know more about the issue of hunting than do its critics; (12) death from hunting is less painful than natural death; (13) shooting a predator eliminates the suffering the prey would otherwise have experienced.

70 Leffingwell, Albert (1845–1916). *An ethical problem, or sidelights upon scientific experimentation on man and animals.* 2d ed. rev. New York: C. P. Farrell, 1916. 374 pp.
Collection of essays, speeches. Animal experimentation is a genuine ethical problem regardless how great the benefits. Critical of unlimited animal experimentation; against secrecy; favors reform through governmental regulation. Critical discussions of John Hunter, François Magendie, Claude Bernard, W. W. Keen. Favorable considerations of John Reid, W. O. Markham, Henry J. Bigelow, William James.

71 Coleridge, Stephen (1854–1936). *Vivisection: A heartless science.* London and New York: John Lane, 1916. 240 pp.
England sustains the shame of having passed a law – the Cruelty to Animals Act 1876 – defending the scientific torturers from any interference by the humane. The whole question of human rights over and duties toward animals is a moral one. Distinguished scientists have no more qualification to claim authority to dictate to us about it than have distinguished musicians, painters, or lawyers. Attacks the appeal to utility: ". . . If the vivisection itself, by which a cure is discovered, entails severe suffering to animals, it is . . . an immoral and cowardly act. . . . Nothing in the world . . . could ever morally justify the artificial production of so horrible a disease as cancer in the body of a miserable animal." Critiques the Research Defence Society, its literature, and Stephen Paget. Criticizes the worship of heartless science.

72 Coleridge, Stephen (1854–1936). *Great testimony against scientific cruelty.* London and New York: John Lane, 1918. 66 pp.
Brief account, with illustrations, of prominent persons' views against animal experimentation: the Seventh Earl of Shaftesbury, Frances P. Cobbe, Cardinal Manning, Robert Browning, Lord Coleridge (Chief Justice of England), John Ruskin, Samuel Johnson, Thomas Carlyle, Alfred Tennyson, Cardinal Newman, Queen Victoria.

73 Lloyd, Bertram, ed. *The great kinship: An anthology of humanitarian poetry.* London: George Allen and Unwin, 1921. 272 pp.
Poems fall into three groups: (1) those which inculcate, or voice the feeling of, justice as ethical duty; (2) those expressing kinship or bond of union between humans and animals; (3) poems evoking emotions, ideas, favorable to the growth of humane feeling. Mainly British, 18th and 19th centuries; also German and French (translated), and American. The 67 poets and translators include: W. Blake, E. Browning, R. Burns, S. T. Coleridge, W. Cowper, W. De la Mare, J. Galsworthy, T. Hardy, V. Hugo, L. Hunt, E. Markham, A. Noyes, H. S. Salt, F. Schiller, P. B. Shelley, R. Southey, A. C. Swinburne, W. Whitman, W. Wordsworth.

74 Schweitzer, Albert (1875–1965). "The ethics of reverence for life" and "The civilizing power of the ethics of reverence for life." (First published in German and English in 1923) In *The philosophy of civilization*, trans. by C. T. Campion, 307–29 and 330–44. New York: Macmillan, 1950.

Schweitzer was an organist, an authority on Bach's music and on organ-building, theologian, philosopher, physician, medical missionary in Gabon, and Nobel Peace Laureate. "Reverence for life" is the usual translation of Schweitzer's expression "der Ehrfurcht vor dem Leben." Develops a cosmic–mystic–spiritual–ethical view emphasizing world-and-life affirmation permeated by a deep respect for all life. Ethics consists in our experiencing the compulsion to show to all will-to-live the same respect as we do to our own will-to-live. "A man is truly ethical only when he obeys the compulsion to help all life which he is able to assist, and shrinks from injuring anything that lives. He does not ask how far this or that life deserves one's sympathy as being valuable, nor, beyond that, whether and to what degree it is capable of feeling. Life as such is sacred to him. . . . The will-to-live in me manifests itself as will-to-live which desires to become one with other will-to-live." Respect for life is a profound attitude which generates no rules; each person must decide actions in the context of this attitude.

75 Nelson, Leonard (1882–1927). "Duties to animals."(A lecture written prior to 1927.) In *System of ethics*, trans. by N. Guterman, 136–44. New Haven: Yale University Press, 1956.

This essay, which is reproduced in [97, pp. 149–55], was published posthumously in Germany in 1932, and is probably the first systematic essay by a professional philosopher defending animal rights. "Under the moral law, all beings who have interests are subject of rights . . ." We have direct duties to animals. Criticizes sophistical arguments used by those who deny animals' rights. ". . . We have merely to ask whether, in considering an action affecting an animal . . ., we would consent to be be used as mere means by another being far superior to us in strength and intelligence." A painless killing of an animal injures that animal's interest in living. "In no event is it permissible to regard the animal's interest as inferior without good reason, and to proceed to injure it." In actual conflicts of interests between humans and animals, the principle of justice must be reaffirmed. Rationality cannot be used to found the claim that in case of conflict a human life ought always be given preference over an animal life.

76 Shaw, George Bernard (1856–1950). "These scoundrels: Vivisection – the 'science' of imbeciles." *The Sunday Express* (London) 7 August 1927.

Distinguishes between science and scoundrelism – the view that experimenters have the unlimited right to harm animals because of an unlimited right to know. Attacks H. G. Wells on animal experimentation. Discusses Queen Victoria's appeal to Lord Lister to make some public declaration in condemnation of animal experimentation, and critiques Lister's reply. An unlimited right to know would justify boiling human infants in order to find out what boiled babies taste like.

77 Salt, Henry S. (1851–1939). *The creed of kinship.* London: Constable, 1935. 118 pp.

Brief, clear overview of humanitarianism, based on kinship view of evolved life forms, with consideration of war, poverty, women's rights, prison reform, theory of punishment, flogging, animal rights, experiments on animals, vegetarianism, hunting, fishing. Shows Salt's humanitarianism vitally concerned with both humans and animals, human rights and animal rights.

78 Salt, Henry S. (1851–1939). "Humanitarianism." In *Encyclopedia of religion and ethics*, ed. by J. Hastings, vol. 6, 836–40. New York: Charles Scribner's, 1961.
Similar to [68].

79 Lamont, W. D. "Duty and interest." *Philosophy* 17 (1942): 3–25.
Duties are based on rights. Rights are based on interests. Argues animals have rights. Possessing a right need not be combined with power to claim in the same individual; a guardian can represent an animal as well as a child. Claims animals have one basic legal right – the right not to be treated cruelly. This is a legal right, in fact, although the law does not verbally admit or say so. Our legal terminology is at fault.

80 Bierens de Haan, Johan A. (1883–?). *Animal psychology: Its nature and its problems*. London: Hutchinson's Library, 1946. 156 pp.
Argues the object of animal psychology is psychic phenomena in animals. The difficulty in knowing subjective experiences is the same in our fellow humans and other animals; our knowledge of both is mainly by observation of behavior, with interpretation based on sympathetic intuition. Concludes all animals (including protozoa) have an inner psychic life, experience sensations, feelings, desires, drives. Criticizes the objectivists (including J. B. Watson) who have no interest in studying psychic phenomena or who think we can have no knowledge of psychic phenomena or who think psychic phenomena do not exist, and who therefore study only observable behavior. Concludes some animals capable of "concrete understanding," "perceptual generalizations" (precursor of abstrations). Discusses animal instinct, learning, intelligence, understanding, ideation, the problem of the animal's world.

81 Hebb, D. O. "Emotion in man and animals: An analysis of the intuitive process of recognition." *Psychological Review* 53 (1946): 88–106.
A two-year attempt to avoid anthropomorphic description of temperament in chimpanzees at Yerkes Laboratories results in a failure to find order or meaning in a series of acts by the animals. By the use of anthropomorphic concepts of emotion and attitude one can easily describe the peculiarities of individual animals. ". . . The true objection to anthropomorphism is not to discover a similarity of mechanism in human and animal behavior, but to inventing similarities that do not exist." Anthropomorphic terminology provides an intelligible and practical guide to behavior. The recognition of emotion in man and animal is not fundamentally different.

82 Lewis, C. S. "Vivisection." (Written in 1947.) In *Undeceptions: Essays on theology and ethics*, ed. by W. Hooper, 182–6. London: Geoffrey Bles, 1971. Also in *God in the dock*, 224–8. Grand Rapids, MI: William B. Eerdmans, 1970.
The charge of sentimentality is as applicable to defenders of animal experimentation as to its critics. Either pain is an evil or it is not an evil; if it is not an evil then the case for animal experimentation falls, since then there is no reason to reduce human suffering; if it is an evil, then infliction of pain, considered in itself, is an evil act. Animal experimentation can only be defended by showing it to be

right that one species should suffer in order to make another species happier. Scientists and Darwinian naturalists who reject the idea of a total difference in kind between humans and animals can find no argument for experiments on animals which is not also an argument for experimenting on humans.

83 MacIver, A. M. "Ethics and the beetle." *Analysis* 8 (1948): 65–70.
Argues, contrary to traditional moral philosophy, that beetles and all animals can have wrong done to them, and can do wrong (but are not blameable). ". . . Their status as moral beings differs from our own . . . only in degree."

84 Shaw, George Bernard (1856–1950). *Shaw on vivisection.* Comp. and ed. by G. H. Bowker. London: George Allen and Unwin, 1949. 65 pp.
Collection of talks, essays, articles, excerpts from plays ("Preface on Doctors" to *The doctor's dilemma; The philanderer*) on animal experimentaton, medicine, attitudes of doctors, vaccination, innoculation, germs. Cautions against attacking animal experimentation because of its uselessness, for this implies that if it were (or turns out to be) useful then the argument collapses. Rather, should attack it on the basis of its immorality. Arguments for animal experimentation's benefits become still stronger arguments for experimenting on humans. Attacks the unlimited-right-to-know argument for experimentation: one does not have the right to know what it feels like to see one's mother boil in oil. Likewise, there are moral restrictions on the right to know about animals. ". . . The pursuit of knowledge should be subject to the same civilized morality and legality as any other activity. . . . It is hardly to be expected that a man who does not hesitate to vivisect for the sake of science will hesitate to lie about it afterwards to protect it from what he deems the ignorant sentimentality of the laity." Persons discussed: I. P. Pavlov, Frances P. Cobbe, Edmund Gurney, Victor Horsley, Edward Jenner, Lord Lister, H. G. Wells.

85 Krutch, Joseph W. (1893–1970). "Reverence for life." In *The great chain of life*, 147–68. Boston: Houghton Mifflin, 1956.
Eloquent expression of reverence-for-life attitude. Critiques hunting, biology, animal experimentation, specimen collecting, nature viewed exclusively for human use, conservation and wildlife policies as antithetical to reverence for life. "When a man wantonly destroys one of the works of man we call him Vandal. When he wantonly destroys one of the works of God we call him Sportsman." When Thoreau allowed himself to be persuaded to send a turtle as specimen to zoologists at Harvard University he felt he had "a murderer's experience in a degree." Humans should look upon sharing the earth with animals a privilege rather than as an irritation. Laboratory biology is least likely to stimulate compassion, love, or reverence for creatures it studies. Are wildlife departments to preserve wildlife or to provide game for hunters to kill? Gives account of officer of a state commission protesting against exhibition in state park of young deer which children allowed to pet because "making pets of wild animals creates a prejudice against hunting."

86 Hume, C. W. (1886–1981). *Man and beast.* London: Universities Federation for Animal Welfare, 1962. 222 pp.

Articles, speeches, 1949–1962. Topics include: trapping, animal experimentation, painless killing of animals, anthropomorphism, bullfights, religion and animals, rights of animals. Main concern is the absence of pain, suffering. Equal pain and suffering are of equal moral importance in humans and animals: "I know of no reason except prejudice for preferring that an animal rather than a random human being should suffer a given amount of pain . . ."

87 Harrison, Ruth. *Animal machines: The new factory farming industry*. London: Vincent Stuart, 1964. 186 pp.
Important first detailed study and critique of factory farming of poultry, animals. Perhaps the first use of the term "factory farming." Restricted to British, but suggestive of European and United States practice. Definition of factory farming: intensive rearing of animals, rapid turnover, high-density stocking, high-degree mechanization, minimum labor, efficient conversion of animal into saleable food products. Discusses maltreatment of poultry, veal calves, pigs, rabbits, cattle. Emphasizes dangers to human health from use of hormones, antibiotics, pesticides, tranquilizers, growth stimulants. Recommends abolition of: battery cages for laying hens, intensive methods of veal production, deficiency diets, permanent tethering, slatted flooring, keeping animals in darkness. Public concern generated by this book resulted in the establishment of the Brambell governmental committee to investigate (see [90]).

88 Morris, Clarence. "The rights and duties of beasts and trees: A law teacher's essay for landscape architects." *Journal of Legal Education* 17 (1964): 185–92.
Interesting, ground-breaking argument for the recognition of legal rights for animals and the natural environment, inviting comparison with C. D. Stone's [107] rationale for legal standing of natural objects. Contrasts the ancient Chinese respect for the harmony of nature (which should be only minimally disturbed by humans) with the modern Western view of nature as instrumental for human use. Argues for a presumption in favor of the natural; the burden of proof is on those who propose to disturb nature. Calls for legal action developing safeguards affirmatively creating nature's legal rights in the form of conservation laws, game laws, forest and park protection – all backed by police, inspectors and judges.

89 Turner, E. S. *All heaven in a rage: A history of the prevention of cruelty in Great Britain*. London: Michael Joseph, 1964. 324 pp.
Title apparently inspired by William Blake [20]. Informative, illustrated historical account of human maltreatment of animals and the development of the animal welfare movement in Great Britain. Significant discussions of: hunting, animal baiting, animal fighting, animal experimentation, William Hogarth's "Four stages of cruelty," Sarah Trimmer, rabbit coursing, "hunting" of carted deer, Lord Erskine, William Windham, Richard Martin, RSPCA, game battue, bird shoots, Frances P. Cobbe, Royal Buck Hounds, beaglers at Eton, Henry S. Salt, trophy hunting, maltreatment of horses, performing animals, maltreatment of birds, trapping and furs.

90 Brambell, F. W. , chairman. *Report of the Technical Committee to Enquire into the Welfare of Animals Kept under Intensive Livestock Husbandry Stystems*. London: HMSO, 1965. Cmnd. 2836. 85 pp.

Popularly known as the Brambell report. This committee was established due to the public concern generated by Ruth Harrison's [87] *Animal machines*. Task of the committee: "to examine the conditions in which livestock are kept under systems of intensive husbandry and to advise whether standards ought to be set in the interests of their welfare, and if so what they should be." Discusses the development of intensive methods, animal welfare legislation in Great Britain, the welfare of animals, stockmanship, education and training. Types of animals studied: poultry, pigs, cattle, sheep, rabbits. Recommendations include: new legislation to safeguard animal welfare; increased spaces for poultry and animals; de-beaking of poultry should be abolished; tail docking of pigs should be prohibited; pregnant sows should not be kept without daily exercise in quarters which do not permit them to turn around and, in any case, should not be tethered indoors; yoking or close tethering of calves should be prohibited. Important article by W. H. Thorpe on pain and distress in animals appended, 71–9 (see [91]).

91 Thorpe, William H. "The assessment of pain and distress in animals." In [90, pp. 71–9].
Essay appended to the Brambell report, 1965. An animal behaviorist, Cambridge University, discusses physiological and ethological evidence for the following in animals: pain, distress, discomfort, stress, fright, anxiety, frustration, apprehension, innate abilities and dispositions, social organization and life. Considers poultry, pigs, sheep, cattle. "There is no doubt that wild and domestic animals feel pain . . ." Many animals remember the past, fear the future. ". . . Modern methods of poultry farming must result in extreme deprivation and . . . conflict and tension in a highly social and quite intelligent animal. . . . It is clearly cruel so to restrain an animal for a large part of its life that it cannot use any of its normal locomotory behaviour patterns."

92 Littlewood, Sydney, chairman. *Report of the Departmental Committee on Experiments on Animals*. London: HMSO, 1965. Cmnd. 2641. 255 pp.
Popularly known as the Littlewood report. Task: "to consider the present control over experiments on living animals, and to consider whether, and if so what, changes are desirable in the law or its administration." History, provisions and administration of the Cruelty to Animals Act 1876; also other laws in Great Britain. Discussion of pain in animals. Conclusions and recommendations summarized in chap. 27, 189–99. Recommends "to extend protection to all animals in, or destined for, laboratories . . . to impose stricter supervision over the granting of licenses for any purpose . . . to make the facts of animal experimentation more accessible to the public. . . . Anyone who makes use of an animal in research incurs a moral responsibility to justify his actions. . . . The present prohibition upon the performance of experiments for the purpose of attaining manual skill should be retained."

93 Brophy, Brigid. "The rights of animals." *Sunday Times* 10 October 1965. Reprinted in *Don't never forget: Collected views and reviews, 15–21*. London: Jonathan Cape, 1966.
". . .Where animals are concerned humanity seems to have switched off its morals and aesthetics." Animal slavery analogous to human slavery. Emphasizes

obligation not to cause pain or kill. Argues for vegetarianism. Attempts to justify harmful animal experimentation will justify (even more so) harmful human experimentation. Precisely because we have imagination, rationality, moral choice, we are under moral obligation to recognize and respect rights of animals.

94 Vyvyan, John. *In pity and in anger: A study of the use of animals in science.* London: Michael Joseph, 1969. 167 pp. Marblehead, MA: Micah Publications, 1987 (reprint, with introduction by Tom Regan and foreword by Roberta Kalechofsky).
Not a dispassionate book; written in pity and anger. Thesis: the humane acquisition of knowledge is indispensable to a civilized society. Strong argument for science to extent not acquired through cruel means, to extent not deny intellectual, aesthetic, emotional, spiritual perspectives of philosophers, artists, poets, mystics. Scientism's conquest and domination must be subject to ethical constraint. If animal sufferings caused by experiments are of no consequence, human sufferings are of no consequence, and that is the end of a civilized ethic. Persons discussed include: Lord Dowding, Claude Bernard, Frances P. Cobbe, Seventh Earl of Shaftestury, Anna Kingsford, Victor Hugo, Queen Victoria, Paul Bert, H. P. Blavatsky, George Hoggan, Samuel Johnson, Emanuel Klein, François Magendie, Edward Maitland, John Ruskin, M. Schiff, Arthur Schopenhauer, Lord Tennyson, Archbishop Thomson, Voltaire, Richard Wagner, Baron Ernst von Weber.

95 Linzey, Andrew. "The politics of animals." *Socialist Commentary* (December 1970): 18–19.
An early argument for animal rights in the current animal rights movement. The way we exploit animals is a problem about which we somehow refuse to think. We exclude animals from morality because we do not consider them to have rights. ". . . Once you have justified cruelty and death to animals then you have also justified it in the case of black people, foreigners, gypsies, mental patients and so on – in fact all those whom we try to regard as culturally, mentally, or educationally inferior. . . . Because we are moral, intelligent humans we should be able to recognize the rights of animals and treat them with respect. . . . It is ludicrous to suppose that we can maintain respect for animals and also exploit them for sport, furs, cosmetic research, biological warfare research, highly artificial means of procuring food, and so on."

96 Godlovitch, Roslind. "Animals and morals." *Philosophy* 46 (1971): 23–33.
Using the conceptual framework of R. M. Hare, attempts "to show that (a) if we claim that certain attitudes we have toward animals are moral, then the application of the consequences of these principles leads us into a rather bizarre, if not outlandish, position, which few would accept as prima facie moral; and (b) if we adopt what can be accepted as a truly moral position with respect to animals, this will turn out to be indistinguishable in kind, if not in degree, from our morality with respect to humans" (23). Explores the consequences of holding or denying different combinations of the following as prima facie moral principles: (1) Human life is more valuable than animal life. (2) When there are no overriding circumstances it is wrong to kill animals. (3) We have a duty to prevent (or not to

cause) animal suffering. ". . . There is no a priori reason to deny that animals can be proper subjects of moral rights" (31).

97 Godlovitch, Stanley and **Roslind**, and **Harris, John**, eds. *Animals, men and morals: An inquiry into the maltreatment of non-humans.* New York: Taplinger, 1972. 240 pp. Also London: Gollancz, 1971.
Thirteen essays regarded by Peter Singer as the manifesto for animal liberation (see [103]). (1) "On factory farming," Ruth Harrison, 11–24. Description of factory farming of animals and summary of recommendations in Brambell report of 1965 (see [90]). (2) "Furs and cosmetics: Too high a price?" Lady Dowding, 25–40. Maltreatment of animals in fur, cosmetic trades, with suggested alternatives. (3) "Experiments on animals," Richard Ryder, 41–82. Nature, extent of animal experimentation; critique of British Cruelty to Animals Act 1876; reform recommendation in Littlewood report (see [92]) of 1965; paradox of experimentation: scientists defend validity of experiments by emphasizing the similarity of humans and animals, and they defend morality of experiments by emphasizing the dissimilarity of humans and animals. Speciesism (a term which Ryder originates) is discrimination on the basis of species membership, analogous to racism. (4) "Alternatives," Terrence Hegarty, 83–93. Recommends maximal use of alternatives to use of animals in experiments: tissue culture, gas chromatography, mass spectrometry, modelling, simulation, qualitative and quantitative analysis. (5) "Killing for food", John Harris, 97–110. Critique of six fallacious arguments often used to defend eating animals; vegetarianism and world hunger; production of protein; eating animals is unjustified. (6) "Beasts for pleasure," Maureen Duffy, 111–24. Critique of hunting, fishing, circus use of animals. (7) "In pursuit of a fantasy," Brigid Brophy, 125–45. Sentient beings have right to life, liberty, pursuit of happiness; critique of fantasy held by those (scientists, the public) who regard experimentation on animals necessary. (8) "Duties to animals," Leonard Nelson, 149–55 (see [75]). Criticizes view that duties to animals are indirect duties to oneself or other humans; argues for direct duties to animals (animal rights) based on animals' interest in living. (9) "Animals and morals," Roslind Godlovitch, 156–72. If humans have natural rights then so do animals; to hold that suffering should be prevented but not to hold that killing is wrong results in the absurd conclusion that we should eradicate all animal life. (10) "Utilities," Stanley Godlovitch, 173–90. Common view is that animals are mere objects, clumps of matter, for human use; given that animals are purposive, striving beings, this common view is based on the functionalist fallacy. (11) "Strategies," David Wood, 193–212. Strategies used by society to keep from worrying about wrongs to animals. (12) "Nature and culture," Michael Peters, 213–31. Critiques attempts to defend human superiority over animals by trying to find an essential difference: use of fire, incest taboo, making tools, intelligence, language. (13) "Postscript," Patrick Corbett, 232–8. ". . . We require *now* to extend the great principles of liberty, equality and fraternity over the lives of animals. Let animal slavery join human slavery in the graveyard of the past!"

98 Vyvyan, John. *The dark face of science.* London: Michael Joseph, 1971. 207 pp. (Forthcoming in 1989: reprint by Micah Publications, Marblehead, MA.)

The dark face rests in indecent, cruel, immoral means of pursuing science by animal experiments, and in the spirit of modern science as conquest and domination. In practice, Cruelty to Animals Act 1876 was turned into protection of experimenters rather than protection of animals. Attempts to justify animal experimentation on bases of promotion of knowledge and benefits to humans can also be used to justify Nazi experiments on humans in World War II. "It will land you in horrors of which you have no conception" (G. B. Shaw quoted). Topics: experiments on animals, Animal Defence and Anti-Vivisection Society, Association for the Advancement of Medicine by Research, British Union for the Abolition of Vivisection, the Brown Dog (monument, riots), International Association against Painful Experiments on Animals, the Littlewood report, Medical Research Council, National Anti-Vivisection Society, Royal Commissions on Vivisection (1875 and 1906–1912), RSPCA, Scottish Society for the Prevention of Vivisection, World League against Vivisection, International Anti-Vivisection and Animal Protection Congress 1909. Persons discussed: George Bernard Shaw, Louise Lind-af-Hageby, Liesa Schartau, Stephen Coleridge, Walter Hadwen, John Cowper Powys, Harvey Metcalfe, Lord Dowding, S. T. Aygun, Claude Bernard, Frances P. Cobbe, John Galsworthy, Goethe, Victor Hugo, Albert Leffingwell, Queen Victoria, Richard Wagner, Alfred Wallace.

99 Brophy, Brigid. "The ethical argument against the use of animals in biomedical research." In *The rational use of living systems in biomedical research*, 51–7. Potters Bar, Herts: Universities Federation for Animal Welfare, 1972. Animal experimenters, *qua* scientists, use the evolutionary meaning of "animal" to include all of us; but *qua* experimenters they switch the meaning of "animal" to exclude sacred humans. "My own view is that it is ethically insupportable to inflict distress, pain, infringement of individuality, disease, mutilation or death on animals unless killing them is the only alternative to their killing you" (53). What would happen if we stop animal experimentation? "We don't know" is the only honest scientific answer. It is just as fallacious to infer from *fact x was discovered by animal experimentation* that fact *x* could have been discovered only by animal experimentation or that in the future facts can be discovered only by animal experimentation, as it would be to infer from *horses were used for transportation* that humans could have used only horses for transportation or that in the future humans can use only horses for transportation. It is just as fallacious for today's scientist to conclude that animal experimentation cannot be eliminated from science as it would have been for the 16th-century scientist to conclude that the atom cannot be split.

100 Russell, George K. "Vivisection and the true aims of education in biology." *American Biology Teacher* 34 (1972): 254–7.
Shows influence of Albert Schweitzer. Criticizes dissection of live animals in high school and college biology classes: knowledge is not advanced, and students do not learn respect for life. Much can be learned from observation of live animals and from alternatives. Encourages students to learn by harmless experiments on themselves. ". . . Biology has largely forgotten that organisms are alive."

101 Ryder, Richard D. *A scientist speaks on the extensive use of animals in non-medical*

research. Edinburgh: Scottish Society for the Prevention of Vivisection, 1972.
8 pp.
A psychologist compares animal researchers today with British slaveowners 200
years ago, especially in regard to secrecy. ". . . We should concentrate our efforts
initially upon abolishing cruel experiments which are *not* in the medical category. . . . I would like to see the immediate prohibition of all non-medical
experiments where there is a risk of pain involved." "Non-medical" includes
experimental psychology, LD-50 test, cosmetic testing, product testing, aerospace engineering, experiments in zoology, ecology, forestry, agriculture. Government should back alternatives to animals in research.

102 Midgley, Mary. "The concept of beastliness: Philosophy, ethics and animal behaviour."*Philosophy* 48 (1973): 111–35.
Analyses and criticizes misuse of mythological concept of animals as beasts (as
lawless, cruel, wanton, murderous, unrestrained, evil, monstrous). Such misuse
results in distortions of philosophical views of humans, animals and ethics. Urges
ethological studies of animals (humans included). Human virtues rest on traits
shared by animals.

103 Singer, Peter. "Animal liberation." *New York Review of Books* (5 April
1973): 17–21. Reprint available from International Society for Animal Rights
[344].
Important first publication by Singer on animal liberation. A review article in
which he characterizes *Animals, men and morals* edited by Stanley and Roslind
Godlovitch and John Harris [97] as the manifesto for an animal liberation movement, analogous to women's liberation and black liberation. Major themes of
Singer's later *Animal liberation* [115] evident.

104 Amory, Cleveland. *Mankind? Our incredible war on wildlife*. New York:
Harper and Row, 1974. 372 pp.
Vivid, sharp attack on hunting, trapping, fur trade, hunters' control of "wildlife"
and "conservation" organizations and governmental "wildlife management"
agencies. Emphasis on maltreatment of the wolf, coyote, bear, seal, deer, otter,
raccoon, fox, kangaroo, feline, snake, skunk, whale, dolphin. 30 photos.

105 Feinberg, Joel. "The rights of animals and unborn generations." In *Philosophy and environmental crisis*, ed. by W. T. Blackstone, 43–68. Athens: University of Georgia Press, 1974.
Many animals have appetites, conative urges, rudimentary purposes, the inte-
grated satisfaction of which constitutes their welfare or good. To have a right is to
have a claim *to* something and *against* someone. It is conceptually intelligible for
animals to have rights. If we hold we ought to treat animals humanely for the
animals' sake, that such treatment is something we owe animals as their due,
something that can be claimed for them, something the withholding of which
would be an injustice and a wrong, then we do ascribe rights to animals.

106 Singer, Peter. "All animals are equal." *Philosophic Exchange* 1 (1974):
103–16.

Race and sex are widely, and correctly, regarded as unacceptable grounds for unequal treatment. Why should species be regarded differently? An examination of the basis of the principle of equality shows that speciesism is as unjustifiable as racism, and that as a consequence we ought to revise many of our current practices, such as eating other animals and experimenting upon them for trivial purposes.

107 Stone, Christopher D. *Should trees have standing? Toward legal rights for natural objects*. Los Altos, CA: William Kaufmann, 1974. 102 pp.
Foreword by Garrett Hardin, ix–xvii. A jurist specifies the criteria for something to have legal rights, to have legal standing: there must be some authoritative body which will review actions and processes of those who threaten it; it can institute legal actions *at its behest*; in determining granting of legal relief, court must take *injury to it* into account; relief must run to *benefit of it*. Legal rights for children, women, incompetents, blacks, Indians, ships, corporations were once unthinkable; now they have them. We are at threshold of transition from unthinkability to actuality of legal rights for natural objects such as wildernesses, rivers, etc. Although there is no emphasis on individual animals, this essay has enormous implications: if a wilderness or a river be granted legal rights there is precedence for granting the same to individual animals.

108 Barkas, Janet. *The vegetable passion*. New York: Charles Scribner's, 1975. 224 pp.
Characterized by one reviewer as "a brightly-coloured rag-mat of tales about vegetarians, and good fun it is." Discusses in relation to vegetarianism: Judaism, Christianity, evolution and human diet, Buddhism, Hinduism, Jainism, Seventh Day Adventism, protein sources, British Vegetarian Society, Fruitlands, Oneida community, Doukhobors, Abkhasians, Gandhi, Da Vinci, Shelley, Annie Besant, G. B. Shaw, Richard Wagner, Albert Schweitzer, John Kellogg, Upton Sinclair, Tolstoy, Porphyry, Charles Wesley, William Lambe, John F. Newton, Anna Kingsford, Hitler, Benjamin Franklin, Sylvester Graham, William Alcott, Bronson Alcott, Pythagoras, Ellen B. White, Thoreau, Plutarch.

109 Blackwelder, Brent F. *A refutation of the major arguments against ascribing rights to animals*. Ph.D. diss., University of Maryland, 211 pp. Ann Arbor, MI: University Microfilms International, 1975.
Concludes there are no good arguments against ascribing rights to animals. Offers reasons for asserting animals meet sufficient conditions for rights possession. Higher animals have interests; such interests can be represented by proxy. Animals are intended beneficiaries of certain laws and can be holders of meaningful legal rights. Existence of legal rights for animals implies animals have moral rights. Capacity for reciprocity is not necessary condition for possession of rights. Animals can be included in J. Rawls' contractual theory in same manner as he includes future generations and legal incompetents.

110 Burr, Stephen I. "Toward legal rights for animals." *Environmental Affairs* 4 (1975): 205–54.
". . . Animals' lives have value to them, and in that sense they are closer to us

than they are to rocks. We should recognize this value, and give animals at least a qualified right to protect themselves. Within a limited area they should have access to courts through legal guardians to assert their interests. The courts, when weighing those interests, should look to the injury suffered by the animal, and to a remedy which would best protect the animal or make it whole. . . . What is needed to make animals holders of legal rights, and therefore truly protected, is a legal system which gives those who would protect them access to the full range of judicial remedies available to humans when threatened with death or injury'' (228–9). Proposes a Model Act to stimulate revision or replacement of the present inadequate anti-cruelty statutes.

111 Hur, Robin. *Food reform: Our desperate need*. Austin, TX: Heidelberg Publishers, 1975. 260 pp.
Technical critique of typical Western diet (animal fat, animal protein, sugar, salt, processed foods) as causative factor in degenerative diseases (cancer, cardiovascular diseases, diseases related to carbohydrate metabolism). Nutritional, ecological arguments for vegan diet of highest quality possible (''diet for those who choose to eat to live, rather than living to eat''), emphasizing raw sprouts, raw dark-leaf greens, algae (B-12), tubers, fruits. Extended discussion of diet and aging, protein requirements. This book heavily influenced Keith Akers' *A Vegetarian sourcebook* [199].

112 Regan, Tom. ''The moral basis of vegetarianism.'' *Canadian Journal of Philosophy* 5 (1975): 181–214. Reprinted in [193].
Important first publication by Regan on animal rights. Argues that if humans have an equal natural right to life on the basis of intrinsic value of satisfaction of interests then animals also have an equal natural right to life on the same basis, in which case vegetarianism becomes morally obligatory.

113 Regenstein, Lewis. *The politics of extinction: The shocking story of the world's endangered wildlife*. New York: Macmillan, 1975. 280 pp.
Critique of hunting, trapping, fur trade, animal experiments (on primates), ''wildlife management'' policies in relation to extinction of wildlife. Details fight to save ocean mammals: dolphins, porpoises, whales, polar bears, sea otters, seals, manatees, dugongs. Discusses the Marine Mammal Protection Act of 1972, US Endangered Species Act of 1969, International Convention on Endangered Species 1973. Emphasizes plight of wolves, grizzly bears, prairie dogs, wild horses, cougars, kangaroos.

114 Ryder, Richard D. *Victims of science: The use of animals in research*. London: Davis-Poynter, 1975. 279 pp. Rev. ed.: London: National Anti-Vivisection Society, 1983. 190 pp. Also New York: State Mutual Books, 1983.
Important work by a psychologist, discussing the nature and extent of, and the moral problems involved in, animal experimentation in Great Britain, United States and worldwide. Ryder originates the term ''speciesism'' to describe the widespread discrimination against other species, and draws parallel with racism. Compares human slavery and animal slavery. ''The capacity to suffer is the crucial similarity between man and animals that binds us all together and places

us all in a similar moral category'' (15). ''If the pain felt by any individual is to be justified it can only be in terms of the benefits accruing to that *same* individual'' (19). All attempts to justify animal experimentation in terms of benefits to other individuals must fail. If it is wrong to cause suffering to human innocents it is also wrong to do this to nonhuman animals. ''The next great step forward in man's moral evolution will be the full recognition of the rights and interests of the animal kingdom'' (26). Critiques Cruelty to Animals Act 1876. History of animal experimentation and excellent history of the animal rights movement (178–247).

115 Singer, Peter. *Animal liberation: A new ethic for our treatment of animals*. New York: New York Review, 1975. 301 pp. New York: Avon Books, 1977. 297 pp. Wellingborough, Northants: Thorsons Publishers, 1983. *Pro mens, pro dier*, Baarn, Netherlands: Anthos, 1977. *Befreiung der tiere*, Munich: Hirthammer, 1982. *Liberación animal*, Chapultepec Morales, Mexico: Asociación de Lucha para Evitar la Crueldad con los Animales, 1985. *Liberazione animali*, Rome: Lega Anti-Vivesezione, 1987. Forthcoming Japanese translation, Gijutsu-to-Ningen, Tokyo.

''The bible'' of the animal liberation movement, written by a philosopher in clear, non-technical language for the benefit of the lay reader, and carefully presented in the context of philosophical principles. Argues that equal pains and equal pleasures should be given equal consideration, regardless of species membership. Failure to comply with this equality principle is speciesism, analogous to sexism and racism. Detailed discussion of animal experimentation, concluding over 99% of animal experimentation as now practiced is morally unjustified. Extensive critique of factory-farming methods in production of animals for food, concluding we should become vegetarians. Short history of speciesism (human dominion). Critiques defenses and rationalizations used by speciesists; answers objections to animal liberation.

116 Davis, William H. ''Man-eating aliens.'' *Journal of Value Inquiry* 10 (1976): 178–85.

Using example of our planet taken over by aliens vastly more powerful and intelligent than humans, and who enjoy eating us, argues we would have only three possible grounds for moral appeal in trying to persuade them not to eat us: appeals to their prudence, sympathy, and conscience. Argues mere presence of rationality or intelligence no ground for moral appeal. Compares our relationship to the animals we eat.

117 Griffin, Donald R. *The question of animal awareness: Evolutionary continuity of mental experience*. Rev. enlarged edition (first edition 1976). New York: Rockefeller University Press, 1981. 209 pp. Bibliography, 173–96.

This work by a cognitive ethologist is important for scientists, most of whom (according to Griffith) tend to regard animals as mechanisms, as unthinking robots, and important for philosophers in that animal consciousness has significant implications for the moral status of animals. Argues behaviorist psychologists have ''blinders'' which result, a priori, in either ignoring or denying awareness in animals. Argues for possibility of mental experience by animals: feelings, wants, desires, having goals, beliefs, acting intentionally, self-awareness, knowing what they are doing. It is not theoretically parsimonious to deny or ignore animal mental experience. It is no more anthropomorphic to postulate mental experience in another species than to compare its bony structure, nervous system, or antibodies with our own.

118 Linzey, Andrew. *Animal rights: A Christian assessment of man's treatment of animals*. London: SCM Press, 1976. 120 pp. Select bibliography, 117–19.
Incorporates a strong animal rights view, similar to one portrayed throughout *Animals, men and morals* [97], into the Christian framework. Argues for sentiency as criterion for the moral right of animals to live as animals on their own terms and in their own way, with freedom of movement and freedom to follow innate behavior patterns. It is immoral to kill animals (even painlessly) except when there are overriding circumstances. Vegetarianism is morally obligatory. No argument for experiments on animals can be found which is not also an argument for experiments on humans. Animal experimentation should be proscribed by law. Critiques arguments used to support animal experiments: (1) that they increase knowledge, (2) that they are useful, (3) that humans are superior to animals, (4) that the welfare of humans (or animals) necessitates them. Discusses animals and animal suffering in relation to theodicy (understanding God's will in relation to the natural world) and eschatology (understanding of the ultimate end of all creation in the pattern of creation, crucifixion and redemption disclosed in the person of Jesus Christ). Considers views of Thomas Aquinas and Albert Schweitzer (reverence for life); also dominion doctrine and question of animal souls.

119 Rachels, James. "Do animals have a right to liberty?" In [121, pp. 205–23]. Defines "liberty" as being able to do as one pleases without being subject to external constraints. Argues humans have right to liberty because of a basic right not to have one's interests needlessly harmed; there is no relevant difference between humans and some animals which would justify denying this right to animals while granting it to humans; therefore some animals also have a right to liberty. Argues animals have right not to be tortured; also a right to property under certain conditions. D. VanDeVeer (1976) critiques this essay.

120 Regan, Tom. "Feinberg on what sorts of beings can have rights." *Southern Journal of Philosophy* 14 (1976): 485–98. Reprinted in [193].
Exploring the implications of Joel Feinberg's theses (that a logically necessary and sufficient condition for a being's possibly possessing rights is that it has or can have interests, that a being without interests cannot be harmed or benefited, cannot have a good or "sake" of its own), argues that by distinguishing two meanings of having an interest (*x* is interested in *y*, and *y* is in *x*'s interest) and by interpreting having a good of its own in terms of inherent value, there is no logical contradiction in the conception of the possession of a right by a plant or an inanimate object. See [105].

121 Regan, Tom and **Singer, Peter**, eds. *Animal rights and human obligations*. Englewood Cliffs, NJ: Prentice-Hall, 1976. 250 pp. Rev. enlarged ed. forthcoming 1988; see [317]. Italian version of 1976 edition under title *Diritti animali*, *obblighi umani*, trans. by P. Garavelli. Torino: Edizioni Gruppo Abele, 1987. Selected readings on animal rights especially intended for use in colleges and universities in ethics, humanities, and interdisciplinary courses. "Introduction," by Tom Regan, 1-20, discusses animal and human nature, and the question whether we have obligations to other animals. Factual articles include "Down on the factory farm," Peter Singer, 23-32, and "Experiments on animals," Richard Ryder, 33-47. Essays on animal and human nature: "How humans differ from other creatures," Aristotle, 53-5; "Differences between rational and other creatures," Thomas Aquinas, 56-9; "Animals are machines," René Descartes, 60-6; "A reply to Descartes," Voltaire, 67-8; "Of the reason of animals," David Hume, 69-71; "Comparison of the mental powers of man and the lower animals," Charles Darwin, 72-81; "The language of animals," Michel de Montaigne, 82-4; "Teaching chimpanzees to communicate," Peter Jenkins, 85-92; "The concept of beastliness," Mary Midgley, 93-106. Selections on moral obligations to animals include: "Animals and slavery," Aristotle, 109-10; "Of eating of flesh," Plutarch, 111-17; "On killing living things and the duty to love irrational creatures," Thomas Aquinas, 118-21; "Duties to animals," Immanuel Kant, 122-3; "A critique of Kant," Arthur Schopenhauer, 124-8; "A utilitarian view," Jeremy Bentham, 129-30; "A defense of Bentham," John Stuart Mill, 131-2; "The ethic of reverence for life," Albert Schweitzer, 133-8; "The humanities of diet," Henry S. Salt, 139-47; "All animals are equal," Peter Singer, 148-62; "A defense of vivisection," Robert J. White, 163-9. Selections on animal rights: "Animal rights," Henry S. Salt, 173-8; 'On the so-called rights of animals," Joseph Rickaby, 179-80; "Why animals do not have rights," D. G. Ritchie, 181-4; "Logic of the larder," Henry S. Salt, 185-9; "Can animals have rights?" Joel Feinberg, 190-6; "Do animals have a right to life?" Tom Regan, 197-204; "Do animals have a right to liberty?" James Rachels, 205-23; "Defending animals by appeal to rights," Donald VanDeVeer, 224-9; "A reply to VanDeVeer," James Rachels, 230-2. Epilogue contains "A modest proposal" by Jonathan Swift, 234-7, and "The limits of Trooghaft" by Desmond Stewart, 238-45.

122 Clark, Stephen R. L. *The moral status of animals*. Oxford: Clarendon Press, 1977. 221 pp. Literature cited, 200-12.
Basic moral principle: it is wrong to cause avoidable suffering. There is no other honest course than the immediate rejection of all flesh-foods and most biomedical animal research. Analyzes eight fallacious arguments used by those who try to avoid the basic moral principle. Animals can be wronged. Criticizes science's loss of respect for nature and animals, and philosophy (Stoicism, Kantianism) and theology (Thomism) which view animals as having no intrinsic value, as being instruments for human use. Sympathetic discussions of Aristotelianism, Neoplatonism, Christianity, Pyrrhonian Scepticism, Mahayana Buddhism, ecology (Gregory Bateson, Aldo Leopold).

123 Haworth, Lawrence. "Rights, wrongs, and animals." *Ethics 88 (1977):* 95-105.
Defines "rights." Specifies necessary and sufficient conditions for rights possession. Some animals fulfil these conditions. Past attempts to regard nonhuman

animals as ineligible for rights (because are not persons, because are non-autonomous, because incapable of a sense of justice) are unconvincing.

124 Rachels, James. "Vegetarianism and 'the other weight problem'." In *World hunger and moral obligation*, ed. by W. Aiken and H. La Follette, 180–93. Englewood Cliffs: Prentice-Hall, 1977.
"The other weight problem" refers to the situation of starving humans in depressed countries (while glutted Americans worry about reducing their waist lines). Argues it is morally wrong for us to eat meat. Appeals to the interests humans have in conserving food resources; also appeals to the interests of the animals. It is hard to think of any plausible rationale for granting a right to life to humans that does not also apply to other animals. If one regards human slavery to be immoral that is sufficient reason to refuse to participate; if one regards the eating of meat to be immoral that is sufficient reason to refuse to participate.

125 Animal Welfare Institute. *Animals and their legal rights*. Washington, DC: AWI, 1978. 215 pp. Extensive appendix giving texts of many laws, pp. i–lxxix. (Rev. ed. forthcoming 1988, with chapter on animals and airlines by F. Brisk.)
Since, technically, animals have no legal rights in the United States (or anywhere else?) perhaps this highly informative book would more correctly be labeled "Animal protection laws." A survey of American laws from 1641 to 1978 by Emily S. Leavitt and Diane Halverson. Additional chapters by the Animal and Plant Health Inspection Service of the US Department of Agriculture (the Twenty-Eight Hour Law); Emily S. Leavitt (humane slaughter laws, cat laws, humane education, organizations for the protection of animals, law enforcement agencies); Christine Stevens (laboratory animal welfare, account of how the Animal Welfare Act 1966 was passed, dog laws, laws regulating sale of small animals and birds, animal fights and baiting, trapping and poisoning, marine mammals, international animal protection); Ruth Harrison (animals in factory farms); Pearl Twyne (horses); Greta Nilsson (birds); Dona Finnley (wildlife laws); Frederick A. Ulmer, Jr. (importation of wild animals and birds); Shirley McGreal (law and the nonhuman primate trade).

126 Clark, Stephen R. L. "Animal wrongs." *Analysis* 38 (1978): 147–9.
In response to R. G. Frey's (1977b) "Animal rights", argues: if babies have rights because they are potentially rational then some animals (chimpanzees, gorillas) which potentially have some rationality will also have rights; if imbeciles have rights because they are similar to us in other respects then, since many animals are similar to us in that they feel, desire, communicate, plan, they will also have rights. Claims we should recognize rights of subnormal humans and animals because they are weak, defenseless, at our mercy, can be hurt, injured, frustrated.

127 Diamond, Cora. "Eating meat and eating people." *Philosophy* 53 (1978): 465–79.
A vegetarian suggests a sense of fellow creaturehood as the direction we should pursue in determining how we should relate to animals. ". . . *Hearing* the moral

appeal of an animal is our hearing it speak – as it were – the language of our fellow human beings.'' The idea of fellow creature is inconsistent with treating an animal as simply a stage in the production of a meat product or as "delicate pieces of machinery" in animal experimentation.

128 Matthews, Gareth B. "Animals and the unity of psychology." *Philosophy* 53 (1978): 437–54.
"The unity of psychology" means the psychology of humans is part of the psychology of animals generally. Defines the Principle of Psychological Continuity as holding that psychological acts, states and functions in lower animals model those in higher animals. Concludes Descartes provided no good reason to reject the Principle of Psychological Continuity and there is no plausible basis for denying the unity of psychology.

129 Midgley, Mary. *Beast and man: The roots of human nature*. Ithaca, NY: Cornell University Press, 1978. 377 pp.
Explores roots of human nature by interdisciplinary approach (ethology, evolutionary biology, sociobiology, sociology, philosophy) to the study of animals and humans. Animal life is far more ordered than previously thought. Humans have tried to deflect attention from their own ferocity by mythically attributing "beastliness" (lawlessness, wantonness, cruelty, sexual indiscrimination, etc.) to animals. We are part of the order of the animal kingdom; this has led not to a brutish state but to our proudest achievements.

130 Morris, Richard K. and **Fox, Michael W.**, eds. *On the fifth day: Animal rights and human ethics*. Washington, DC: Acropolis Books, 1978. 240 pp. Also New York: Centaur Books.
Twelve essays: (1) "Of man, animals, and morals: A brief history," Robert S. Brumbaugh, 6–25. Greek, Roman, Christian, Cartesian, Lockean, Kantian, utilitarian, evolutionist views of animals. (2) "Man and animals: Some contemporary problems," Richard K. Morris, 26–44. Anthropocentrism in Western world; Eastern world view (cosmic unity, *ahimsa*) could correct. (3) "Human duties and animal rights," Joel Feinberg, 45–69. Legal theory and practice should change to recognize animals' legal rights and legal standing. Humans and animals have an equal moral right not to be treated cruelly. (4) "Thinking and being with beasts," Carleton Dallery, 70–92. Favors phenomenological philosophy (Edmund Husserl, Maurice Merleau-Ponty), emphasizing primitive perception and direct engagement with the world, realizing community between humans and all living things. (5) "Is man innately aggressive?" Ashley Montagu, 93–110. No. Animal societies essentially cooperative, peaceful. Humans project their own violent tendencies upon animals, resulting in myth of the beast. (6) "Man and nature: Biological perspectives," Michael W. Fox, 111–27. Continuity, interrelatedness of life forms; consciousness in humans and animals; kinship of humans and animals; biospiritual ethic based on humane stewardship, benevolence, reverence for life. (7) "Are we right in demanding an end to animal cruelty?" Roger Caras, 128–36. It is wrong to cause preventable pain, fear; to allow such is as bad as causing it. Critiques fur trade, hunting. (8) "Beyond anthropocentrism in ethics and religion," John B. Cobb, Jr., 137–53. Only

experience, whether human or animal, has intrinsic value. We should always act to maximize intrinsic value. (9) "Foundations for a humane ethics," Charles Hartshorne, 154–72. Intrinsic value of humans, animals lies in their contribution to the beauty, cosmic drama of the whole of reality. Human, animal rights based on intrinsic value. Process philosophy. Panpsychism. (10) "Naturalistic realism and animate compassion," F. S. C. Northrop, 173–204. Opts for Gautama Buddha's view of compassion for suffering fellowship of humans and animals, in contrast with Western metaphysical views. (11) "A game for all seasons," Amy Freeman Lee, 205–18. Humans brutal to animals (bullfighting, rodeos, hunting) brutalize themselves. (12) "What future for man and earth? Toward a biospiritual ethic," Michael W. Fox, 219–30. In next stage of evolution humans will not view nature as a resource for humans but will regard humans and nature as of one earth and one spirit; eco-consciousness rather than ego-consciousness.

131 Rollin, Bernard E. "Beasts and men: The scope of moral concern." *Modern Schoolman* 55 (1978): 241–60.
Critiques attempts to draw distinctions between humans and animals with regard to the possession of rights or candidacy for moral concern on the basis of possession of a soul, human dominion, rationality, linguistic capacity. Using rationality and linguistic ability as basis for rights has the consequence of leaving out human infants, the mentally retarded, the insane, the brain-damaged. Argues that interests, goals, needs and wants which are subject to fulfillment, nurture or impediment are basis for being object of moral concern. It may well turn out that much of our ordinary practice is immoral – the caging of animals, eating meat, experimenting on animals, keeping of pets.

132 Rollin, Bernard E. "Updating veterinary medical ethics." *Journal of the American Veterinary Medical Association* 173 (1978): 1015–18.
Criticizes the veterinary profession for failing to face the important moral issues and for concentrating instead on questions of professional etiquette (as reflected in *Principles of veterinary medical ethics* issued by the American Veterinary Medical Association, the AVMA code of ethics, and the veterinarian's oath). "To whom does the veterinarian owe primary allegiance, owner or animal?" Argues the goals expressed in the veterinarian's oath are incompatible.

133 Ruesch, Hans. *Slaughter of the innocent.* New York: Bantam, 1978. 432 pp.
History and sharp criticism of animal experimentation and testing in medical and drug industries, with thesis that such experiments are doing more harm to humans than good.

134 Singer, Peter. "Animal experimentation: Philosophical perspectives." In *Encyclopedia of bioethics*, ed. by W. T. Reich, vol. 1, 79–83. New York: Free Press, 1978.
Nature, extent of animal experimentation. Case for and against. Legislation. Moral status of animals.

135 Sussman, Vic S. *The vegetarian alternative: A guide to a healthful and humane diet.* Emmaus, PA: Rodale Press, 1978. 286 pp.

Explains fundamentals of sensible vegetarian diet for those who wish to de-emphasize flesh diet, for potential vegetarians, for parents agonizing over children who want to become vegetarians, for established vegetarians wondering how to answer questions about their diets and beliefs. Covers nutrition, protein requirements, health, world food crisis, recipes, kitchen techniques.

136 Ulrich, Roger E. "Letter to editor on animal research." American Psychology Association *Monitor* (March 1978).
A psychologist discovers that the results of his earlier research on aggression in animals do not justify its continuance. "Instead I began to wonder if perhaps financial rewards, professional prestige, the opportunity to travel, etc., were the maintaining factors and if we of the scientific community (supported by our bureaucratic and legislative system) were actually a part of the problem. . . . Animal research has become a sacred institution almost disconnected from the relief of suffering it supposedly serves."

137 Auxter, Thomas. "The right not to be eaten." *Inquiry* 22 (1979): 221–30.
Argues for teleological ethic: the highest good has as essential constituent properties harmony, diversity, subtlety of response in maximum development of all the more highly organized beings consistent with diversification of nature. Conclusion: wild animals have right not to be eaten and we should discontinue wasteful practice of domesticating animals for meat production.

138 Clark, Stephen R. L. "The rights of wild things." *Inquiry* 22 (1979): 171–88.
Critiques D. G. Ritchie's (⟨1894⟩ 1952) *reductio ad adsurdum* argument which can be formulated: (1) Assume wild animals have rights. (2) Therefore we are obligated to protect rabbits (prey) from wolves (predators). (3) But (2) is absurd. (4) Therefore (1) is absurd. (5) Therefore wild animals cannot have rights. Clark argues either (2) does not follow from (1), or (2) follows only in the abstract but not in practice, or (2) is not absurd; therefore, wild animals may have rights, even rights of autonomy. "Where there is massive and unusual danger [to wild animals] we should act . . . but for the most part we should leave well enough alone. . . . The rules are not very different from those we should apply to the troubles of human independents."

139 Giehl, Dudley. *Vegetarianism: A way of life.* New York: Harper and Row, 1979. 252 pp. Foreword by Isaac Bashevis Singer, vii–ix. Copious notes, 222–42.
Topics in relation in vegetarianism: types of vegetarianism; nutrition; protein myth; health; economic and ecological and world-hunger implications; ethics and religion; international vegetarian movement (organizations). Dangers of flesh diet. Inherent cruelty of keeping and slaughtering animals for food (poultry, calves for veal, branding and castration of cattle). Analyzes subterfuges used by meat-eaters to assuage guilt feelings: ritual, semantics, repression, rationalizations (might is right; two wrongs make a right; animals love to be eaten; follow the bandwagon). Persons discussed: Porphyry, Leonardo da Vinci, Tolstoy, G. B. Shaw, Gandhi, Isaac Bashevis Singer, Byron, Shelley, Thoreau, Seneca,

Plutarch, Tennyson. Religions covered: Egyptian, Christianity, Judaism, Gnosticism, Manichaeanism, Albigensianism, Hinduism, Buddhism, Jainism, Islam.

140 Hoff, Christina M. *The moral domain: An inquiry into its extent and limits.* Ph.D. diss., Brandeis University. 211 pp. Ann Arbor, MI: University Microfilms International, 1979.
Analyzes roles of moral agents, moral patients in moral theory. Moral patients can be wronged. Criticizes view that moral patients must be moral agents. Concludes moral domain includes many nonhuman animals. A non-arbitrary demarcation of the moral domain is a condition of adequacy for moral theories. Coherent account of moral domain requires us to include animals among those whom we can wrong.

141 Johnson, Edward. *Species and morality.* Ph. D. diss., Princeton University, 1976. 251 pp. Ann Arbor, MI: University Microfilms International, 1979.
Animals are objects of direct moral concern (moral patients) since they possess interests. Social contract theories (John Rawls) and respect-for-persons theories (Kant) provide no good reason for supposing humans as moral agents have any special moral status. Equal interests should be given equal consideration. The practice of raising and killing animals for food is morally wrong. We ought to become vegetarians. We are never justified in inflicting serious suffering or harm on a being (without consent) merely in order to increase knowledge. We are not in general justified in discriminating against a particular class of beings in order to benefit others. Since animals are not able to consent, it is rarely if ever permissible to perform harmful experiments on them. Most experiments on animals should stop.

142 McGinn, Colin. "Evolution, animals, and the basis of morality." *Inquiry* 22 (1979): 81–99.
Humans (but not animals) have capacity "to rebel against our genes." Rationality is conducive to survival. Rationality necessarily brings with it rational morality (disinterested altruism; universalization of moral principles). Consistency requires application of moral principles to members of all species possessing morally relevant characteristics. Therefore, evolution theory, properly interpreted, gives no justification for speciesism (giving greater weight to interests of members of our own species merely because of such species membership). Contends our eating animals and a large proportion of animal experimentation are immoral.

143 Paterson, David and **Ryder, Richard**, eds. *Animals' rights: A symposium.* Fontwell, Sussex: Centaur Press, 1979. 244 pp. Preface by Peter Singer, xi–xii. Bibliography and notes, 218–35. Also New York: Centaur Books, 1981.
27 papers presented at first international academic conference on animal rights, Trinity College, Cambridge, 18 and 19 August 1977. As reported by P. Godfrey (1977) in *The Times*, "The rights of animals: A declaration against speciesism" was signed by some 150 people at the time of the conference (reproduced on p. viii of this anthology, and also in Appendix A to this *Keyguide*). (1) "The struggle

against speciesism," Richard D. Ryder, 3–14. History of British animal welfare movement. 70 notes, 218–28, very informative and surveying many important historical works. (2) "Man's place in nature," John Aspinall, 15–21. Humans have deified their own species. (3) "Buddhist attitudes toward animal life," Jack Austin, 25–33. The principle of *ahimsa*, non-harming. (4) "Animals and moral theology," Andrew Linzey, 34–41. Status of animals in Christian tradition. (5) "Animals and moral theology," Eric Turnbull, 43–7. St Paul: the whole natural order is to be rescued from suffering. (6) "Animal rights and nature liberation," Michael W. Fox, 48–60. Suggests go beyond animal rights to theology of nature/earth. (7) "The Darwinist's dilemma," Brigid Brophy, 63–72. In abolishing the barrier between humans and other animals we institute a sort of egalitarianism between all species; we cannot justify any sense for "lower" and "higher" animals. (8) "Exploring the idea of animal rights," Tom Regan, 73–86. Going beyond the "be kind to animals" view, the rights view recognizes duties the performance of which can be justly demanded of us. (9) "The animal welfare movement and the foundations of ethics," Timothy L. S. Sprigge, 87–95. A genuine grasp of the fact that another suffers necessarily involves taking account of it in deciding what to do, in the same kind of way as one would if one directly felt it oneself. (10) "How to calculate the greater good," Stephen R. L. Clark, 96–105. Disagrees with those who treat animals according to utilitarian morality and humans according to Kantian morality; but argues that even those who follow this mistaken principle must forgo factory-farmed meat and most animal experimentation. (11) "What has sentiency to do with the possession of rights?" R. G. Frey, 106–11. The claim that sentiency is a basis for rights needs substantiation. (12) "Life, liberty and the pursuit of happiness," Maureen Duffy, 112–14. The three rights mentioned in title apply to humans and animals. (13) "Killing for food," John Harris, 117–21. Economic and moral prospects for vegetarianism. (14) "Ethical questions concerning modern livestock farming," Ruth Harrison, 122–30. Maltreatment in factory farming of animals. (15) "The experts say this is not cruel . . ." Peter Roberts, 131–4. Criticizes factory farming. (16) "Dietethics: Its influence on future farming patterns," Jon Wynne-Tyson, 135–42. Ethics of diet; ecology, world hunger, duties to animals, vegetarianism. (17) "Humane education," David A. Paterson, 143–6. Need for humane education; critique of dissection by students. (18) "Altruism and aggression in animals," W. J. Jordan, 147–53. There is altruism in nature; nature not cruel, not "red in tooth and claw." (19) "Animal exploitation in human recreation," John M. Bryant, 154–64. Critique of hunting, blood sports. (20) "The management and conservation of carnivores: A plea for an ecological ethic," David W. Macdonald and L. Boitani, 165–77. Wolves, seals, badgers. (21) "Animal experiments: Time for a new approach," Bernard Dixon, 178–86. Plea that scientists join animal welfarists in promoting alternatives. (22) "Controversial aspects of current animal experimentation," L. Goldman, 187–93. Search for criteria to distinguish justified, unjustified experiments. (23) "Research," Jenny Remfry, 194–5. How can scientists be encouraged to have concern and minimize experiments on animals? (24) "Scientists and their experimental animals," David Sperlinger, 196–200. What can be done to make scientists, and other animal exploiters, change their ways of treating animals? (25) "Animal Welfare Year in retrospect," Clive Hollands, 203–8. Putting animals into politics in Great

Britain on the centenary of the Cruelty to Animals Act 1876. (26) "Animals and the law: Moral and political issues," Lord Houghton, 209–15. Animal welfare must become a matter of law. (27) "Political perspectives: The national petition for the protection of animals," Bill Brown, 216–17. Argues for a national petition for reform.

144 Regan, Tom. "An examination and defense of one argument concerning animal rights." *Inquiry* 22 (1979): 189–219. Reprinted in [193].
Defends the argument from marginal cases: higher animals cannot be denied basic moral rights if humans, including infants and the mentally enfeebled, are assumed to have them, whereas these humans will lack such rights if these animals are denied them. Suggests the most reasonable criterion for rights-possession to be inherent value: an individual has basic moral rights if and only if such individual has value logically independently of being of value to, or valued by, another.

145 Ryder, Richard D. *Speciesism: The ethics of animal abuse*. Horsham, Sussex: Royal Society for the Prevention of Cruelty to Animals, 1979. 7 pp.
". . . If I cause it [pain] to another creature then I had better be absolutely sure that I have good reason for doing so." If the pain felt by any individual is to be justified it can best be done in terms of benefits accruing to that same individual. We have no more right to exploit an ape than we have to exploit a mentally retarded child. "Surely, if we are all God's creatures, if all animal species are capable of feeling, if we are all evolutionary relatives, if all animals are on the same biological continuum, then we should also be on the same moral continuum – and if it is wrong to inflict suffering upon an innocent and unwilling human, then it is wrong to do it to a member of another species. To deny this logic is to be guilty of the prejudice of speciesism."

146 Singer, Peter. "Killing humans and killing animals." *Inquiry* 22 (1979): 145–56.
It is one thing to say that the suffering of nonhuman animals ought to be considered equally with the like suffering of humans; quite another to decide how the wrongness of killing nonhuman animals compares with the wrongness of killing human beings. Argues that while species makes no difference to the wrongness of killing, the possession of certain capacities, in particular the capacity to see oneself as a distinct entity with a future, does. This is not, however, the only factor to be taken into account. Pleasant or happy life is itself good. Discusses killing animals for food; also infanticide.

147 Singer, Peter. "Not for humans only: The place of nonhumans in environmental issues." In *Ethics and problems of the 21st century*, ed. by K. E. Goodpaster and K. M. Sayre, 191–206. Notre Dame and London: University of Notre Dame Press, 1979.
When our actions which change the environment are likely to make animals suffer that suffering must count equally with a like amount of suffering of humans. Since species as such are not conscious and do not have interests, the only reasons for being more concerned about the interests of animals from endangered species are

those which relate the preservation of species to benefits for humans and other animals.

148 Singer, Peter. *Practical ethics*. Cambridge: Cambridge University Press, 1979. 237 pp.
Three chapters on animals. Chap. 3: "Equality for animals?" 48–71. Argues the principle of equality (equal interests should be given equal consideration) applies to humans and animals. Speciesists give greater weight to the interests of members of their own species. Factory farming of animals for food and nearly all animal experimentation are speciesistic. Takes seriously "the argument from marginal cases" which concludes that if experimentation on sentient animals is justified then experimentation on infants or severely retarded humans would also be justified. Chap. 4: "What's wrong with killing?" 72–92. Discusses, in the context of utilitarianism, problems in determining the values of different types of lives (members of the species *homo sapiens*, persons, conscious beings which are not persons, non-conscious lives) and in determining whether it is wrong to kill. Chap. 5: "Taking life: Animals," 93–105. Some animals are persons (aware of themselves as distinct entities existing over time); some animals are conscious but not persons. The case against killing animal persons (whales, for example) is strong. The case against killing animals which are not persons (chickens?) is weaker. Concludes utilitarianism will not justify the killing of factory-farmed animals or poultry for food.

149 Singer, Peter. "Unsanctifying human life." In *Ethical issues relating to life and death*, ed. by J. Ladd, 41–61. New York: Oxford University Press, 1979.
Using examples of refusal to painlessly take the life of a hopelessly deformed infant and approval of taking the life of any nonhuman animal, argues medical ethics is inconsistent or discriminatory. Traces history of doctrine of sanctity of human life (view that human life has extreme value; nonhuman animal lives have no value) to Christian belief humans have immortal souls, animals do not. A consistent, non-discriminatory ethic will require radical changes in our attitudes, treatment of deficient humans and nonhuman animals, with corresponding changes in law.

150 Singer, Peter. "Animals and human beings as equals." *Animal Regulation Studies* 2 (1979/80): 165–74.
Applies the equality principle (equal interests should be given equal consideration, regardless of species membership) to animal experimentation and use of animals for food. Only those experiments on animals can be justified which would also be justified if performed on an orphaned, irreparably retarded human at a comparable level of sentience, awareness. Factory farming of animals for food is morally unjustified.

151 Sprigge, Timothy L. S. "Metaphysics, physicalism, and animal rights." *Inquiry* 22 (1979): 101–43.
Basic principle: treat each animal which is a subject at center of consciousness (especially mammals, birds, reptiles) not merely as an object but also as expression of another equally real version of the world in which she/he is the subject at the center and you are an object. We should not eat animals produced by

intensive farming methods. Harmful animal experiments should be totally prohibited, since the result of prohibition would be preferable to current experimentation practice.

152 VanDeVeer, Donald. "Interspecific justice." *Inquiry* 22 (1979): 55–79.
Argues for "two factor egalitarianism" which requires consideration of (1) level of importance of interests to each individual in a conflict of interests and (2) psychological capacities (complexities) of parties whose interests conflict. Concludes much of prevailing wholesale disregard of basic interests of higher animals unconscionable.

153 Wynne-Tyson, Jon. *Food for a future: The complete case for vegetarianism.* (First published 1975.) New York: Universe Books, 1979. 160 pp. Fontwell, Sussex: Centaur Press, 1979.
Approaches vegetarianism and veganism not as isolated "isms" but as parts of a fundamental way – an eco-*logical* way – of life, taking into consideration economics, population, social obligation, ecology, health, moral obligations to animals, moral and spiritual development, nutrition and dietethics, preventive medicine. The tone and theme of this scholarly and compassionate book are captured by the quotation from Victor Hugo: "In the relations of man with animals, with the flowers, with all the objects of creation, there is a whole great ethic [*toute une grande morale*] scarcely seen as yet, but which will eventually break through into the light and be the corollary and the complement to human ethics" (13).

154 Bowd, Alan D. "Ethical reservations about psychological research with animals." *Psychological Record* 30 (1980): 201–10.
A psychologist argues psychologists pay little attention to ethical issues relating to painful experimentation on animals because of widespread acceptance of traditional (non-scientific) view of human superiority over animals because of a failure to consider that sentient animals have interests deserving consideration. Discusses role of psychologists' language in disguising and disregarding animal sentience, pain, suffering. "Animals in psychological experiments are simply complex research tools." Psychologists' dilemma: if animals are not like us, experiments on them are of no use; if animals are like us, we ought not perform any experiment which would be considered outrageous if performed on a human. Critiques benefits to humans and increase of knowledge as justifications for painful research on animals. Endorses principle: animals should not be forced to accept suffering greater than humans would accept.

155 Burghardt, Gordon M. and **Herzog, Harold A. Jr.** "Beyond conspecifics: Is Brer Rabbit our brother?" *Bioscience* 30 (1980): 763–8.
Two psychologists reveal an understanding and appreciation of the moral issues involved in animal experimentation. A descriptive, rather than proscriptive, analysis of the issues surrounding animal liberation, intended to sharpen discussion. Many animal behavior researchers are clearly ambivalent about the scientific and ethical aspects of certain kinds of experiments. "We must not discredit ourselves by ignoring, in self-interest, the grounding of 'animal rights' in an evolutionary continuity among all living things, while using the same continuity to justify our research. . . . We need to develop an 'ethological ethics' divorced

from the self-serving apologetics and *ad hominem* counter-attacks so often typical of agribusiness, drug, and cosmetic companies, the "anything is justified to save one human life" emotionalism too often found in medical circles. . . . All of us should personally address the difficult challenge of 'Brer Rabbit' – both as scientists and as human beings'' (767). Valuable list of references cited.

156 Carpenter, Edward, convener. *Animals and ethics: A report of the Working Party*. London: Watkins, 1980. 44 pp.
Working Party (mainly theologians, scientists, veterinarians) includes Edward Carpenter, Angela Bates, Trevor Beeson, Michael Brambell, Kenneth Carpenter, Lilian Carpenter, David Coffey, Ruth Harrison, Sydney Jennings, Andrew Linzey, Hugh Montefiore, W. H. Thorpe. Carefully prepared position paper in 94 numbered paragraphs presenting guidelines for human attitudes, treatment of animals. Albert Schweitzer's reverence-for-life principle implicit throughout. Dignity of animals requires respect for their needs: (1) freedom to perform natural physical movement, (2) association with other animals, where appropriate, of their own kind, (3) facilities for comfort activities, e.g. rest, sleep and body care, (4) provision of food and water to maintain full health, (5) ability to perform daily routines of natural activities, (6) opportunity for the activities of exploration and play, especially for young animals, (7) satisfaction of minimal spatial and territorial requirements including a visual field and "personal" space. Application of the guidelines: (a) preclusion of intensive systems such as battery-cages, sow-stalls, veal crates; (b) knowledgeable and responsible pet ownership, reduction in numbers and types of pets, virtual elimination of destruction of pet animals; (c) substantially reduced number of animals in experiments, improvement in lives of experimental animals, preclusion of some experimental procedures, cease using animals for testing non-essential products (adornment articles, tobacco, etc.), cease experiments designed to prove the obvious; (d) cease pleasure killing in all forms; (e) cease dog fighting, rodeos, some uses of animals in films; (f) cease importation of wild exotic animals for use as pets. ". . . In complex situations where no authoritative judgment can be made the animals should be given the benefit of the doubt.''

157 Clark, Stephen R. L. ''The rights of animals.'' (In Polish.) *Etyka* 18 (1980): 77–86.
The arguments which led to legislation to protect the interests of nonhuman animals were of three kinds: moralistic, utilitarian, judicial. If these laws are interpreted as being concerned with human character they should perhaps be repealed. If moralism is rejected, their point is to prevent animal suffering or to protect the rights of animals even against utilitarian calculation. That only ''rational'' beings have rights is a rule excluding too many; that all ''sentient'' beings have equal rights includes too much. The attribution of rights should be considered a response to the challenge of really existing creatures within ''Earth's Household.''

158 Curtis, Patricia. *Animal rights: Stories of people who defend the rights of animals*. New York: Four Winds Press, 1980. 148 pp. Reading list, 140–3; animal magazines, 144; national organizations, 145–8.

For teenagers. Fictional people (but whose experiences and observations are based on actuality) tell stories of defending animals. First-year medical student on animal experimentation. Humane organization lawyer on treatment of pets. Two young whale lovers on whales. Wildlife illustrator on hunting, trapping. Veterinarian on factory farming. Curator on zoos. ASPCA law enforcement officer on animals for entertainment.

159 Dawkins, Marian S. *Animal suffering: The science of animal welfare*. London: Chapman and Hall, 1980. 149 pp. 212 references, mainly scientific, 131–44.
How can we determine whether, and to what extent, an animal is suffering? Defines suffering as wide range of unpleasant subjective states including pain, fear, frustration, anxiety, conflict, etc. Suggests criteria for determination of suffering: (1) physical health, ill-health; (2) "natural," "unnatural" living conditions; (3) physiological state (including stress, heart rate, hormone levels, etc.); (4) normal, abnormal behavior (vacuum activity, stereotypy, displacement activity, self-mutilation, etc.); (5) animal preferences (choices); what animals find positively, negatively reinforcing; "animals may not be able to talk, but they can vote with their feet"; (6) analogies with ourselves. Heavily criticizes using productivity as a criterion. Argues no single criterion adequate but simultaneous use of several or all provides scientific basis for determining suffering.

160 Fox, Michael W. *Returning to Eden: Animal rights and human responsibility*. New York: Viking Press, 1980. 281 pp. Sources and reading list, 219–27.
Eden: situation where humans conscious of the evolutionary kinship with all other forms of life, in harmony with biosphere, respect all life forms, stewards of environment. Present distance from Eden measured by human abuse of animals and nature. One absolute right: the right of all life to a whole and healthy biosphere; human and animal rights are relative to this absolute right. Human species is "an evolutionary experiment . . . that may be a mistake, a tragic error." Unless humans "return to Eden" they will become extinct.

161 Hollands, Clive. *Compassion is the bugler: The struggle for animal rights*. Edinburgh: Macdonald, 1980. 201 pp.
Detailed account of successes, failures, hopes of two British campaigns. (1) Animal Welfare Year 1976–77. Participation by 67 animal welfare groups. Four areas accented: pet animals, laboratory animals, farm animals, transit of animals. Aims: to bring to public's attention animal welfare legislation of past 100 years, to focus public attention on animal exploitation, to develop public support for members of Parliament to revise animal protection legislation. (2) Putting Animals into Politics 1978–79. Supported by five joint consultative bodies: Christian Consultative Council for the Welfare of Animals, Committee for the Reform of Animal Experimentation, Farm Animal Welfare Co-ordinating Executive, Humane Education Council, National Joint Equine Welfare Committee. Succeeded in getting the three major political parties in Britain (Conservative, Labour, Liberal) to include animal welfare and protection in election manifestos. Roles of Lord Houghton, Richard Ryder, Clive Hollands prominent.

162 Magel, Charles. *Humane experimentation on humans and animals, or, muddling*

through. Chicago: National Anti-Vivisection Society, 1980. 24 pp.
Extry, an extraterrestrial, visits Terry, a terrestrial, in a deserted salt mine in Utah. In Extraterrestria there is no animal experimentation. Extry engages Terry in dialogue to learn about animal experimentation, its nature and purposes. Extry is alarmed to find that extraterrestrials cannot justify their meticulous protection of humans in contrast to "anything goes" in animal experimentation. Terrestrials admit to "muddling through" without moral justification. Extry returns to outer space disillusioned. Extensive notes.

163 Mason, Jim and **Singer, Peter**. *Animal factories*. New York: Crown, 1980. 174 pp. Japanese translation, Gendai Shokan, Tokyo, 1983.
Well-documented, heavily illustrated descriptions of mechanized, intensive producton of "biomachines" (especially poultry, pigs, cattle). Emphasize ethical costs to animals (confinement, stress, boredom, frustration, mutilation, suffering, disease), dangers to consumers, economic inefficiency, ecological damage, victimization of farmers. Cessation of factory farming of animals would result in better way of life for consumers, farmers, farm animals.

164 Orlans, Barbara. "Humaneness supercedes curiosity." In (H. McGiffin and N. Brownley 1980, 106–18).
The ethical costs to the animal are too high to justify invasive experiments on animals at the high school level. Describes a wealth of projects which are biologically instructive but do not harm animals. Descriptions, illustrations of unacceptable, acceptable science fair projects.

165 Regan, Tom. "Animal rights, human wrongs." *Environmental Ethics* 2 (1980): 99–120. Reprinted in [193].
Using examples of whaling, capturing gibbons, Draize test, veal factory farming, analyzes and critiques three approaches to these wrongs: cruelty account, utilitarian account, Kantian account. Argues for animal rights account based on the inherent value of animal lives. Animals have the right not to be harmed; the onus of justification is on anyone who violates this right.

166 Regan, Tom. "Cruelty, kindness, and unnecessary suffering." *Philosophy* 55 (1980): 532–41.
Argues concepts of cruelty and kindness are inadequate as basis for determining our moral obligations to animals since they both essentially refer to the mental states of the agent and do not capture the sense of obligations being *owed to* the animals. That an act causes unnecessary suffering is relevant to assessing its morality. Distinguishes two meanings of "unnecessary suffering": (1) suffering in excess of what is required to achieve a chosen goal, (2) suffering which cannot be morally justified.

167 Regan, Tom. "The debate over animal rights." In (H. McGiffin and N. Brownley 1980, 145–51).
Moral rights and legal rights. Do animals have moral rights? Grounds for possession of moral rights. Should animals have legal rights?

168 Russell, George K. "Reverence for life: An ethic for high school biology curricula." In (H. McGiffin and N. Brownley 1980, 27–34).
There is no demonstrable necessity to justify infliction of pain or killing of vertebrate animals in high schools. Injurious experiments not only fail to promote reverence for life but tend to destroy it. No animal experiments or demonstrations in high schools advance human knowledge in the slightest. Experiments are more likely to destroy than nurture the medical and scientific interests of young people. Humane alternatives should be emphasized: use of plant pathogens, using students as experimental subjects in harmless experiments, mechanical models, human cells (tissue culture), biological studies using methods of non-intervention.

169 Sapontzis, Steve F. "Are animals moral beings?" *American Philosophical Quarterly* 17 (1980): 45–52.
Animals are not moral agents in Kantian sense, but do act virtuously, warranting moral respect, with right to life, right to dignity, right to a fulfilling life.

170 Singer, Peter. "Animals and the value of life." In *Matters of life and death*, ed. by Tom Regan, 218–59. New York: Random House, 1980.
Criticizes traditional views which hold that human lives have much greater value than animal lives. Defining "person" as a self-conscious being aware of itself as a distinct entity existing over time, argues some animals are persons, not all humans are persons. Discusses utilitarianism and moral rights theories.

171 Stubbs, Anne C. "Morality and our treatment of animals." *Philosophical Studies* (Ireland) 27 (1980): 29–39.
Animals and humans share capacity for suffering; proscription against unnecessary suffering holds for both; infliction of suffering cannot be considered necessary unless in the interests of the sufferer. Animals and humans are pursuers of projects, loci of interests, ends in themselves, deserving respect, should not be exploited. Kant to the contrary, rational agency not required for deserving respect.

172 Braunstein, Mark M. *Radical vegetarianism: A dialectic of diet and ethics*. Los Angeles: Panjandrum Books, 1981. 140 pp.
A dialectic of diet and ethics which must be read to be appreciated. Why not to eat flesh. Why to eat fruit. What to eat and how to eat it. What not to eat and how not to eat it. Why not to drink milk. Why animals have a right to life. Why whoever lets animals live will live longer. How to kill less by eating fruits and eating raw. How animals have been denied the right to live. Why humans also have rights.

173 Hartbarger, Janie C. and **Neil J**. *Eating for the eighties: A complete guide to vegetarian nutrition*. Philadelphia: Saunders Press, 1981. 331 pp.
Discusses nutrition: carbohydrates, fat, protein, vitamins and minerals. "A normal, healthy adult need only get enough calories from a variety of foods and the protein will take care of itself" (8). Four eating styles. Special cases considered: pregnancy, babies and children, athletes, weight-loss diet. Is vegetarianism healthier? "Meat is not a particularly useful part of a good diet. As a matter of fact, it has some powerful disadvantages, both from the point of view of its direct

effect on health and from the point of view of trying to eat a well-balanced diet. Whatever your reasons for becoming vegetarian, you can add health benefits to the list. Meat is simply not good for you'' (230).

174 Heim, Alice. ''The desensitization of teachers and students.'' In [178, pp. 37–45].
Discusses blunting of sensibilities in schools with respect to suffering animals. Examples mainly from experimental psychology. Paradox in experimental psychology: although (so it is claimed) the ''distress'' of animals cannot possibly compare with what humans would suffer, experiments on ''stress'' in animals are extrapolated to humans. Reports accounts of laughter in laboratories at animal suffering.

175 Linzey, Andrew. ''Moral education and reverence for life.'' In [178, pp. 117–25].
Recommends reverence for life as basis for moral education. Defends Albert Schweitzer's concept of reverence for life against criticisms which have been brought against it: (1) that it cannot consistently be practiced, (2) that it refuses to accept one form of life as more valuable than another, (3) that it extends reverence to non-sentient life, (4) that it is merely a feeling. Reverence for life is more an attitude of mind than a moral law; it has a mystical connotation, meaning awareness of a claim made upon one; it is an intuitive experience of obligation as we acknowledge the value of ''the other''; it is an intuition combining intellect and emotion, incorporating limitless responsibility to all that lives.

176 Magel, Charles. *A bibliography on animal rights and related matters*. Washington, DC: University Press of America, 1981. 602 pp. 3,210 entries. Name index, 559–602. Also New York: Centaur Books, 1983.
Comprehensive, non-annotated, non-selective bibliography on animal rights and related subjects, from Biblical times through 1980, English-language sources. Topics and entry numbers: literature on animals before 19th century (1–50); nature of animals (51–196, 453–988); attitudes toward animals and nature (197–204, 989–1042); animals and religion (205–19, 1043–99); animals and ethics (220–42, 1107–303); animal experimentation (271–400, 1353–650, 1934–43); animals used for food, including factory farming of animals (401–3, 1651–719); hunting (438–40, 1854–901); other uses of animals (243–70, 441–4, 1304–52, 1801–2025); educational uses of animals (1840–53); vegetarianism (404–36, 1720–800); animal welfare movement (445–52, 2172–213); environmental ethics and ecology (2026–171); animals and law (2236–321); animals and literature and art and music (2322–594); conferences (2595–607); college courses (2608–22); biographies and autobiographies (2231–5); government documents (2623–87); films (2688–718); organizations (2719–3132); magazines and journals (3133–40); vegetarian cookbooks (3141–210).

177 National Association for the Advancement of Humane Education. *People and animals: A humane education curriculum guide*. Edited by Kathleen Savesky and Vanessa Malcarne. East Haddam, CT: NAAHE. 140 pp.
Four-book curriculum guide for preschool through sixth grade, intended to assist

children in developing compassion, a sense of justice, and a respect for all living creatures. Developed under the supervision of the Project Development Team consisting of 28 educators and educational administrators. Prior to publication, the guide was field tested by 350 teachers in 17 states and Ontario, Canada. 400 activities designed to interpret and explore relationships between humans and other animals, to develop skills or teach content in language arts, social studies, mathematics, health/science. Four general topics: human/animal relationships, pet animals, wild animals, farm animals. Resource materials (including audio-visuals) and humane education resource organizations are indicated. The topics of animal experimentation and animal safety-testing are not covered significantly. 35 humane themes permeate the guide: (1) humans are animals; (2) animals, like humans, have certain rights; (3) animals, like humans, react physically to their environment; (4) some animals, like humans, have and display emotions; (5) humans' different attitudes sometimes affect the way humans treat animals; (6) humans use other animals for a variety of purposes; (7) domestication is a process humans have used to make animals that were once wild suitable for human use; (8) humans sometimes choose alternatives to the use of animals or animal products; (9) laws exist to govern the keeping of animals; (10) laws exist to protect some animals; (11) humans have the responsibility to provide proper care for animals in public or private facilities; (12) careers exist that involve working with and for animals; (13) humans raise and keep pet animals to fulfill emotional needs; (14) some pet animals once met or now meet needs other than emotional fulfillment; (15) the factors considered in pet selection can affect the welfare of the animal selected; (16) not all animals make good pets; (17) pet animals need to be trained and controlled to live safely in the human world; (18) when a pet owner is irresponsible, the pet's health or life may be in danger; (19) when a pet owner is irresponsible, the pet may cause problems in the human and natural environments; (20) excessive breeding of dogs and cats causes pet overpopulation problems; (21) abandoned pets are the products of irresponsible owners; (22) humans share the earth with other animals; (23) in nature all things, living and non-living, are connected; (24) humans have the responsibility to preserve and allow for the development of natural habitats for wildlife; (25) humans have the responsibility to maintain a healthy environment for humans and other living things; (26) humans have the responsibility to allow wild animals in captivity to live as naturally as possible; (27) humans often destroy wild animal habitats; (28) some species of animals have become endangered or extinct as the result of human interference; (29) humans have different attitudes about the killing of animals for sport or profit; (30) humans raise and keep farm animals to fulfill physical needs; (31) humans have the responsibility to provide for farm animals' physical and behavioral needs; (32) farm animals can suffer if their basic needs are not met; (33) raising food for human use affects the natural environment; (34) humans have formed organizations to protect and control some animals; (35) pets depend on responsible owners to fulfill their needs.

178 Paterson, David, ed. *Humane education: A symposium.* Burgess Hill, West Sussex: Humane Education Council, 1981. 146 pp.
Proceedings of First International Symposium on Humane Education, Sussex University, August 1980. Eighteen presentations. (1) ''Welcome to humane

education," David Paterson, 1-4. (2) "Speciesism: Psychological and moral aspects," Richard D. Ryder, 5-14 (see [182]). (3) "Animals in British schools," David Paterson, 15-23. (4) "Animals in British universities," Gill Langley, 25-35. (5) "The desensitization of teachers and students," Alice Heim, 37-45 (see [174]). (6) "Pet psychotherapy," David Heather, 47-56. (7) "Humane education and the Council for Environmental Education," John Baines, 57-62. (8) "The work of Edinburgh Interlink," Robert J. Ollason, 63-6. (9) "Wild animals in captivity," S. A. Omrod, 67-73. ". . . Most [zoos] are simply peep-shows, the animals merely goods displayed to the public in return for hard cash." (10) "Children's ideas on animals: A preliminary study," David Paterson, 75-80. (11) "Dogs in society," Lesley S. Ordish, 81-90. (12) "Interdependence: Food animals and society," Damaris Hayman, 91-6. (13) "Natural cosmetics in a humane society," E. Joseph, 97-100. (14) "Animals and the media: Interest or concern," Pat Chapman, 101-7. (15) "The basis of social and moral responsibility," Alan Wynne, 109-15. Christianity and animals. (16) "Moral education and reverence for life," Andrew Linzey, 117-25 (see [175]). (17) "The animal welfare societies," Clive Hollands, 127-32. (18) "Thoughts for the future," Lord Douglas Houghton, 133-7. Plea for effective use of media, education, unity, professionalism, leaders to achieve political power for animal reform.

179 Regan, Tom. "Animal rights and animal experimentation." In *Rights and responsibilities in modern medicine*, ed. by M. D. Basson, 69-83. New York: Alan R. Liss, 1981.
Distinguishes between moral rights and legal rights. Discusses various grounds for human rights. Concludes the most plausible ground for human rights implies many animals also have rights. Those who would use animals in research must always justify doing so.

180 Richards, Stewart. "Forethoughts for carnivores." *Philosophy* 56 (1981): 73-88.
Accepts Peter Singer's equality principle (equal interests should be given equal consideration regardless of species) and his analogy of speciesism to racism and sexism. Equal interests can be resolved only through biological evidence concerning evolutionary development. Concludes normally preferable to refrain from being party to killing animals when unnecessary for fulfillment of human life. Those who are opposed only to cruelty to animals are generally unjustified in eating their flesh. ". . . Any individual who reflects honestly on this question will be obliged, for utilitarian reasons alone, to cease eating factory-farmed flesh."

181 Rollin, Bernard E. *Animal rights and human morality*. Buffalo, NY: Prometheus Books, 1981. 182 pp. Bibliography, 179-82.
Defends a theory of rights for humans and animals based on awareness, having interests, and having a nature or *telos*, a set of activities intrinsic to the organism evolutionarily determined and genetically imprinted. Animals and humans have a right to life and also a right to the kind of life which their nature (*telos*) dictates. In practice, animal experimentation is imbedded so heavily in our culture it is impossible to put the animal rights theory into effect; as a result we should apply the utilitarian principle to animal experimentation; any justified research on an

animal should be conducted in such a way as to maximize the animal's potential for living its life according to its nature or *telos*, and certain fundamental rights should be preserved as far as possible, given the logic of the research, regardless of consideration of cost. In theory, animal rights win over utilitarianism; in practice, utilitarianism wins over animal rights. Discusses pet animals in terms of an implicit "social contract" between humans and animals.

182 Ryder, Richard D. "Speciesism: Psychological and moral aspects." In [178, pp. 5–14].
Defines speciesism as human arrogance in assuming humans different in kind from other species, that humans have rights or interests which other sentient creatures can be denied. Dissecting live animals in schools can lead to trauma, "hardening," sadism. Characterizes experimental psychology as "one of the most jejune, cruel and useless of sciences." Children typically see animals as friends, colleagues, brothers, sisters; speciesist adults and education erode this attitude. Animal rights movement as revolutionary as Copernican revolution. We should stop eating animals, experimenting on them, caging them in zoos, hunting and trapping them. Legally, animals perhaps should be put on equal footing with children, mentally handicapped.

183 Schonfeld, Victor and **Alaux, Myriam**, directors. *The animals film*. London: Slick Pics International, 1981. 16 mm color, 136 minutes. Narration by Julie Christie. Also video-cassette. Available from The Cinema Guild, 1697 Broadway, New York, NY 10019 or Slick Pics International, 331 Goswell Road, London, EC1. Also available from International Society for Animal Rights [344].
Powerful feature-length documentary on maltreatment of animals in scientific research, military testing, product testing, factory farming of animals for food, pet shops, whaling, hunting, stray pets, fur industry. Covers alternatives, animal liberation movement.

184 Singer, Peter. "The concept of moral standing." In *Ethics in hard times*, ed. by A. L. Caplan and D. Callahan, 31–45. New York: Plenum Press, 1981.
Uses the universalizability principle (to decide whether an action is right, imagine yourself living, one after another, the lives of all those affected by the action; if, under these conditions, you still want the action done, you have satisfied the universalizability principle) and sentience as basic components in the criterion for moral standing (not synonymous with legal standing). Concludes persons, mammals, vertebrates, invertebrates have moral standing, and that rocks, trees, streams, species, corporate entities do not have moral standing.

185 Sperlinger, David, ed. *Animals in research: New perspectives in animal experimentation*. Chichester and New York: John Wiley, 1981. 373 pp.
Sixteen essays by scientists, philosophers, animal welfarists, journalists, all seeming to agree animals have significant moral status. (1) "British legislation and proposals for reform," Richard D. Ryder, 11–38. Royal Commission on Vivisection 1876, Cruelty to Animals Act 1876, second Royal Commission on Vivisection 1906–1912, Littlewood report, "Houghton–Platt Memorandum,"

General Election Coordinating Committee for Animal Protection 1978–79, Halsbury Bill 1979, Fry Bill 1979, proposals by Committee for Reform of Animal Experimentation (CRAE) 1979. (2) "European animal experimentation law," Richard W. J. Esling, 39–61. Denmark, Norway, Sweden, Federal Republic of Germany, Netherlands, Belgium, France, Italy, Austria, Switzerland, Council of Europe, European Convention on the Protection of Laboratory Animals. (3) "Legislation and practice in the United States," Margaret Morrison, 63–78. Animal Welfare Act 1966 and revisions; laws on animal testing. (4) "Natural relations: Contemporary views of the relationship between humans and other animals," David Sperlinger, 79–101. Animals are our natural relations, distinct individuals with needs and interests; implications for animal rights theories and animal experimentation. (5) "The medical sciences," Louis Goldman, 105–21. Naive to assume no regulation is necessary because of conscience of experimenters and peers. (6) "The biological sciences," Jenny Remfry, 123–39. Overview of animal experimentation in biology, with seven unanswered questions. (7) "The use of animals in experimental cancer research," Harold B. Hewitt, 141–74. The experimenter must deny himself knowledge, however valuable, which cannot be obtained without the infliction of suffering. (8) "Animal experimentation in the behavioural sciences," Robert Drewett and Walia Kani, 175–201. Moral significance of captivity, death, pain of animals in psychological research. (9) "Ethology: The science and tool," David MacDonald and Marian Dawkins, 203–23. Ethical implications of ethological studies, experiments. (10) "The use of animals in schools of Britain," David Paterson, 225–38. Animal usage in primary, secondary schools; laws governing. (11) "Live-animal science projects in U.S. schools," Michael W. Fox and Heather McGiffin, 239–54. Critique of animal usage in biology classrooms, science fairs. (12) "Alternatives and laboratory animals," Andrew N. Rowan, 257–83. Toxicity testing and alternatives, "alternatives" defined as any technique replacing animals or reducing number or reducing suffering through refinement. (13) "The 'defined' animal and the reduction of animal use," Michael F. W. Festing, 285–306. Encourages reduction of use, of suffering of animals through precisely defining animals microbiologically and genetically in well-designed experiments. (14) "The fallacy of animal experimentation in psychology," Don Bannister, 307–17. Problem of reflexivity (experiment and experimenter have effect on response of experimental subject, human or animal – an effect which psychologists must but cannot account for) has resulted in cruel deaths of countless animals in vain in psychological experiments. (15) "Why knowledge matters," Mary Midgley, 319–36. Value of knowledge for its own sake must be considered in context of other values, costs, including costs to animals in experiments. (16) "Experimenting on animals: An ethical problem," Cora Diamond, 337–62. Argues for moral scrutiny of animal experimentation.

186 Taylor, Paul W. "The ethics of respect for nature." *Environmental Ethics* 3 (1981): 197–218.
Opposing human-centered ethics, presents foundation for biocentric egalitarianism. Respect for nature as an ultimate moral attitude. All organisms have a good (welfare, well-being) of their own, have equal inherent worth. Species impartiality. Critiques three classical arguments for human superiority: Judeo-

Christian, Greek, Cartesian. Not asserting animals or plants have moral rights; there is no reason they could not be ascribed legal rights. For development of this theory see [274].

187 Wood-Gush, David G. M., Dawkins, Marian S. and **Ewbank, R.**, eds. *Self-awareness in domesticated animals*. Herts: Universities Federation for Animal Welfare, 1981. 55 pp.
Seven essays. (1) "The problem of distinguishing awareness from responsiveness," Donal R. Griffin, 4–10. Birds, mammals have some degree of awareness; we are almost obliged to postulate some degree of self-awareness as well. (2) "Awareness and self-awareness," Stephen R. L. Clark, 11–18. Most animals are aware; some are self-aware. (3) "Neuropharmacology and awareness of the body in rats," D. M. Vowles, 19–21. Hypothesis that rats possess rudimentary type of self-consciousness based on awareness of body needed for motor control. (4) "Pain sensations and pain reactions," David Bowsher, 22–8. Much we don't know about mechanisms of pain, suffering in humans, animals. (5) "Methods for studying cognition in the chimpanzee," Guy Woodruff, 29–36. Experiments show chimpanzees capable of cause–effect inference, perceiving abstract relationships underlying concepts of number and proportion, making inferences about others, choosing to communicate accurate or false information. Can chimpanzees be psychologists (attribute different abilities or states of knowledge to others)? This question unresolved. (6) "Having feelings and showing feelings," N. K. Humphrey, 37–9. Ethology, evolution theory support view if animals have feelings they will advertise them and if animals advertise them they have them. (7) "The social skills of dogs as an indicator of animal awareness," Roger A. Mugford, 40–4. Case studies in context of evolution theory provide evidence of self-awareness in dogs (and probably in other species).

188 Cave, George P. "Animals, Heidegger, and the right to life." *Environmental Ethics* 4 (1982): 249–54.
Criticizes utilitarianism's inability to resolve conflicts of interests, to prove painless killing of animals morally wrong. Suggests Heidegger's concept of *care* as basis for criterion higher than pleasure/pain principle. Life matters to animals; they *care* about what happens to them; they are concerned for their own existence. Hence we have a duty not to kill animals.

189 Clark, Stephen R. L. *The nature of the beast: Are animals moral?* Oxford and New York: Oxford University Press, 1982, 127 pp. Bibliography, 119–24.
Two basic questions: (1) What is the nature of animals? Ethological studies within evolutionary context deny sharp qualitative gulf between animals and humans. Are similarities and great differences (especially in use of abstract language and in degree, complexity of self-awareness). (2) Are animals moral? Are they altruistic? Selfish? Concerned about welfare of others? Aggressive? Warlike? Cruel? Sadistic? Affectionate? Caring parents? Social? Loyal? Restrained in sexuality? Domineering? Competitive? Acquisitive? Territorial? Organized hierarchically? Capable of feeling grief, shame? Finds tendencies in animals to behave in ways suggestive of what we would judge to be moral (or immoral) behavior; some

similarities to humans, but great differences (especially in human use of moral principles to evaluate actions).

190 Dyer, Judith C. *Vegetarianism: An annotated bibliography*. Metuchen, NJ: Scarecrow Press, 1982. 280 pp. Author index, 233–55; subject index, 256–80. List over 200 vegetarian cookbooks, 217–32.
1,412 annotated entries. Part I, early works through 1959, pp. 3–46. Part II, 1960–1980, pp. 47–232, organized under topics: general interest, history of vegetarianism, athletics and endurance, planning vegetarian diet (adults, infants, children, pets), food technology, institutional food service, children's materials, reference sources, position papers on vegetarian diets, philosophical aspects of diet (including economics, ecology, ethics, religion, animal rights), medical aspects of vegetarian diets (including general interest, cardiovascular system, cancer, digestive system, diabetes, skeletal system, protein, vitamins B12 and D, mental health, infants and children and young adults, vegans).

191 Jamieson, Dale and **Regan, Tom**. "On the ethics of the use of animals in science." In *And justice for all*, ed. by T. Regan and D. VanDeVeer, 169–96. Totowa, NJ: Rowman and Littlefield, 1982.
Reject two extreme positions on animal experimentation: (1) The Unlimited Use Position which states it is permissible to use any animal for any scientific purpose so long as no human being is wronged; and (2) The No Use Position, which claims no use of any animal for any scientific purpose is morally permissible. Analyze two less extreme positions: (3) Modified Innocence Principle, claiming it is wrong to harm an innocent individual unless it is reasonable to believe that doing so is the only realistic way of avoiding equal harm for many other innocents; and (4) Principle of Utility, claiming we ought to act so as to bring about the greatest possible balance of good over evil for everyone affected. Conclusion: (3) and (4) proscribe much scientific use of animals as morally wrong; (3) is more proscriptive than (4). ". . . The burden of proof must always be on those who cause harm to animals in scientific settings." S. F. Sapontzis (1987) responds to this essay.

192 McCarthy, Vincent P. "The changing concept of animals as property." *International Journal for the Study of Animal Problems* 3 (1982): 295–300.
Compares the property status of slaves to the property status of animals, arguing there are indications of evolution in animal law similar to the evolution of slave law which led to emancipation. Market value as purchase price minus depreciation is a principle which has been applied to both slaves and animals. An increased awareness of the intrinsic value of animals will result in the beginning of law to focus on the specific interests of animals themselves. "An animal will then be seen as an autonomous being, with interests that are worthy of consideration equal to those of human beings. . . . Inevitably, some owner or animal group will eventually introduce a breakthrough case, on behalf of an animal, in which a court will award damages for the loss to the animal himself" (299).

193 Regan, Tom. *All that dwell therein: Animal rights and environmental ethics*. Berkeley: University of California Press, 1982. 249 pp. Bibliography by Tom Regan and Charles Magel, 241–6.
Ten essays and lectures from period 1975–1981, most of them formerly published.

Regan provides introduction for each essay, citing relevant literature in agreement and disagreement with the argument. (1) "The moral basis of vegetarianism," 1-39 [112]. (2) "Utilitarianism, vegetarianism, and animal rights," 40-60. Criticizes Peter Singer's attempt to base vegetarianism on utilitarianism. (3) "Animal experimentation: First thoughts," 61-74. Analysis and critique of use of the ideas of cruelty and kindness to animals by animal welfarists in their attempts to curb animal experimentation; argues animal rights is a better basis. (4) "Animal rights, human wrongs," 75-101 [165]. (5) "Why whaling is wrong," 102-12. Whaling wrong on the basis of pain inflicted in the killing and on the basis of the wrongness of killing. (6) "An examination and defense of one argument concerning animal rights," 113-47 [144]. (7) "Animals and the law: The need for reform," 148-64. (Published in Proceedings of *Internationalen vereinigung für rechts- und sozial-philosophie*, World Congress, 1979, vol. 2.) Argues that the concept of legal rights for animals is intelligible, that animals at present have no legal rights, and that, given that human interests are protected by law, likewise animal interests should be protected through recognition of the legal status (standing) of animals and the recognition of animal legal rights. (8) "What sorts of beings can have rights?" 165-83 [120]. (Formerly published under different title: "Feinberg on what sorts of beings can have rights.") (9) "The nature and possibility of an environmental ethic," 184-205. (Published in *Environmental Ethics* 3 (1981): 19-34.) Explores the nature of an environmental ethic (must hold that there are nonhuman beings that have moral standing, must hold that the class of those beings that have moral standing includes but is larger than the class of conscious beings) and argues for the possibility of such an environmental ethic on the basis of postulating the inherent value of beings having moral standing. (10) "Environmental ethics and the ambiguity of the Native Americans' relationship to nature," 206-39. (Paper presented at Moorhead State University, Minnesota, March 1981.) Argues there is a fundamental ambiguity in Amerinds' relationship to nature, that the evidence does not prove Amerinds to be shallow environmentalists (the view that nature exists for *Homo sapiens* and has no value in its own right) and does not prove them to be deep ecologists (view that nature has value in its own right, apart from human interests).

194 Ruesch, Hans. *Naked empress or the great medical fraud*. Zurich: Buchlervag CIVIS Publications, 1982. 202 pp. Illustrations, 163-202.
Argues the empress (modern medicine) is naked in the sense that instead of fulfilling its promise to improve public health it has become the principal cause of disease. Improvement of health would result from emphasis on prevention of disease, abolition of animal experimentation and testing, and drastic reduction of drugs.

195 Sapontzis, Steve F. "The moral significance of interests." *Environmental Ethics* 4 (1982): 345-58.
Several philosophers (H. J. McCloskey, J. Narveson, B. Steinbock, L. and R. Norman, R. G. Frey, M. Williams, R. Cigman) opposed to animal rights have recently sought to justify their opposition by arguing epistemic differences between human and animal interests (often referred to as "taking an interest" vs. "having an interest") constitute a morally significant difference. Details various

forms of having an interest and of taking an interest. Evaluates moral significance of these differences from utilitarian and deontological viewpoints. Concludes epistemic differences between human and animal interests not morally significant.

196 Sapontzis, Steve F. "Must we value life to have a right to it?" *Ethics and Animals* 3 (March 1982): 2–11.
Purpose of essay to refute following argument: (1) only those who can suffer the misfortune of death can have a right to life; (2) only those who can value life can suffer the misfortune of death; (3) animals cannot value life; (4) therefore, animals cannot have a right to life. Argument is refuted by showing that (2) is false. Critique of R. Cigman's (1981) "Death, misfortune, and species inequality."

197 Schwartz, Richard H. *Judaism and vegetarianism*. Smithtown, NY: Exposition Press, 1982. 158 pp.
". . . The conditions under which animals are raised today are completely contrary to the Jewish ideals of compassion and avoiding *tsa'ar ba'alei chayim*" (24). "In view of the strong Jewish mandates to be compassionate to animals, preserve health, help feed the hungry, preserve and protect the environment, and seek and pursue peace, and the very negative effects flesh-centered diets have in each of these areas, how do you justify not becoming a vegetarian?" (129). Biographies of famous Jewish vegetarians. Jewish vegetarian organizations and activities.

198 Westerlund, Stuart R., ed. *Humane education and realms of humaneness: Readings*. Washington, DC: University Press of America, 1982. 271 pp.
41 articles and editorials selected from issues of the National Association for the Advancement of Humane Education *Journal*, 1974–1977. The concept of humaneness is unifying theme, and there is no consideration of animal rights. Basic topics: philosophy of humaneness, theory of humane education, practice of humane education, international perspectives. Three most important selections: (1) "Of man, animals, and morals," Ashley Montagu, 3–15. "The principle which should obtain in our relationships to all other living creatures is *as we would have others do unto us so should we do unto all living creatures* . . ." (14). (2) "From kinship to mastery: A study of American attitudes toward animals," Stephen R. Kellert, 61–8. Identifies seven distinct attitudes: naturalistic, ecologistic, humanistic, moralistic, scientistic, aesthetic, and dominionistic. (3) "Vivisection and the true aims of education in biology," George K. Russell, 197–204 [100].

199 Akers, Keith. *A vegetarian sourcebook*. New York: G. P. Putnam's, 1983. 229 pp.
Peter Singer's judgment: ". . . Most useful single volume I know covering all the arguments about vegetarianism." Three approaches: nutritional, ecological, ethical. Ethical approach discusses suffering, deaths of food animals, Hinduism, Buddhism, Jainism, Judaism, Christianity, Plato, Pythagoras, Empedocles, Plutarch, Porphyry, Descartes, Kant, Peter Singer.

200 Benney, Norma. "All of one flesh: The rights of animals." In *Reclaim the earth: Women speak out for life on earth*, ed. by L. Caldecott and S. Leland, 141–51. London: Women's Press, 1983.

"The overthrowing of the patriarchy is the feminist's *raison d'être*. We write, organise, activate, oppose patriarchal life-patterns and edicts, and work towards an overthrow of the system. But if while aiming for this change we do not become aware of the sufferings of non-humans, then I feel we will not have understood the concept of liberty. If we struggle to free ourselves, without realising that we are also crushing the most oppressed and exploited creatures on the planet, we can only fail." Animal experimentation; factory farming; vegetarianism; animal rights movement.

201 Caplan, Arthur L. "Beastly conduct: Ethical issues in animal experimentation." *Annals of the New York Academy of Sciences* 406 (1983): 159–69.
Clear exposition of the moral issues in the controversy over animal experimentation. Animals which are sentient and purposive have prima facie rights to live and to be let alone. The burden of proof is always on the experimenter to give good moral reasons for overriding these prima facie rights.

202 Fretz, Sada. *Going vegetarian: A guide for teen-agers*. New York: William Morrow, 1983. 278 pp. Bibliography, 259–70. Cookbooks, 271–3.
Informative source for aspiring young vegetarians who cannot rely on "folk wisdom" of their meat-eating families. The case against meat. Vegetarian nutrition. Vegetarian cooking.

203 Gold, Mark. *Assault and battery: What factory farming means for humans and animals*. London and Australia: Pluto Press, 1983. 172 pp.
Detailed factual study, critique of factory farming of animals in British context. Attacks five myths used to defend factory farming. Factory farming not only immeasurably cruel but also economically unnecessary, wasteful, unhealthful, and damaging to the cause of alleviating human hunger.

204 Johnson, Lawrence E. "Can animals be moral agents?" *Ethics and Animals* 4 (1983): 50–61.
Some animals (monkeys for example) can sometimes act as moral agents. They act from morally relevant motivations. Awareness of moral principle is not necessary for moral agency. Moral agency does not require linguistic ability or human levels of intelligence. Any argument against the possibility of moral agency on the part of animals can also be applied to humans, or is implausible on other grounds.

205 Johnson, Lawrence E. "Do animals have an interest in life?" *Australian Journal of Philosophy* 61 (1983): 172–84.
The case that killing an animal violates the animal's interests is as strong as the case that killing a human violates the human's interest. Preference utilitarianism does not show that only humans have an interest in life. Animals have an interest in continuing to live. Equal interests are to be treated equally. Killing animals for meat violates their interest in continuing to live.

206 Midgley, Mary. *Animals and why they matter*. Athens: University of Georgia Press, 1983. 158 pp.

Attacks views of others who try to argue that animals do not matter morally because it is wrong to be emotional about animals, because evolution teaches us that we are locked into life and death competition with other species, because animals without reason or language have no moral standing, because any attempt to understand conscious inner life of animals vitiated by anthropomorphism. In contrast to a rights view or equality principle, opts for a model with overlapping, interconnected factors: kinship, special need, justice, special responsibility, prudence, gratitude, admiration and wonder, fellowship. Concludes animals do matter morally. Gives the reader little or no guidance how we should treat animals or how we should weigh human interests against animal interests when they conflict.

207 Miller, Harlan B. and **Williams, William H.**, eds. *Ethics and animals.* Clifton, NJ: Humana Press, 1983. 400 pp. Bibliography, 381–9.
Papers presented by scientists, philosophers, animal rightists and welfarists at conference on ethics and animals, Virginia Polytechnic Institute and State University, 24–27 May 1979. (1) "Introduction," Harlan B. Miller, 1–14. History of philosophical traditions underlying issue of moral status of animals, and discussion of seven factors accounting for the current strong interest in animals and ethics. (2) "Animal rights, human wrongs," Tom Regan, 19–43 [165]. (3) "Animal rights revisited," Jan Narveson, 45–59. Favors contractarian rational egoist theory allowing no moral status for animals; criticizes Tom Regan's moral rights theory. (4) "Knowing our place in the animal world," Annette C. Baier, 61–77. Applies David Hume's moral theory to question how we should treat animals. (5) "The clouded mirror: Animal stereotypes and human cruelty," Thomas L. Benson, 79–90. Conflicting stereotypes prevent us from understanding nature of animals, often resulting in maltreatment. Typical stereotypes regard animals as aliens, as children, as moral paragons, as demons, as machines. (6) "Moral community and moral order," James M. Buchanan, 95–102. Animals may be treated as members of the human moral community but they have no place in the human "moral order." (7) "The legal and moral bases of animal rights," Bernard E. Rollin, 103–18. There is no morally significant difference between humans and animals on basis of which moral rights possessed by humans can be denied to animals. Legal rights based on moral rights. Animals should be granted legal rights. (8) "Life, death, and animals," Edward Johnson, 123–33. To any conscious being its life is as important to it as is any other conscious being's life to it, regardless of varying complexity of consciousness (self-consciousness for example). We have no basis for saying mental complexity is an ethically significant factor. (9) "Killing persons and other beings," Dale Jamieson, 135–46. Argues consciousness, simple or reflexive, sufficient for imposing on us a prima facie obligation not to kill its subject. (10) "Interspecific justice and animal slaughter," Donald VanDeVeer, 147–62. Extending John Rawls' "veil of ignorance" in such way that rational, self-interested contractors do not know which species of sentient animals they will belong to, argues contractors would agree to two principles: (a) no sentient creature should have forced upon it (by a rational being) treatment that makes its life not worth living; and (b) no rational being should deliberately cause to exist a sentient creature with a life not preferable to no life at all. (11) "Humans, animals, and 'animal behavior'," Stephen R. L. Clark, 169–82. Critiques utilitarianism and Stoicism as bases for adequate morals in regard to

animals. An adequate morality must allow due weight to both sentiment and rationality. (12) "Ecology, morality, and hunting," Peter S. Wenz, 183–97. Argues we have a prima facie obligation to protect environment for its own sake; hunting is inconsistent with this obligation. (13) "Humans as hunting animals," Patrick F. Scanlon, 199–205. Humans, as natural predators, practice hunting as part of the ecological process. The position of universal vegetarianism can be argued only from ignorance regarding ecology. (14) "Apes and language research," Duane M. Rumbaugh and Sue Savage-Rumbaugh, 207–17. Description of ape-language research at Yerkes Regional Primate Research Center of Emory University. (15) "The priority of human interests," Lawrence C. Becker, 225–42. Argues for the moral priority, for humans, of human interests over comparable ones in animals. (16) "Comments on 'The priority of human interests'," James Cargile, 243–9. Comments on Becker's paper. (17) "The case against raising and killing animals for food," Bart Gruzalski, 251–65. Makes the case against raising and killing animals for food on the basis of classical utilitarianism. Defends his view against five objections. (18) "Do animals have a right to life?" James Rachels, 275–84. "Having a life" (not just being alive but having a biography, hopes, plans, memories) is the morally relevant characteristic for having a right to life. Since many animals have a life they have a right to life. (19) "On why we would do better to jettison moral rights," R. G. Frey, 285–301. Argues against moral rights theory for both humans and animals. (20) "Philosophy, ecology, animal welfare, and the 'rights' question," Michael W. Fox, 307–15. We should move from anthropocentric to an ecocentric view. Given humans have rights, animals have them also. The basic right is freedom of animals to pursue their natural potentials in environment for which they are best suited or pre-adapted. (21) "Deciding what to kill," T. Nicolaus Tideman, 317–22. We must kill to live. Plants are conscious too. (22) "Chicken-environment interactions," W. B. Gross, 329–37. Report of research on the effect of genetic endowment and environmental changes on chickens. (23) "Against a scientific justification of animal experiments," Deborah G. Mayo, 339–59. Criticizes animal experiments as irrelevant and invalid. Justifications given for experimenting on animals can be used to justify experiments on humans. (24) " 'Animal liberation' as crime: The Hawaii dolphin case," Gavan Daws, 361–71. In 1977 two employees of University of Hawaii release two dolphins from experimental situation to the ocean. Legal defense argues (unsuccessfully) that dolphins are persons and therefore cannot be stolen property, and that therefore liberation justified. (25) "Fighting for animal rights: Issues and strategies," Henry Spira, 373–77. Tactics, strategies for effective animal liberation. ". . . We must sharply focus on a single significant injustice, on one clearly limited goal at a time. . . . And the goal must be winnable. . . . One criterion for choosing a target is that the mere statement of the issue tends to place the adversary on the defensive. . . . Do not start off being personally hostile to your potential adversary. Suggest reasonable options, realistic collaborative approaches."

208 Regan, Tom. *The case for animal rights.* Berkeley: University of California Press, 1983. 425 pp. Notes, 401–17.
By far the most rigorous, sophisticated, comprehensive work defending moral

rights for animals. Written for intelligent lay persons, philosophers, scientists. Helpful "summary and conclusion" at end each chapter. Critique of Descartes' denial of animal awareness. Develops cumulative argument for animal consciousness. Discusses complexity of awareness in animals (perception, memory, desire, belief, self-consciousness, concepts, intentional action). Analyzes animal welfare in terms of autonomy, interests, benefits and harms. Critiques indirect duty views: rational egoism (Jan Narveson), contractarianism (John Rawls), humanity as an end in itself (Kant). Critiques direct duty views: cruelty–kindness view, hedonistic utilitarianism, preference utilitarianism. Using principles of justice and equality, develops a theory of moral rights for humans and animals, based on equal inherent value of individuals which are subjects of a life. Emphasizes the right not to be harmed, arguing the infliction of death to be the ultimate harm. Concludes: vegetarianism is morally obligatory; hunting and trapping are morally wrong; harmful experiments and testing on animals should cease.

209 Rollin, Bernard E. "Morality and the human–animal bond." In *New perspectives on our lives with companion animals*, ed. by A. H. Katchen and A. M. Beck, 500–10. Philadelphia: University of Pennsylvania Press, 1983.
In addition to their instrumental value, companion animals possess intrinsic value. They are living, feeling, sentient creatures whose lives matter to them. We are bonded to them by the bounds of morality. Each animal species has a unique set of interests, genetically programmed, which determines its nature (*telos*). Animals have a right to life and a right to live in accordance with their nature. There is a strong implicit social contract between humans and companion animals. Examples of violations of rights described. Our legal and educational systems should recognize animal rights.

210 Rollin, Bernard E. *The teaching of responsibility*. Potters Bar, Herts: Universities Federation for Animal Welfare, 1983. 30 pp.
Moral reasoning and moral philosophy are desperately needed in biomedicine and biomedical education. Animals are objects of moral concern, ends in themselves, whose interests are determined by their *telos*. Ideally, we must conclude that animals have a basic moral right to life if people do, and a basic moral right to live their lives in accordance with their natures. Animals have intrinsic value, not merely instrumental value.

211 Sprigge, Timothy L. S. "Vivisection, morals and medicine." *Journal of Medical Ethics* 9 (1983): 98–101.
Argues for commensurability of pain, pleasure in humans and animals. Concludes complete ban on harmful experiments on animals (and humans) will result in greater welfare of sentient world than existing practice of experimenting on animals.

212 Thomas, Keith. *Man and the natural world: A history of the modern sensibility.* New York: Pantheon Books, 1983. 426 pp. Voluminous notes, 305–403. Also London: Allen Lane, 1983.
History of human (mainly British) views of and attitudes toward natural environment, especially animals, 1500–1800. Thousands of sources cited, especially in

natural history, literature, theology, science. 16th-century anthropocentrism comes into question by 1800 due to natural science, impossibility of finding a rigid boundary between animals and humans, moral indignation over cruelty, aesthetic contemplation. Topics include relations between farmers and animals, growth of pet-keeping, origin of vegetarianism, whether animals have souls. Thomas provides fascinating, vivid account of British mental history ranging from George Cheyne's claim that Creator made the horse's excrement smell sweet because he knew that man would often be in its vicinity to John Dryden's:

> Take not away the
> life you cannot give:
> For all things have an
> equal right to live.

213 Clark, Stephen R. L. "Animal rights and the peaceable kingdom." in *From Athens to Jerusalem*, 158–79. Oxford: Clarendon Press, 1984.
Could there be a peaceable kingdom in which all claims to life and liberty and pursuit of happiness be fully satisfied? And could we live by the rules of that kingdom? Clark's answer seems to be "literally, no." However, he provides suggested life-styles premissed on the basis of a belief in justice. "We are the children both of earth and heaven, and all living creatures are the same."

214 Dombrowski, Daniel A. *The philosophy of vegetarianism.* Amherst: University of Massachusetts Press, 1984. 188 pp. Notes and discussions, 141–66. Bibliography, 168–83.
Uses concepts and insights of contemporary philosophy to better understand strengths, weaknesses of ancient philosophical vegetarianism in Greece and Rome (Pythagoras, Plato, Empedocles, Theophrastus, Plotinus, Plutarch, Porphyry). Uses wisdom of ancient vegetarians as basis for analysis, critique of contemporary views (Stephen R. L. Clark, Peter Singer, Tom Regan, Richard Rorty, Charles Hartshorne).

215 Duffy, Maureen. *Men and beasts: An animal rights handbook.* London: Granada, 1984. 160 pp.
Sensitive, rational, pragmatic discussion of virtually all aspects of British animal rights movement. Considers ethical issues, vegetarianism, animals used for food, pets, wildlife, experiments on animals, tactics and methods of protest, goals of animal rights movement. Poem following each chapter. Appendices: Animal Liberation Front direct actions; principal British animal rights and welfare organizations.

216 Hall, Rebecca. *Voiceless victims.* Hounslow, Middx: Wildwood House, 1984. 288 pp.
Foreword by Brigitte Bardot. A "what can I do?" book in regard to maltreatment of animals: cruel sports (hunting, coursing, beagling, fishing, bullfighting, badger digging and baiting, trapping), factory farming and slaughtering of animals for food (including Jewish and Muslim methods), animals in entertainment (films, television, circus), horses (including export and horse-meat trade),

domestic pets (dogs, cats), experiments and testing on animals, conservation. Following each chapter a list of things the reader can do. Gives detailed information on history, activities and goals of over 70 organizations (mainly British). Chap. 7 contains interview with a doctor, J. D. Whittall, who agrees with Gandhi that animal experimentation is the blackest of all black crimes. Chap. 10, based on an interview with Henry Spira, discusses strategy in animal rights activism.

217 O'Connor, Karen. *Sharing the kingdom: Animals and their rights.* New York: Dodd, Mead, 1984. 144 pp.
For junior high, high school students. Well-written, informational, illustrated. Based on interviews with students, workers in animal rights, researchers, factory farmers. Covers animals in films, television, zoos, rodeos, factory farms, trapping, hunting, research, testing, adoption centers, wildlife, companion animals, alternatives to animal experiments. List of organizations and addresses.

218 Regan, Tom. "Ethical vegetarianism and commercial animal farming." In *Agriculture, change and human values,* ed. by R. Haynes and R. Lanier, 279–94. Gainesville, FL: Humanities and Agricultural Program, 1984.
Traditional moral anthropocentrism bequeathed to us by humanism and theism is morally bankrupt. Utilitarianism does not succeed in showing either that we have an obligation to be vegetarians or that commercial animal agriculture is morally to be condemned. Ecological holism (Aldo Leopold's theory) implies that individuals are of no consequence apart from their role as "members of the biotic team," is environmental fascism. The rights view, based on inherent value of human and animal lives, calls for total abolition of commercial animal agriculture and a switch to vegetarianism.

219 Rollin, Bernard E. "How I put the horse before Descartes: An autobiographical fragment." *Between the Species* 1 (Winter 1984–85): 44–50.
Autobiography of a philosopher and animal rightist especially concerned about the use of animals in experimentation and in veterinary medicine and education.

220 Rowan, Andrew N. *Of mice, models, and men: A critical evaluation of animal research.* Albany: State University of New York Press, 1984. 323 pp. Bibliography, 287–312.
A concerned biochemist urges reform. Claims ultimate goal of scientists is the abolition of animal research; current abolitionists and research scientists differ on the time scale and strategies. Ethical cost to animals (pain, suffering, death) must be weighed in cost–benefit analysis. Psychologists face ethical paradox: the better the animal model the more restricted its use should be. Strong argument for alternatives, ethics education for animal researchers, ethical review committees on animal experimentation analogous to review boards for human experimentation. Recommends legislative regulation of animal experimentation. Informative not only for scientists but also for non-scientists to gain scientific perspective. Especially illuminating on toxicity testing and alternatives.

221 Sandys-Winsch, Godfrey. *Animal law in England and Wales.* 2d ed. London: Shaw, 1984. 260 pp. Table of statutes, xvii–xxvii; Table of statutory

instruments, xxix–xxx; Table of cases, xxxi–xxxiv. 12 appendices, 211–38. Detailed index, especially by type of animal, 241–60.
Covers animal law as of October 1983 in England and Wales on quadrupeds, excluding birds, fishes, insects, but including seals, rare wild creatures. Excludes slaughterhouses, horse and greyhound racing. Written for legal practitioners, government officers, court officials, police, lay persons. Topics include owner-ship, theft, owner's responsibilities, sale, agistment, import, export, movement of animals, pet animals, horses and farm animals, dangerous wild animals, animals as game, protection of animals, prevention of cruelty (abandonment, transporta-tion, cruelty to livestock, docking and nicking, dogs as draught animals, drugging and poisoning, experiments on animals, fighting and baiting, operations and anaesthetics, traps, killing or injuring animals), animal diseases, performances and public exhibitions, pests. Extensive documentation, references to acts of Parliament, statutory instruments, statutory rules and orders.

222 Sapontzis, Steve F. "Predation." *Ethics and animals* 5 (1984): 27–38.
Deals with whether animal rights entail interfering with predation in nature and with the place of *reductio ad absurdum* arguments in ethics. Several different senses of "absurdity" are considered; a rule for practical reasoning based on the Kantian principle that "ought implies can" is proposed; and it is concluded that predation should be prevented when that can be done without occasioning even greater suffering.

223 Sapontzis, Steve F. "Some reflections on animal research." *Between the Species* 1 (Winter 1984–85): 18–24.
Critiques two arguments: (1) Pro-animal argument, contending since animals cannot consent to participate in research, such research is immoral. (2) Pro-researcher argument, contending since humans a higher form of life, it is morally permissible to harm animals in research for human benefits. Concludes: (1) is trivially unsound but easily remedied; (2) is fundamentally unsound. The same moral regulations which govern human research should govern animal research.

224 Spira, Henry. "Getting at the numbers." *Animals' Agenda* (May/June 1984): 4–5, 36.
Animal rights activist Spira, interviewed by Jim Mason, describes strategies for reducing harm to animals as applied to experiments on cats at the Museum of Natural History, the LD50 test, the Draize test, repeal of New York State's Metcalf–Hatch pound seizure law, alternatives to safety testing on animals, etc. "We choose the right target on the basis of common sense. We are aware of the politics of numbers. . . . The objectives must be winnable. . . . A coalition brings little bits of power together and makes a great power. . . . I don't compromise with injustice. I want to see a world where no human or nonhuman is harmed. . . . The only moral issue I see is our obligation to work in the most effective way possible to most rapidly bring down the pain and the death. . . . We can liberate the nonhuman animals and, in the process, ourselves, for we can't be free while billions of our kin are imprisoned and their minds and bodies continu-ously violated."

225 Sprigge, Timothy L. S. "Non-human rights: An idealist perspective."
Inquiry 27 (1984): 439–61.
An absolute idealist argues for animal rights, defining having a right as having
intrinsic value which imposes obligations on those who can appreciate this value to
foster it. Animals are centers of consciousness in same general sense as are
humans; the flourishing of such centers is inherently good and its non-flourishing
inherently evil. Animals "have rights which are violated in a whole range of
experimental uses to which they are presently put, and in factory and other kinds
of farming which involve cruelty. I am convinced that man would be behaving
much more morally if there were a total ban on all experimentation on animals
which involves pain of any sort" (447).

226 Terrace, Herbert. "And now . . . the thinking pigeon." In *The understanding of animals*, ed. by G. Ferry, 261–71. Oxford: Basil Blackwell and New
Scientist, 1984.
A cognitive psychologist argues, Descartes to the contrary, that animals can think
without the use of language. There is evidence to support Darwin's view of
continuity between the mental abilities of animals and humans. I. P. Pavlov and
B. F. Skinner to the contrary, animal thinking cannot be reduced to thoughtless
reactions to stimuli. Animals can create their own internal representation of past
events and use these representations in formulating solutions to problems. Rats
can reflect upon past experience; they can represent past situations. Monkeys can
think about stimuli that are not physically present. Monkeys can think the
abstract concepts same and different and make judgments of sameness and difference. Pigeons can readily master concepts such as "tree," "water," "fish,"
"pigeons," "people." We do not know how to program the most sophisticated
computer to master the deceptively simple types of concepts pigeons can learn in a
matter of days. Pigeons can represent past sequences of events. The fundamental
question: how does an animal think without language? ". . . We have only just
begun to glimpse the nature of many long-neglected mental abilities of animals."

227 Wenz, Peter S. "An ecological argument for vegetarianism." *Ethics and
animals* 5 (1) (March 1984): 2–9.
Argues that if healthy ecosystems are of value, and the value of an ecosystem is
positively related to its degree of health, then people have prima facie obligations
to avoid harming, to repair damage and to improve the health of ecosystems.
Using land to grow large quantities of food impairs the health of the ecosystems
involved, so people have a prima facie obligation to meet their nutritional needs
through minimal use of land. Because vegetarianism enables people to do this,
they have a prima facie obligation to be vegetarians. For healthy people in our
society, the countervailing considerations are shown to be generally of little
weight. People therefore have an obligation that is not merely prima facie to try
vegetarianism for a length of time sufficient to become habituated to it.

228 Baker, Ron. *The American hunting myth.* New York: Vantage Press, 1985.
287 pp.
Comprehensive attack on American wildlife management policy and recreation
hunting. Attacks "pseudobiological" arguments used by hunters who claim

hunting is justified because (1) wildlife management is necessary to maintain healthy populations of both hunted and non-hunted species and (2) hunting maintains a system of "checks" on game populations. Attacks "nuisance" and "pseudoecological" arguments used by hunters who claim hunting is justified because (3) it eliminates "nuisance wildlife" which interfere with human interests; (4) hunters are natural predators filling an ecological niche helping to keep nature in balance; (5) "game" animals are abundant; relatively few species are legal game; endangered species are not hunted; (6) hunters, rather than extinguishing or endangering species, conserve wildlife; (7) hunters establish new areas of protected wilderness; (8) hunters' money supports wildlife restoration. Attacks slob hunter argument: (9) hunting is justified because few hunters break game laws or disrespect landowners' rights. Attacks "pseudoethical" arguments used by hunters who claim hunting is justified because (10) hunters are no more cruel than predators are to their prey; (11) humans were given dominion over animals by God; (12) animals, governed by instinct, have little emotion, pain; (13) there is no way to draw a line in evolutionary scale between animals which should be protected and those which should not. Baker finds unworthy of comment simplistic arguments used by hunters who claim that hunting is justified because (14) rights apply only to humans; (15) hunting is an American tradition based on the constitutional "right to bear arms"; (16) hunting is simply a method of securing food; (17) the primary objective is not killing but communion with nature; (18) hunters admire, respect their quarry; (19) hunting is a challenge to outsmart an animal. Wildlife management means "controlled killing of wild animals for consumption by hunters" and treats animals as species rather than individuals. Wildlife management should not be based on animals as renewable resources for human use but as sentient beings with right to live unmolested in natural surroundings.

229 Clark, Stephen R. L. "Rights of the wild and the tame." *Chronicles of Culture* 9 (8) (August 1985): 20–2.
"They [birds and animals] are our evolutionary relatives and like us do not know where they came from nor where they are going." Our relations to the wild should be governed by a vision of a sort of cosmic democracy, the ecosystemic community. Our treatment of domesticated animals should be assessed by the principle of asking whether they would rationally have consented to the bargain they live under. Domestic animals should be regarded as partners, paying their way, and being owed care and affection.

230 Fox, Michael W. "Designer animals, built-in cruelty." *Animals' Agenda* (June 1985): 30–1, 35.
"Since many of the genetic disorders of purebred cats and dogs have been created by a combination of human ignorance, egotistical self-indulgence and commercial greed, it is clear that animals' rights are being violated. . . . Let's make it ethical as well as fashionable to choose a *mongrel* or mixed breed over a purebred cat or dog. And ideally, we should obtain our companion animal from the local pound or animal shelter. . . . The case against purebred pets is based on reality and not on animal rightists' fantasies."

231 Fox, Michael W. "Duty and the beast: Treatment, empathy, and global sympathy." In *The human/animal connection,* ed. by R. L. Eaton, 52–76. Incline Village, NV: *Carnivore Journal* and Sierra Nevada College Press, 1985.

Insightful critique of our dominionistic, patriarchal values in relation to natural world which are leading to a nemesis of human civilization and which threaten survival of human species. The nemesis of science and medicine results from emphasis on interventive, mechanistic, non-holistic approach, in contrast to the preventive outlook. Nemesis of agriculture is resulting from factory farming of animals, poisoning life-support systems, loss of top soil, depletion of water supplies. Our life styles and eating habits must change; we must revolutionize agriculture, industry and medicine. The lack of respect for animal and human rights and for the sanctity and dignity of all life is a cause of our nemeses.

232 Galvin, Roger W. "What rights for animals? A modest proposal." *Pace Environmental Law Review* 2 (1985): 245–54.

Emphasizing that animals, considered as personal property, currently have no legal rights, lays out five criteria for a working definition of a legal right. Proposes three basic rights minimally necessary to ensure justice for animals (including humans): right to live out their lives in accordance with their nature, instincts, and intelligence; right to live in a habitat ecologically sufficient for normal existence; right to be free from exploitation. ". . . We do not need to eat their flesh, wear their skins, hunt or trap them, amuse ourselves at their expense, or experiment on them" (254).

233 Giannelli, Michael A. "Pro-people, pro-science, anti-vivisection." *Cogitations on Law and Government* 2 (1985): 75–83.

A psychologist criticizes United States federal laws and policies, and state laws, as inadequately protecting animals in experiments. Criticizes experiments on animals: proclaimed benefits are highly exaggerated; reliability of extrapolating animal data to humans questionable. Experimenters tend to scare people into believing that without harmful experiments on animals we would all be dead or dying. Human health is much more dependent on societal and environmental and life-style factors than on medicine. The majority of laboratory animals are in context of commercial, industrial or military testing, not in medical research. The era of unchallenged scientific exploitation of animals is over. Harmful experiments which induce diseases, inflict injuries, cause pain violate the first principle of medical ethics: "first do no harm."

234 Giannelli, Michael A. "Three blind mice, see how they run: A critique of behavioral research with animals." In (M. W. Fox and L. D. Mickley, eds. 1985, 109–64).

A psychologist reviews growing criticisms of behavioral experiments on animals, examines the responses of orthodox psychology. Animal research can and often does become an end-in-itself, a self-perpetuating industry. Claims N. E. Miller (1985) and others greatly inflate the importance of animal research to the development of therapeutic psychological techniques. Critiques the American Psychological Association's *Ethical principles for psychologists* as lip-service and paper shuffling posing as ethical guidelines. Ethical standards for animal research should be analogous to the standards now in use for experiments on humans. "... I am grieved to see my beloved profession glorify and engage in behavior so unbecoming of *civilized* humanity" (156).

235 Kellert, Stephen R. and **Berry, Joyce K.** *A bibliography of human/animal relations.* Lanham, MD: University Press of America, 1985. Not paginated.
3861 numbered, unannotated citations in alphabetical order by author, mainly 1960 through 1983, emphasizing scientific and scholarly publications in English language on human/animal relations. 66 journals and 20 major databases searched. Each citation is coded by one or more of 62 subject labels. There is an index of citation numbers under each subject label. Major emphasis on ecological interactions between humans and animals; little emphasis on human use of animals in experimentation or for use as food (factory farming of animals). Subject labels: agriculture, amphibians–reptiles, animal control, attitudes (over 700 citations), bears, bibliography-proceedings, birds, canids, children, commercial exploitation, commercial fish, communications, cross-cultural, deer, demographic characteristics of animal users, domestic animals, economic values, education (over 90 citations), endangered species, energy-minerals, environmental organizations, equids, ethics (about 300 citations), exotic-feral animals, felids, fish, fishing, forestry, history, human injury–disease, human disturbance–land use, hunting (over 475 citations), invertebrates, knowledge, landowners, laws-regulation (about 200 citations), marine mammals, mustelids, native Americans, nonconsumptive uses, off-road recreation vehicles, passerines, pets, policy, pollution, protected areas, raptors, recreation, research methods, rodents, sheep–goats, shore birds, species preference–symbolic perceptions, trade, transportation, trapping, upland game birds, urban, urbanization, water use, waterfowl, zoos–museums–aquariums.

236 Linzey, Andrew. *The status of animals in the Christian tradition.* Birmingham: Woodbrooke College, 1985, 32 pp. Informative notes and references, 28–32.
Explores twelve important ideas within Christian tradition influencing our understanding of animals: animals as creation, value of animals, dominion concept, animal sacrifice, covenant with animals, redemption of all creation, souls and rationality, sentiency and pain, duties to and rights of animals, love of creation, unity of creation, responsibility for creation. Three traditions emphasized: Biblical, Scholastic (Thomistic), saintly. "Our recognition of animal rights is at heart a question about the recognition of God's moral claim upon us to have all creatures treated with respect." Summarizes eight grounds within Christian tradition for a positive, rights approach to animals.

237 Magel, Charles. "Animals: Moral rights and legal rights." *Between the Species* 1 (Spring 1985): 9–14.
Should animals have moral standing? Should animals have legal standing? Historical views answering negatively to these questions analyzed. Contemporary arguments for answering positively presented. Views of Peter Singer, Tom Regan, Ronald Dworkin, Christopher Stone included. Analogy drawn between human slavery and animal slavery.

238 Moran, Victoria. *Compassion the ultimate ethic: An exploration of veganism.* Wellingborough, Northants: Thorsons Publishers, 1985. 128 pp. Organizations, 112–14. Bibliography, 121–5.
Interprets veganism broadly: a way of living excluding all forms of exploitation of animal kingdom, including a reverence for life, living on products of plant kingdom to exclusion of flesh, fish, fowl, eggs, honey, animal milk and its derivatives. Encourages use of alternatives to all commodities derived from animals. Discusses Albert Schweitzer and Christianity, Gandhi and *ahimsa*. Veganism in relation to world hunger, ecology, nutrition, health, losing weight, rearing children.

239 Pacheko, Alex (producer) and **Newkirk, Ingrid** (narrator). *Unnecessary fuss.* Washington, DC: People for Ethical Treatment of Animals, 1985? (Available from Focus on Animals, P.O. Box 150, Trumbull, CT 06611.)
29-minute video distilled from 70 hours of videotapes confiscated by the Animal Liberation Front from the animal research laboratory at University of Pennsylvania where Thomas Gennarelli conducted head-injury experiments, at taxpayers' expense, on baboons. The severity of the experiments, as well as the negative attitudes to animals expressed by personnel in the laboratory, have generated much "fuss" in animal rights and scientific and governmental circles. Thomas Gennarelli: "I am not willing to go on the record to discuss the laboratory studies because it has the potential to stir up all sorts of unnecessary fuss among those who are sensitive to these kinds of things." Symposium by Federation of American Societies for Experimental Biology (1986) heavily influenced by this videotape.

240 Psychologists for the Ethical Treatment of Animals. *Position papers by the dozen.* Lewiston, ME: PsyETA, 1985. 25 pp. Many references.
The American Psychological Association's *Guidelines for ethical conduct in the care and use of animals* fail to acknowledge individual animal interests and rights for their own sake. Students should have option not to conduct procedure with animals if ethically unacceptable to them. Sale of shelter animals (pound seizure) for research opposed. Harmful experiments on Great Apes cannot be justified ethically. Supports research into possibility of including animal abuse in a diagnostic definition of antisocial personality. Too many animals are used in psychological research; is too much suffering, gross abuse exists; such abuse is not dealt with adequately in the profession. Maternal deprivation experiments on primates (H. F. Harlow, S. J. Suomi) involving prolonged separation are unethical. Psychologists have recognized in their guidelines the priority of protecting human experimental subjects over unlimited academic inquiry; now, psychologists must develop principles and techniques protecting rights and welfare of research animals within context of academic freedom.

241 Rollin, Bernard E. "Animal pain." In (M. W. Fox and L. D. Mickley, eds. 1985b, 91–105).
Dilemma of pain research: scientists are loath to speak of animals experiencing pain but their work presupposes the existence of pain. The important issues on pain in animals are not scientific ones; they are moral, philosophical, conceptual. Science can no longer ignore moral status of animals.

242 Rollin, Bernard E. ''The moral status of animals in psychology.'' *American Psychologist* 40 (1985): 920–6.
Science is not value-free. No clear morally relevant differences exist to exclude animals from moral concern. Animals are ends in themselves. If animals are sufficiently similar to humans to be good models, what right do we have to do to them what we would not do to humans?

243 Rollin, Bernard E. ''Seven pillars of folly: Barriers to reason in laboratory animal welfare.'' *ATLA Alternatives to Laboratory Animals* 12 (1985): 243–7.
Discusses seven barriers blocking a rational approach to ethical questions pertaining to the use of animals in science: (1) the issues are highly emotional and tend to provoke extreme, knee-jerk reactions; (2) the ideology or common sense of science: ''science deals only with facts''; ''science is value-free''; (3) the absence of a coherent moral perspective on animals; (4) the effect of custom, habit, tradition; (5) ignorance of highly relevant information outside one's area of expertise; (6) failure to communicate across disciplines; (7) emotional, sensational polarization of opposing positions; for example, the ''Fido or the kid'' defense of animal experimentation.

244 Sapontzis, Steve F. ''Moral community and animal rights.'' *American Philosophical Quarterly* 22 (1985): 251–7.
Deals with most common objection to extending moral rights to animals: ''But they're just animals!'' Critiques three attempts to justify that intuition, all of which are based on a sense of moral community: the requirement that rights-holders must respect the rights of others, the requirement that rights-holders must be moral agents, and the requirement that rights-holders must participate in a political, economic, familial life with us. All three of these animal-excluding criteria for having moral rights are rejected, leaving the common presumption that animals are not worthy of moral rights in need of justification, if it is not to be merely an expression of anthropocentrism.

245 Singer, Peter. *The animal liberation movement: Its philosophy, its achievements, and its future.* Nottingham: Old Hammond Press, 1985? 21 pp. Reading list. Organizations.
Overview of animal liberation movement: animal equality in relation to suffering, killing; goals of movement; implications for animal research, animals as food; future of animal liberation.

246 Singer, Peter, ed. *In defense of animals.* Oxford and New York: Basil Blackwell, 1985. 224 pp. Also New York: Harper and Row, 1986. *Verteidigt der tiere,* Vienna: Neff, 1986. *Dierenactiboek,* Baarn, Netherlands: Anthos, 1986. *In difesa degli animali,* Rome: Lucarini, 1987. Japanese translation, Gi jutsu to Ningen, Tokyo, 1986.
Seventeen essays providing excellent introduction to ideas, problems, activist strategies in animal liberation movement. (1) ''Prologue: Ethics and the new animal liberation movement,'' Peter Singer, 1–10. Brief history Western antecedents to new animal liberation movement; morally condemns speciesism's denial of equal consideration of similar interests regardless species membership.

(2) "The case for animal rights," Tom Regan, 13-26. Human, nonhuman animals have equal moral rights based on equal inherent value of lives based on being experiencing subjects of a life; harmful scientific uses of animals, commercial animal agriculture, sport hunting, trapping should cease. (3) "The scientific basis for assessing suffering in animals," Marian S. Dawkins, 27-40. Definition of suffering: experiencing one of wide range of extremely unpleasant subjective (mental) states; three evidential sources for determining suffering: physical health, physiological signs, behavior. (4) "Good dogs and other animals," Stephen R. L. Clark, 41-51. "Good animal" does not mean "animal serving human interests" but should be interpreted as referring to virtues of character possessed by animal. (5) "Persons and non-persons," Mary Midgley, 52-62. "Person" not synonymous with "human being"; criterion for personhood should include social and emotional complexity, fellowship, rather than intellectual capacity. (6) "Images of death and life: Food animal production and the vegetarian option," Harriet Schleifer, 63-73. Critique of meat industry; ethical, ecological, world-hunger arguments for vegetarianism. (7) "Speciesism in the laboratory," Richard D. Ryder, 77-88. Nature, extent of animal experimentation; tactics in animal liberation; reform, alternatives, control, abolition. (8) "Brave new farm?" Jim Mason, 89-107. International movement against factory farming of animals; consumption of factory farm products should cease; 13 suggested changes in agricultural, food policy. (9) "Against zoos," Dale Jamieson, 108-17. Since liberty an important interest for most animals, the usual arguments for zoos (amusement, education, scientific research, species preservation) not strong enough to justify captivity. (10) "Animal rights, endangered species and human survival," Lewis Regenstein, 118-32. History, extent, causes of extinction, endangerment of animal species, plants; losses to animals and humans (including threat to survival). (11) "The Silver Spring monkeys," Alex Pacheko, 135-47. Detailed account of Pacheko's role in rescue of 17 monkeys from E. Taub's laboratory, Silver Springs, Maryland; trials and appeals, termination of Taub's grant by National Institutes of Health. (12) "The island of the dragon," Dexter L. Cate, 148-56. Account of Cate's attempt to stop Japanese fishermen from slaughtering thousands of dolphins (the fishermen claimed they destroyed the fish supply); Cate imprisoned, convicted, given suspended sentence, allowed to leave Japan. (13) "A matter of change," Donald J. Barnes, 157-67. Account of how Barnes in "conditioned ethical blindness" spent 16 years radiating monkeys at US Air Force School of Aerospace Medicine; his transformation into an animal rights activist. (14) "Animal rights in the political arena," Clive Hollands, 168-78. How British animal welfare movement put animals into politics; the necessity of compromise in politics. (15) "Militant voices," Philip Windeatt, 179-93. Interviews with activists: Kim Stallwood (British Union for the Abolition of Vivisection), Val Veness (Labour Member, Islington Council), Lin Murray (Hunt Saboteurs Association), Dick Course (League Against Cruel Sports), Ronnie Lee (Animal Liberation Front). (16) "Fighting to win," Henry Spira, 194-208. Spira's role in cessation of New York American Museum of Natural History mutilation experiments on cats, repeal of New York State pound seizure law, coalitions to abolish Draize and Lethal Dosage 50 tests; tactical suggestions for successful activism. (17) "Epilogue," Peter Singer, 209-11. "The animal liberation movement is here to stay."

247 Singer, Peter. "Ten years of animal liberation." *New York Review of Books* (17 January 1985): 46–52.
Overview of animal liberation movement 1975–1985: its literature, activities, achievements, goals, organizations. Reviews nine books: M. W. Fox's *Farm animals: Husbandry, behavior, and veterinary practice* (1984), A. N. Rowan's *Of mice, models, and men* [220], R. D. Ryder's *Victims of science* [114], W. Patons's *Man and mouse* (1984), T. Regan's *All that dwell therein* [193] and *The case for animal rights* [208], M. Midgley's *Animals and why they matter* [206], R. G. Frey's *Rights, killing, and suffering* (1983b) and *Interests and rights* (1980).

248 Spira, Henry. "Winning with Archimedian principles." *ATLA Alternatives to Laboratory Animals* 13 (1985): 117–22.
Describes strategies for making animal rights a significant part of scientific thinking. "Archimedian" in the sense that specific, winnable actions are used as fulcrums and levers to move progressively larger problem-weights. Examples: stopping cat-mutilation sex experiments at American Museum of Natural History; repeal of New York Metcalf–Hatch Act (pound seizure); Coalition to Abolish the LD50 and Draize Tests; establishment of Johns Hopkins Center for Alternatives to Animal Testing.

249 Wynne-Tyson, Jon, comp. *The extended circle: A dictionary of humane thought.* Fontwell, Sussex: Centaur Press, 1985. 436 pp. New York: Paragon House, 1988. Introduction, ix–xx. Bibliography, 433–6.
Impressive, massive collection of passages from thinkers of all ages, expressive of Albert Schweitzer's insight that until humans extend the circle of compassion to all living things, humans will not find peace. Arranged alphabetically by author from George D. Abraham to Émile Zola, with hundreds between. As much an anthology for the general reader as a dictionary for teachers and students of humane education.

250 Alprin, Stanley I. "Teaching reverence for life." *The Review* (publication of The Ohio Council for the Social Studies) 22 (Spring 1986): 20–5.
A professor of education explains how *becoming reverent toward life* could well become an organizing concept providing continuity for social studies instruction throughout the grades. Reverence toward life requires understanding the major forms of irreverence toward life: racial and ethnic exploitation, environmental damage, economic exploitation, maltreatment of animals, over-consumption, sexism, etc. Unless each of us gives immediate attention to these basic forms of irreverence "neither we nor our students are likely to find life worth living" (20). Sixteen suggested classroom activities described. Writings of Albert Schweitzer on the ethics of reverence for life stressed. Alprin teaches a Social Studies Methods course at Cleveland State University based on three fundamental concepts: compassion, interdependence, and reverence toward life.

251 Altman, Nathaniel. *Eating for life: The ultimate diet.* New York: Vegetus Books, 1986. 176 pp.
Heavily factual account of meat-free diet, permeated by an ethical concern for animals. Scientific nutrition (proteins, carbohydrates, fats, minerals, vitamins).

Comparative anatomy and physiology (carnivora, omnivora, herbivora, frugivora). "We can conclude that the human being is naturally neither a carnivore, omnivore, nor herbivore. Instead we are anatomically, physiologically, and instinctively suited to a diet of fruits, vegetables, nuts, and grains" (44). Advantages of a vegetarian diet and its superiority in regard to nutrition, health, strength, endurance, hygiene, economics, ecology, world food supply. "There are no sound scientific or ethical arguments in favor of meat-eating" (125). Appendices include high protein suggestions, vegetarian recipes, veganism, comparative food values of foods from plant and animal origins, vegetarian societies, vegetarian publications.

252 Barnes, Donald J. "The case against the use of animals in science." In
    (M. W. Fox and L. D. Mickley, eds. 1986, 215–25).
Psychologist Barnes spent fifteen years at US Air Force School of Aerospace Medicine, responsible for irradiation of over 1,000 monkeys and baboons. Breaking out of what he calls "conditioned ethical blindness," argues against "the ends justify the means" rationalization for experiments on animals. The only "humane" research possible is clinical research, accomplished for the sake of the individual animal (human or nonhuman) being studied.

253 Carlsson, Birgitta. "Ethical issues in animal experimentation: View of the
    animal rightist." *Acta Physiologica Scandinavica* 128 Supplementum 554 (1986):
    50–68.
"The basic stand-point of the animal rightist is that other animals than man are living beings also capable of feeling pain, distress, pleasure and joy. . . . Since sentience is a characteristic of other animals as well as man, logically the ethics applied to mankind must be extended to encompass *all* animals. For the animal rightist it is apparent that not only man, but other animals, too, must be attributed an intrinsic value. Consequently, using animals in procedures to which they would not consent, if they were able to speak for themselves, and which are carried out solely because of the means of power man possesses and the other animals lack, and are used to exploit those who are less powerful . . . is of the same brand as racism or sexism, but was given its own name, symptomatically, only 15 years ago, namely speciesism."

254 Favre, David. "Laboratory Animal Act: A legislative proposal." *Pace Environmental Law Review* 3 (1986): 123–64.
Proposes federal act governing animal experimentation, presupposing basic premisses: (1) Animals are in an evolutionary continuum with humans, with basic similarities to humans and having interests and preferences. (2) Animals feel pain in the same general sense as we do. (3) The ethical interests of animals must be weighed in considering whether and when animal experiments are justified. (4) Society, through government, should decide in weighing the arguments of the scientists against the interests of the animals, thus providing legal due process. The proposed Act controls all primate research; primates are not to be used in any research except under most extraordinary circumstances. Certain kinds of procedures and techniques will not be permitted on any animals. Painful testing procedures will be phased out within two years; Draize eye test and LD50 test

become unlawful. Violations punishable by imprisonment not more than two years or fine not more than $10,000.

255 Ferré, Frederick. "Theodicy and the status of animals." *American Philosophical Quarterly* 23 (1986): 23–34.
Theistic environmentalists are in crisis situation; times are ripe for revolution in theory. Free will defense by John Hick (1978) and George Wall (1983) of suffering in world trivializes animal suffering. Fundamental to ethics is principle of non-maleficence: any being with interests should not, all other things being equal, be subjected to frustration of those interests, and any being capable of feeling pain should not, all other things being equal, be made to feel it. Failure to incorporate this principle leaves theology vulnerable to the abuses of speciesism. A redrawing of our ethical maps, a reform in traditional doctrines of God may be required.

256 Fox, Michael W. *Agricide: The hidden crisis that affects us all*. New York: Schocken Books, 1986. 194 pp. Bibliography, 185–9.
Sharp critique of intensive farming practices. We cannot go on as we have been; we are killing the earth, killing the animals, killing ourselves; this is the true meaning of agricide. Although author a vegetarian, and "completely humane meat-eating is a contradiction in terms," endorses major reforms in farm animal husbandry, given the fact that society is (and will continue to be so for some time) omnivorous. Chapter 5, "The matter of conscience," 108–35, summarizes the ethical view.

257 Fox, Michael W. "The trouble with zoos." *Animals' Agenda* (June 1986): 8–12.
". . . Many zoos thoroughly *mis*educate; they exhibit unhealthy, neurotic animals that in no way represent the true, full range of behavior of the species. . . . Zoos are becoming facsimiles—or perhaps caricatures – of how animals once were in their natural habitat. . . . As to the claim that the best zoos are helping save species from extinction by breeding them in captivity, it may be best to let these animals become extinct if there is no place for them in the wild. . . . To put animals on exhibit as 'specimens' and 'social groups' torn from the very fabric of the ecosystems and bio-fields in which they evolved and which shaped their being as an inseparable part of the seamless web of creation, is a violation of the biological and spiritual unity of all life."

258 Grandy, John W. "Providing humane stewardship for wildlife: The case against sport hunting." In (M. W. Fox and L. D. Mickley, eds. 1986, 295–302).
"Sport hunting has no place on the National Wildlife Refuges of this nation. To even consider it is an affront to the concept of a refuge, the right of wild animals to safe haven, and the wishes of society . . . We are moving more and more to a view that wildlife should be treated with the same dignity, respect, and freedom from avoidable cruelty that we would ask for ourselves. That process can be moved miles ahead if we eliminate sport hunting—killing for fun—now" (300).

259 Humane Society of the United States. "The HSUS condemns psychological experimentation on animals." *Close-up Report*. Washington, DC: HSUS, 1986.

"Animals have been blinded and returned to the wild to test their ability to survive. They've been placed in tanks of water to record how long they will struggle against an inevitable drowning. They have been subjected to all manner of unnatural conditions, stress, and pain to see how much they can take before being driven to cannibalism. . . . Experimental psychology is particularly fiendish because it's the only area of research in which animals are deliberately tortured as part of the experiment's design. . . . It is time to condemn actively, without question or qualification, all use of animals in psychological experimentation . . . . We are presenting testimony to Congress asking that no funding be given to psychological experiments that use laboratory animals."

260 Lockwood, Randall. *Animal rights, animal welfare, and human–animal relationships: An annotated bibliography for higher education.* Washington, DC: Humane Society of US, 1986. 37 pp.

Annotated bibliography emphasizing works likely to be available in bookstores or libraries, designed to complement Lockwood's (1985b) model syllabus for a course in human–animal relationships. Nine categories: history of the humane movement and the treatment of animals, ethical and philosophical issues, laboratory animals and alternatives, farm animal welfare and humane diet, animal consciousness and the origins of intelligence, animals in captivity, ethology and sociobiology, wildlife ecology and environmental ethics, the human–animal bond.

261 Mickley, Linda D. and **Fox, Michael W.** "The case against intensive farming of food animals." In (M. W. Fox and L. D. Mickley, eds. 1986, 257–72).

Analyze two examples of farm animal systems: battery-caging of laying hens, tethering and/or crating of brood sows. Health and well-being of animals are sacrificed in name of efficiency and productivity. Ecological damage. Human costs in terms of occupational diseases and consumer health hazards. Alternatives should allow freedom of natural physical movement and activity, association with own kind, facilities for rest and sleep and body care, food and water to maintain full health, opportunity for exploration and play, reasonable spatial and territorial provisions including a visual field of "personal" space. When all costs are considered, intensive farming of animals is uneconomic.

262 Midgley, Mary. "Embarrassing relatives: Humans and other intelligent animals." *Encounter* 66 (March 1986): 40–3.

Charles Darwin and George Romanes were not embarrassed by intelligent animal relatives. The theory of evolution implies physiological and mental continuity, no qualitative distinction between humans and other animals. Later scientists, viewing animals as machines reducible to mechanistic physics, fell into a bias from which it became easy to tag ordinary views of people who work and live with animals as being "anthropomorphic," "sentimental," "anecdotal," and therefore unscientific. Ethologists (Donald Griffin, Jane Goodall, Konrad Lorenz) do not find intelligent animal relatives embarrassing.

263 Regan, Tom. ''The bird in the cage: A glimpse of my life.'' *Between the Species* 2 (Winter 1986) 42–9 and (Spring 1986): 90–9. Reprinted in [296].
Autobiography of a philosopher and animal rightist and activist.

264 Regan, Tom. ''The case for animal rights.'' In (M. W. Fox and L. D. Mickley, eds. 1986, 179–89).
Clear summary of views, arguments, themes developed in Regan's *The case for animal rights* [208]. Critiques contractarianism which holds that rights are generated by an agreement among voluntary agents to follow a set of rules intended to maximize the self-interests of the contractors; under this view all our duties regarding animals are indirect duties to humans. Criticizes the cruelty-kindness approach to animals because this view emphasizes the motive of the agent rather than the rightness or wrongness of actions. Critiques utilitarianism which holds we should do that act which will bring about the best balance between satisfaction and frustration for every individual affected by the outcome; this view recognizes no value of individual lives and can result in harming the few for the benefit of the many. Argues humans and nonhuman animals have equal moral rights, based on equal inherent value of individual lives, based on fact that individuals are experiencing subjects of a life. Harmful scientific use of animals, commercial animal agriculture, sport hunting, trapping should cease.

265 Regan, Tom. ''On civil disobedience.'' Humane Society of the United States *News* 31 (2) (Spring 1986): 2.
The time has come for every person seriously committed to the struggle for animal rights to consider taking steps leading to nonviolent civil disobedience.

266 Regan, Tom. ''Pigs in space.'' In *Heaven and earth: Essex essays in theology and ethics*, ed. by A. Linzey and P. J. Wexler, 104–18. Worthing, West Sussex: Churchman Publishing, 1986.
If one of our astronauts were to find pigs in space, exactly similar to terrestrial pigs, how should they be treated? (1) As domesticable renewable resources (things) merely for human use? (2) Or as individuals which experience pleasure and pain, have desires, beliefs, can act purposively and intentionally, are experiencing subjects of a life, have a well-being, can be harmed or benefited, whose lives have inherent value warranting respect? Regan argues for (2), urging that we radically switch from (1) to (2) in regard to terrestrial pigs as well as to extraterrestrial pigs.

267 Regan, Tom. ''The rights of humans and other animals.'' *Acta Physiologica Scandinavica* 128 Supplementum 554 (1986): 33–40.
Critique of traditional Western moral approaches to animals: Plato, Thomas Aquinas, Descartes, Kant, D. G. Ritchie, J. Bentham and J. S. Mill (utilitarianism). Claims many contemporary scientists are ''closet Cartesians'' who, blatantly at odds with common sense and Charles Darwin, deny awareness, awareness of pain, to animals. The equal inherent value of the lives of human and other animal individuals means that the violation of their rights through harmful experiments must cease. ''It is not a bigger but an empty cage we seek. . . . We do not despise either science or humanity. Only injustice'' (39–40).

268 Regan, Tom, writer and director. *We are all Noah.* 16 mm color film, also video, 29 minutes. Raleigh, NC: Culture and Animals Foundation, 1986. (Available from Focus on Animals, P.O. Box 150, Trumbull, CT 06611; also from Ecuvision, 10–12 High Street, Great Wakering, Essex, England SS3 OEQ.)
Explores ethical teachings of Judaism and Christianity in human–animal relationships (science, agriculture, hunting, trapping, companion animals) and asks how sensitive, informed Jews and Christians should think and act in regard to animals. Representative thinkers from Jewish and Christian religious communities participate. Like Noah, contemporary Jews and Christians must take responsibility for the fate of nonhuman animals. This film took the Silver Medal in the International Film and Television Festival of New York.

269 Regan, Tom, ed. *Animal sacrifices: Religious perspectives on the use of animals in science.* Philadelphia: Temple University Press, 1986. 270 pp.
Nine papers presented at international conference Religious Perspectives on the Use of Animals in Science, London, 25–27 July 1984. (1) "Introduction: Religions and the rights of animals," John Bowker, 3–14. Six important points, in regard to animals, on which religions can and do agree. (2) "The use of animals in science," Sidney Gendin, 15–60. Types, extent of animal experimentation, testing; alternatives; legislation in Australia, Canada, United Kingdom, United States. (3) "Judaism and animal experimentation," J. David Bleich, 61–114. Judaic view, attitudes, literature on use of animals. (4) "The place of animals in creation: A Christian view," Andrew Linzey, 115–48. From theological notion of the worth of creation concludes the subjugation of any being (human, fetal, or animal) to experimental procedures against its own interests morally wrong. (5) "The relevance of animal experimentation to Roman Catholic methodology," James Gaffney, 149–70. Discusses moral status of animals in Roman Catholic thought. (6) "Animal experimentation: The Muslim viewpoint," Al-Hafiz B. A. Masri, 171–97. Islamic view of animals in relation to humans; animal welfare; laws; the same moral, ethical, and legal codes should apply to the treatment of animals as are applied to humans. (7) "Hindu perspectives on the use of animals in science," Basant K. Lal, 199–212. Doctrinal Hinduism, strictly speaking, does not permit medical or exploratory or cosmetic use of animals; popular Hinduism has weaker views. (8) "Noninjury to animals: Jaina and Buddhist perspectives," Christopher Chapple, 213–35. Role of principle of noninjury (*ahimsa*) in Buddhism and Jainism in human attitudes and treatment of animals. (9) "Of animals and man: The Confucian perspective," Rodney L. Taylor, 237–63. Classical Confucianism and Neo-Confucianism on humans and animals.

270 Rollin, Bernard E. "Animal consciousness and scientific change." *New Ideas in Psychology* 4 (1986): 141–52.
Why did science change from the C. Darwin/G. Romanes affirmation of animal consciousness to behavioristic/positivistic denial or disregard? Common sense, evolution theory, physiological and behavioral analogies support animal mentation. Study of nature of conscious animals has tremendous moral implications for treatment of animals. Psychological animal research must become a moral science, much as medical research on human subjects has become.

271 Serpell, James. *In the company of animals: A study of human–animal relationships.* Oxford: Basil Blackwell, 1986. 215 pp.

An animal behaviorist studies the paradoxes and moral dilemmas inherent in our conflicting attitudes toward different types of domesticated animals, pigs and dogs for example. Critiques and contrasts the case often given against pets with an alternative view of pets as friends and companions, conducive to health. Illuminating discussion of distancing devices used in reacting to the moral dilemma: detachment, concealment, misrepresentation, shifting the blame. In recognizing animals as companions, friends and social beings, we unwittingly undermine the artificial barriers which we have set up through distancing; moral concern and feelings of guilt result. Historically informative. Notes, 188–209, valuable in introducing reader to extensive literature on domestication of animals and human–animal relationships, especially companion animals.

272 Sharpe, Robert. "The cruel deception." In (M. W. Fox and L. D. Mickley, eds. 1986, 9–18).

A scientist emphasizes the deceptive nature of claims made by vested interest groups that animal experimentation has had great benefits and will achieve major advances in human health. Increase in life expectancy is mainly due to improvements in nutrition, living and working conditions, hygiene, sanitation. Mortality for nearly all the infectious diseases was declining before specific therapies became available. If major advances in health are to be achieved, the emphasis must be on prevention; animal experimentation could have only a marginal impact. Despite the enormous scale of animal experimentation in recent years, our overall health appears to be declining. Research should be conducted humanely without animals.

273 Singer, Peter. "Animal liberation: A personal view." *Between the Species* 2 (3) (Summer 1986): 148–54.

Autobiography of a philosopher, animal liberationist, activist. The animal liberation movement should follow the examples of Gandhi and Martin Luther King (nonviolent civil disobedience).

274 Taylor, Paul W. *Respect for nature: A theory of environmental ethics.* Princeton: Princeton University Press, 1986. 329 pp. Bibliography, 315–23.

Argues for transition from anthropocentrism to egalitarian biocentrism. All living organisms have equal inherent worth; each is a unique individual pursuing its own good (welfare, well-being) in its own way. Respect for inherent worth results in four duties which we have to living organisms, owed to them as their due: (1) the duty not to harm, (2) the duty not to interfere with, (3) the duty not to break trust, (4) the duty to provide restitution when one has been wronged. Considers five priority principles for fair resolution of conflicting claims of living organisms. Legal rights for living organisms are possible. Claims the Endangered Species Act of 1973 ascribes to certain species-populations legal right to exist; claims laws prohibiting hunting, fishing, trapping in designated areas provide to animals the legal right not to be hunted, trapped, or caught by fishers. Psychologically, ethics of respect for nature requires profound moral reorientation. Argues for vegetarianism on basis of biocentrism. Although it is conceivable to ascribe moral rights (in a modified version) to animals and plants, concludes respect for inherent worth is sufficient, and recommends dropping language of moral rights for animals and plants. Interesting discussion of hunting, trapping, fishing as violations of our duty not to break trust, not to interfere with.

275 Wise, Steven M. "Of farm animals and justice." *Pace Environmental Law Review* 3 (1986): 191–227.
Examines and criticizes unjust state of present law as it concerns farm animals and the homocentricity that underlies it. Discusses erroneous ways in which society thinks about farm animals and the ways in which law drives this thinking, and the ways in which this thinking drives the law. Farm animals have no legal rights for they have no standing to litigate their interests. "Because farm animals suffer in great numbers, they make out a prima facie case both for moral and legal rights. . . . The factory-farming and genetic engineering of farm animals, based as it is upon their unregulated institutionalized exploitation in a manner that inherently and unnecessarily infringes their basic needs and concerns, is unjust. Because it is unjust it should be abolished."

276 Epstein, Robert. "A spiritual approach to the question of leather." *Between the Species* 3 (1) (Winter 1987): 19–24.
In contrast to moral, utilitarian, economic, or aesthetic points of view, approaches leather question on basis of spirituality (J. Krishnamurti's "you are the world"; Albert Schweitzer's "reverence for life"), the sacredness of being-one-with-life. Spirituality, involving non-attachment and expanded compassion, is a "pathless path"; there are no prefabricated answers. Question of what to do with one's leather possessions must be individually resolved (give away? bury? continue wearing?).

277 Fox, Michael A. "Animal experimentation: A philosopher's changing views." *Between the Species* 3 (1987): 55–60, 75, 80, 82.
Candid account of the psychology and rationale of Fox's "awakening from his dogmatic slumbers" on animal experimentation. In *The case for animal experimentation*, Fox (1986a) argued that more valuable humans may use less valuable species as means to their ends; we have no duty to prevent animal suffering; animals cannot have value in themselves. Changed view: animals are capable of faring well or ill; we harm them when we cause them to experience pain or suffering, when confining them, when depriving them of ability to behave in ways natural to their species, when killing them; no species is inherently superior or inferior to any other; no general moral justification of animal experimentation can be given. Scientists never even ask the basic moral question: is it ever morally acceptable for some beings to benefit from the harms they cause to other beings, assuming that these beings' welfare also matters? Benefiting from harms caused to other animals is prima facie wrong; it means the search for a whole new way of life, learning to live in harmony with nature. Former views were given by Fox (1978a) (1978b) (1978c) (1979–80) (1984) (1986a).

278 Fox, Michael W. "Do fish have feelings?" *Animals' Agenda* (July/August 1987): 24–5, 28–9.

". . . Many people believe that cold-blooded fish have no feeling. . . . And to some people, fish (like amphibians, reptiles, and insects) aren't even regarded as 'animals' per se, but as something more akin to insensitive motile vegetables. . . . The degree to which we are surprised at – and resistant to – the convincing evidence that fish are sentient beings capable of experiencing pain and suffering is surely a measure of how anthropocentric and empathetically detached we have become from the rest of creation. Argues for the existence of fear, as well as pain, in fish."

279 Free, Ann Cottrell. *No room, save in the heart: Poetry and prose on reverence for life – animals, nature and humankind.* Washington, DC: Flying Fox Press, 1987. 120 pp.
Nearly 100 poems and fragments of prose permeated by Albert Schweitzer's philosophy of reverence for life, reflecting "moments of deep sorrow and bright joy over the animal, nature and human condition – a distillation of tears, anger, and an aching heart." Who but a poet could capture the stir-craziness of the laboratory dog?

> Beagle, Beagle
> Circle, circle
> Circle within your cage . . .

In portraying those unfortunate beings for whom there is "no room, save in the heart," Free exemplifies her view that fifty words of powerful poetry may well have more efficacy in motivating the public to aid the animals than 5,000 words of abstract prose (Free 1987).

280 Friedman, Ruth. *Animal experimentation and animal rights.* Oryx Science Bibliographies, vol. 9. Phoenix: Oryx Press, 1987. 75 pp. Author index.
An annotated bibliography, 245 entries, preceded by a research review of animal experimentation. Emphasis on recent materials; obscure sources avoided; only materials at the undergraduate level chosen; highly technical or extremely general articles excluded. Topics with entry numbers: bibliographies, 1–3; animal experimentation issues, 4–28; philosophy, ethics, morality, 29–59; history, 60–2; US federal laws, regulations, guidelines and proposed legislation, 63–101; US state legislation, 102–5; the international scene, 106–28; laboratory tests, experiments, 129–42; primate experimentation, 143–8; experimentation in the classroom, 149–61; animal welfare activism, 162–70; specific animal experimentation cases, 171–202; alternatives, 203–45.

281 Goodall, Jane. "Spanning the gap." *Animals' Agenda* 7 (October 1987): 6–11, 51.
Goodall is interviewed by Wayne Pacelle. "I hope that the chimpanzee will act as a bridge, spanning the gap – which is only a conceptual gap – between humans on the one hand and the rest of the animal kingdom. . . . I hope that the chimpanzee will help us to understand all life . . . is entitled to freedom and dignity, and is worthy of our compassion, respect, and love. . . . Much of what goes on behind locked doors of labs is unethical. . . . I don't even like to see chimps in a zoo . . ."

282 Gruen, Lori, Singer, Peter and **Hine, David**. *Animal Liberation: A graphic guide*. London: Camden Press, 1987. 159 pp. Bibliography, 147–9. Organizations, 151–3. Cruelty-free products, 155–6. Direct action groups, 157.
Text by Gruen and Singer. Over 75 powerful graphics by Hine. Ideal for all types of reader: the intellectual will find it enlightening; the teenager will find it as gripping as an adventure-thriller but will be shocked to realize "it is for real." A dash of humor pervades portrayal of alarming facts and development of philosophical argument. Covers animal liberation movement (especially Animal Liberation Front, and People for Ethical Treatment of Animals) in United States and United Kingdom; analysis of speciesism and intellectual basis for animal liberation; maltreatment of wildlife, animals in experiments, animals used for food; suggested shift to cruelty-free life style and recommended tactics for effective activism.

283 Hare, R. M. "Moral reasoning about the environment." *Journal of Applied Philosophy* 4 (1987): 3–14.
Using basic themes from the Christian law of *agape*, Kantianism and utilitarianism, argues that the only class of beings to whom duties are owed directly is the class of sentient beings. Sentient animals (human and nonhuman) have morally relevant interests, rights. Non-sentient animals, plants, ecosystems, the biosphere, the universe have no morally relevant interests, no rights. When we make decisions, duties to sentient beings can be ascertained fairly by weighing their interests impartially, strength for strength.

284 Humane Society of the United States. "The HSUS launches campaign to end sow, hen suffering." *Close-up Report*. Washington, DC: HSUS, 1987.
"The Humane Society of the United States is fed up with America's pork and egg producers. . . . Behind virtually every slice of bacon and every innocuous egg lurks a long, hidden history of unbearable suffering. . . . For a staggering 266 million hens . . . life is spent behind the closed doors of 'factory farms' in cages so crowded that birds barely have room to move. . . . In constant discomfort, caged birds become aggressive; fighting, feather-pulling, and pecking erupt. . . . Millions of sows used for breeding endure life inside metal crates so small that they are prevented from ever turning around. Many sows are actually chained to the floor. . . . The HSUS is enlisting consumers' help to end the misery for millions of hogs and hens. . . . Be sure to mail the enclosed postcards to the National Pork Producers Council and the United Egg Producers, informing them of your pledge not to eat the breakfast of cruelty and demanding humane reforms."

285 Inglis, Jane. *Some people don't eat meat*. Potters Bar, Herts: Oakroyd Press, 1987. 31 pp. Illustrations by Henry Lees.
Perhaps the only book for children under twelve explaining the vegetarian life style and why some people follow it. Can serve as basis for parents and children to explore the topic. Appropriate for primary and elementary school libraries.

286 Linzey, Andrew. *Christianity and the rights of animals*. London: SPCK, 1987. 191 pp. New York: Crossroad/Ungar/Continuum, 1987.

A deeper theological approach to animal rights than in Linzey's earlier *Animal rights* [118]. Divine creation as gift, as source of intrinsic value, as source of the freedom of the creature to be itself before the Creator serves as foundation for Theos-rights ultimately grounded in God's right to have creation respected. ''. . . It is not that the Christian tradition has faced the question about animals and given unsatisfactory answers, rather it is that the question has never really been put. . . . The thinking . . . *has yet to be done*'' (23). Interprets dominion christologically in terms of humility and sacrificial love and service to the powerless, rather than in terms of tyranny. Interprets covenant as community including animals and as redemption including animals. Defines animal (and human) rights in terms of Spirit-filled individuals composed of flesh and blood. Applies theological theory to ways of liberation: from wanton injury, from institutionalized suffering (intensive farming, harmful experimentation, fur trapping), from oppressive control (captive animals, companion animals, culling and control), from primary and by-products of slaughter through vegetarianism.

287 Linzey, Andrew and **Regan, Tom.** *Getting it taped: The rights of animals.* Essex: Ecuvision (10–12 High Street, Great Wakering, Essex, England SS3 OEQ), 1987.
Set of three audio cassettes containing six study sessions, with study booklet, providing a comprehensive guide to the animal rights issues. Theologian Linzey and philosopher Regan are interviewed.

288 McArdle, John. ''Argumentation and anti-vivisection mythologies.'' New England Anti-Vivisection Society *Reverence for Life* 72 (5) (Nov.–Dec. 1987): 4–6, 15.
A scientist argues there is no need to use any of the anti-vivisection mythologies of the past, such as (1) ''all vivisection is scientific fraud''; (2) ''vivisection has never benefited anyone''; (3) ''all biomedical researchers are sadists''; (4) ''there are alternatives for all uses of laboratory animals.'' ''Most defenders of vivisection continue to rely on their own arrogance, social status and fear tactics, rather than accurate information. They can be defeated with a few well-chosen and clearly understood examples. . . . Vivisection is a complex issue that requires serious consideration and responses. Ethical, factual and scientific evidence all support the abolition of vivisection.''

289 McArdle, John. ''Studying death to understand life: Dissension on dissection.'' *Animals' Voice – The California Connection* 2 (September 1987): 8–9, 31.
A scientist concludes: ''Students who refuse to kill animals in order to obtain an education are showing a healthy respect for life that should be encouraged and adopted by others participating in the system. Vivisection and dissection in the classroom are not necessary consequences of obtaining a degree in biology, but rather the continuation of a tradition that no longer serves a useful or desirable purpose.''

290 Masri, Al-Hafiz B. A. *Islamic concern for animals.* Petersfield, Hants: The Athene Trust, 1987. 37 pp. in English; 54 pp. in Arabic.
A Muslim scholar draws upon the Koran and the Hadith, concluding that ''Islam

wants us to think and act in the positive terms of accepting all species as communities like us in their own right and not to sit in judgment on them according to our human norms and values'' (vii). This work is to form the basis of a larger book on animals in Islam. Topics include human dominion over animals, animals' place in nature, conservation of species, experiments on animals, factory farming of animals, beasts of burden, slaughter of food animals.

291 Moran, Victoria. ''Classroom dissection: The right to refuse.'' *Animals' Agenda* 7 (September 1987): 41.
''It is a very definite right of every student to be educated without having to perform acts that conflict with his or her personal ethics.'' Discusses procedures for students to follow in asserting such right.

292 Rachels, James. ''Darwin, species, and morality.'' *Monist* 70 (1987): 98–113.
Claims Charles Darwin, on basis of human–animal kinship and view that humans and animals differ only in degree, had more insight into the threat to traditional morality (which holds humans and animals are in separate moral categories) than did some scientists and philosophers. Criticizes unqualified speciesism held by R. Nozick (1983) and qualified speciesism (for example, view that only humans warrant full moral consideration because rationality and autonomy are correlated with human species membership). Opts for moral individualism: how an individual (human or animal) may be treated is determined, not by considering group membership but by considering the individual's particular characteristics. Discusses four stages in historical process by which ''the gradual illumination of men's minds'' of the sort provided by Darwin's theory leads to the rejection of speciesism. Agrees with Peter Singer and Tom Regan, in opposition to Nozick, that traditional morality's view of animals indefensible.

293 Regan, Tom, director. *Voices I have heard.* 56-minute film; also video. Raleigh, NC: Culture and Animals Foundation, 1987.
Emphasizes ways in which some of our more mature citizens are remedying conditions causing animal suffering – a challenge to the elderly to find fulfillment in service to animals. Documents the pro-animal activities of Cleveland Amory, Christine Stevens, Marjorie Anchel, Herbert Rackow, William and Eleanor Cave, Ethel Thurston, Hope Sawyer Buyukmichi, Dallas Pratt, Gladys Sargent, Margaret Owings, Gwenyth Snyder, Jo Stallard, Rachel Rosenthal, Virginia Fisk, Edna and Bill Mills, Clement Droz, Mary Abby, Helen Nearing, David Brower.

294 Regan, Tom. ''Animal rights and the law.'' *Saint Louis University Law Journal* 31 (1987): 513–17.
Regan applies the theory developed in *The case for animal rights* [208] to law. The moral weave of society is changing; there is growing recognition of our direct duties to animals. This growing consensus requires changes in the law. ''Real change – pervasive change – is coming.''

295 Regan, Tom. ''Ill-gotten gains.'' In *Health care ethics*, ed. by D. VanDeVeer and T. Regan, 239–64. Philadelphia: Temple University Press, 1987. It is legal for medical researchers to induce heart attacks in and experiment on and kill healthy chimpanzees for the purpose of benefiting humans with heart conditions. It is illegal to do the same to humans. Why, morally, the difference? Argues there are no morally relevant differences between chimpanzees and humans to justify such difference in treatment. Chimpanzees and humans are subjects of a life, are individuals with lives of equal inherent value, have an individual experiential welfare. Any gains from experimenting on chimpanzees (and mammals generally) for the benefit of humans are morally ill-gotten and such experiments should cease.

296 Regan, Tom. *The struggle for animal rights.* Clarks Summit, PA: International Society for Animal Rights, 1987. 208 pp. Introduction by Colman McCarthy. Informal essays and addresses conveying author's struggle "to find myself" while struggling for animal rights. (1) "The bird in the cage: A glimpse of my life," 3–43. See [263]. (2) "The case for animal rights," 44–63. See [264]. (3) "But for the sake of some little mouthful of flesh," 64–82. Moral indefensibility of eating animals. Critique of defenses used by animal eaters. Reasons for not eating animals. (4) "Animals are not our tasters; we are not their kings," 83–101. Critique of harmful experiments and safety-testing on animals. Argues for abolition. Gains we receive from using animals are morally ill-gotten, not well-gotten. (5) "The other victim," 102–6. Argues there was a violation of Goobers' (the baboon whose heart was removed for transplant in Baby Fae) rights. "What we must not do . . . is violate the rights of some in order to benefit others." (6) "Against sealing," 107–12. Testimony before Royal Commission on Seals and the Sealing Industry, March 1985. (7) "The abolition of pound seizure," 113–19. Testimony at meeting of a subcommittee of North Carolina General Assembly, 1985. ". . . Allowing pound seizure undermines the historic moral mission of our pounds and shelters. That mission is simple: to serve as the last safe haven for animals who are the victims of human irresponsibility." (8) "The role of culture in the struggle for animal rights," 120–35. Takes the offensive by appealing to the convictions of the best in our cultural heritage: Leonardo da Vinci, Mark Twain, Oscar Wilde, Walter de la Mare, John Steinbeck, William Cowper, John Ruskin, Robert Browning, C. S. Lewis, Richard Wagner, George Bernard Shaw, Luther Burbank, Porphyry, Jean Jacques Rousseau, Ovid, Oliver Goldsmith, Percy Bysshe Shelley, Pythagoras, Plutarch, Seneca, Thomas Merton, Lincoln, William Wordsworth, Isaac Bashevis Singer. (9) "Students' rights in the lab," 136–51. Testimony before Faculty Senate, North Carolina State University, 1984. Students' right not to violate the rights of animals should be protected. (10) "The promise and challenge of religion," 152–63. Animal rights must be put on the agenda of the religious community. "No movement of social justice will succeed . . . without the active participation of the religious community." (11) "Animal rights and the law," 164–73. See [193, pp. 148–64]. (12) "Civil disobedience," 174–83. Suggestions for wise use of Gandhian-type civil disobedience in struggle for animal rights. Description of June 1985 sit-in at National Institutes of Health leading to closing of Head Injury Laboratory at University of Pennsylvania (see [239]). (13) "A summing up," 184–97. Interview with Patrice Greanville on present status of animal rights movement.

297 Robbins, John. *Diet for a new America: How your food choices affect your health, happiness and the future of life on earth.* Walpole, NH: Stillpoint Publishing, 1987. 423 pp. Animal rights and environmental organizations, 384–6.

Declining the opportunity to take over Baskin–Robbins, the world's largest ice cream company, the author criticizes the "Great American Food Machine" (meat–egg–dairy industries), and spiritedly and factually argues for a vegetarian life style in the interests of humans, animals and the ecological welfare of the planet. "All creatures are endowed with the same will-to-live which we possess. . . . All God's creatures have a place in the choir." Condemns factory-farming methods of producing animals for food (chickens, pigs, cattle) and the myths promoted by lobbying organizations such as National Livestock and Meat Board, National Dairy Council, National Commission on Egg Nutrition. Reveals how the meat, dairy and egg industries have fostered a false and harmful "protein obsession." Presents studies linking animal high-protein and high-fat diets with degenerative diseases: arteriosclerosis, osteoporosis, cancer.

298 Rollin, Bernard E. "Animal pain, scientific ideology, and the reappropriation of common sense." *Journal of the American Veterinary Medical Association* 191 (1987): 1222–7.

Calls attention to scientists' neglect of animal pain, its control, and ethical issues surrounding its infliction. Scientific ideology rests on mistaken assumptions that science is value-free, that ethics is a matter of taste and preference and emotion but not reason, that animal consciousness is outside the purview of science. The common sense view affirms the reality of animal pain and consciousness. Growing moral and social pressure is forcing scientists to face moral issues in animal experimentation.

299 Rollin, Bernard E. "Environmental ethics and international justice." In *Ethics and international justice*, ed. by S. Luper-Foy. Boulder, CO: Westview Press, 1988 forthcoming.

Argues for moral concern for individual animals and humans primarily based on sentience; animals enjoy some moral value in virtue of the fact that what we do to them matters to *them*, even if they serve no purpose to anyone else. Since what we do to non-sentient natural objects (rivers, species, habitats, eco-systems) does not harm them in ways which matter to them, the value of natural objects should be interpreted as instrumental – instrumental for the use of individual sentient humans and animals. Explores international dimensions of environmental concerns and the possibilities of achieving international justice.

300 Rosen, Steven. *Food for the spirit: Vegetarianism and the world religions.* New York: Bala Books, 1987. 120 pp. Bibliography, 111–14.

Isaac Bashevis Singer, in the preface (i–ii), presents a vegetarian interpretation of religion and finds Rosen's book in confirmation. Discusses world religions (Christianity, Judaism, Islam, Zoroastrianism, Sikhism, Jainism, Buddhism, Hinduism) in relation to vegetarianism. Argues vegetarianism not merely a way to better health but an important means for developing true spiritual life. "Followers of all faiths can come to see universal compassion and its concomitant vegetarianism as a thread uniting their religions." Interesting thesis that mistranslations and literal interpretations of Christian symbolism in New Testament resulted in later Christian rationalizations for eating flesh. A chapter on early Christianity explores the life and teachings of Jesus on basis of Dead Sea Scrolls and Essene texts, supportive of vegetarianism.

301 Sapontzis, Steve F. "Everyday morality and animal rights." *Between the Species* 3 (1987): 107–18.
Abridged version of chapter 6 of Sapontzis' *Morals, reason, and animals* (see [303]). Argues for animal liberation on basis of three generally accepted moral goals: virtue (development of moral character), minimizing suffering and maximizing enjoyment, and fairness.

302 Sapontzis, Steve F. "The evolution of animals in moral philosophy." *Between the Species* 3 (1987): 61–5, 74–5.
Discusses three stages of status of animals in moral philosophy: (1) animals as natural resources, as tools to which anything can be done; (2) the be-kind-to-animals stage; (3) animal liberation stage, emphasizing justice and equality.

303 Sapontzis, Steve F. *Morals, reason, and animals.* Philadelphia: Temple University Press, 1987. 302 pp.
Argues for animal liberation on the basis of fundamental conceptions (fairness, making the world a happier place, developing moral character) in currently accepted moral tradition. Criticizes over-emphasis upon reason in traditional philosophy, concluding other factors in addition to reason determine moral value of actions, denying only rational beings can be moral, affirming some animals are virtuous agents. Argues against humanist principle, the view that all and only persons (humans) merit basic moral rights. Defends analogy between animal liberation and human liberation from racism and sexism. The burden of proof is on those who oppose animal liberation, since well-established standards of fairness, minimizing suffering and maximizing happiness, and virtue point to animal liberation. Although accepting R. G. Frey's claim that only beings with interests can have rights, attacks claim that only rational beings can have interests. Criticizes view that moral rights originate in and are restricted to a community of similarly interested, rational beings. Killing an animal painlessly is a harm to the animal because life is necessary for happiness. The dietary consequences of liberating animals will closely approximate vegetarianism. Since animals can show whether or not they desire to participate in research, a consent requirement could meaningfully be applied to animal experiments. Animal research should be governed by same moral principles which govern experiments on humans. Discusses utilitarianism (Peter Singer), moral rights theory (Tom Regan), animal liberation in relation to animal predation and environmental ethics.

304 Singer, Peter. "Animal liberation or animal rights?" *Monist* 70 (1987): 3–14.
Defends animal liberation based on utilitarian position based on equal consideration of equal interests as recognizing the inherent value of human and animal individuals. Argues Tom Regan has not shown that respect for inherent value of subjects-of-a-life is a reason for embracing a rights view rather than a utilitarian view.

305 Singer, Peter. "Letter on animal liberation." *Animals' Agenda* 7 (December 1987): 3.

". . . I have consistently stated that I support claims about 'the rights of animals' when they are used to support a political campaign. . . . Since the animal rights movement is a political, campaigning movement, there is no error in people regarding [my] *Animal liberation* [115] as the 'bible' of the movement . . . In the political arena, the terms 'animal rights movement' and 'animal liberation movement' are interchangeable." Claims asserting that animals have rights are "handy political slogans." It is theoretically conceivable that the equality principle and utilitarianism could justify some harmful research on animals so that humans benefit, also some harmful research on humans so that animals benefit. "In practice, though, I am convinced that the best way to advance the interests of animals and humans would be to stop all harmful research on animals, and use the money thereby saved in other, more productive, ways."

306 Association of Veterinarians for Animal Rights. *Position statements.* Winters, CA: AVAR, 1988. 23 pp.

Carefully stated positions on 21 aspects of animal rights. "AVAR operates under the premise that all animals have interests and inherent values that are independent of the interests and values of others. Each animal is an end in herself/himself and not simply a means to another's end. In this light, it is inappropriate to consider animals as property. Nor may the present Veterinary Oath be appropriate since it seems to predicate animal care on the basis of its effects on society and not primarily out of concern for the individual animal. . . . AVAR is opposed to declawing, ear cropping, tail docking, tail myotomies, tongue myectomies, hot iron branding, and castration or dehorning of large animals without benefit of anesthesia. . . . AVAR is opposed to so-called sport hunting and fishing, bow and arrow hunting, and all forms of trapping. AVAR does not condone hunting or fishing for food, but recognizes this will continue until vegetarianism is universal. . . . AVAR is philosophically opposed to the use of animals in research that is not directed at helping the individual subject. Although AVAR promotes an end to the dependence on animals in other types of research, it recognizes that this will continue into the foreseeable future. In the meantime, AVAR feels that certain uses of animals in research are not justifiable or appropriate and should be eliminated now. These include research into human behavior, drug addiction, and trauma. . . . AVAR is opposed to the use of animals in product testing. . . . AVAR is opposed to all so-called factory farming methods and promotes the conversion to a non-animal product based lifestyle. . . . AVAR is opposed to forms of entertainment in which injury of the animal is the object or where this is a likely or unavoidable occurrence. AVAR is opposed to the incarceration of animals in zoos or similar establishments." See [473].

307 Dombrowski, Daniel A. *Hartshorne and the metaphysics of animal rights.* Albany: State University of New York Press, 1988.

Primarily about the relationship between Hartshorne's theory of God and his thought on animals. Secondarily an attempt to use Hartshorne's process metaphysics to defend philosophic vegetarianism, to force us to take animal rights seriously, and to present a way of resolving disputes between animal rightists who emphasize value of individuals and holistic ecologists who emphasize value of species or ecosystems. Hartshorne's thought is unique in that, given his extension of low-grade sentience or feeling throughout nature, he can extend value throughout creation *and* maintain the requirement that moral patients must be conscious. Behind Hartshorne's views of God and animals is a highly reflective romanticism suggestive of Plato and Wordsworth.

308 Fox, Michael A. ''The philosopher who came in from the cold: Interview with Michael Allen Fox by Marly Cornell.'' *Animals' Agenda* 8 (March 1988): 7–10.
Candid interview with Fox, author of the only major philosophical book, *The case for animal experimentation* (1986a), defending animal experimentation, who has changed his position and now radically disagrees with several theses in that book. Fox no longer believes a general justification of animal experimentation from an ethical viewpoint is possible. ''Complete abolition [of animal experiments] in my view is possible within 15 to 25 years but a target of 50–100 years from now is more realistic and feasible. . . . If the notion of animal rights is established in law (legal standing for animals à la Christopher Stone) then people will start thinking about the moral status of animals. The notion of animal rights is becoming well established.''

309 Fox, Michael A. ''Animal research reconsidered: A former defender of vivisection struggles with his radical change of heart.'' *New Age Journal* (Jan.–Feb.1988): 14–15, 18, 20–1.
Fox shares with the reader the process of his gestalt shift or new world-view in relation to animal experimentation. A stinging attack on his *The case for animal experimentation* (1986a) by a feminist, and a critical review by a philosopher (J. Tannenbaum 1986a) led to the stunning revelation that he had compart-mentalized feeling and thought. ''. . . I had been playing the philosopher's traditional game of supposing I was a rational being above all else, a cerebrum on stilts. . . . I eventually came to believe that our basic moral obligation to avoid causing harm to other people should be extended to animals. And since I could not see any justification for our benefiting from harm caused other humans, I inferred it would likewise be wrong for us to benefit from the suffering of animals. . . . I have adopted a vegetarian diet, something that long seemed more an eccentricity than a necessity. I've also begun to change my lifestyle so that it is less dependent upon animals and animal products and is more ecologically responsible.''

310 Jacobs, Lynn. ''Amazing graze: How the livestock industry is ruining the American West.'' *Animals' Agenda* 8 (Jan/Feb 1988): 12–16, 46.
''. . . From an environmental perspective, livestock grazing is nothing short of disaster.'' Ranchers and government agencies ''are perpetuating a system – often described as 'welfare ranching' – which consumes tax dollars as quickly as range livestock consume the environment.'' Overgrazing has helped put about ten percent of the land in the United States, all in the West, in a state of severe or very severe desertification. We taxpayers subsidize the welfare ranchers through low grazing fees, predator control, fire management, soil erosion control, low property taxes, road networks. Heavy grazing adversely affects the water

cycle. ". . . The grazing industry's 'predator control' programs have been nothing less than a ruthless campaign of genocide against many animal species."

311 Linzey, Andrew and **Regan, Tom,** eds. *Animals and Christianity: A book of readings*. London: SPCK, forthcoming 1988. New York: Crossroad/ Continuum, forthcoming 1988.
Intended for use in courses at Christian colleges and universities and seminaries and by theologians and members of the Christian community in addressing the basic question: "What do we owe to the animals?" Over 50 selections: from Bible, and by saints, theologians, philosophers of religion, Christian scholars. Major topics: attitudes to creation, the problem of pain (theodicy), the question of animal redemption, reverence and responsibilities and rights, practical issues (animal experimentation, hunting, intensive farming of animals, killing animals for food, vegetarianism).

312 Linzey, Andrew and **Regan, Tom,** eds. *Compassion for animals: Readings and prayers*. Approx. 130 pp. London: SPCK, forthcoming 1988.
An anthology of biblical readings, quotations from the saints, theologians and poets, together with prayers for animals. In addition to the introduction, "Preaching the Gospel to every creature," selections are organized under the headings: creation, communion, responsibility, compassion, redemption. Also a guide to educational resources.

313 Linzey, Andrew and **Regan, Tom,** eds. *The song of creation: Poetry in celebration of animals*. Basingstoke, Hants: Marshall Pickering, forthcoming.
Over 100 poems arranged chronologically, beginning with selections from the Old and New Testaments and mainly drawing from English and American poetry in the 17th through 20th centuries. The collection is about and for animals, intended to increase understanding of their moral status, to celebrate the nonhuman creation, to promote the liberation of animals from human cruelty and oppression, to reveal profound insights into the relationship between humans and animals. Index of first lines and of over 55 poets.

314 McArdle, John. "Data and delusion: The myth of objectivity in biomedical research." *Animals' Agenda* 8 (Jan/Feb 1988): 40–2.
A scientist critiques claimed objectivity in biomedical animal research. "The image of the scientist searching for knowledge, guided only by objective analysis of the facts, is one of the great myths of our times. Biomedical researchers are basically no different than other members of society, and are just as likely to stretch the facts, manipulate information, and act as irrationally as anyone else when under attack or in defending a comfortable way of life." Identifies and discusses persistent biases characterizing most animal research: reductionism (tendency to reduce biology to a study of parts of animals or animals divorced from their natural environments); treating animals as machines; over-confidence in inter-specific extrapolations when using animal models; excessive repetition of animal experiments resulting in redundancy; white-coat syndrome (belief that laboratory research using sophisticated equipment resulting in quantification is better science than non-mechanistic investigations such as ecology and ethology);

tendency to give higher status to research on animals closest (in the evolutionary scale) to humans; tendency to make research projects "relevant" to human disease ("disease status").

315 Pluhar, Evelyn. "Moral agents and moral patients." *Between the Species* 4 (1988): 32–45.
Are we, as moral agents, all morally considerable? Are we all equally morally significant? Are there any moral patients (beings who are not moral agents but are morally considerable)? If so, are they as morally significant as we are? Critiques Tom Regan's moral rights theory. Adapts A. Gewirth's (1978) transcendental derivation of rights (the right to well-being, the right to freedom) from the concept of what it is to be an agent – a being with purposes or desires. Unlike Gewirth, applies this rights theory to animals as agents, and also as patients. Claims this Gewirthian type view applied to animals goes as far as, perhaps even further than, Regan's rights view.

316 Randall, Dick. "Wyoming's predator defender." *Animals' Agenda* 8 (Jan/ Feb 1988): 4–8.
Interviewed by Wayne Pacelle. After ten years of intensive killing of predators while in the employ of the US Fish and Wildlife Service, Randall changed his mind and is into his second decade of work with Defenders of Wildlife [482]. "The theory behind the predator killing is still there: if you kill lots of predators, especially coyotes, foxes, mountain lions, bears, then cows and sheep can sleep in peace. It's time we recognize that this philosophy has never worked, and it never will. . . . It's time we began protecting livestock, not killing predators." We taxpayers are subsidizing the cattle industry and indirectly supporting the fur industry in that when Federal agents trap predators the Fish and Wildlife Service auctions the hides to fur traders.

317 Regan, Tom and **Singer, Peter,** eds. *Animal rights and human obligations.* 2d ed. rev. and enlarged. Englewood Cliffs, NJ: Prentice-Hall, forthcoming. (See [121] for 1st ed.)
Tentative contents: (1) The Bible, "Selections." (2) Aristotle, "Animals and slavery." (3) Plutarch, "Of the eating of flesh." (4) Saint Thomas Aquinas, "Differences between rational and other creatures"; "On the killing of things and the duty to love irrational creatures." (5) René Descartes, "Animals are machines." (6) Voltaire, "A reply to Descartes." (7) Immanuel Kant, "Duties in regard to animals." (8) Jeremy Bentham, "A utilitarian view." (9) Charles Darwin, "Comparison of the mental powers of man and the lower animals." (10) Henry S. Salt, "Animals' rights." (11) D. G. Ritchie, "Why animals do not have rights." (12) Albert Schweitzer, "The ethic of reverence for life." (13) R. G. Frey, "Why animals lack beliefs and desires." (14) Bernard Rollin, "Thought without language." (15) Donald R. Griffin, "Ethology and the mental life of animals." (16) Stephen Walker, "Animal and human thought." (17) Bernard Rollin, "Animal pain." (18) Eric Eckholm, "Language acquisition in nonhuman primates." (19) Mary Midgley, "Emotion, emotiveness and sentimentality." (20) Peter Singer, "All animals are equal." (21) Lawrence Becker, "The priority of human interests." (22) James Rachels, "Darwin, species and

morality.'' (23) Tom Regan, "The case for animal rights.'' (24) R. G. Frey, "The case against animal rights.'' (25) Alan White, "Why animals cannot have rights.'' (26) James Rachels, "Why animals have a right to liberty.'' (27) Edward Johnson, "Life, death and animals.'' (28) Ruth Cigman, "Why death does not harm animals.'' (29) Tom Regan, "Why death does harm animals.'' (30) Thomasine Kushner, "Interpretations of *life* and prohibitions against killing.'' (31) Peter Singer, "Down on the farm.'' (32) Stanley Curtis, "The case for intensive farming of food animals.'' (33) Bart Gruzalski, "The case against raising and killing animals for food.'' (34) R. G. Frey, "Two conceptions of the status of vegetarianism.'' (35) Jan Narveson, "A defense of meat eating.'' (36) Sidney Gendin, "The use of animals in science.'' (37) C. R. Gallistel, "The case against governmental regulation of research using animals.'' (38) Mary Midgley, "The case for government regulation of research using animals.'' (39) R. G. Frey and Sir William Paton, "Vivisection, morals and medicine: An exchange.'' (40) Carl Cohen, "The case for the use of animals in biomedical research.'' (41) Edwin C. Hettinger, "Cohen's Defense of using animals in biomedical research: A reply.'' (42) Paul and Anne Ehrlich, "Extinction.'' (43) J. Baird Callicott, "An ecoholistic critique of animal liberation/animal rights.'' (44) Holmes Rolston III, "The value of species.'' (45) Lily-Marlene Russow, "Why do species matter?'' (46) Marti Kheel, "Nature and feminist sensitivity.'' (47) David A. Jessup, "A defense of trapping.'' (48) Nedim Buyukmichi, "A critique of trapping.'' (49) Dale Jamieson, "Against zoos.'' (50) David Chiszar, James B. Murphy, Warren Iliff, "For zoos.'' (51) Desmond Stewart, "The limits of Trooghaft.'' (52) Andrew Linzey, "Argument for animal rights within context of Christianity.'' (53) *Catholic dictionary*, "Argument against animal rights within context of Christianity.''

318 Rollin, Bernard E. *Animal consciousness, animal pain, and scientific change.*
(Title may change) Oxford: Oxford University Press, forthcoming 1989.
Argues major obstacle to getting scientists to deal with moral issues relevant to animal use is the ideology of science which is rooted in positivism and behaviorism, and which declares that science is value-free and that one cannot scientifically deal with mental states in animals. Shows how this idea arose as an historical accident. Claims highly questionable valuational changes led to abandonment of Darwinian view that animal consciousness is knowable. Discusses implications for scientific views of animal pain, also social forces which are militating in favor of a "reappropriation of common sense." Surveys progress of psychology and ethology in relation to these issues. Includes discussions of: anthropomorphism, Charles Darwin, George Romanes, C. L. Morgan and his canon, E. L. Thorndike, J. B. Watson, W. McDougall, Ludwig Wittgenstein, K. Lorenz, Noam Chomsky, Cyril Burt, R. B. Joynson, Ernest Hilgard, Donald Griffin, Marian Dawkins, G. G. Gallup, E. Titchener, J. von Uexküll, F. J. Buytendijk, W. Kohler, H. S. Jennings, R. J. Herrnstein, E. C. Tolman.

319 Ryder, Richard D. *Animal revolution: Changing attitudes towards speciesism.*
Oxford: Basil Blackwell, forthcoming.
Uses history as a framework to discuss the struggle against speciesism. Includes moral, psychological, sociological and political comment. The revolution, to a

large extent, is about the concept of "animal" itself. Topics include RSPCA, animal experimentation, wildlife, conservation, seals and whales, factory farms, the Animal Liberation Front.

320 Wenz, Peter S. *Environmental justice.* Albany, NY: State University of New York Press, 1988.
By means of a "challenge–response" technique (somewhat similar to debate or dialogue) develops a pluralistic theory of justice, providing framework within which to make just decisions consonant with environmental protection. Animals, especially endangered species, are included in consideration of benefits and burdens generated by environmental decisions and actions. Argues for a pluralistic theory of justice, using a concentric-circle perspective, including both negative rights (such as right to liberty, to life, to pursuit of happiness) and positive rights (such as right to food, to medical care). Argues wild animals have only negative rights, that domestic animals have positive rights (but domestication generally violates animals' negative right to liberty). Extended discussions of theory of moral rights for humans and animals (especially Tom Regan) and utilitarianism (Peter Singer). Also considers theories of Paul Taylor and John Rawls.

321 Akeret, Julie, director/producer. *In defense of animals.* Thirty-minute documentary film, forthcoming. (For information contact Nalith Pacific Foundation [497].)
Documentary film featuring Peter Singer, providing for the general audience the principles behind animal liberation. On-the-street interviews and clips from feature films will explore our attitudes toward animals.

322 Arnold, Sue. "Sermon in celebration of World Week of Prayer for Animals." (Given at Sydney University Wesley College Chapel, Australia, 4 October 1987.) *Between the Species* (1988 forthcoming).
"In several churches I have been told . . . 'We don't pray for animals; we pray for humans'. The Christian church stands accused of hypocrisy, of practicing apartheid against the animal kingdom. . . . If Jesus Christ walked the earth today, what would He say when He saw the way we treat His creation? Would He condone the silence of the Christian church and its congregations? Would He approve of the churches who only pray for humans? . . . Would Christ agree that the human kingdom can only advance by using, abusing and torturing the other members of His precious creation? . . . I pray for the mercy of God's love for the animal kingdom; for an end to their suffering; and I pray that the hearts of humankind will be opened to the beauty, the immeasurable magnificent beauty of the oneness and unity of His creation."

323 Lockwood, Jeffrey A. "Not to harm a fly: Our ethical obligations to insects." *Between the Species* (1988 forthcoming).
An entomologist reviews the literature on the question of sentience in insects. "Considerable empirical evidence supports the assertion that insects feel pain and are conscious of their sensations." Proposes a minimum ethic: "We ought to refrain from actions which may be reasonably expected to kill or cause nontrivial pain in insects when avoiding these actions has no, or only trivial, cost to our own

welfare.'' The burden of justification is on those who harm insects. Applies the proposed ethical principle to research and teaching, to technology. Extensive list of references cited.

324 Castignone, Silvana and **Battaglia, Luisella,** eds. *I diritti degli animali.* Genova: Centro di Bioetica, 1986. 255 pp.
Proceedings of national conference, Genova, Italy, 23–24 May 1986. 31 presentations by philosophers, scientists, jurists, historians, literati, writers, representatives of animal rights and anti-vivisection societies. (1) ''Di alcune difficoltà culturali e di una tentazione perversa inerenti ai 'diritti degli animali','' Uberto Scarpelli, 7–10. (2) ''Oltre la 'Grande Catena dell' Essere' per un'etica interspecifica,'' Silvana Castignone, 11–22. (3) ''I diritti degli animali e una nozione di progresso in etica,'' Salvatore Veca, 23–34. (4) ''Gli antichi fisici e i moderni animalisti,'' Giorgio Imbraguglia, 35–8. (5) ''La protezione degli animali: anticipazioni nel pensiero antico,'' Rosanna Muratori, 39–42. (6) ''Spunti di riflessione in materia di diritti degli animali,'' Lilia Capocaccia, 43–8. (7) ''Difficoltà e aporie lungo le ipotesi suscitate da alcune acquisizioni della psicobiologia,'' Menico Torchio, 49–56. (8) ''Una carente situazione normativa. La tutela degli animali da maltrattamenti e sevizie nel nostro ordinamento giuridico,'' Maurizio Santoloci, 57–60. (9) ''Sulle fonti dell'art. 727 Codice Penale,'' Renato Sgrò, 61–8. (10) ''Lo spirito della dichiarazione universale dei diritti dell'animale: dall'etica alla politica,'' Laura Girardello, 69–76. (11) ''La protezione giuridica degli animali di interesse zootecnico,'' Giulio Vignoli, 77–100. (12) ''Nuovi indirizzi legislativi per la tutela degli animali,'' Jacopo Virgilio, 101–18. (13) ''Diritti degli animali e orientamenti filosofico-giuridici,'' Patrizia Borsellino, 119–22. (14) ''Intervento,'' Mario Jori, 123–6. (15) ''Intervento,'' Luigi Lombardi-Vallauri, 127–8. (16) ''Uomini e animali: per una nuova alleanza,'' Giuliana Lanata, 129–32. (17) ''Animali quarto mondo,'' Gianni Vattimo, 133–8. (18) ''Le ragioni del vegetarismo. Etica e politica,'' 139–164. (19) ''Una filsofia pubblica per animali non-umani,'' Sebastiano Maffettone, 165–72. (20 ''Alla radice del rapporto uomo-animale: competizione e diversità interspecifiche,'' 173–84. (21) ''Intervento,'' Kim Buti, 185–90. (22) ''Vivisezione e diritti degli animali: quali interventi?'' Santa Giuffrida, 191–4. (23) ''Intervento,'' Adriana Beverini, 195–6. (24) ''Intervento,'' Gian Felicetti, 197–8. (25) ''L'animale maestro,'' Franco Cardini, 199–206. (26) ''Lupi, gatti e grilli parlanti,'' Carla Salviati, 207–22. (27) ''Uomini e animali: quale armonia?'' Luisella Carretta, 223–8. (28) ''Gli animali nel cinema tra immaginario e utopia,'' Maurizio Del Ministro, 229–40. (29) ''Animali delinquenti,'' Anna Mannucci, 241–8. (30) ''L'iconografia del mondo animale,'' Carlo Cormagi, 249–54. (31) ''Conclusione,'' Vico Faggi, 255–.

325 Goodwin, Frederick K. ''Reflections following the 9/28/87 meeting on the animal rights movement.'' Memorandum from Director of Intramural Research [Goodwin], National Institute of Mental Health, to Lowell T. Harmison, Deputy Assistant Secretary for Health, US Department of Health and Human Services, dated 29 September 1987. (Copies of this three-page memorandum available from People for Ethical Treatment of Animals [503]). One measure of the strength of the animal rights movement is implicit in the sensitivity and responses of the animal research community. "The stakes are enormous. The animal rights movement threatens the very core of what the Public Health Service is all about. . . . The 'bunker' strategy is no longer tenable. . . . The health research community must participate in a more pro-active posture . . ." Recommends public funding of "out front" activities – the health research community working in concert with patient groups, voluntary health organizations, the American Medical Association. "The PHS should prepare a list of Senators and Congressmen who have a special interest in health research on a particular disease. . . . It might be possible to fund special *fellowships in research advocacy*. . . . A corollary would be the creation of *research advocacy awards* that could convey some of the prestige available for traditional research awards. . . . The Department of Education should be contacted concerning infiltration of high schools by the animal rights people. . . . PHS should sponsor counter-educational efforts . . ."

326 Jones, Helen. "Autobiographical notes." *Between the Species* 4 (1988): 69–76. A life-long animal rights activist, founder and President of the International Society for Animal Rights [344], presents not only autobiography but an illuminating biography of the animal rights movement.

327 Brunois, Albert, ed. *Les droits de l'animal et la pensée contemporaine.* Colloque du vendredi 12 octobre 1984. 54 pp. Paris: Institut de France, 1984.
Eight papers by four scientists, a philosopher, jurist, doctor, pastor on the philosophical and historical aspects of the concept "animality," animals and Christianity, genetic proximity of humans and other animals, brain and thinking in humans and animals, animals in biology and medicine, rights of animals and psycho-physiological evolution, animals and the law (French, international), history and nature and status of the Universal Declaration of the Rights of Animals (see Appendix B to this *Keyguide* for an English translation of this universal declaration). (1) "Le concept d'animalité; aspects philosophiques et historiques," Françoise Armengaud, 3–8. (2) 'L'animal et la pensée religieuse," Etienne Mathiot, 9–16. (3) "Arguments génétiques de la proximité de l'homme et des autres animaux," Bernard Dutrillaux, 17–26. (4) "Cerveau et pensée chez l'homme et chez l'animal," François Lhermitte, 27–30. (5) "La pensée scientifique et l'animal, en biologie et en médecine," Etienne Wolff, 31–6. (6) "Droits de l'animal et évolution psycho-physiologique," Georges Chapouthier, 37–40. (7) "L'animal, sujet du droit," Albert Brunois, 41–8. (8) "Émergence de la Déclaration Universelle des Droits de l'animal," Jean-Claude Nouët, 49–54.

328 Castignone, Silvana, ed. *I diritti degli animali: Prospettive bioetiche e giuridiche.* Bologna: Il Mulino, 1985. 251 pp.
16 essays mainly by philosophers, all except the introduction translated from English essays previously published, on human dominion, chimpanzee communication, intensive farming of animals, animal experimentation, ethics and animals, animal rights. (1) "Introduzione," Silvana Castignone, 9–32. (2) "Vennero i Troog e dominarono la terra," Desmond Stewart, 33–42. (3) "Gli scimpanzé a scuola di comunicazione," Peter Jenkins, 43–54. (4) "Gli allevamenti intensivi," Peter Singer, 55–66. (5) "La vivisezione," Hans Ruesch,

67–78. (6) "Rispetto per la vita," Albert Schweitzer, 79–84. (7) "Il movimento per il benessere degli animali e il fondamento della morale," Timothy Sprigge, 85–92. (8) "La giustizia interspecifica," Donald VanDeVeer, 93–120. (9) "Gli animali e la liberazione della natura," Michael W. Fox, 121–8. (10) "Tutti gli animali sono uguali," Peter Singer, 129–44. (11) "Pro e contro i diritti degli animali," Tom Regan, 145–74. (12) "Il diritto di non soffrire," Tom Regan, 175–88. (13) "Il diritto di vivere," Tom Regan, 189–96. (14) "Diritto alla libertá?", James Rachels, 197–218. (15) "Gli animali possono avere diritti?", Joel Feinberg, 219–26. (16) "L'esigenza di una riforma," Tom Regan, 227–44. (17) "Bibliografia," 245–51.

329 Sharpe, Robert. *The cruel deception: The use of animals in medical research.* Wellingborough, Northants: Thorsons Publishers, 1988 forthcoming. Foreword by Julie Christie.
The author is a research chemist. The book demonstrates, using documented historical facts, how animal experiments are generally irrelevant to real advances in health. It is asserted that animal experimentation can not only prove dangerously misleading with regard to human safety but diverts attention and resources from more reliable sources of information. Part 1 is "Prevention is better than cure" and deals with the dramatic increase in life expectancy over the past 150 years, mainly in Britain but also in the United States and other countries. Part 2 is "Vivisection – The myth" and shows how misleading animal experiments can prove in medical research, drug evaluation, physiology and in the development of surgical techniques. Detailed critique of the drug industry. The final part "The alternative" looks at how most of the key discoveries throughout history were really based on human studies. A detailed examination of current alternatives is presented and the scope for real advances in health illustrated if resources could be shifted toward these approaches.

330 Moss, Douglas. "Animal rights: Broadening our perspective, broadening our base." *Between the Species* (1988 forthcoming).
Autobiography of an animal rightist and "biography" of *The Animals' Agenda*, national journal of animal rights in the United States.

331 Cave, George P. "Up from the roots." *Between the Species* (1988 forthcoming).
Autobiography of a philosopher turned animal rights activist, with perspective on the animal rights movement and an account of the origin and activities of Trans-Species Unlimited [512].

332 Dolan, Edward F. Jr. *Animal rights.* New York: Franklin Watts, 1986. 144 pp.
Intended for grades 7–10, provides information on abuses to animals in experimentation and testing, factory farming, trapping, hunting, zoos, rodeos, circuses, movies. Raises animal rights issues in non-technical manner. Provides names and addresses of organizations; recommended reading list.

333 Brockhaus, Wilhelm, et al. *Das recht der tiere in der zivilisation: Einführung in naturwissenschaft, philosophie und einzelfragen des vegetarismus.* München: F. Hirthammer Verlag, 1975. 309 pp.

20 collaborators join Brockhaus in a variety of approaches to animal rights with special emphasis on vegetarianism. Biological and historical approaches to nutrition. Economic and moral grounds for vegetarianism. Discussion of Leonard Nelson's argument for animal rights (see [75]). Religious perspectives on vegetarianism: Judaism, Christianity, Hinduism, Sikhism, Buddhism.

334 Cooper, Margaret E. *An introduction to animal law.* London: Academic Press, 1987. 213 pp.
Scholarly guide providing the lay person an understanding of the basic concepts of animal law and providing the lawyer, who is a lay person in animal science, an introduction to relevant concepts and literature. Current. Very informative. Extensive references and recommended reading lists. Mainly deals with law in Great Britain but chap. 9 is a useful, brief treatment of international legislation (Council of Europe, European Economic Community) and national laws (United States, Belgium, Norway, France, Denmark, Switzerland, Federal Republic of Germany, Canada) related to animal welfare, animals used in research, animal health, treatment and care of animals, conservation. Preface contains: extended table of statutes and table of statutory instruments for Great Britain; brief table of statutes in other nations, Council of Europe, European Economic Community; international conventions and treaties. Main categories of British laws: welfare legislation (chap. 3), animals used for scientific purposes (chap. 4), animal health (chap. 5), treatment and care of animals (chap. 6), conservation (chap. 7). Appendix 1 is a list of useful addresses of organizations, British and international.

335 Beauchamp, Tom L. and **Regan, Tom,** eds. "Animals in research." *Journal of Medicine and Philosophy* 13 (2) (May 1988): 121–221.
The entire issue is devoted to analytical essays on ethical issues inherent in biomedical and behavioral research. (1) "Introduction," Tom L. Beauchamp, 121–2. (2) "Standards for animal research: Looking at the middle," Rebecca Dresser, 123–44. Analysis of reform positions between absolute freedom of inquiry and abolition of animal experimentation. (3) "Institutional animal care and use committees: A new set of clothes for the emperor?" Lawrence Finsen, 145–58. Explores advantages and disadvantages of relying on institutional animal care and use committees to subject research proposals to ethical scrutiny. (4) "Animal welfare and animal rights," L. W. Sumner, 159–76. Argues for a moderation in the gap between the utilitarian moral outlook and the animal rights approach to animal liberation. (5) "On justifying the exploitation of animals in research," S. F. Sapontzis, 177–96. Critique of attempts to justify harmful animal experimentation; criticizes the claim that human life is more worthy than animal life, also the inference from superior worth to being entitled to exploit one's inferiors. (6) "Sinking the research lifeboat," Susan Finsen, 197–212. Argues that there is no inconsistency between Tom Regan's conclusion that in a lifeboat situation it may be necessary to sacrifice a dog in order to save human life and the demand for abolition of animal experimentation. (7) "The question is not 'Can they talk?' " Gene Namkoong and Tom Regan, 213–21. Argue that the possession of linguistic ability is not a necessary condition for possession of rights by animals.

PART III

List of selected organizations

List of Selected Organizations

The *Encyclopedia of associations* (Detroit, MI: Gale Research 1988) lists and describes a number of the larger organizations: Vol 1, National Organizations of the US; Vol. 4, International Organizations. C. R. Magel's [176] bibliography, entries 2719–3132, contains an extended list of organizations "interested in animals." *The animals' diary*, published annually by Animus, 34 Marshall St, London W1, lists many organizations (national, international) with names of publications. The Vegetarian Society (UK) Ltd. [456] publishes a list of organizations (British and international) located in the United Kingdom: "Organizations List: Food, Agriculture and Environment, Health, Animal Welfare and Third World." K. A. Reece's (1988–89) *Animal organizations and services directory*, published every other year, lists over 400 United States national and state animal welfare organizations, providing addresses, phone numbers, branch offices, year established, staff names, membership information, objectives, and materials available by mail. *The animal rights resources catalog* issued by The Fund for Animals [487] provides a wealth of information (films, books, literature, lesson plans, membership data, objectives) by assembling brochures and fliers provided by United States organizations.

Harvard University (1982) and D. Macauley (1987–88) provide useful analyses of United States organizations in the animal rights movement. Several books contain lists of organizations: [114] [158] [215]–[217] [245] [251] [282] [332]. G. Nilsson (1986) lists, along with their publications, United States and international organizations concerned about conservation and endangered species. D. Johnson (1988) provides an informative survey of worldwide organizations opposed to animal experimentation; also a table giving addresses of 40 such organizations.

The selections in the following list are drawn from a large inventory of national and international organizations. Descriptive information is provided for most of the selected organizations located in English-speaking countries. Little information is given on organizations located in non-English-speaking nations. The reader should make no inference from the absence of descriptive information to any conclusion regarding the importance of such organizations. The omission of a number of countries means only that the author had no information; probably there are important organizations in all countries. The absence of organizations from this selective list has no implication for the importance of organizations so omitted.

There are hundreds – probably thousands – of organizations in the inventory of regional, state, county, municipal, and various local groups. There has recently been an impressive proliferation of animal rights and welfare organizations. Student animal rights groups are developing at various levels: junior high school, high school, college and university, professional school.

Addresses change frequently. The nature of organizations changes with shifts in membership. "Takeovers" are not restricted to industrial corporations; they also occur in animal organizations due to the phenomenal growth and influence of the contemporary animal rights movement.

International and Multi-regional Organizations

336 European Council for Animal Welfare
c/o RSPCA United Kingdom Contact Office, Causeway, Horsham, West Sussex RH12 1HG, England.
Principal animal welfare organizations in member nations of the Council of Europe. Objectives: secure recognition as the main advocate of animal welfare in the European Community; seek introduction and enforcement of legislation protecting animals.
Publications: *Summary of legislation relative to animal welfare at the levels of the European Community and the Council of Europe.*

337 Europäische Union gegen den Missbrauch der Tiere
c/o Max Keller, Salomon-Vogelin-Strasse 3, CH-8038 Zurich, Switzerland.
National organizations and individuals concerned about the well-being and treatment of animals.
Publications: *EUMT Informationen* (quarterly); monographs.

338 Greenpeace
1611 Connecticut Ave NW, Washington, DC 20009, USA. Offices worldwide.
Objectives: protect marine life and environment.
Publications: *Greenpeace Magazine* (6/year).

339 International Association Against Painful Experiments on Animals
P.O Box 215, St Albans, Hertfordshire AL3 4RD, England.
Animal welfare organizations united to abolish painful experiments on animals.
Publications: information bulletins; films.

340 International Fund for Animal Welfare
P.O. Box 193, Yarmouth Port, MA 02675, USA.
Objectives: protect endangered animal species; mitigate animal suffering. Active

in stopping seal hunt. Campaign against maltreatment of dogs used for food in Philippines.

341 International Jewish Vegetarian Society
Bet Teva, 855 Finchley Road, Golders Green, London NW11 8LX, England.
Objectives: promote ethical vegetarianism as related to Jewish religious teachings; foster respect for all life.
  Publications: *Jewish Vegetarian* (quarterly); Jewish vegetarian cookbook.

342 International Network for Religion and Animals
P.O. Box 33061, Washington, DC 20033, USA.
Network of religious organizations including Christian, Buddhist, Jewish, Hindu, and Moslem groups, seeking to apply the moral principles of these religions to human interaction with animals.
  Publications: *Network News.*

343 International Primate Protection League
P.O. Box 776, Summerville, SC 29484, USA.
Objectives: conserve and protect nonhuman primates; protect primate habitat; reduce primate trade; improve conditions of primates in zoos and laboratories.
  Publications: *Newsletter* (quarterly); special reports.

344 International Society for Animal Rights
421 So. State St, Clarks Summit, PA 18411, USA.
Objectives: achieve rights for animals in law and practice; abolish experiments on animals. Sponsors seminars for activists; organizes demonstrations; serves as informational source for media and writers; maintains video cassette rental film library; drafts legislation, coordinates National Committee for Pet Protection to secure passage of federal legislation prohibiting National Institutes of Health from funding research involving dogs and cats acquired directly or indirectly from shelters.
  Publications: *ISAR Report* (6/year); *Educational materials on animal rights; Animals' rights* [49] by H. S. Salt; *The struggle for animal rights* [296] by T. Regan; *Experimental psychology: Experiments using animals* by J. Diner; video film *Animal liberation from laboratories*; reprints of P. Singer's review article "Animal liberation" and C. R. Magel's address "Human rights and animal rights"; various monographs.

345 North American Vegetarian Society
P.O. Box 72, Dolgeville, NY 13329, USA.
Organizes and coordinates vegetarian movement in the United States and Canada, including annual week-long conference. Sells wide variety of books and literature.
  Publications: *Vegetarian Voice* (quarterly); *Facts of vegetarianism.*

346 Europäische Union gegen den Missbrauch der Tiere
Scheuchzerstrasse 14a, CH 8006 Zurich, Switzerland.

347 World Society for the Protection of Animals
106 Jermyn St, London SW1Y, 6EE, England.

National animal welfare societies in countries worldwide organized to promote conservation and protection of animals both domestic and wild. Hold world conferences.

Publications: *Animals International* (irregular journal).

Organizations by Country

Argentina

348 Asociación para la Defensa de Los Derechos del Animal
Julian Alvarez n. 143, 1414 Buenos Aires.

349 Federacion Argentina de Entidades Protectoras de Animales
Quito 4378/3A, Codigo 1212, Buenos Aires.

350 Sociedad Argentina Protectora de Los Animales
Lavalle 1334 – Piso 30, Buenos Aires.

Australia

351 Action for Animals
P.O. Box 519, Eltham, Victoria 3095.
Direct action group; rescues animals from factory farms and laboratories; raids fur shops.

352 Animal Liberation
National Australian organization with state branches: 20 Enmore Road, Newton, New South Wales 2402; Room 16, Floor 5, 37 Swanston St, Melbourne 3000, Victoria; P.O. Box 1787, Brisbane 4001, Queensland; 118 Hutt St, Adelaide 5000, South Australia; P.O. Box 146, Inglewood 6052, Western Australia; P.O. Box 1875, Canberra City 2601, Australian Capital Territory; Environment Centre, 102 Bathurst St, Hobart 7000, Tasmania; P.O. Box 49277, Casuarina 5792, Northern Territory.
Opposes factory farming of animals for food and animal experiments in accordance with principles expressed in P. Singer's *Animal liberation* [115]. Declares animal rights: freedom to move and exercise, to fulfil behavioral instincts, to not be mutilated; right to suitable habitat and wholesome diet. Promotes vegetarianism.

Publications: *Animal Liberation Magazine* (quarterly); brochures; assists in publication of submissions to Australian Senate Select Committee of Inquiry into Animal Welfare.

353 Australian and New Zealand Federation of Animal Societies
P.O. Box 200, Greensborough 3088, Victoria, Australia, and P.O. Box 60208, Titirangi, New Zealand.
Organization of animal welfare societies and individuals to unify animal movement and to establish federal inquiry into animal welfare. Makes recommendations for statutory and other reform.

Publications: news bulletins; three volumes of documented evidence to the Australian Senate Select Committee of Inquiry into Animal Welfare.

354 Australian Association for Humane Research
Box 356, Broadway 2007, New South Wales.
Objectives: promotion of alternatives to uses of animals in medical, scientific and commercial research; eventual phasing-out of all experiments using animals.
Publications: *Newsletter* (quarterly).

355 Vegan Society
Box 467, Broadway 2007, New South Wales.

356 W. A. Group Against Vivisection
GPO Box T1798, Perth 6001, Western Australia.

Austria

357 Arbeitskreis gegen Tierversuche
Alpestrasse 43, A-6890 Lustenau.

Belgium

358 Chaîne Bleue Mondiale pour la Protection des Animaux et de la Nature
39, rue de Vise, B-1050 Brussels.
Individuals concerned with all aspects of animal welfare and nature protection. Educational programs and seminars. Distributes films.
Publications: *The Blue Chain* (quarterly).

Brazil

359 Sociedade Zoofila Educativa
Rua Dona Delfina 11, Tijuca, Cep 20 5 11, Rio de Janeiro.

Canada

360 Animal Liberation Collective
P.O. Box 148, South Durham, Quebec, JOH 2CO.

361 ARK II
542 Mount Pleasant Road, Suite 103, Toronto, Ontario M4S 2M7.
Canadian coast-to-coast animal rights network. Non-violent, civil-disobedient, direct action. Demonstrations against animal experimentation, furs.

362 Canadian Federation of Humane Societies
101 Champagne Ave, Ottawa K1S 4P3.
Membership limited to animal societies across Canada. Concerned with whaling, factory farming, transportation, pets, hunting, trapping, sealing, animals in research, humane education.
Publications: *Animals Canada* (quarterly).

363 Canadian SPCA
5215 Jean-Talon St West, Montreal, Quebec H4P 1X4.
Oldest animal welfare society in Canada. Objectives: prevention of cruelty and promotion of alternatives to use of animals in teaching and research. Concerned with companion animals and factory farming.

364 Lifeforce
Box 3117, Main Post Office, Vancouver V6B 3X6.
Branches: Box 825, North Hollywood, CA 91603, USA, and Box 210345, San Francisco, CA 94121, USA.
Motto: respect for all life. Objective: to secure animal rights around the world. Attacks animal experimentation as violation of health rights of both animals and humans. Organizes picketing, demonstrations; brings lawsuits; collects photo-documentation of harmful experiments on animals, prepares educational packets.
    Publications: *Lifeforce News; Critique of spinal cord research using animals;* special reports. Video films: *Broken promises* (spinal cord experiments on animals at University of California, Los Angeles), *Primates: Far from home* (capture, transport, experiments), *Beau & Captain: Let them live* (eye research on primates at University of California, San Francisco), *Canada: Part of the Pain* (Canadian animal research).

365 National Animal Rights Association
P.O. Box 461, Port Credit Postal Station, Mississauga, Ontario L5G 4M1.
Objectives: promote welfare of animals and a healthy, natural environment. Nonhuman animals are due the same moral consideration as humans. Special concerns: seal hunt, laboratory animals, surplus pets, fur industry, seizure of pets from animal pounds and shelters.
    Publications: *Experiments on animals: A review of the Scientific Literature.*

Chile

366 Unión de Amigos de los Animales
Casilla 3675, Santiago.

Colombia

367 Sociedad Colombiana para el Bienestar de los Animales
Carrera 30, No. 45. A. 88, Bogotá D.E.

Denmark

368 Foreningen til Dyrenes Beskyttelse i Danmark
Alhambravej 18, 1826 Frederiksberg C.
Largest and oldest animal protection organization in Denmark. Concerned about pets, farm animals, wild animals, etc.

369 Humanitarian Nordisk Samfund til Benaempelse of Misburg as Dyr
Blichers alle 32, 6700 Esbjerg.

370 Komiteen mod Dyreforsog
Malmogade 2, 2100 København.

371 Nordic Council for Animal Protection
c/o Foreningen til de Dyrenes Beskyttelse i Danmark, Alhambravej 18, DK-1826 Frederiksberg C.
Objectives: discuss problems of animal welfare in Nordic countries and to establish regulations governing animal welfare.

Finland

372 Koe-eläinten suojelu ry
Mäkelänkatu 8, 00550 Helsinki.

373 Vihrea Rists Grona Korset
Vironkatu 5c 33 SF, SF-00170 Helsinki 17.

France

374 Fondation Brigitte Bardot
83990 Saint Tropez.

375 Ligue Antivivisectionniste de France et de Défense des Animaux Martyrs
9, rue Paul Feval 75018 Paris.

376 Ligue Française contre la Vivisection
Siège Social, 4 Quai de la Fontaine 30, Nimes.

377 Ligue Française des Droits de l'Animal
21, rue Jacob 75006 Paris.
Maintains all animals possess rights and that human violation of these rights morally unjustified. Campaigns for the adoption of the universal declaration of the rights of animals.
Publications: *Les droits de l'animal et la pensée contemporaine* [327], *Déclaration universelle des droits de l'animal* (see Appendix B for English translation), *La tauromachie en France, L'animal et l'école, Violence et droits de l'animal, Dossier d'information*.

378 Notre Dame de Toute Pitié (Association Catholique pour le Respect de la Création Animale)
36 bd. Foch, 28000 Chartres.

379 Société Nationale pour la Défense des Animaux
BP 105, 94304 Vincennes.

Germany (Federal Republic)

380 Berliner Tierschutzverein für Berlin (Tierheim Lankwitz)
Dessauerstrasse 21–27, 1000 Berlin 46.

381 Bundesverband der Tierversuchsgegner
Postfach 170 110, 5300 Bonn.

382 Gesellschaft für Tierrechte e.V.
Postfach 53 66, D-7500 Karlsruhe 1.

383 Mobilization for Animals e.V.
Postfach 2626, 3400 Göttingen.

Greece

384 Hellenic Animal Welfare Society
12 Pasteur St, Athens 602.

Hong Kong

385 Royal Society for the Prevention of Cruelty to Animals
Harcourt Road, Hong Kong.

Hungary

386 Association Hongroise pour la Protection des Animaux
V. Beloiwsz, 7, Budapest.

India

387 Bombay Humanitarian League
Dayamandir, 123–27 Mumbadevi Road, Bombay 3.

388 India Welfare Board
1 First Main Road, Gandhinager 600020.
Implements the Prevention of Cruelty to Animals Act 1960 and advises the Government on amendments. Coordinates animal welfare organizations.
    Publications: *Animal Citizen* (quarterly).

Ireland

389 Irish Council Against Blood Sports
Lower Bridge St, Callan Co, Kilkenny.

390 Irish Society for the Prevention of Cruelty to Animals
1 Grand Canal Quay, Dublin 2.
Federation of member societies covering most of the counties in Ireland.

Israel

391 Animal Liberation
P.O. Box 519, Givatayim 53104.

Italy

392 Lega Anti-vivisezione
Via dei Portoghesi, 18–00186 Rome.
Publications: *Liberaimo la Cavia.*

393 Lega Antivivisezionista Campagna
Via Leopardi 90, Naples.

394 Lega Antivivisezionista Lombarda
Via Settala, 2–20129 Milan.

395 Lega Italiana dei Diritti dell'Animale
Viale del Vignola 75, 00196 Rome.

396 Unione Antivivisezionista Italiana
Corso di Porta Nuova 32, 2121 Milan.

Japan

397 Japan Animal Rights Center
4C Kama Building, 16–5 Izumi-cho, Kanagawa, Yokohama City.
Promotes animal rights throughout Japan, focusing on animal experimentation, factory farming, treatment accorded domestic and wild animals. Promotes vegetarianism.
Publications: *Newsletter.*

398 Japan Animal Welfare Society
No. 5 Tanizawa Building 7A, 3–1–82 Moto-Azabu, Minato-Ku, Tokyo 106.

Malaysia

399 Sahabat Alam Malaysia
37 Lorong Birch, Penang.

Mexico

400 Asociación de Lucha para Evitar la Crueldad con los Animales
Av. Presidente Masarik 350–201, Col. Polanco Chapoltepec, 11560, Mexico S.D.F.
Publications: *La Voz de los Animales* (4/year); *Liberacion animal* by P. Singer.

Morocco

401 Union Marocaine pour la Protection des Animaux
48, rue Colbert, Casablanca.

Netherlands

402 Anti Bont Comite
Postbus 589, 8901 BV, Leeuwarden.

403 Blue Peace
Postbus 213, Lochem.

404 De Anti-Vivisectie-Stichting
Stadhouderslaan 100, 2517 JC The Hague.

405 Dierenbevrijding een uitgave van Vrienden van DBF
Oude Gracht 36, 3511AP, Utrecht.

406 Kritisch Faunabeheer
Postbus 76, 1243 ZH 's-Graveland.

407 Lekker Dier
Jansveld 30, 3512 BG Utrecht.

408 Nederlands Bond tot Bestrijding van de Vivisectie
Jan van Nassaustraat 81, 2596 BR The Hague.

New Zealand

409 New Zealand Anti-Vivisection Society
P.O. Box 2065, Wellington.
Publications: *Mobilise*.

410 Save Animals from Experiments
P.O. Box 30139, Takapuna North, Auckland 9.
Publications: *Safeguard*.

Norway

411 Anti-Viviseksjon'en
Pilestredet 30 C, Oslo 1.

412 Dyrenes Beskytter
Arbiensgt 1, Oslo 2.

413 Natur og Ungdom
Stenersg 16, Oslo 1.

414 Nordisk Samfunn mot Smerteveoldende Dyrefosok
Hansteensgate 9, Oslo 2.

415 Norsk Liga for Dyrs Rettigheter
Box 8380 Hammersborg, Oslo 1.

Peru

416 Amigos de los Animales
Avda La Paz, 434 Of. 100, Lima.

417 Sociedad Protectors de Animales y Plantas del Peru
Manuel Bonilla 168, Miraflores, Lima.

Poland

418 Towarzystwo Opieki nad Zwierzetami
nl. Noakowskiego 4, Warsaw 00–666.

Singapore

419 Society for the Prevention of Cruelty to Animals
31 Mount Vernon Road, Singapore 1336.

South Africa

420 Animal Anti-Cruelty League
P.O. Box 49007, Rosettenville, Transvaal.

421 South African Association Against Painful Experiments on Animals
P.O. Box 430, Claremont, 7735, Cape.

Spain

422 Alternativa para la Liberación Animal
Apdo. postal 38.109–28080 Madrid.

423 Asociación para la Asistencia y el Control de los Animales
Mariano Cubi 78–80, Barcelona 6.

424 Asociate para la Defensa de los Derechos del Animal
Rambla de Catalauna 92, 470a, Barcelona 8.

Sri Lanka

425 Animals' Welfare and Protection Association
59 Gregory's Road, Colombo 7.

426 Sri Kapila Humanitarian Society
257 Circular Road, Magalle, Galle.
Promotes vegetarianism on basis of economics, medicine, ethics, religion. Acts against cruelty to animals.
Publications: *Sathuta* (annual magazine).

Sweden

427 Aktion Radde Valarna
Odens vag 40D, 517 00 Bollebygd.

428 Foreningarna Djurens Vänners Riksorganisation
c/o Ingrid Persson, Box 7029, S 250 07, Helsingborg.

429 Nordiska Samfundet mot Plagsamma Djurforsok
Drottninggatan 102, 111 60 Stockholm.
Members are individuals belonging to Nordic anti-vivisection and animal rights groups. Aims to stop painful experiments on animals. Promotes alternatives to using animals in research. Conducts grass roots campaigns for animal rights.
    Publications: *Djurens Ratt* (6/year), *InternInfo* (6/year), *Djurfront* (quarterly), *Brutus* (irregular).

Switzerland

430 Bund zum Schutze der Tiere und Verein gegen die Vivisektion
Schillerstrasse 30, CH 4053, Basel.

431 Stiftung Fonds für Versuchstierfreie Forschung
Biberlinstrasse 5, 8032 Zurich.

United Kingdom

432 Anglican Society for the Welfare of Animals
10 Chester Ave, Hawkesbury, Tunbridge Wells, Kent, England.
Works specifically for members of the Church of England but membership open to all Christians.
    Publications: *Bulletin*.

433 Animal Aid
7 Castle St, Tonbridge, Kent TN9 1BH, England.
Radical, activist, non-violent, grass roots organization with branches across United Kingdom, working for total abolition of experiments on animals. Also against factory farming of animals and all other animal abuses. "Meat Means Misery" campaign. Organizes demonstrations and protest marches. Sponsors an Animal Aid Youth Group.
    Publications: *Outrage* (6/year); *Blinded by science: Facts about sight deprivation experiments on animals* by G. Langley.

434 Animal Liberation Front
BCM Box 1160, London WC1N 3XX, England.
Umbrella group for cells of activists committed to animal rescues from laboratories, factory farms, hunts; economic sabotage against animal abuse industries.

435 The Athene Trust
3A Charles St, Petersfield, Hants GU32 3EH, England.
An educational charity to promote harmony between animals, the natural world and humans. Organizes conferences with international speakers. Provides educational packets with slide sets, videos and Teachers' Notes for schools.
Publications: *Islamic concern for animals* by Al-hafiz B. A. Masri; *Does close confinement cause distress in sows?*

436 Beauty Without Cruelty
11 Lime Hill Road, Tunbridge Wells, Kent TN1 1LJ, England.
Stresses alternatives to clothing using animal parts, and to cosmetics and products tested on animals or containing animal ingredients. Branches worldwide.
Publications: *Compassion*.

437 British Union for the Abolition of Vivisection.
16a Crane Grove, Islington, London N7 8LB, England.
Radical campaigning organization committed to total abolition of experiments on animals. Stands for animal rights. Large-scale protests at animal laboratories, including Unilever and Porton Down. "Choose Cruelty-Free" campaign for alternatives to products tested on animals or containing animal ingredients.
Publications: *Liberator* (6/year); *The military abuse of animals*; *What is vivisection?*

438 Catholic Study Circle for Animal Welfare
39 Onslow Gardens, London E18, England.
Objective: "To bring our relations with the creatures of God into harmony with His will and purpose for them and us. To try to learn from the Holy Scriptures, the example of the Saints, the rules and customs of the Church how God would have us think of His creatures and treat them. . . . There is a woeful ignorance and muddle-headedness among Catholics on the whole question of our rights and duties with regard to the entire animal creation."
Publications: *The Ark* (quarterly).

439 Chickens' Lib
P.O. Box 2, Holmfirth, Huddersfield HD7 1QT, England.
Active group dedicated to the abolition of the battery cage for laying hens. Campaign against retailers who do not sell humanely produced eggs. Demonstrate outside churches and at headquarters of large battery egg concerns.
Publications: *Newsletter*.

440 The Christian Consultative Council for Animal Welfare
c/o Revd A. Wynne, Archbishop Tenison's Grammar School, Kennington, London SE11, England.
Co-ordinates the work of the Christian animal welfare societies. Produces policy statements and prayer leaflets.

441 Committee for the Reform of Animal Experimentation
10 Queensferry St, Edinburgh EH2 4PG, Scotland.
Committee drawn from both Houses of Parliament and from the fields of animal

welfare, science and medicine, and devoted to the reform of law relating to the care and use of living animals in research.

442 Compassion in World Farming
20 Lavant St, Petersfield, Hants GU32 3EW, England.
Campaigns against violence in agriculture, be it directed toward animals, the soil, plants or humans. Attacks livestock production by intensive means. Aims at ban on the export of live animals for food. Prepares film and educational materials.
Publications: *Agscene* (6/year). Videos: *Screaming for change* (close confinement of pregnant sows) and *Hopping madness* (frogs' legs trade).

443 Farm Animal Welfare Council
Block "B", Government Buildings, Hook Rise South, Tolworth, Surbiton, Surrey KT6 7NF, England.
Co-ordinates efforts to improve farm animal welfare. Prepares policy statements and recommendations for legislative change.

444 FRAME (Fund for the Replacement of Animals in Medical Experiments)
Eastgate House, 34 Stoney St, Nottingham NG1 1NB, England.
Aim: to promote methods of research which help to reduce or eliminate the need for laboratory animals without disputing the ethics of animal experimentation. Seeks out and publishes technical information on practical alternatives.
Publications: *FRAME News* (quarterly); *ATLA* (Alternatives to Laboratory Animals): technical but also generally informative on alternatives; *The use of non-human laboratory animals in Great Britain*.

445 Hunt Saboteurs Association
P.O. Box 19, London SE22 9LR, England.
Seeks an end to all blood sports. Disrupts fox and stag hunts, and harasses anglers. Sponsors foxcubs for young people.
Publications: *Howl* (quarterly).

446 Jewish Vegetarian Society
855 Finchley Road, London NW11 8LX, England.
Promotes practice of vegetarianism within Judaic tradition.
Publications: *The Jewish Vegetarian*.

447 League Against Cruel Sports
83–87 Union St, London SE1 1SG, England.
Works to oppose hunting of all animals and buys land to create sanctuaries where hunting is prohibited.
Publications: *Cruel Sports* (quarterly).

448 London Vegans
7 Deansbrook Road, Edgware, Middx HA8 9BE, England.
Publications: *London Vegan* and restaurant guide.

449 National Anti-Vivisection Society
51 Harley St, London W1N 1DD, England.
Seeks to awaken the conscience of mankind in all parts of the world to the iniquity
of painful experiments on animals and to obtain legislation totally prohibiting all
such experiments and, subject to the aforesaid remaining the primary object of the
Society, to support, sponsor and otherwise assist any meaningful legislation for
lesser measures than total prohibition of such experiments.
Publications: *The Campaigner and Animals' Defender*

450 Quaker Concern for Animal Welfare
Webb's Cottage, Saling, Braintree, Essex CM7 5DZ, England.
Co-ordinates concern for animals among members of the Society of Friends. "Let
the law of kindness know no limits. Show a loving consideration for all God's
creatures."
Publications: *Newsletter*; brochure: *Regarding Animals: Some Quakers consider our
treatment of animals in the modern world.*

451 Royal Society for the Prevention of Cruelty to Animals
Causeway, Horsham, West Sussex RH12 1HG, England.
Founded in 1824, the oldest and largest animal welfare organization. Acts as law
enforcement agency against animal cruelty; provides practical help and assistance
to animals through animal homes and clinics; produces educational material for
distribution to schools. ". . . People should keep [companion] animals only if
they care for them properly. . . . The RSPCA is opposed to all farming methods
which result in the animals suffering and which do not allow them to enjoy their
natural environment. . . . The RSPCA is in principle opposed to the taking or
killing of wild animals or making them suffer. . . . The RSPCA is opposed to all
experiments or procedures which cause pain, suffering or distress."
Publications: *RSPCA Today* (for all members); *Animal World* (for ages 12–17);
Animal Ways (for ages 7–11); variety of booklets and educational material.

452 The Scottish Anti-Vivisection Society
121 West Regent St, Glasgow G2 2SD, Scotland.
Objectives: the total suppression of vivisection on animals, children and
unconsenting adults; the promotion of kindness to and protection of animals.
Publications: *Newsletter* (quarterly).

453 Scottish Society for the Prevention of Vivisection
10 Queensferry St, Edinburgh EH2 4PG, Scotland.
Objectives: the protection of animals from cruelty, the prevention of the infliction
of suffering, and the abolition of vivisection. A prime mover in the Animal
Welfare Year campaign 1976–77 and the campaign to "Put Animals into Politics" 1978–79.
Publications: *Annual Pictorial Review*.

454 Universities Federation for Animal Welfare
8 Hamilton Close, South Mimms, Potters Bar, Herts EN6 3QD, England.
"UFAW is a scientific society. Its function is to solve technical problems by

making calm, rational judgements based on the available facts and by carrying out investigations to increase the knowledge available. Emotion, although a great motivator, plays no part in the making of such judgements. UFAW belongs to the realist school of thought which looks mainly at the behaviour of animals with a view to reducing their suffering and improving their lot. . . . UFAW does not believe that animals have rights in the legal sense. . . . The Federation shall not engage on either side in public controversies relating to the legitimacy of making scientific experiments on animals . . . Throughout UFAW's history, realism, as opposed to sentimentality, has been the keynote of its policy." Members are college or university graduates or undergraduates, or staff members of colleges or universities, or persons with professional qualifications. Conducts symposia and workshops.

Publications: See "Universities Federation for Animal Welfare" entry in Literature Cited for a list of recent publications.

455 Vegan Society
33–35 George St, Oxford OX1 2AY, England.
Seeks to further knowledge and interest in veganism – a way of living on the products of the plant kingdom to the exclusion of flesh, fish, fowl, eggs, and animal milk and its derivatives.

Publications: *The Vegan* (quarterly); *The Cruelty-Free Shopper* (United Kingdom guide to 100% animal-free foods, toiletries, cosmetics, household goods); monographs and vegan cookery books.

456 The Vegetarian Society (UK) Ltd.
53 Marloes Road, Kensington, London W8 6LA, England. Also Vegetarian Centre and Bookshop at same address.
Aim: to improve knowledge of the benefits which a vegetarian diet has to offer in terms of ethics, health, economics, ecology and a reduction in famine in the Third World countries. Provides free literature; sponsors research; runs vegetarian cookery courses; provides speakers; issues press releases; organizes symposia, lectures, courses, exhibitions; operates mail order book service; sponsors Young Vegetarians. Video lending library.

Publications: *The Vegetarian* (6/year); *International Vegetarian Handbook* (restaurants, accommodations, travel, additives, cosmetics).

457 Zoo Check
Cherry Tree Cottage, Coldharbour, nr Dorking, Surrey RH5 6HA, England.
Aims: to prevent abuse to captive animals and wildlife; to promote conservation of animals in their natural habitat; to end the taking of animals from the wild; to phase out zoos and, where appropriate, support conservation centers.

Publications: *Newsletter*.

United States

458 Actors and Others for Animals
5510 Cahuenga Blvd, North Hollywood, CA 91601.
Individuals (with emphasis on members of the entertainment industry) united to

alleviate animal suffering through direct emergency aid and pet adoption, to promote "zero pet population" growth, to protect endangered species. Sponsors Annual Celebrity Fair.

Publications: *Actors and Others Newsletter* (annual).

459 American Anti-Vivisection Society

Noble Plaza, Suite 204, 801 Old York Road, Jenkintown, PA 19046.

Advocates abolition of experiments on animals and sponsors research on alternatives to the use of animals in research. Opposes pound seizure laws. Provides filmstrips, films, other educational material.

Publications: *The AV Magazine* (monthly); *The truth behind the discovery of insulin* by B. Reines. Co-publisher of *A critique of animal experiments on cocaine abuse* by M. L. Stephens and *A compendium of alternatives* by J. Diner.

460 American Fund for Alternatives to Animal Research

175 West 12th St, New York, NY 10011.

Stimulates and encourages the development of research and testing methods without the use of live animals; funds research grants.

Publications: *AFAAR News Abstracts* (3/year).

461 American Humane Association

9725 East Hampden Ave, Denver, CO 80231.

Objective: to prevent cruelty to animals and children. Provides educational materials. Serves as consulting and supervisory agency for use of animals in films and television. Provides materials on animal care and control.

Publications: *Directory of Animal Care and Control Agencies* (weekly); *Shoptalk* (6/year); *Advocate* (quarterly).

462 American Vegan Society

501 Old Harding Highway, Malaga, NJ 08328.

Goals: abstinence from animal products; harmlessness with reverence for life; service to humans, nature and creation.

Publications: *Ahimsa* (quarterly).

463 The American Society for the Prevention of Cruelty to Animals

441 East 92nd St, New York, NY 10028.

America's oldest animal welfare society. In addition to protecting companion animals, efforts are directed to animals bred and used for experiments, food, fur, entertainment, exhibitions and work.

Publications: *ASPCA Report* (quarterly).

464 Animal Legal Defense Fund

333 Market St, Suite 2300, San Francisco, CA 94105.

Attorneys and law students seeking to promote animal rights, and protect the lives and interests of animals through the use of legal skills. Maintains an animal rights "lawyers' network" with a listing of attorneys available for animal-related legal assistance. Sponsors annual conference on animals and the law. Offers summer legal internships for law students.

Publications: *Newsletter* (quarterly); *The animals' advocate: Investigating animal abuse.*

465 Animal Liberation Front

Underground organization whose objective is to end all forms of exploitation of animals. Conducts raids on laboratories (for example, the Head Injury Clinical Research Laboratory, University of Pennsylvania, where head-injury experiments on baboons were conducted under the supervision of Thomas Gennarelli; see [239]), factory farms and fur industries; liberates animals. Maintains student arm known as the Band of Mercy.

466 Animal Political Action Committee

P.O. Box 2706, Washington, DC 20077.

Supports the election and re-election campaigns of legislators committed to acting in the interests of animals.

Publications: *Voter's Guide* (listing records of congressional candidates and their positions regarding animal protection legislation).

467 Animal Protection Institute of America

P.O. Box 22505, Sacramento, CA 95822.

Conducts educational and informational programs to promote humane treatment of animals. Areas of concentration: slaughter of marine mammals, dog and cat population surplus, leg hold traps, distribution of humane-oriented materials to schools.

Publications: *Mainstream* (quarterly).

468 Animal Rights Information Service, Inc.

P.O. Box 20672, Columbus Circle Station, New York, NY 10023.

Produces and distributes weekly 30-minute video programs on animal rights. See Appendix C.

469 Animal Rights Coalition, Inc.

P.O. Box 20315, Minneapolis, MN 55420.

Promotes animal rights through educational and outreach programs including national conferences and demonstrations and by networking with international, national and local animal rights and environmental groups.

Publications: *ARC Newsletter.*

470 Animal Rights Network

P.O. Box 5234, Westport, CT 06881.

Objectives: to foster greater cooperation and unity within the animal rights/welfare movement; inform the public about animal rights issues.

Publications: *The Animals' Agenda* (monthly).

471 Animal Welfare Institute

P.O. Box 3650, Washington, DC 20007.

Promotes humane treatment of animals. Primary concerns include cruel trapping devices, destruction of whales and other endangered species, excessive confinement and deprivation of animals used for food, and mistreatment of animals used for experiments and tests. Presents annual Albert Schweitzer Medal for outstanding contributions to animal welfare.

Publications: *A WI Quarterly; Annual Report; Facts about furs; The bird business; Comfortable quarters for laboratory animals; Animals and their legal rights [125]; Endangered species handbook; Physical and mental suffering of experimental animals; Beyond the laboratory door; A bibliography for the use of non-affiliated members of institutional animal care and use committees; Humane biology projects;* a "Publications and Films" list.

472 Argus Archives
228 East 49th St, New York, NY 10017.
Maintains files on animal organizations in the United States and abroad; also collection of books, magazines, newspaper clippings, film reviews. Available for use by writers, researchers and members of organizations engaged in humane work.

Publications: *Animal films for humane education* and *Alternatives to pain in experiments on animals*, both by D. Pratt.

473 Association of Veterinarians for Animal Rights
530 East Putnam Ave, Greenwich, CT 06830.
Founded in 1981 under the assumption that veterinarians, by virtue of their training and career motivation, must be at the forefront in ethical issues surrounding the use of nonhuman animals. See [306] for statement of principles and positions. Provides testimony on animal-related legislation.

Publications: *Animal Rights: News and Views; Position statements*.

474 Beauty Without Cruelty USA
175 West 12th St, New York, NY 10011.
Opposed to the painful and destructive use of animals in the production of wearing apparel and toiletries. Sponsors fashion shows of simulated fur garments and other garments without fur. Provides information where to obtain cruelty-free apparel and toiletries.

Publications: *News Abstracts* (3/year); *The Compassionate Shopper* (3/year).

475 Buddhists Concerned for Animals
300 Page St, San Francisco, CA 94102.
Buddhists and other individuals concerned with society's treatment of animals. Focuses on wildlife and farm and laboratory animals. Has filed suit against the US Department of Agriculture and the University of California at Berkeley in regard to alleged use of animals under illegal conditions. Organizes grass roots activities and demonstrations.

Publications: *Newsletter; Animal Care and Animal Care Policy*.

476 Center for Animals
Tufts University School of Veterinary Medicine, 203 Harrison Ave, Boston, MA 02111.
Co-ordinates programs dealing with ethical, legal, scientific and social issues relating to the status of animals in society. Topics: veterinary ethics, veterinary

jurisprudence, companion animal demographics and control, human/animal relations, wildlife policy issues, animal research ethics, etc. Organizes seminars, conferences, workshops, research programs.

Publications: *Center for Animals Newsletter* (quarterly); *Animals and society* (proceedings of first annual conference); *Animal control* (proceedings of workshop).

477 Coalition to Abolish the LD50
P.O. Box 214, Planetarium Station, New York, NY 10024.
Organizations co-ordinated by Henry Spira, focusing on abolishing the LD50 (Lethal Dose 50%) test. LD50 measures the amount of any substance, including cosmetics, pesticides, and household products, that poisons or gasses to death 50% of a test group of laboratory animals. Has achieved a consensus among the US scientific community, regulatory agencies, and trade associations that the test serves no useful purpose and should therefore be abolished.

478 Coalition to Stop Draize Rabbit Blinding Tests
P.O. Box 214, Planetarium Station, New York, NY 10024.
Organizations co-ordinated by Henry Spira, campaigning against the Draize test which forces caustic chemicals into the eyes of conscious rabbits to observe the subsequent damage. Conducts boycotts and demonstrations. Encourages corporate funding to develop innovative nonanimal methods. Works to phase out all animal testing methods.

479 Coalition to End Animal Suffering in Experiments
P.O. Box 27, Cambridge, MA 02238.
All-volunteer, activist organization dedicated to the liberation of animals from suffering caused by abuse in animal experiments and testing, and in other areas. Conducts demonstrations against experiments and testing, against furs, against circuses, against factory farming of animals. Promotes vegetarianism.

480 Committee to Abolish Sport Hunting
Box 43, White Plains, NY 10605.
Under the leadership of Luke A. Dommer, works to abolish all forms of recreational hunting through public education and lobbying. Seeks to change current government wildlife management programs designed to provide recreational opportunities for hunters at taxpayers' expense. Runs refuge in Catskill Mountains, New York. Patrols other wildlife refuge areas. Conducts demonstrations and maintains speakers' bureau. Brings lawsuits against hunter-dominated wildlife management boards.

Publications: *Exploring the Abolition of Sport Hunting;* brochures and pamphlets.

481 Culture and Animals Foundation
3509 Eden Croft Drive, Raleigh, NC 27612.
Fosters the growth of intellectual and artistic endeavors that are united by their positive concern for animals. Entirely educational and cultural, funds research program (scholarly research into the lives and works of thinkers and artists who have expressed positive concern for animals), creativity program (original works by artists and thinkers expressing positive concern for animals), performance

program (performance and presentation of intellectual and artistic works compatible with concern for animals). Sponsored the film *We are all Noah* (see [268]) and Rachel Rosenthal's stage presentation of "The Others."

482 Defenders of Wildlife
1244 Nineteenth St NW, Washington, DC 20036.
Promotes wildlife conservation. Strives to reform the government's tax-supported predator control program which destroys thousands of bobcats, raccoons, badgers, coyotes and other animals each year. Recommends improvements in public land wildlife policies, particularly on national wildlife refuges. Works to protect marine mammals. Fights to preserve wilderness lands and wildlife refuges in Alaska.
Publications: *Defenders* (6/year); *Action Alerts*.

483 Farm Animal Reform Movement
P.O. Box 70123, Washington, DC 20088.
Purpose is to eliminate abuse of farm animals and the adverse impact of animal agriculture on human health, world hunger, environmental quality, natural resources, and national economy. Sponsors conferences to train animal rights activists in promoting public respect for animal rights. Holds demonstrations and radio and television interviews. Monitors pertinent legislation and regulations. Formed national Veal Boycott Coalition and organized picketing of restaurants serving veal.
Publications: *The FARM Report* (quarterly).

484 Focus on Animals
P.O. Box 150, Trumbull, CT 06611.
Resource center for purchase and rental of films and videotapes on animal rights and animal welfare. Teachers' guides available for each film and videotape. (See Appendix C.)
Publications: *Catalog of Films and Videotapes; Educators' Newsletter.*

485 Food Animal Concerns Trust
P.O. Box 14599, Chicago, IL 60614.
A growing program organized by Robert A. Brown to improve the welfare of farm animals by setting humane standards, finding farmers willing to follow these standards, and assisting farmers to market their products under registered trademarks. Present projects include reforms in the production of eggs and veal. Laying hens have room to move about, litter for scratching, a wholesome drug-free diet, and nest boxes for laying eggs; eggs are marketed in New York, Chicago and other metropolitan areas under the trademark NEST EGGS. Calves are raised on pasture, with a shelter, in small social groups, receiving milk and solid food, with no need for routine medication; free-range veal is sold under the trademark RAMBLING ROSE BRAND. Future plans call for similar programs in the raising of broiler chickens and pigs. FACT lobbies for federal and state legislation banning crates for raising calves.
Publications: *FACT Acts; FACT Sheets.*

486 Friends of Animals
P.O. Box 1244, Norwalk, CT 06856.
Works to reduce the number of stray animals by educating pet owners to prevent the birth of unwanted pets. Active in: banning of steel jaw leg-hold traps and US seal slaughter; elimination of wildlife destruction; boycotting of furs. Opposes hunting and animal experiments.

Publications: *Action Line* (5/year).

487 Fund for Animals
200 West 57th St, New York, NY 10019.
Regional offices in many states. Uses its resources to protect both domestic and wild animals, and to fight cruelty wherever it occurs. Projects include: saving starving horses in Texas by relocating them to the Black Beauty Ranch, saving burros scheduled to be shot in the Grand Canyon and initiating an adoption program, campaign to end the killing of dolphins in tuna fishing nets, campaign against seal hunts. Opposes animal experiments and pound seizure laws. Attacks hunting, trapping, fur trade, hunters' control of wildlife management policy.

Publications: *Newsletter; Animal Rights Resources Catalog.*

488 Humane Farming Association
1550 California St, San Francisco, CA 94109.
Produces educational materials on inhumane practices currently used in animal breeding and farming, including factory farming, genetic engineering, and slaughterhouses. Organizes national demonstrations to advocate veal boycotts; has introduced state legislation outlawing the veal crate.

489 Humane Society of the United States
2100 L St NW, Washington, DC 20037.
Committed to the prevention of cruelty to animals. Major goals include: reducing the overbreeding of cats and dogs; opposing sports hunting and trapping; educating people to respect all living things; eliminating animal abuse in entertainment; correcting inhumane conditions in zoos and other exhibitions; stopping cruelty in biomedical research and testing; strengthening anticruelty laws and their enforcement; extending animal protection into areas where there is none; monitoring federal laws to protect animals. "It is wrong to use animals for medical, educational, or commercial experimentation or research unless the following criteria are met: absolute necessity; no available alternative methods; and no pain or torment caused the animals. It is wrong to maintain animals that are to be used for food in a manner that causes them discomfort or denies them an opportunity to develop and live in conditions that are reasonably natural for them." "It is time to condemn actively, without question or qualification, all use of animals in psychological experimentation . . ." (see [259]). See [284] on the HSUS campaign to end sow and hen suffering.

Publications: *The Humane Society News* (quarterly); *Close-Up Reports; Shelter Sense* (10/year); *Kind News* (for youth, 5/year); *Children and Animals* (for teachers, quarterly); *Animal Activist Alert* (quarterly); variety of educational material (booklets, brochures, posters, films, filmstrips, etc.).

490 In Defense of Animals
21 Tamal Vista Blvd, Corte Madera, CA 94925.
Takes direct action to protect animals from cruel treatment in the name of science.
Conducts national demonstrations and protests at experimental laboratories.
   Publications: *Perspective* (quarterly).

491 Institute for the Study of Animal Problems
2100 L St NW, Washington, DC 20037.
A scientific division of the Humane Society of the US. Uses scientific methods to
analyze and investigate animal welfare issues. Studies companion animals, farm
animals, laboratory animals, and wild animals with the aim of reconciling the
needs of animals with those of humans. Holds seminars, conferences and
symposia; maintains library and speakers' bureau.
   Publications: *Advances in Animal Welfare Science* (annually, 1984/85, 1985/86,
1986/87, but discontinued); monographs.

492 Jewish Vegetarians of North America
P.O. Box 1463, Baltimore, MD 21203.
Goals: to promote vegetarianism within the Judaic tradition; to explore relation-
ship between Judaism, dietary laws and vegetarianism. Organizes Jewish veg-
etarian conferences.
   Publications: *Newsletter*.

493 Massachusetts Society for the Prevention of Cruelty to Animals
350 South Huntington Ave, Boston, MA 02130.
Founded in 1868, the MSPCA is a nonprofit animal-protection organization,
providing a wide range of services: education, legislative lobbying, publications,
law enforcement, emergency rescue operations, a farm for retired horses, a pet
cemetery, eight animal shelters and three animal hospitals.
   Publications: *Animals* (6/year); *MSPCA Animal Action* (quarterly).

494 Medical Research Modernization Committee
P.O. Box 6036, Grand Central Station, New York, NY 10163–6018.
Organization of doctors and scientists with the primary function of providing
scientific critiques of medical research using animal models. ''We have found that
many models are irrelevant or obsolete and should be replaced with alternatives to
live animal use . . .'' Advocates alternatives to animals on *scientific* rather than
any other grounds. Sponsors summer research fellowships for medical and veterinary students.
   Publications: *MRMC Newsletter* (quarterly).

495 Millennium Guild
40 Central Park South, New York, NY 10019.
Vegetarians who believe that all creatures have a right to life. Opposes killing of
animals for food, use of animals in research, furs, feathers from slain birds,
leather, ivory. Sponsors radio broadcasts; distributes books and leaflets; bestows
awards.

496 Ministries for Animals
1442A Walnut St, Berkeley, CA 94709.
Encourages exploration of animal rights issues by members of religious groups. Has initiated an interdenominational resolution on animal rights. Attempts to raise consciousness within the religious community through education. Encourages programs supporting animal ministries, a ministry to all of creation. Also plans to develop curriculum and educational materials for use in seminaries. Developing book collection on animals.
Publications: *Anima/l: A Magazine of Religion and Animal Rights*.

497 Nalith Pacific Foundation
2649 Benvenue Ave, Berkeley, CA 94704.
Objective: to promote wholistic culture, including respect for the rights of human and animal life. Emphasizes inter-species relationships, animal rights, vegetarianism, ecologically sensitive agriculture. Projects include a print and audiovisual library, assistance to students working toward degrees, establishment of vegetarian organic-foods restaurant, workshops in animal rights, vegetarianism and organic agriculture. Is supporting a film on animal liberation featuring Peter Singer (see [321]).
Publications: *Commonsense* (journal).

498 National Alliance for Animal Legislation
P.O. Box 77012, Washington, DC 20013.
An informational and "empowering" resource offering legislative seminars, workshops and publications to grass roots groups across the nation. Goal: the building of a self-sustaining network of informed and active citizens in every district in the nation which could eventually translate into an effective "animal rights constituency."

499 National Anti-Vivisection Society
53 West Jackson Blvd, Suite 1550, Chicago, IL 60604.
Objectives: to eliminate the use of animals in biomedical research and to encourage nonanimal alternatives. Provides educational material and organizes rallies and demonstrations.
Publications: *NAVS Bulletin* (quarterly). Monographs: *Reverence for life: An ethic for high school biology curricula, Personal care with principle: A guide to choosing cruelty-free cosmetics and products from major manufacturers, Toward an ethic of animal use in psychology research by J. Diner, Military madness* by J. Diner, *Animal rites: A research perspective* by J. Diner, *Test tubes with whiskers* by J. Diner. Co-publisher of: *A critique of animal experiments on cocaine abuse* by M. L. Stephens, *A compendium of alternatives* by J. Diner, *Maternal deprivation experiments in psychology* by M. L. Stephens.

500 National Association for the Advancement of Humane Education
P.O. Box 362, East Haddam, CT 06423.
A division of the Humane Society of the United States. Seeks to improve education programs nationally by providing leadership, practical ideas and materials. Holds regional and professional development workshops.
Publications: *Kind News* (children's newspaper, 5/year); *Children and Animals*

(quarterly); *National Humane Education Curriculum Guide* (see [177]); brochures for teachers and students.

501 National Coalition to Protect Our Pets

3123 Cahuenga Boulevard West, Los Angeles, CA 90068.
Coalition of eleven groups working to ban nationwide use and procurement of pound and shelter animals for scientific purposes.

Informational packet: "Sacrificing pound or shelter animals for medical or veterinary school training: A needless waste." Also informational packet on scientific disadvantages and false economy of using random source animals for research and testing.

502 The New England Anti-Vivisection Society

333 Washington St, Suite 850, Boston, MA 02108.
Goal: total abolition of the use of live animals for research, experimentation or testing. Three major activities: education, legislative action, search for alternative methods of research.

Publications: *Reverence for Life* (5/year). Monographs: *Environmental experiments on animals* by B. Kuker-Reines, *Psychology experiments on animals* by B. Kuker-Reines. Co-publisher of: *A critique of animal experiments on cocaine abuse* by M. L. Stephens and *Maternal Deprivation experiments in psychology* by M. L. Stephens.

503 People for the Ethical Treatment of Animals

Box 42516, Washington, DC 20015.
Educational and activist group opposing all forms of oppression and exploitation of animals. Conducts rallies and demonstrations against major institutionalized forms of maltreatment: the exploitation and abuse of animals in experimentation and testing, and the factory farming of animals for food. Uses photos and video-taped evidence of maltreatment of animals in laboratories (for example, the Head Injuries Laboratory using baboons at the University of Pennsylvania; see [239]). Also campaigned against the shooting of animals at the US Defense Department Wound Laboratory. Promotes vegetarianism. Sells cruelty-free soaps and health care products, books on animal rights and vegetarianism.

Publications: *PETA News* (6/year); *PETA Kids* (first issue Spring 1988; interesting, heavily illustrated, for elementary students and their teachers); *How to be an activist* (64 pages of ideas, illustrated with cartoons); *Animal liberation* (record album, also in cassette and compact disc).

504 Psychologists for the Ethical Treatment of Animals

P.O. Box 87, New Gloucester, ME 04260.
Seeks to ensure proper treatment of animals used in psychological research and education. Urges revision of curricula to include ethical issues in the treatment of animals. Works for reduction in numbers of animals used, and promotes use of alternative methods. Has developed a scale of invasiveness that reliably classifies, in terms of pain and harm, the range of contemporary experimental procedures involving animals.

Publications: *PsyETA* (2/year); *Position papers by the dozen* (see [240]); *Humane innovations and alternatives in animal experimentation* (annual).

505 Schweitzer Center of the San Francisco Bay Institute
   P.O. Box 254, Berkeley, CA 94701.
Is an activity of the Congress of Cultures, a California nonprofit public benefit corporation. Sponsors lectures on interspecies issues. Conducts a humane education research project in several elementary schools.
   Publications: *Between the Species* (quarterly interdisciplinary and philosophical journal); *Earning a degree in interspecies studies or humane education* (pamphlet outlining strategies for earning degrees from both traditional and non-traditional academic institutions; also describing the Schweitzer Center's own certificate programs and study offerings).

506 Scientists Center for Animal Welfare
   4805 St Elmo Ave, Bethesda, MD 20817.
Organization of scientists believing that humane concern for animals should be incorporated into all areas of science. Seeks alternatives to use of animals where possible. Provides forum for the discussion of public accountability, public policy, and the scientist's responsibilities regarding animal care and use. Monitors legislation on laboratory animal welfare; conducts conferences, workshops, training for investigators; maintains speakers' bureau.
   Publications: *Newsletter* (quarterly); *Effective animal care and use committees; Scientific Perspectives on Animal Welfare.*

507 Scientists' Group for Reform of Animal Experimentation
   147-01 Third Ave, Whitestone, NY 11357.
Physicians and veterinarians; research scientists; students. Promotes a humane approach to animal experimentation in biological research, testing and education. Encourages the development and use of alternatives to animal experimentation. Opposes pound seizure of animals for experiments. Opposes invasive and distressing experiments on vertebrate animals by high school and college students.
   Publications: position papers.

508 Sea Shepherd Conservation Society
   P.O. Box 7000-S, Redondo Beach, CA 90277. Also Box 48446, Vancouver, British Columbia V7X 1A2, Canada and Box 114, Plymouth PL1 1DR, England.
A nonviolent direct action group, under the leadership of Paul Watson, owning and operating its own ships, policing illegal whaling activities; sinks and/or destroys illegal whaling ships, but without injury to human life. Campaigns to end whaling, sealing and destructive wildlife exploitation. Was the first to "paint" white seal pups with a harmless yet indelible dye to protect them from club-swinging sealers. Organizing a boycott of Danish goods as a result of the continuing slaughter of pilot whales in the Danish Faroe Islands. Plans to confront Japanese whalers in the Antarctica. Is pressuring Sea World to release four killer whales captured in Iceland.
   Publications: *Sea Shepherd Log.*

509 Society for Animal Protective Legislation
   P.O. Box 3719, Georgetown Station, Washington, DC 20007.

Objectives: to help enact legislation that will provide protection for animals. Compiles information for Congress and sends letters to members urging support for particular national and state legislation.

510 Society for the Study of Ethics and Animals

c/o Department of Philosophy, Virginia Polytechnic Institute and State University, Blacksburg, VA 24061-0126.

Organizes programs for meetings of the Society in conjunction with annual meetings of the American Philosophical Association.

Publications: SSEA *Newsletter*.

511 Student Action Corps for Animals

P.O. Box 15588, Washington, DC 20003-0588.

Assists young people to become animal activists. High school, junior high and college students comprise its membership. Aids in organization of student animal rights groups; provides information on animal rights issues. Co-ordinates a Stop Dissection Campaign. "Saying 'no' to dissection is a matter of *rights*: the animal's right and the student's right! The animal has a right not to be harmed and killed. The student has a right to act on his/her beliefs." Attacks factory farming of animals for food and encourages vegetarianism.

Publications: *SACA News* (quarterly); *Suggestions for Student Groups; Say no to dissection; Live and let live* (teacher guide, grades 4–8); *Action Alerts;* informative posters.

512 Trans-Species Unlimited

Box 1553, Williamsport, PA 17703. Branch offices: Box 20697, Columbus Circle Station, New York, NY 10023; P.O. Box 81, Staten Island, NY 10312; 215 Godwin Ave, Box 152, Midland Park, NJ 07432; P.O. Box 27762, Philadelphia, PA 19118; P.O. Box 805859, Chicago, IL 60680.

Nonviolent, grass roots, activist, educational national organization (see [331]). Objectives: to see the total elimination of animal exploitation and abuse, to elucidate and articulate the interconnections between human and nonhuman rights, and to provide a bridge between philosophical concern with animal rights as a moral issue and grass roots activism for the liberation of animals, both human and nonhuman. Recent campaigns include: a legislative ban on the use of the decompression chamber (used in animal euthanasia) in Pennsylvania; joint Canadian/United States protest against Woodstream Corporation (the principal manufacturer of leg-hold traps); promotion of spaying/neutering to prevent over-population of companion animals; strengthening of regulations for the protection of laboratory animals; co-ordination of Humans Against Rabbit Exploitation (international coalition against commercial exploitation of rabbits for meat and fur); campaign against barbiturate addiction experiments on cats at Cornell University; campaign for a Fur-Free America; campaigns against bird shoots and factory farming of animals for food. Offers free university course, film series, and presentations on animal rights.

Publications: *T S Update;* action alerts and fliers.

513 United Action for Animals
205 East 42nd St, New York, NY 10017.
Promotes research using modern, sophisticated methods in place of live animals. Seeks legislation to provide federal funding of existing alternatives and the development of new alternatives.

Publications: Reports; recent brochures: *Animal agony in addiction research; Your child or your dog?* ("The argument 'Your child or your dog' is nothing but a sham.")

514 Vegetarian Information Service, Inc.
Box 5888, Washington, DC 20014.
Educational organization to inform the public on the merits of a vegetarian way of life. The educational programs focus on government agencies, mass media, and vegetarian activists. Issues news releases; books appearances on radio and television interview shows.

Publications: *Newsletter*; leaflets.

515 The Voice of Nature Network, Inc.
P.O. Box 68, Westport, CT 06881.
A new venture, attempting to reach a mass television audience on a regular basis on animal rights and ecology. Produces, co-produces, fosters and distributes television programming, including documentaries, TV news-magazines, interview shows, dramas, public service announcements, and commercials. Use of cable television will be maximized. Three rules governing approach: (1) Educate, entertain and inspire; avoid preachiness. (2) Produce quality programming suitable for broadcasting by commercial and public stations. (3) Show people that practicing the ethic of equal consideration toward animals and nature need not preclude enjoying life to the fullest.

Publications: flier. Possible VNN programs include Children's "Prestige" Series; "Crossfire"–Type Debate on Animal, Environmental and Social Issues; Animal Hospital Show; Video Magazine – A TV version of *The Animals' Agenda*; Spotlight on Humane and Environmentalist Leaders and Organizations; Helping Animals in Distress.

Venezuela

516 Amigos de los Animales
Apartado Postal 47.651, Caracas 104–A.

Yugoslavia

517 Medobcinsko Drustvo Proti Mucenju Zivali
Jubljanske Regije, 61000 Ljubljana, Trubarjeva 16.

Literature Cited

Works annotated in Part II are not included in this list. Twenty-five items in this list are not cited elsewhere in the text; either they were discovered too late or they do not logically fit into the structure of the *Keyguide*; such items are identified by the expression "(Not cited)". The notation "⟨   ⟩" is used to indicate either when the item was written or when it was first published (for example "Kant, I. ⟨1785⟩ 1962").

Abse, J. 1980. *John Ruskin*. London: Quartet Books.
Acton, H. B. 1950. *Aristotelian Society Proceedings* 24: 95–110.
———. 1961. Animal pleasures. *Massachusetts Review* 2: 541–8.
Adams, R. 1978. *The plague dogs*. New York: Knopf.
Addis, W. E. and Arnold, T. 1957. *A Catholic dictionary*. (See "Animals, lower.") St Louis, MO: B. Herder.
Adler, J. and Hager, M. 1988. Emptying the cages. *Newsweek* 111 (23 May): 59–60. (Not cited.)
Adler, M. J. 1967. *The difference of man and the difference it makes*. New York: Holt, Rinehart and Winston.
———. 1985. *Ten philosophical mistakes*. New York: Macmillan.
Aelian. ⟨3rd cent.⟩ 1958–59. *On the characteristics of animals*. 3 vols. Trans. A. F. Scholfield. London: Heinemann.
Agius, A. 1970. *God's animals*. London: Catholic Study Circle for Animal Welfare.
Aiken, W. 1980. Animals and rights: A reply to Regan. (In Polish.) *Etyka* 18: 119–23.
Albright, J. L. 1986. Animal welfare and animal rights. *National Forum* 66 (Winter): 34–7.
Alcott, W. A. 1838. *Vegetable diet*. Boston: Marsh, Capen and Lyon.
Alfort. 1895. *Zoophilist* 15: 259–64.
Allen, D. W. 1983. The rights of nonhuman animals and world public order: A global assessment. *New York Law School Law Review* 28: 377–429.
American Association for the Advancement of Science. 1986. *Effects of regulation on the use of animals in biomedical research*. Washington, DC: AAAS.

American Medical Association. 1923. *Defense of research pamphlets*. Chicago: AMA. (By 1923 the Bureau on Protection of Medical Research had published 29 pamphlets, emphasizing the benefits of animal research in various areas of medicine. Included: (1) "The ethics of animal experimentation," J. R. Angell, 8 pp. (2) "Fruits of Medical research with aid of anesthesia and asepticism," C. W. Eliot, 16 pp. (3) "What vivisection has done for humanity," W. W. Keen, 16 pp. (4) "Medical control of vivisection," W. B. Cannon, 8 pp. (5) "Some characteristics of antivivisection literature," W. B. Cannon, 16 pp. (6) "Animal experimentation and its benefits to mankind," W. B. Cannon, 24 pp. (7) "The influence of antivivisection on character," W. B. Cannon, 43 pp. (8) "Antivivisection legislation: Its history, aims, and menace," W. B. Cannon, 11 pp.)
American Veterinary Medical Association. n.d. *Food animal welfare*. Schaumberg, IL: AVMA.
Animal Legal Defense Fund. 1987. *The animals' advocate: Investigating animal abuse*. San Francisco: ALDF.
Animal Welfare Institute. 1985. *Beyond the laboratory door*. Washington, DC: AWI.
———. 1987. *Factory farming: The experiment that failed*. Washington, DC: AWI.
Anscombe, G. E. M. 1958. *Intention*. Oxford: Blackwell.
Aquinas, T. ⟨13th cent.⟩ 1947. *Summa theologica*. Vol. 2. Trans. Fathers of the English Dominican Province. New York: Benziger Brothers.
———. ⟨13th cent.⟩ 1956. *On the truth of the Catholic faith: Summa contra gentiles*. Vol. 3, pt. 2. Trans. V. J. Bourke. New York: Hanover House.
Aristotle. ⟨4th cent. BC⟩ 1908–52. *The works of Aristotle*. 12 vols. Ed. W. D. Ross. Oxford: Clarendon Press.
Armstrong, D. M. 1973. *Belief, truth and knowledge*. Cambridge: Cambridge University Press.
Armstrong, S. B. 1976. *The rights of nonhuman beings: A Whiteheadian study*. Ph.D. diss., Bryn Mawr College. Ann Arbor, MI: University Microfilms International.
Armstrong-Buck, S. 1986. Whitehead's metaphysical system as a foundation for environmental ethics. *Environmental Ethics* 8: 241–59.
Arnold, E. V. 1958. *Roman Stoicism*. New York: Humanities Press.
Aronson, L. R. and Cooper, M. L. 1976. Letter on cat sex experiments at American Museum of Natural History. *Science* 194: 784–5.
Association for Biomedical Research. 1984. *State laws concerning the use of animals in research*. Waltham, MA: ABR.
Attfield, R. 1983a. Methods of ecological ethics. *Metaphilosophy* 14: 195–208.
———. 1983b. *The ethics of environmental concern*. Oxford: Basil Blackwell.
———. 1983c. Christian attitudes to nature. *Journal of the History of Ideas* 44: 369–86.
Augustine. ⟨4th–5th cents.⟩ 1964. *On free choice of the will*. Trans. A. S. Benjamin and L. H. Hackstaff. Indianapolis, IN: Bobbs-Merrill.
———. ⟨4th–5th cents.⟩ 1966. *The Catholic and Manichaean ways of life*. Trans. D. A. and I. J. Gallagher. Washington, DC: Catholic University of America Press.
Austin, J. B. 1887. *The duties and rights of man*. London: Trübner.
Austin, P. 1885. *Our duty towards animals*. London: Kegan, Paul.

Bacon, F. ⟨1627⟩ 1907. *The essays: The wisdom of the ancients, New Atlantis*. London: Cassell.
Baky, J. S., ed. 1980. *Humans and animals*. The Reference Shelf, vol. 52, no. 4. New York: H. W. Wilson. (Not cited.)
Balls, M. et al., eds. 1983. *Animals and alternatives in toxicity testing*. London: Academic Press.
Balz, A. G. A. 1951. Cartesian doctrine and the animal soul. In *Cartesian studies*, 106–57. New York: Columbia University Press.
Banton, M. 1987. *Animal rights*. New York: Franklin Watts. (For grades 7–9.)
Barad, J. 1988 forthcoming. Aquinas' inconsistency on the nature and treatment of animals. *Between the Species*.

Barbour, I. G., ed. 1972. *Earth might be fair*. Englewood Cliffs, NJ: Prentice-Hall.
——. 1973. *Western man and environmental ethics*. Reading, MA: Addison-Wesley Publishing.
Bargen, R. 1979. *The vegetarian's self-defense manual*. Wheaton, IL: Quest Books.
Barnard, N. D. 1987. AIDS research: Problems with the animal model. *Animals' Agenda* (September): 44-6.
Bateson, P. 1986. When to experiment on animals. *New Scientist* 109 (20 February): 30-2.
Bayle, P. ⟨1697⟩ 1734-38. *Dictionary, historical and critical*. 5 vols. London: J. J. and P. Knapton.
Bean, M. J. 1983. *The evolution of national wildlife law*. New York: Praeger.
Becker, L. C. 1983. The priority of human interests. In *Ethics and animals*, ed. by H. B. Miller and W. H. Williams, 225-42. Clifton, NJ: Humana Press.
Benison, S. 1970. In defense of medical research. *Harvard Medical Alumni Bulletin* 44 (3): 16-23.
Benison, S. et al. 1987. *Walter B. Cannon*. Cambridge, MA: Belknap Press.
Benn, S. I. 1967a. Equality, moral and social. In *The Encyclopedia of philosophy*, ed. by P. Edwards, vol. 3, 38-42. New York: Macmillan and Free Press.
——. 1967b. Egalitarianism and equal consideration of interests. In *Equality*, ed. by J. R. Pennock and J. W. Chapman, 61-78. New York: Atherton.
——. 1977. Personal freedom and environmental ethics: The moral inequality of species. In *Equality and freedom*, ed. by G. Dorsey, 401-24. Dobbs Ferry, NY: Oceana Publications.
Bennett, E. R. 1985. Logic and the limits of animal liberation. In *Advances in animal welfare 1984*, ed. by M. W. Fox and L. D. Mickley, 89-99. Boston: Martinus Nijhoff.
Bennett, J. 1964. *Rationality*. London: Routledge and Kegan Paul.
——. 1976. *Linguistic behaviour*. London: Cambridge University Press.
——. 1988 forthcoming. Thoughtful brutes. *Proceedings and addresses of the American Philosophical Association*, vol. 62, Supplement.
Bennon, R. 1984. Research guide for animal welfare and animal rights. *Legal Reference Services Quarterly* 4 (Fall): 3-31.
Benson, J. 1975. Hog in sloth, fox in stealth: Man and beast in moral thinking. In *Nature and conduct*, ed. by R. S. Peters, 265-80. London: Macmillan.
——. 1978. Duty and the beast. *Philosophy* 53: 529-49.
Bentham, J. ⟨18th-19th cents.⟩ 1891. *Theory of legislation*. Trans. from French of E. Dumont by R. Hildreth. London: Kegan Paul, Trench, Trübner.
——. ⟨18th-19th cents.⟩ 1962. *The works of Jeremy Bentham*. 11 vols. Ed. J. Bowring. New York: Russell and Russell.
——. ⟨18th-19th cents.⟩ 1970. *Of laws in general*. In *The collected works of Jeremy Bentham*, ed. by H. L. A. Hart. London: University of London, Athlone Press.
Berdoe, E. 1903a. *Broken gods: A reply to Mr. Stephen Paget's "Experiments on animals"*. London: Swan Sonnenschein.
——. 1903b. *A catechism of vivisection*. London: Swan Sonnenschein.
Berman, L. A. 1982. *Vegetarianism and the Jewish tradition*. New York: KTAV Publishing House.
Bernard, C. ⟨1865⟩ 1949. *An introduction to the study of experimental medicine*. Trans. H. C. Greene. New York: Henry Schuman.
Berry, R., Jr. 1979. *The vegetarians*. Brookline, MA: Autumn Press.
Bestiary: A book of beasts. ⟨12th cent.⟩ 1960. Trans. by T. H. White from a 12th-century Latin version. New York: G. P. Putnam's.
Bigelow, H. J. ⟨1871⟩ 1977. Medical education in America. In *Surgical anaesthesia: Addresses and other papers*. (Reprint of 1900 ed.) Boston: Longwood Press.
Birch, C. and Cobb, J. B., Jr. 1981. An ethic of life. In *The liberation of life*, 141-75. Cambridge: Cambridge University Press.

Bishop, J. 1980. More thought on thought and talk. *Mind* 89: 1–16.

Black, J. N. 1970. *The dominion of man*. Edinburgh: Edinburgh University Press.

Blackstone, W. T. 1980. The search for an environmental ethic. In *Matters of life and death*, ed. by T. Regan, 299–335. New York: Random House.

———. ed. 1974. *Philosophy and environmental crisis*. Athens, GA: University of Georgia Press. (Not cited.)

Blount, M. 1974. *Animal land: The creatures of children's fiction*. London: Hutchinson.

Boakes, R. 1984. *From Darwin to behaviourism: Psychology and the minds of animals*. Cambridge: Cambridge University Press.

Board of Social Responsibility of the Church of England. 1970. Man and animals. In *Man in his living environment*, 18–25. London: Church Information Office.

Boas, G. 1933. *The happy beast in French thought of the seventeenth century*. Baltimore: Johns Hopkins Press.

———. 1973. Theriophily. In *Dictionary of the history of ideas*, ed. by P. P. Wiener, vol. 4, 384–9. New York: Charles Scribner's.

Bodson, L. 1983. Attitudes toward animals in Greco-Roman antiquity. *International Journal for the Study of Animal Problems* 4: 312–20.

Bowd, A. D. 1980. Reply to Gallup and Suarez. *Psychological Record* 30: 423–5.

———. 1986. Are there alternatives to the use of animals in psychological research? Psychologists for the Ethical Treatment of Animals. *PsyETA Bulletin* (Spring): 5–6.

———. 1987. A decade of debate on animal research in psychology: Room for consensus? Paper presented at annual convention, Canadian Psychological Association, Vancouver.

Bowditch, H. P. 1896. Vivisection justifiable. *Sanitarian* 38: 229–43.

Boylan, C. R. and Bowd, A. D. 1985. Enhancing students' respect for animal life through the teaching of science. *Australian Science Teachers Journal* 30: 18–23.

Brabazon, J. 1975. *Albert Schweitzer: A biography*. New York: G. P. Putnam's.

Bradley, F. H. ⟨1876⟩ 1927. *Ethical studies*. 2d ed. rev. Oxford: Clarendon Press.

Brandt, R. B. 1959. *Ethical theory*. Englewood Cliffs, NJ: Prentice-Hall.

Bretschneider. H. 1962. *Der streit um die vivisektion im 19. jahrhundert: Verlauf, argumente, ergebnisse*. Stuttgart: Gustav Fisher Verlag.

Brinton, H. H. 1960. Quakers and animals. In *Then and now*, ed. by A. Brinton, 188–99. Philadelphia: University of Pennsylvania Press.

British Veterinary Association. n.d. *Animal Welfare Foundation*. London: BVA. AWF.

Broadie, A. and Pybus, E. M. 1974. Kant's treatment of animals. *Philosophy* 49: 375–83.

Bronars, J. R. 1970. Tampering with nature in elementary school science. In *Readings in the philosophy of education*, ed. by J. R. Martin, 274–9. Boston: Allyn and Bacon.

Broom, D. M. 1986. Indicators of poor welfare. *British Veterinary Journal* 142: 524–6.

Brophy, B. 1964. *Hackenfeller's ape*. London: Secker and Warburg.

———. 1979. The way of no flesh. In *The genius of Shaw*, ed. by M. Holroyd, 94–112. London: Hodder and Stoughton.

Burch, R. W. 1977. Animals, rights, and claims. *Southwestern Journal of Philosophy* 8: 53–9.

Burdon-Sanderson, J. et al. 1873. *Handbook for the physiological laboratory*. 2 vols. London: J. and A. Churchill.

Bures, J. et al. 1976. *Techniques and basic experiments for the study of brain and behavior*. Amsterdam and New York: Elsevier Scientific Pub.

———. 1978. Teaching vivisection. *New Scientist* 77: 872.

Burghardt, G. M. 1985. Animal awareness: Current perceptions and historical perspective. *American Psychologist* 40: 905–19.

Butler, S. ⟨1890⟩ 1967. Thought and language. In *The humour of Homer and other essays*, ed. by R. A. Streatfield, 209–44. Freeport, NY: Books for Libraries Press.

———. ⟨1872⟩ 1970. *Erewhon*. Harmondsworth: Penguin Books.

Callicott, J. B. 1979. Elements of an environmental ethic: Moral considerability and the biotic community. *Environmental Ethics* 1: 71–81.

———. 1980. Animal liberation: A triangular affair. *Environmental Ethics* 2: 311–38.

———. 1984a. Non-anthropocentric value theory and environmental ethics. *American Philosophical Quarterly* 21: 299–309.

———. 1984b. Reply to S. F. Sapontzis' review of "Animal liberation: A triangular affair." *Ethics and Animals* 5: 135–40.

———. 1985a. The search for an environmental ethic. In *Matters of life and death*, ed. by T. Regan, 380–424. 2nd ed. New York: Random House.

———. 1985b. Review of T. Regan's *The case for animal rights*. *Environmental Ethics* 7: 365–72.

———. 1986. On the intrinsic value of nonhuman species. In *The preservation of species*, ed. by B. G. Norton, 138–72. Princeton, NJ: Princeton University Press.

Canadian Council on Animal Care. 1980–84. *Guide to the care and use of experimental animals*. 2 vols. Ottawa: CCAC.

Cannon, W. B. 1908. The opposition to medical research. *Journal of the American Medical Association* 51: 635–40.

Caplan, A. L. 1983. Animals do have rights. *Nature* 306: 110.

Carrier, L. S. 1980. Perception and animal belief. *Philosophy* 55: 193–210.

Carson, G. 1972. *Men, beasts, and gods: A history of cruelty and kindness to animals*. New York: Charles Scribner's.

Cartmill, M. 1986. Animal rights and wrongs. *Natural History* 95: 66–9.

Carus, P. 1897. The immorality of the anti-vivisection movement. *Open Court* 11: 370–6, 694–5.

———. 1898. Vegetarianism. *Open Court* 12: 565–70.

Castignone, S. 1983. I diritti degli animali: La prospettiva Utilitarista. *Materiali Per Una Storia Della Cultura Giuridica* 13: 397–421.

———. 1987. Per i diritti degli animali. *Biblioteca Della Libertà* 22: 87–93.

Cave, G. P. 1982. On the irreplaceability of animal life. *Ethics and Animals* 3 (December): 106–16.

———. 1985. Rational egoism, animal rights, and the academic connection. *Between the Species* 1 (2) (Spring): 21–3, 25–7.

Cebik, L. B. 1981. Can animals have rights? No and yes. *Philosophical Forum* (Boston) 12: 251–68.

Christensen, H. N. 1986. Children's stories and adult attitudes toward the use of animals in biomedical research and testing. *Perspectives in biology and medicine* 29: 573–87.

Cicero. ⟨1st cent. BC⟩ 1887. *The treatises of M. T. Cicero*. Trans. C. D. Yonge. London: George Bell.

Cigman, R. 1981. Death, misfortune, and species inequality. *Philosophy and Public Affairs* 10: 47–64.

Clair, J. B. 1987. Animal rites and justice. *Between the Species* 3: 190–5.

Clark, K. 1977a. *Animals and men: Their relationship as reflected in Western art from prehistory to the present day*. London: Thames and Hudson.

———. 1977b. Animals and men. *Smithsonian* (September): 52–61. (Not cited.)

Clark, R. W. 1984. *The survival of Charles Darwin*. New York: Random House.

Clark, S. R. L. 1976. Licensed torture? *Journal of Medical Ethics* 2: 125–6.

———. 1978. Animal wrongs. *Analysis* 38: 147–9.

———. 1983a. Gaia and the forms of life. In *Environmental philosophy*, ed. by R. Elliot and A. Gare, 182–97. University Park, PA: Pennsylvania State University Press.

———. 1983b. Nature, theology and. In *A new dictionary of Christian theology*, ed. by A. Richardson and J. Bowden, 394–5. London: SCM Press.

———. 1985a. Hume, animals and the objectivity of morals. *Philosophical Quarterly* 35: 117–33.

———. 1985b. Animals in ethical tradition. In *Animal experimentation*, ed. by N. Marsh and S. Haywood, 1-6. Nottingham: FRAME.

———. 1986. Christian responsibility for the environment. *Modern Churchman* 28 (2): 24-31.

———. 1987a. The description and evaluation of animal emotion. In *Mindwaves*, ed. by C. Blakemore and S. Greenfield, 139-50. Oxford: Basil Blackwell.

———. 1987b. Animals, ecosystems, and the liberal ethic. *Monist* 70: 114-33.

Clifton, M. 1988. Chucking zoo animals overboard. *Animals' Agenda* 8 (March): 14-22, 53-4. (Not cited.)

Cobbe, F. P. 1895. The ethics of zoophily. *Contemporary Review* 68: 497-508.

Cohen, B. J. 1981. Animal rights and animal experimentation. In *Rights and responsibilities in modern medicine*, ed. by M. D. Basson, 85-92. New York: Alan R. Liss.

Cohen, C. 1986. The case for the use of animals in biomedical research. *New England Journal of Medicine* 315: 865-70.

———. 1987. Letter on use of animals in biomedical research. *New England Journal of Medicine* 316: 553.

Cohen, H. 1983a. Letter: Animal rights. *New York Times Book Review* (18 December): 30.

———. 1983b. Some preliminary thoughts on permitting animals to sue in contract and tort. *International Journal for the Study of Animal Problems* 4: 284-5.

———. 1987. The legality of the Agriculture Department's exclusion of rats and mice from coverage under the Animal Welfare Act. *St Louis University Law Journal* 31: 543-9.

Cohen, L. D. 1936. Descartes and Henry More on the beast-machine: A translation of their correspondence pertaining to animal automatism. *Annals of Science* 1: 48-61.

Cohen, N. J. 1976. *Tsa'ar ba'ale hayim: The prevention of cruelty to animals*. 2d ed. Jerusalem and New York: Feldheim Publishers.

Coile, D. C. and Miller, N. E. 1984. How radical animal activists try to mislead humane people. *American Psychologist* 39: 700-1.

Collingwood, R. G. 1946. *The idea of history*. Oxford: Clarendon Press.

Collins, A. W. 1968. How one could tell were a bee to guide his behaviour by a rule. *Mind* 77: 556-60.

Compassion in World Farming. 1987. European success. *Agscene* (Newsletter) (June):5.

Conly, J. L. 1986. *Rasco and the rats of NIMH*. New York: Harper and Row.

Cottingham, J. 1978. "A brute to the brutes?": Descartes' treatment of animals. *Philosophy* 53: 551-61.

Council for Agricultural Science and Technology. 1981. *Scientific aspects of the welfare of food animals*. Ames, IA: CAST.

Council of the European Communities. 1978. Council decision of 19 June 1978 concerning the conclusion of the European Convention for the Protection of Animals Kept for Farming Purposes (text of the Convention annexed). *Official Journal of the European Communities* 21, No. L 323 (17 November): 12-17.

———. 1986a. Council directive of 24 November 1986 regarding the protection of animals used for experimental and other scientific purposes. *Official Journal of the European Communities* 29, No. L 358 (18 December): 1-13.

———. 1986b. Council directive of 25 March 1986 laying down minimum standards for the protection of laying hens kept in battery cages. *Official Journal of the European Communities* 29, No. L 95 (10 April): 45-8.

Covino, J. Jr. 1987. *Lab animal abuse: Vivisection exposed!* Berkeley, CA: New Humanity Press. (Not cited.)

Cowley, G. 1988. The wisdom of animals. *Newsweek* 111 (23 May): 52-9. (Not cited.)

Cox, P. 1986. *Why you don't need meat*. Wellingborough, Northants: Thorsons.

Crisp, R. 1985a. A comment on "On behalf of a moderate speciesism" by Alan Holland. *Journal of Applied Philosophy* 2: 279-80.

———. 1985b. The minds of non-human animals. Thesis, Bachelor of Philosophy, Oxford University.

Cuny, H. 1966. *Louis Pasteur.* Trans. P. Evans. New York: Paul S. Erikson.

Curtis, S. E. 1980. Who should regulate animal care and research? *Journal of Animal Science* 51: 479–82.

———. 1982. What constitutes animal well-being? In *Animal stress*, ed. by G. P. Moberg, 1–12. Bethesda, MD: American Physiological Society.

———. 1986. The case for intensive farming of food animals. In *Advances in animal welfare science 1986/87*, ed. by M. W. Fox and L. D. Mickley, 245–55. Washington, DC: Humane Society of US.

———. 1987. Animal well-being and animal care. *Veterinary Clinics for North America: Food Animal Practice* 3: 369–82.

Dalton, J. C. 1867. *Vivisection: What it is, what it has accomplished.* New York: Baillière.

———. ⟨1875⟩ 1980. *John Call Dalton on experimental method.* (Reprint) New York: Arno Press.

Darwin, C. ⟨19th cent.⟩ 1977. *The collected papers of Charles Darwin.* 2 vols. Ed. P. H. Barrett. Chicago: University of Chicago Press.

Darwin, F., ed. 1887. *The life and letters of Charles Darwin.* 3 vols. London: John Murray.

Data Notes Publishing Staff. 1983. *Vegetarian associations, organizations, periodicals: Directory.* Houston, TX: Prosperity and Profits.

Davidson, D. 1975. Thought and talk. In *Mind and language*, ed. by S. Guttenplan, 7–23. Oxford: Clarendon Press.

———. 1985. Rational animals. In *Actions and events*, ed. by E. Le Pere, 473–81. Oxford: Blackwell.

Davis, K. 1988. Farm animals and the feminine connection. *Animals' Agenda* 8 (Jan–Feb): 38–9.

Dawkins, M. S. 1987. Minding and mattering. In *Mindwaves*, ed. by C. Blackmore and S. Greenfield, 151–62. Oxford: Basil Blackwell.

Day, D. 1981. *The doomsday book of animals: A natural history of vanished species.* New York: Viking. (Not cited.)

DeBakey, M. E. 1985. Medical advances resulting from animal research. In *The contributions of laboratory animal science to the welfare of man and animals*, ed. by J. Archibald et al., xix–xxvi. New York: G. Fischer Verlag.

Dennett, D. C. 1983. Intentional systems in cognitive ethology: The "Panglossian paradigm" defended. *Behavioral and Brain Sciences* 6: 343–55.

DeRosa, W. 1984. *An annotated bibliography of research relevant to humane education.* East Haddam, CT: National Association for the Advancement of Humane Education.

Descartes, R. ⟨17th cent.⟩ 1911–12. *The philosophical works of Descartes.* 2 vols. Trans. E. S. Haldane and G. R. T. Ross. Cambridge: Cambridge University Press.

———. ⟨17th cent.⟩ 1970. *Descartes: Philosophical letters.* Trans. A. Kenny. Oxford: Clarendon Press.

Devall, B. and Sessions, G. 1985. *Deep ecology: Living as if nature mattered.* Salt Lake City, UT: Gibbs M. Smith.

Devine, P. E. 1978. The moral basis of vegetarianism. *Philosophy* 53: 481–505.

Dewar, J. 1969. *The rape of Noah's ark.* London: William Kimber. (Not cited.)

Dewey, J. 1926. The ethics of animal experimentation. *Atlantic Monthly* 138: 343–6. Also in *The later works*, ed. by J. A. Boydston and B. A. Walsh, vol. 2, 99–103. Carbondale, IL: Southern Illinois University Press, 1984.

Dichter, A. 1978. Legal definitions of cruelty and animal rights. *Environmental Ethics* 7: 147–64.

Dierauer, U. 1977. *Tier und mensch im denken der antike: Studien zur tierpsychologie, anthropologie und ethik.* Amsterdam: Grüner.

Diner, J. 1979. *Physical and mental suffering of experimental animals.* Washington, DC: Animal Welfare Institute.

———. 1985. *Toward an ethic of animal use in psychology research*. Chicago: National Anti-Vivisection Society.

———. 1986. *Test tube with whiskers*. Chicago: National Anti-Vivisection Society.

———. 1987. *Experimental psychology: Experiments using animals*. Clarks Summit, PA: International Society for Animal Rights.

———. n. d. *A compendium of alternatives to the use of live animals in research and testing*. Jenkintown, PA: American Anti-Vivisection Society.

Dodds, W. J. and Orlands, F. B., eds. 1982. *Scientific perspectives on animal welfare*. New York: Academic Press.

Dolan, E. F. 1986. *Animal rights*. New York: Franklin Watts. (For grades 7–12.)

Dombrowski, D. A . 1983. Rorty on pre-linguistic awareness in pigs. *Ethics and Animals* 4: 2–5.

———. 1984a. Was Plato a vegetarian? *Apeiron* 18: 1–9.

———. 1984b. Vegetarianism and the argument from marginal cases in Porphyry. *Journal of the History of Ideas* 45: 141–3.

———. 1985. The Jesuits and the zoophilists, again. *Irish Theological Quarterly* 51: 232–41.

———. 1986a. Thoreau, sainthood and vegetarianism. *American Transcendental Quarterly* Issue no. 60 (June): 25–36.

———. 1986b. The ancient mariner, God, and animals. *Between the Species* 2: 111–15.

———. 1988. Individuals, species, ecosystems: A Hartshornian view. *Between the Species* 4 (1988): 3–10.

Donaghy, K. 1974. Singer on speciesism. *Philosophic Exchange* 1: 125–27.

Dresser, R. 1985. Research on animals: Values, politics and regulatory reform. *Southern California Law Review* 58: 1147–201.

———. 1988 forthcoming. Assessing harm and justification in animal research: Federal policy opens the door. *Rutgers Law Review* (June).

Drewett, R. F. 1977. On the teaching of vivisection. *New Scientist* 76: 292.

Droeven, A. M., ed. 1985. *Irrweg tierversuch: Fakten, daten, hintergrunde*. Basel: Lenos Verlag.

Dryden, J. ⟨1700⟩ 1958. Of the Pythagorean philosophy, from Ovid's *Metamorphoses* Book XV. In *The poems of John Dryden*, ed. by J. Kinsley, vol. 4, 1717–36. Oxford: Clarendon Press.

Duffy, M. 1973. *I want to go to Moscow*. London: Hodder and Stoughton. Also under title *All heaven in a rage*. New York: A. A. Knopf, 1973.

Dukes, E. F. 1987. The Improved Standards for Laboratory Animals Act. *St Louis University Law Journal* 31: 519–42.

Duncan, I. 1973. Can the psychologist measure stress? *New Scientist* 60: 173–5.

Duncan, I. J. 1981. Animal rights – animal welfare: A scientist's assessment. *Poultry Science* 60: 489–99.

Dunheim, D. 1981. Donald Barnes joins the ranks of animal activists. *Animal's Agenda* (July–August): 1, 4.

Eaton, R. L., ed. 1985. *The human/animal connection*. Incline Village, NV: Carnivore Journal. (Not cited.)

Edwards, R. B. and Marsh, F. H. 1978. Reasonableness, murder and modern science. *Phi Kappa Phi Journal* 58 (Winter): 24–29.

Ehrlich, P. and A. 1981. *Extinction*. New York: Random House. (Not cited.)

Elliot, R. 1984. Rawlsian justice and non-human animals. *Journal of Applied Philosophy* 1: 95–106.

———. 1987. Moral autonomy, self-determination and animal rights. *Monist* 70: 83–97.

Epstein, R. 1985. A benefactor of his race: Thoreau's "Higher laws" and the heroics of vegetarianism. *Between the Species* 1 (Summer): 23–8.

Ernst, H. C. 1902. *Animal experimentation*. Boston: Little, Brown.

Estes, C. and Sessions, K. W., eds. 1983–84. *Controlled wildlife.* 3 vols. Lawrence, KS: Museum of Natural History.

Etherington, G. F. 1842. *Vivisection investigated and vindicated.* Edinburgh: P. Rickard.

Evans, E. P. ⟨1906⟩ 1987. *The criminal prosecution and capital punishment of animals.* Winchester, MA: Faber and Faber.

Ewbank, R. 1973. The trouble with being a farm animal. *New Scientist* 60: 172–3.

Ewer, T. 1973. Farm animals in the law. *New Scientist* 60: 178–9.

Fairholme, E. G. and Pain, W. 1924. *A century of work for animals: The history of the RSPCA, 1824–1924.* London: John Murray.

Falkin, L. 1985. Taub v. State: Are state anti-cruelty statutes sleeping giants? *Pace Environmental Law Review* 2: 255–69.

Fallaci, O. 1967. The dead body and the living brain. *Look* 31 (28 November): 99–101, 104–6, 108, 110, 112, 114.

Favre, D. S. 1979. Wildlife rights: The ever-widening circle. *Environmental Law* 9: 241–82.

Favre, D. S. and Loring, M. 1983. *Animal law.* Westport, CT: Quorum Books.

Federation of American Societies for Experimental Biology. 1986. Government, media and the animal issue: Proceedings of a symposium. *Federation Proceedings* 45 (11): 7a–14a; 45 (12): 9a–16a; 45 (13): 5a–10a.

Feeney, D. M. 1987. Human rights and animal welfare. *American Psychologist* 42: 593–9.

Feezell, R. M. and Dombroski, D. A. 1984. A dialogue on philosophical vegetarianism. *American Philosophical Association Newsletter on Teaching Philosophy* (Late autumn): 8–10.

Felthous, A. R. 1980. Aggression against cats, dogs, and people. *Child Psychiatry and Human Development* 10: 169–77.

Felthous, A. R. and Kellert, S. R. 1986. Violence against animals and people: Is aggression against living creatures generalized? *Bulletin of the American Academy of Psychiatry and the Law* 14: 55–69.

———. 1987. Childhood cruelty to animals and later aggression against people: A review. *American Journal of Psychiatry* 144: 710–17.

Fern, R. L. 1981. Human uniqueness as a guide to resolving conflicts between animal and human interests. *Ethics and Animals* 2: 7–21.

Ferré, F. 1986. Moderation, morals, and meat. *Inquiry* 29: 391–406.

Ferry, G., ed. 1984. *The understanding of animals.* Oxford: Basil Blackwell and New Scientist. (Not cited.)

Field-Fisher, T. G. 1964. *Animals and the law.* Potters Bar, Herts: Universities Federation for Animal Welfare.

Finsen, L. and Finsen, S. 1988 forthcoming. How clever was the old fox? *Between the Species.*

Finsen, S. 1988. Making ends meet: Reconciling ecoholism and animal rights individualism. *Between the Species* 4 (1988): 11–20.

Fleming, D. 1954. *William H. Welch and the rise of modern medicine.* Boston: Little, Brown.

Flowers, F. H. 1983. Research animal care in Canada: Its control and regulation. *Annals of the New York Academy of Science* 406: 144–9.

Fölsch, D. W., ed. 1978. *The ethology and ethics of farm animal production.* Basel: Birkhauser Verlag.

Ford, E. K. 1908. *The Brown Dog and his memorial.* London: Animal Defence and Anti-Vivisection Society.

Foreman, D. 1987. A discussion with Dave Foreman of Earth First! (interviewed by W. Pacelle). *Animals' Agenda* 7 (December): 6–9, 52–3.

Forward, C. W. 1898. *Fifty years of food reform.* London: Ideal Publishing Union.

———. 1904. *The food of the future.* London: George Bell.

Foster, R. N. 1897. Vivisection and morality. *Open Court* 11: 689–93.

Foundation for Biomedical Research. 1987a. *The biomedical investigator's handbook for researchers using animal models.* Washington, DC: FBR.

———. 1987b. *The new research environment*. Washington, DC: FBR. Training package and materials: (1) *The biomedical investigator's handbook*. (2) *Health benefits of animal research* ed. by W. I. Gay. (3) Videotapes: (a) 14-minute documentary on the animal rights movement and its threat to biomedical research. (b) Three 10-minute segments on Animal Care and Use Committees, handling laboratory animals, surgical procedures. (c) *Will I be all right, doctor?* Patients and doctors explain how animal research benefits humans. (4) Issue papers: (a) Caring for laboratory animals. (b) The use of pound animals in biomedical research and education. (c) The use of animals in biomedical research and testing. (5) Speaker's kit. (6) *FBR Newsletter*, quarterly. (7) *NABR Alert* (National Association for Biomedical Research, a lobbying group). (8) *CIRA Newsletter* (Center for Information on Research with Animals).

Fox, M. A. 1978a. "Animal liberation": A critique. *Ethics* 88: 106–18.

———. 1978b. Animal suffering and rights: A reply to Singer and Regan. *Ethics* 88: 134–8.

———. 1978c. Animal rights: Misconceived humaneness. *Dalhousie Review* 58: 230–9.

———. 1979–80. On justifying the use of animals for human ends. *Animal Regulation Studies* 2: 191–203.

———. 1984. Ethical considerations in painful animal research. In *Advances in pain research and therapy*, ed. by H. L. Fields et al., vol. 9, 685–94. New York: Raven Press.

———. 1986a. *The case for animal experimentation*. Berkeley: University of California Press.

———. 1986b. Letter (in response to reviews of Fox's *The case for animal experimentation* by R. E. Burke and J. Tannenbaum). *The Scientist* 1 (15 December).

Fox, M. W. 1976. *Between animal and man*. New York: Coward, McCann and Geoghegan.

———. 1980a. *Factory farming*. Washington, DC: Humane Society of the US.

———. 1980b. Intensive "factory farming" and the question of animal rights. *Animal Regulation Studies* 2: 175–90.

———. 1981. Experimental psychology, animal rights, welfare and ethics. *Psychopharmacology Bulletin* 17 (April): 80–4.

———. 1983. *Farm animal welfare and human diet*. Washington, DC: Humane Society of the US.

———. 1984. *Farm animals: Husbandry, behavior, and veterinary practice*. Baltimore: University Park Press.

———. 1985. The bio-politics of sociobiology and philosophy. *Between the Species* 1 (4): 3–7.

———. 1986a. On the genetic manipulation of animals: A response to Evelyn Pluhar. *Between the Species* 2: 51–2.

———. 1986b. *Laboratory animal husbandry*. Albany: State University of New York Press.

———. 1987. Genetic engineering: Nature's cornucopia or Pandora's box? *Animals' Agenda* 7 (March): 9–15.

———. 1988 forthcoming. Francis Bacon: Father of technocracy. *Between the Species*.

Fox, M. W. and Mickley, L. D., eds. 1985a. *Advances in animal welfare science 1984*. Dordrecht: Martinus Nijhoff.

———. 1985b. *Advances in animal welfare science 1985/86*. Washington, DC: Humane Society of the US.

———. 1986. *Advances in animal welfare science 1986/87*. Washington, DC: Humane Society of US.

Fox, M. W. and Mickley, L. D. 1986. The case against intensive farming of food animals. In *Advances in animal welfare science 1986/87*, ed. by M. W. Fox and L. D. Mickley, 257–72. Washington, DC: Humane Society of US.

Francione, G. L. 1988 forthcoming. The constitutional status of restrictions on experiments involving nonhuman animals: A comment on Professor Dresser's analysis. *Rutgers Law Review* (June).

Frankena, W. K. 1979. Ethics and the environment. In *Ethics and problems of the 21st century*, ed. by K. E. Goodpaster and K. M. Sayre, 3–20. Notre Dame, IN: University of Notre Dame Press.

Franklin, B. ⟨18th cent.⟩ 1875. *The life of Benjamin Franklin*, ed. by J. Bigelow. Vol. 1. Philadelphia: J. B. Lippincott.

Frazier, J. M. et al. 1987. *A critical evaluation of alternatives to acute ocular irritation testing.* Alternative Methods in Toxicology, vol. 4. New York: Mary Ann Liebert.

Free, A. C. 1987. Reaching the general public through poetry. *Between the Species* 3: 208–9.

Freeman, K. 1962. *Ancilla to the Pre-Socratic philosophers: A complete translation of the Fragments in Diels, "Fragmente der vorsokratiker".* Oxford: Basil Blackwell.

French, R. D. 1975. *Antivivisection and medical science in Victorian society.* Princeton: Princeton University Press.

——. 1978. Animal experimentation: Historical aspects. In *Encyclopedia of bioethics*, ed. by W. T. Reich, vol. 1, 75–9. New York: Free Press.

Freshel, M. R. L., comp. 1933. *Selections from three essays by Richard Wagner.* New York: Millennium Guild.

Frey, R. G. 1977a. Interests and animal rights. *Philosophical Quarterly* 27: 254–9.

——. 1977b. Animal rights. *Analysis* 37: 186–9.

——. 1979. Rights, interests, desires and beliefs. *American Philosophical Quarterly* 16: 233–9.

——. 1980. *Interests and rights: The case against animals.* Oxford: Clarendon Press.

——. 1983a. Vivisection, morals and medicine. *Journal of Medical Ethics* 9: 95–104.

——. 1983b. *Rights, killing, and suffering: Moral vegetarianism and applied ethics.* Oxford: Basil Blackwell.

——. 1987. Autonomy and the value of animal life. *Monist* 70: 50–63.

Friedman, R. 1988 forthcoming. Animal rights: Periodical publications. *Serial Librarian.*

Friend, C. E. 1974. Animal cruelty laws: The case for reform. *University of Richmond Law Review* 8: 201–31.

Frisch, K. von. 1967. *The dance language and orientation of bees.* Trans. L. Chadwick. Cambridge: Harvard University Press.

Frucht, K. 1979. Animals and children: Image and imagination. *Animal Regulation Studies* 2: 259–73.

Fuchs, A. E. 1981. Duties to animals: Rawls' alleged dilemma. *Ethics and Animals* 2: 83–7.

Fuller, B. A. G. 1949. The messes animals make in metaphysics. *Journal of Philosophy* 46: 829–38.

Gallistel, C. R. 1981. Bell, Magendie, and the proposals to restrict the use of animals in neurobehavioral research. *American Psychologist* 36: 357–60.

Gallup, G. G., Jr. 1983. Toward a comparative psychology of mind. In *Animal cognition and behavior*, ed. by R. L. Mellgren, 473–510. Amsterdam: North-Holland Publishing.

Gallup, G. G., Jr. and Suarez, S. D. 1980. On the use of animals in psychological research. *Psychological Record* 30: 211–18.

——. 1985. Animal research versus the care and maintenance of pets. *American Psychologist* 40: 968.

Gandhi, M. K. 1927. Experiments in dietetics. In *The story of my experiments with truth*, 137–45. Ahmedabad: Navajivan Press.

——. 1949. *Diet and diet reform.* Ahmedabad: Navajivan Publishing.

——. 1954. *How to save the cow.* Ahmedabad: Navajivan Publishing.

Geach, P. 1957. *Mental acts.* London: Routledge and Kegan Paul.

——. 1977. Animal pain. In *Providence and evil*, 67–83. Cambridge: Cambridge University Press.

Gendin, S. 1988. Animal rights and ecoholism are not compatible. *Between the Species* 4 (1988): 23–7.

Gewirth, A. 1978. *Reason and morality.* Chicago: University of Chicago Press.

Gill, J. E. 1969. Theriophily in antiquity. *Journal of the History of Ideas* 30: 401–12.

Giraud, R. 1984–85. Rousseau and Voltaire: The Enlightenment and animal rights.

Between the Species 1 (Winter): 4–9, 24.

Girdlestone, E. D. 1884. *Vivisection: In its scientific, religious, and moral aspects.* London: Simpkin, Marshall.

Glacken, C. J. 1967. Interpreting man's dominion over nature. In *Traces on the Rhodian shore,* 295–302. Berkeley: University of California Press.

Godfrey, P. 1977. RSPCA gives animals charter of rights. *The Times* (20 August): 3. (Not cited.)

Godlee, R. J. 1918. *Lord Lister.* London: Macmillan.

Goldberg, A. M. 1986. Alternatives in toxicology: Problems and alternatives. In *Chemicals testing and animal welfare,* Proceedings from the International Seminar, 249–60. Stockholm: National Chemicals Inspectorate.

Goldberg, A. M. ed. 1984. *Acute toxicity testing: Alternative approaches.* New York: Mary Ann Liebert.

——. 1987. *In vitro toxicology: Approaches to validation.* Alternative Methods in Toxicology, vol. 5. New York: Mary Ann Liebert.

Goldsmith, O. ⟨1760⟩ 1934. *The citizen of the world.* London: J. M. Dent.

Goodall, J. 1986. *The chimpanzees of Gombe: Patterns of behavior.* Cambridge: Belknap Press of Harvard University.

Goodpaster, K. E. 1978. On being morally considerable. *Journal of Philosophy* 75: 308–25.

——. 1979. From egoism to environmentalism. In *Ethics and problems of the 21st century,* ed. by K. E. Goodpaster and K. M. Sayre, 21–35. Notre Dame, IN: University of Notre Dame Press.

Goodrich, T. 1969. The morality of killing. *Philosophy* 44: 127–39.

Gossel, P. P. 1985. William Henry Welch and the antivivisection legislation in the District of Columbia, 1896–1900. *Journal of the History of Medicine and Allied Sciences* 40: 397–419.

Gray, J. A. 1987. The ethics and politics of animal experimentation. In *Psychology Survey 6,* ed. by H. Beloft and A. Colman, 218–33. Leicester: British Psychological Society.

Gray, J. C. ⟨1909⟩ 1963. *The nature and sources of the law.* Boston: Beacon Press.

Greanville, P. 1988a. In the name of humanity. *Animals' Agenda* 8 (Jan/Feb): 36–7.

——. 1988b. Agrijournals: News from the super farms. *Animals' Agenda* 8 (May): 40–1.

Great Britain. 1876–77. *Report of the Royal Commission on the practice of subjecting live animals to experiments for scientific purposes.* Cmnd. 1397, 1864. London: HMSO.

——. 1907–12. *Royal Commission on Vivisection Reports.* Cmnd. 3326, 3461, 3462, 3756, 3757, 3954, 3955, 4146, 4147, 6114. London: HMSO.

——. 1980. *Report of the Select Committee on the Laboratory Animals Protection Bill (H. L.),* House of Lords. 2 vols. London: HMSO.

——. 1981. *Report on animal welfare in poultry, pig and veal calf production.* The House of Commons Select Committee on Agriculture. London: HMSO.

——. 1983. *Scientific procedures on living animals.* Secretary of State for the Home Department. Cmnd. 8883. London: HMSO.

——. 1985. *Scientific procedures on living animals.* Secretary of State for the Home Department. Cmnd. 9521. London: HMSO.

Green, T. H. ⟨1885⟩ 1960. *Lectures on the principles of political obligation.* London: Longmans.

Grice, G. R. 1967. *The grounds of moral judgement.* Cambridge: Cambridge University Press.

Griffin, D. R. 1978. Prospects for a cognitive ethology. *Behavioral and Brain Sciences* 1: 527–37.

——. 1982. Animal communication as evidence of thinking. In *Language, mind, and brain,* ed. by T. W. Simon and R. J. Scholes, 241–50. Hillsdale, NJ: L. Erlbaum Associates.

——. 1984. *Animal thinking.* Cambridge: Harvard University Press.

Griffin, D. R., ed. 1982. *Animal mind - Human mind.* Berlin: Springer-Verlag.

Griffin, J. 1986. *Wellbeing.* Oxford: Clarendon Press.

Griffiths, R. 1982. *The human use of animals.* Bramcote, Notts: Grove Books.

Gross, J. and Freifeld, K. 1983. *The vegetarian child*. Secaucus, NJ: Lyle Stuart.

Grotius, H. ⟨1625⟩ 1901. *The rights of war and peace*. Trans. A. C. Campbell. New York: M. Walter Dunne.

Grunewald, C. and Mason, J. 1985. The head injury lab break-in. *Animals' Agenda* 5 (May): 1, 8–11.

Gunderson, K. 1964. Descartes, La Mettrie, language and machines. *Philosophy* 39: 193–222.

Gunn, A. S. 1983. Traditional ethics and the moral status of animals. *Environmental Ethics* 5: 133–54.

Gunn, B. 1987. *Entering the gates of hell: Laboratory cruelty you were not meant to see*. St Albans, Herts: International Association Against Painful Experiments on Animals.

Gustafson, D. 1971. The natural expressions of intention. *Philosophical Forum* (Boston) 2: 299–315.

Guthrie, W. K. C. 1962. *The earlier Presocratics and the Pythagoreans*. A History of Greek Philosophy, vol. 1. Cambridge: Cambridge University Press.

———. 1965. *The Presocratic tradition from Parmenides to Democritus*. A History of Greek Philosophy, vol. 2. Cambridge: Cambridge University Press.

Hadwen, W. R. 1914. *Experiments on living animals: Useless and cruel*. London: British Union for the Abolition of Vivisection.

———. 1926. *The difficulties of Dr. Deguerre*. London: C. W. Daniel.

Haldane, J. B. S. 1928. Some enemies of science. In *Possible worlds and other papers*, 261–71. New York: Harper and Brothers.

Hamilton, I. 1980. *The beagle brigade*. Hicksville, NY: Exposition Press.

Hampshire, S. 1959. *Thought and action*. London: Chatto and Windus.

Hampson, J. E. 1978. Animal experimentation, 1876–1976. Ph.D. diss., University of Leicester.

———. 1985? *Laboratory animal protection laws in Europe and North America*. Horsham, West Sussex: RSPCA.

Hare, R. M. 1963. *Freedom and reason*. New York: Oxford University Press.

Harrison, R. 1970. Steps toward legislation in Great Britain. In *Factory farming: A symposium*, ed. by J. R. Bellerby, 3–16. London: British Association for the Advancement of Science. (Not cited.)

Hart, B. L., ed. 1976. *Experimental psychobiology: A laboratory manual*. San Francisco: W. H. Freeman.

Hart, H. L. A. 1955. Are there any natural rights? *Philosophical Review* 64: 175–91.

———. 1963. *Law, liberty and morality*. Stanford, CA: Stanford University Press.

———. 1980. Death and utility. *New York Review of Books* (15 May): 25–32.

Hartshorne, C. 1979. The rights of the subhuman world. *Environmental Ethics* 1: 49–60.

Harvard University. 1982. *The animal rights movement in the United States: Its composition, funding sources, goals, strategies and potential impact on research*. Cambridge, MA: Harvard University Office of Government and Community Affairs. (Reprinted by and available from International Society for Animal Rights, Clarks Summit, PA [344].)

Harwood, D. 1928. *Love for animals and how it developed in Great Britain*. New York: Columbia University.

Hastings, H. 1936. *Man and beast in French thought of the eighteenth century*. Baltimore, MD: Johns Hopkins Press.

Haussleiter, J. 1935. *Der vegetarismus in der antike*. Berlin: Alfred Töpelmann.

Hearne, V. 1986. *Adam's task: Calling the animals by name*. New York: Knopf.

Hebb, D. O. 1946. Emotion in man and animal. *Psychological Review* 53: 88–106.

Hegarty, T. W. 1976. Comments on the paper "The ethics of animal experimentation" by W. Lane-Petter. *Journal of Medical Ethics* 2: 122–4.

Hegel, G. W. F. ⟨1821⟩ 1958. *Hegel's philosophy of right*. Trans. T. M. Knox. Oxford: Clarendon Press.

———. ⟨1830⟩ 1970. *Hegel's philosophy of nature*. Vol. 3. Trans. M. J. Petry. London: George Allen and Unwin.

———. ⟨1807⟩ 1978. *Hegel's philosophy of subjective spirit*. Vol. 3. Trans. M. J. Petry. Dordrecht: D. Reidel.

Heim, A. 1979. The proper study of psychology. *New Universities Quarterly* 33: 135–54.

Heinroth, K. and Burghardt, G. M. 1977. The history of ethology. In *Grzimek's encyclopedia of ethology*, ed. by K. Immelmann, 1–22. New York: Van Nostrand Reinhold.

Herman, L. M. 1980. Cognitive capacities of dolphins. In *Cetacean behavior*, ed. by L. M. Herman, 363–429. New York: Wiley.

Herman, L. M. et al. 1984. Comprehension of sentences by bottlenosed dolphins. *Cognition* 16: 129–219.

Herodotus. ⟨5th cent. BC⟩ 1961. *Herodotus*. 4 vols. Trans. A. D. Godley. Cambridge: Harvard University Press.

Herrnstein, R. J. 1985. Riddles of natural categorization. In *Animal intelligence*, ed. by L. Weiskrantz, 129–44. Oxford: Oxford University Press.

Herscovici, A. 1985. *Second nature: The animal rights controversy*. Toronto: CBC Enterprises.

Heyes, C. M. 1987. Contrasting approaches to the legitimation of intentional language within comparative psychology. *Behaviorism* 15 (Spring): 41–50.

Hick, J. 1978. *Evil and the God of love*. New York: Harper and Row.

Hilgard, E. 1980. Consciousness in contemporary psychology. *Annual Review of Psychology* 31: 1–26.

Hitt, J. 1988. Just like us? Toward a notion of animal rights. *Harper's* 277 (August): 43–52. Hitt moderates a discussion with A. Caplan, G. Francione, R. Goldman, I. Newkirk. (Not cited.)

Hoage, R. J. and Goldman, L., eds. 1986. *Animal intelligence*. Washington, DC: Smithsonian Institution Press.

Hobbes, T. ⟨17th cent.⟩ 1962. *The English works of Thomas Hobbes*. 11 vols. Ed. W. Molesworth. Aalen, Germany: Scientia.

Hobhouse, L. T. 1901. *Mind in evolution*. London: Macmillan.

Hoff, C. 1983. Kant's invidious humanism. *Environmental Ethics* 5: 63–70.

Holland, A. F. 1984. On behalf of moderate speciesism. *Journal of Applied Philosophy* 1: 281–92.

Hollands, C. 1986. Animal experimentation: The Animals (Scientific Procedures) Act 1986. *Lancet* 2 (5 July): 32–3.

———. 1987. The Animals (Scientific Procedures) Act 1986. In The Scottish Society for the Prevention of Vivisection *Annual pictorial review 1987*, 11–37. Edinburgh: SSPV.

Holmes, O. W. 1881. *The common law*. Boston: Little, Brown.

Hospers, J. 1985. Review of *The case for animal rights* by T. Regan. *Reason Papers* 10: 113–24.

Hume, C. W. 1957. *The status of animals in the Christian religion*. London: Universities Federation for Animal Welfare.

Hume, D. ⟨1740⟩ 1888. *A treatise of human nature*, ed. by L. A. Selby-Bigge. Oxford: Oxford University Press.

———. ⟨1751⟩ 1946. *An enquiry concerning the principles of morals*. La Salle, IL: Open Court.

Humphrey, N. K. 1976. The social function of intellect. In *Growing points in ethology*, ed. by P. P. G. Bateson and R. A. Hinde, 303–17. Cambridge: Cambridge University Press.

———.1980. Nature's psychologists. In *Consciousness and the physical world*, ed. by B. D. Josephson and V. S. Ramachandran, 57–80. New York: Pergamon Press.

———. 1982. Consciousness: A just-so story? *New Scientist* 95: 474–7.

———. 1983. *Consciousness regained: Chapters in the development of mind*. Oxford: Oxford University Press.

Hurnik, J. F. 1980. Animal welfare and modern agriculture. *Animal Regulation Studies* 2: 145–54.
Hurnik, J. F. and Lehman, H. 1982. Unnecessary suffering: Definition and evidence. *International Journal for the Study of Animal Problems* 3: 131–7.
Hurwitz, J. 1978. *Much ado about Aldo*. New York: Morrow.
Hutchings, M. and Caver, M. 1970. *Man's dominion: Our violation of the animal world*. London: Rupert Hart-Davis.
Huxley, T. H. 1893. On the hypothesis that animals are automata, and its history. In *Collected essays*, vol. 1, 199–250. London: Macmillan.
———. 1897. The mental phenomena of animals. In *Essays*, vol. 6, 121–33. New York: D. Appleton.
Hyde, W. W. 1916. The prosecution and punishment of animals and lifeless things in the Middle Ages and modern times. *University of Pennsylvania Law Review* 64: 696–730.

Institute of Laboratory Animal Resources. 1977. *The future of animals, cells, models, and systems in research, development, education and testing*. Washington, DC: National Academy of Sciences.
International Association against Painful Experiments on Animals. 1977. *The moral, scientific and economic aspects of research techniques not involving the use of living animals*. London: National Anti-Vivisection Society.

Jaini, P. S. 1979. *The Jaina path of purification*. Berkeley: University of California Press.
James, D. N. 1988. Dombroski on individuals, species, and ecosystems. *Between the Species* 4 (1988): 27–31.
James, W. ⟨1890⟩ 1981. *The principles of psychology*. 3 vols. Cambridge: Harvard University Press.
———. ⟨1891⟩ 1948. *Essays in pragmatism*, ed. by A. Castell. New York: Hafner.
———. 1909. Letter to the Secretary of The Vivisection Reform Society. In *The humane movement*, by R. C. McCrea, 274–5. New York: Columbia University Press, 1910. (This letter also published in *New York Evening Post*, 22 May 1909.)
Jamieson, D. 1981. Rational egoism and animal rights. *Environmental Ethics* 3: 167–71.
———. 1983. Review of B. E. Rollin's *Animal rights and human morality*. *Ethics and Animals* 4: 13–18.
———. 1985. Experimenting on animals: A reconsideration. *Between the Species* (Summer): 4–11.
Jamieson, D. and Regan, T. 1985. Whales are not cetacean resources. In *Advances in animal welfare science 1984*, ed. by M. W. Fox and L. D. Mickley, 101–11. Boston: Martinus Nijhoff.
Jeffrey, R. 1985. Animal interpretation. In *Actions and events*, ed. by E. Le Pere, 482–7. Oxford: Blackwell.
Jesse, G. R. 1875. *Evidence given before the Royal Commission on Vivisection*. London: B. M. Pickering. (Not cited.)
Joad, C. E. M. and Lewis, C. S. ⟨1950⟩ 1970. The pains of animals: A problem in theology. In *God in the dock*, by C. S. Lewis, 161–71. Grand Rapids, MI: William B. Eerdmans.
Johnson, D. 1988. Worldwide action for animals. British Union for the Abolition of Vivisection *Liberator* (March/April): 24–8.
Johnson, E. 1981. Animal liberation versus the land ethic. *Environmental Ethics* 3: 265–73.
Jolly, A. 1985. A new science that sees animals as conscious beings. *Smithsonian* 15 (March): 66–75.
Jones, G. E. 1972. *Concern for animals as manifest in five American churches: Bible Christian, Shaker, Latter-day Saint, Christian Scientist and Seventh-day Adventist*. Ph.D. diss., Brigham Young University. Ann Arbor, MI: University Microfilms International.

———. 1983. Singer, animal rights and consistency. *International Journal of Applied Philosophy* 1: 67–70.

Jones. J. 1957. Transcendental grocery bills: Thoreau's *Walden* and some aspects of American vegetarianism. *University of Texas Studies in English* 36: 141–54.

Jordan, W. J. 1975. Animals have rights. *Contemporary Review* 226: 82–6.

Juergensmeyer, M. 1984–85. Gandhi and the cow. *Between the Species* (Winter): 11–17.

Kagan, C. 1979. *Rationality of animals*. Ph.D. diss., University of Oklahoma. Ann Arbor, MI: University Microfilms International.

Kaleschofsky, R. 1985. *Haggadah for the liberated lamb*. Marblehead, MA: Micah Publications. (English and Hebrew/English editions.)

Kant, I. ⟨1785⟩ 1962. *Kant's groundwork of the metaphysic of morals*. Trans. H. J. Paton. London: Hutchinson.

———. ⟨1780⟩ 1978. *Lectures on ethics*. Trans. L. Infield. Gloucester, MA: Peter Smith.

Kaplan, H. F. 1988 forthcoming. *Philosophic des vegetarismus: Kritische würdigung und weiterführung von Peter Singers ansatz*. Frankfurt am Main: Verlag Peter Lang.

Kapleau, P. 1982. *To cherish all life: A Buddhist case for becoming a vegetarian*. San Francisco, CA: Harper and Row.

Katcher, A. H. and Beck, A. M., eds. 1983. *New perspectives on our lives with companion animals*. Philadelphia: University of Pennsylvania Press.

Katz, E. 1988. Methodology in applied environmental ethics: Comments on Dombrowski and Finsen. *Between the Species* 4 (1988): 20–3.

Kaufman, L. and Mallory, K., eds. 1986. *The last extinction*. Cambridge: MIT Press. (Not cited.)

Kaufman, S. R. 1987. The clinical relevance of the LD-50. *Veterinary and Human Toxicology* 29: 39–40.

Keehn, J. D., ed. 1982. *The ethics of psychological research*. Oxford: Pergamon Press.

Keen, W. W. 1914. *Animal experimentation and medical progress*. Boston: Houghton Mifflin.

Kellert, S. R. and Felthous, A. R. 1985. Childhood cruelty toward animals among criminals and noncriminals. *Human Relations* 38: 1113–29.

Kellogg, J. H. 1923. *The natural diet of man*. Battle Creek, MI: Modern Medicine Publishing.

Kelly, J. A. 1986. Psychological research and the rights of animals: Disagreement with Miller. *American Psychologist* (July): 839–41.

Kiley-Worthington, M. 1977. *Behavioral problems of farm animals*. London: Oriel Press.

King, F. A. 1984. Animals in research: The case for experimentation. *Psychology Today* (September): 56–8.

———. 1986. Philosophical and practical issues in animal research involving pain and stress. *Annals of the New York Academy of Science* 467: 405–9.

King-Farlow, J. 1978. Man, beast and mental acts. In *Self-knowledge and social relations*, 37–58. New York: Science History Publications.

King-Farlow, J. and Hall, E. A. 1965. Man, beast, and philosophical psychology. *British Journal for the Philosophy of Science* 16: 81–101.

Kingston, A. R. 1967. Theodicy and animal welfare. *Theology* 70: 482–8.

Kirk, R. 1967. Rationality without language. *Mind* 76: 369–86.

Klug, B. 1982. Language, science and the abuse of farm animals: A review of the CAST report on farm animal welfare. *Animals' Agenda* (Sept–Oct): 22–4.

———. 1983a. Lab animals, Francis Bacon and the culture of science. *Listening* 18 (Winter): 54–72.

———. 1983b. Language, science, and the abuse of farm animals. *California Veterinarian* 37 (January): 61–2.

Kotzwinkle, W. 1976. *Doctor Rat*. New York: Alfred A. Knopf.

Kuker-Reines, B. 1982. Psychology experiments on animals: *A critique of animal models of*

human psychopathology. Boston: New England Anti-Vivisection Society.
————. 1984. *Environmental experiments on animals: A critique of animal models of hypoxemia, heat injury and cold injury*. Boston: New England Anti-Vivisection Society.
————. 1985. *Heart research on animals: A critique of animal models of cardiovascular disease*. Jenkintown, PA: American Anti-Vivisection Society.
Kulstad, M. 1981. Leibniz, animals, and apperception. *Studia Leibnitiana* 13: 25–60.

Laertius, D. ⟨3rd cent.⟩ 1958. *Lives of eminent philosophers*. Vol. 2. Trans. R. D. Hicks. Cambridge: Harvard University Press.
Lamb, D. 1982. Animal rights and liberation movements. *Environmental Ethics* 4: 215–33.
Lane-Petter, W. 1972. The rational use of living animals in biomedical research. In *The rational use of living systems in biomedical research*, by Universities Federation for Animal Welfare, 37–41. Potters Bar, Herts: UFAW.
————. 1976. The ethics of animal experimentation. *Journal of Medical Ethics* 2: 118–22.
Langley, G. 1987. *Blinded by science: The facts about sight deprivation experiments on animals*. Tonbridge, Kent: Animal Aid Society.
Lansbury, C. 1985. *The old brown dog: Women, workers and vivisection in Edwardian England*. Madison, WI: University of Wisconsin Press.
Lappé, F. M. 1982. *Diet for a small planet*. New York: Ballantine Books.
LaRene, S. 1987. *Michigan Humane Society handbook of animal cruelty law*. Detroit, MI: MHS.
Lawler, J. G. 1965. On the rights of animals. *Anglican Theological Review* 47: 180–90.
Leader, R. W. and Stark, D. 1987. The importance of animals in biomedical research. *Perspectives in Biology and Medicine* 30: 470–85.
Lecky, W. E. H. ⟨1859⟩ 1869. *History of European morals from Augustus to Charlemagne*. 2 vols. London: Longmans, Green.
Lederer, S. E. 1987. *An ethical problem: The controversy over human and animal experimentation in late nineteenth-century America*. Ph.D. diss., University of Wisconsin. Ann Arbor, MI: University Microfilms International.
Leffingwell, A. J. 1880. Does vivisection pay? *Scribner's Monthly* 20: 391–9.
————. 1907. *The vivisection question*. Chicago: The Vivisection Reform Society.
Leibniz, G. W. F. ⟨1714⟩ 1965. *Monadology and other philosophical essays*. Trans. P and A. Schrecker. Indianapolis, IN: Bobbs-Merrill.
————. ⟨1716⟩ 1949. *New essays concerning human understanding*. Trans. A. G. Langley. LaSalle, IL: Open Court.
Leon, D. 1949. *Ruskin: The great Victorian*. London: Routledge and Kegan Paul.
Leopold, A. 1949. The land ethic. In *A Sand County almanac*, 201–26. New York: Oxford University Press.
Levin, M. E. 1977a. Animal rights evaluated. *Humanist* 37 (July–Aug): 12, 14–15.
————. 1977b. All in a stew about animals: A reply to Singer. *Humanist* 37 (Sept–Oct): 58.
Lewis, C. S. 1943. Animal pain. In *The problem of pain*. London: Geoffrey Bles.
Liddell, G. 1985. The consistency-from-marginal-cases argument for animal rights: A critical examination. *Victoria University of Wellington Law Review* 15: 147–55.
Limburg, J. 1971. What does it mean to "have dominion over the earth"? *Dialog* 10: 221–3.
Lind af Hageby, L. and Schartau, L. K. 1903. *The shambles of science*. London: Ernest Bell.
Lindeboom, G. A. 1978. *Descartes and medicine*. Amsterdam: Rodopi.
Linden, E. 1974. *Apes, men, and language*. New York: Saturday Review Press.
————. 1986. *Silent partners: The legacy of the ape language experiments*. New York: Times Books.
Lindgren, P. et al., eds. 1983. *First CFN symposium: LD50 and possible alternatives*. Acta Pharmacologica et Toxicologica 52 Supplement 2: 1–302.
Linzey, A. 1985. *Christian attitudes to animals*. London: Christian Education Movement. Horsham, West Sussex: RSPCA.
————. 1986. Animals. In *The Westminster Dictionary of Christian Ethics*, ed. by J. Childress and J. Macquarrie, 28–33. Philadelphia: Westminster Press.

Lloyd, G. 1980. Spinoza's environmental ethics. *Inquiry* 23: 293–311.

Locke, J. ⟨1690⟩ 1966. *Two treatises of government*, ed. by P. Laslett. Cambridge: Cambridge University Press.

———. ⟨1706⟩ 1975. *An essay concerning human understanding*, ed. by P. H. Nidditch. Oxford: Clarendon Press.

———. ⟨17th cent.⟩ 1968. *The educational writings of John Locke*, ed. by J. L. Axtell. Cambridge: Cambridge University Press.

Lockwood, M. 1979. Singer on killing and the preference for life. *Inquiry* 22: 157–70.

Lockwood, R. 1985a. Anthropomorphism is not a four-letter word. In M. W. Fox and L. D. Mickley (1985b, 185–99).

———. 1985b. *A model syllabus for a course in human–animal relationships.* Washington, DC: Humane Society of US.

Loew, F. M. 1987. The animal welfare *bête noire* in veterinary medicine. *Canadian Veterinary Journal* 28: 689–92.

Loftin, R. 1985. The medical treatment of wild animals. *Environmental Ethics* 7: 231–9.

Loftin, R. W. 1983. Comments on Jones' and Perry's "On animal rights." *International Journal of Applied Philosophy* 1: 83–6.

Lombardi, L. G. 1983. Inherent worth, respect, and rights. *Environmental Ethics* 5: 257–70.

Long, T. A. 1963. Hampshire on animals and intentions. *Mind* 72: 414–16.

Lorenz, K. 1952. *King Solomon's ring: New light on animal ways.* Trans. M. K. Wilson. New York: Crowell.

———. 1954. *Man meets dog.* Trans. M. K. Wilson. London: Methuen.

———. 1971. Do animals undergo subjective experience? In *Studies in animal and human behavior*, vol. 2, 323–37. Cambridge: Harvard University Press.

———. 1978. *The year of the Greylag goose.* Photos by S. and K. Kalas. Trans. R. Martin. New York: Harcourt Brace Jovanovich.

Lovejoy, A. O. and Boas, G. ⟨1935⟩ 1965. *Primitivism and related ideas in antiquity.* New York: Octagon Books.

Lowry, J. W. 1975. Natural rights: Men and animals. *Southwestern Journal of Philosophy* 6: 109–22.

Lyster, S. 1985. *International wildlife law.* Cambridge: Grotius Publications.

McArdle, J. 1984. Psychological experimentation on animals: Not necessary, not valid. Humane Society of the US *Humane Society News* (Spring).

———. 1986. Lies by the pound: How scientists justify the use of pound animals in research. *Animals' Agenda* 6 (October): 32–4.

Macauley, D. 1987–88. Political animals: A study of the emerging animal rights movement in the United States. *Between the Species* 3: 119–27, 177–89; 4: 55–68.

Macauley, J. 1875. *Plea for mercy to animals.* London: Religious Tract Society.

McCarthy, R. F. and Bennett, R. E. 1986. Statutory protection for farm animals. *Pace Environmental Law Review* 3: 229–55.

McCloskey, H. J. 1965. Rights. *Philosophical Quarterly* 15: 115–27.

———. 1969. *Meta-ethics and normative ethics.* The Hague: Martinus Nijhoff.

———. 1975. The right to life. *Mind* 84: 403–25.

———. 1979. Moral rights and animals. *Inquiry* 22: 23–5.

———. 1983. Animal rights? How they would bear on ecological ethics. Political implications thereof. In *Ecological ethics and politics*, 62–9, 121–3. Totowa, NJ: Rowman Littlefield.

———. 1987. The moral case for experimentation on animals. *Monist* 70: 64–82.

McCulloch, M. J. 1978. The veterinarian and human health-care systems: Issues and boundaries. In *Implications of history and ethics to medicine: Veterinary and human*, ed. by L. B. McCullough and J. P. Morris III, 53–65. College Station, TX: Centennial Academic Assembly, Texas A&M University.

Macdonald, A. D. 1972. The ethical arguments for the use of animals in bio-medical research. In *The rational use of living systems in bio-medical research.* 47–50 (Universities Federation for Animal Welfare 1977–1987).

McGiffin, H. and Brownley, N., eds. 1980. *Animals in education: Use of animals in high school biology classes and science fairs.* Washington, DC: Institute for the Study of Animal Problems.

McKenna, V. et al., eds. 1987. *Beyond the bars: The zoo dilemma.* Wellingborough, Northants: Thorsons Publishers. (Not cited.)

Mackintosh, N. 1987. Animal minds. In *Mindwaves*, ed. by C. Blakemore and S. Greenfield, 111–22. Oxford: Basil Blackwell.

McLachlan, H. V. 1980. The moral case of a carnivore. *Contemporary Review* 237: 19–24.

McLaughlin, R. J. 1985. Men, animals and personhood. *Proceedings of the American Catholic Philosophical Association* 59: 166–81.

Macphail, E. 1987. Intelligence: A comparative perspective. In *Mindwaves*, ed. by C. Blakemore and S. Greenfield, 177–93. Oxford: Basil Blackwell.

Magel, C. R. and Regan, T. 1979. A select bibliography on animal rights and human obligations. *Inquiry* 22: 243–7.

Maitland, E. 1896. *Anna Kingsford.* 2 vols. 2d ed. London: George Redway.

Malcolm, N. 1967. Wittgenstein, Ludwig Josef Johann. In *The encyclopedia of philosophy*, ed. by P. Edwards, vol. 8, 327–40. New York: Macmillan.

——. ⟨1972–73⟩ 1977. Thoughtless brutes. In *Thought and knowledge*, 40–57. Ithaca: Cornell University Press.

Mandelbaum, M. 1943. A note on "anthropomorphism" in psychology. *Journal of Philosophy* 40: 246–8.

Marcuse, F. L. and Pear, J. J. 1979. Ethics and animal experimentation: Personal views. In *Psychopathology in animals*, ed. by J. D. Keehn, 305–29. New York: Academic Press.

Margolis, J. 1974. Animals have no rights and are not the equal of humans. *Philosophic Exchange* 1: 119–23.

——. 1975. Mental states. *Behaviorism* 3: 23–31.

——. 1978. Propositional content and the beliefs of animals. In *Persons and minds*, 146–70. Dordrecht: D. Reidel.

Marsh, N. and Haywood, S., eds. 1985. *Animal experimentation: Improvements and alternatives: Replacement, refinement and reduction.* Nottingham, England: FRAME.

Martin, M. 1976. A critique of moral vegetarianism. *Reason Papers* 3: 13–43.

——. 1979. Vegetarianism, the right to life and fellow creature-hood. *Animal Regulation Studies* 2: 205–14.

Martinengo-Cesaresco, E. 1904a. The Greek conception of animals. *Contemporary Review* 85: 430–9.

——. 1904b. Animals at Rome. *Contemporary Review* 86: 225–34.

——. 1909. *The place of animals in human thought.* London: T.F. Unwin.

Mason, W. A. 1979. The role of primates in research. US National Institutes of Health *Research Resources Reporter* 3 (May): 11–14.

Mendel, L. B. 1903–04. Some historical aspects of vegetarianism. *Popular Science Monthly* 64: 457–65.

Mendus, S. 1980. Personal identity: The two analogies in Hume. *Philosophical Quarterly* 30: 61–8.

Merrill, G. F. 1986. The case for the use of animals in medicine. In M. W. Fox and L. D. Mickley, eds. (1986, 227–43).

Metz, H. 1986. Suffer the little animals. *Student Lawyer* 15 (October): 12–20.

Midgley, M. 1979. Brutality and sentimentality. *Philosophy* 54: 385–94.

——. 1985. The vulnerable world and its claims on us. In *Evolution as a religion*, 148–62. London: Methuen.

Mighetto, L. 1986. John Muir and the rights of animals. Preface to *Muir among the animals*, ed. by L. Mighetto, xi–xxviii. San Francisco, CA: Sierra Club Books.

Mill, J. S. ⟨19th cent.⟩ 1963–1986. *Collected Works*. 25 vols. Toronto: University of Toronto Press.

Miller, N. E. 1983. Understanding the use of animals in behavioral research. *Annals of the New York Academy of Sciences* 406: 113–18.

———. 1985. The value of behavioral research on animals. *American Psychologist* 40: 423–40.

———. 1986. The morality and humaneness of animal research on stress and pain. *Annals of the New York Academy of Science* 467: 402–4.

Mills, W. 1898. *The nature and development of animal intelligence*. New York: Macmillan.

———. 1899. The nature of animal intelligence and the methods of investigating it. *Psychological Review* 6: 262–74.

Montague, P. 1980. Two concepts of rights. *Philosophy and Public Affairs* 9: 372–84.

Montaigne, M. ⟨16th cent.⟩ 1958. *The complete essays of Montaigne*. Trans. D. M. Frame. Stanford, CA: Stanford University Press.

Montefiore, H., ed. 1975. *Man and nature*. London: Collins.

Moretti, D. S. 1984. *Animal rights and the law*. London: Oceana Publications.

Morgan, C. L. 1886. On the study of animal intelligence. *Mind* 11: 174–85.

———. 1890. *Animal life and intelligence*. London: Edward Arnold.

———. ⟨1894⟩ 1977. *An introduction to comparative psychology*. Washington, DC: University Publications of America.

———. 1896a. *Habit and instinct*. London: Edward Arnold.

———. 1896b. Animal automatism and consciousness. *Monist* 7: 1–17.

Morse, M. 1968. *Ordeal of the animals*. Englewood Cliffs: Prentice-Hall. (Not cited.)

Moseley, Ray E. 1984. *Animal rights: An analysis of the major arguments for animal rights*. Ph.D. diss., Georgetown University. Ann Arbor: University Microfilms International.

Moss, A. W. 1961. *Valiant crusade: The history of the RSPCA*. London: Cassell.

Moss, T. H. 1984. The modern politics of laboratory animal use. *Science, Technology, and Human Values* 9 (Spring): 51–6.

Muir, J. ⟨1838–1914⟩ 1986. *Muir among the animals: The wildlife writings of John Muir*, ed. by L. Mighetto. San Francisco, CA: Sierra Club Books.

Murphy, J. G. 1972. Moral death: A Kantian essay on psychopathy. *Ethics* 82: 284–98.

Muscari, P. G. 1986. Is man the paragon of animals? *Journal of Value Inquiry* 20: 303–8.

Myers, N. 1979. *The sinking ark: A new look at the problem of disappearing species*. Oxford: Pergamon. (Not cited.)

Naess, A. 1977. Spinoza and ecology. *Philosophia* 7: 45–54.

———. 1979. Self-realization in mixed communities of humans, bears, sheep, and wolves. *Inquiry* 22: 231–41.

———. 1980. Environmental ethics and Spinoza's ethics. *Inquiry* 23: 313–25.

Nagel, T. 1974. What is it like to be a bat? *Philosophical Review* 83: 435–50.

Narveson, J. 1977. Animal rights. *Canadian Journal of Philosophy* 7: 161–78.

———. 1983. Animal rights revisited. In [207, 45–59].

———. 1987. On a case for animal rights. *Monist* 70: 31–49.

Nash, R. 1967. *Wilderness and the American mind*. New Haven: Yale University Press.

National Anti-Vivisection Society. 1977. *The moral, scientific and economic aspects of research techniques not involving the use of living animals*. London: NAVS.

Nearing, H. and S. 1970. *Living the good life*. New York: Schocken.

———. 1979. *Continuing the good life*. New York: Schocken.

Nelson, J. A. 1982. Review of Sapontzis' recent work on animal rights. *Ethics and Animals* 3: 117–23.

———. 1985. Recent studies in animal ethics. *American Philosophical Quarterly* 22: 13–24.

———. 1986. Critical notice of *Rights, killing and suffering* by R. G. Frey. *Between the Species* 2: 70–80.

Nelson, J. O. 1983. Do animals propositionally know? Do they propositionally believe? *American Philosophical Quarterly* 20: 149–60.

——. 1987. Brute animals and legal rights. *Philosophy* 62: 171–7.

Newman, J. H. 1858. *Sermons preached on various occasions*. London: Burns and Lambert.

Niemi, S. M. and Dodds, W. J. 1986. Animals in research. *National Forum* 66 (Winter): 25–9.

Nietzsche, F. ⟨19th cent.⟩ 1964. *Complete works of Friedrich Nietzsche*, ed. by O. Levy. New York: Russell and Russell.

Nilsson, G. 1986. *The endangered species handbook*. Washington, DC: Animal Welfare Institute.

Nolan, F. R. 1929. *The doctor's nightmare*. Belfast: William Brown.

Norman, R. and Francis, L. P. 1978. Some animals are more equal than others. *Philosophy* 53: 507–27.

Nozick, R. 1974. *Anarchy, state and utopia*. New York: Basic Books.

——. 1983. About mammals and people. *New York Times Book Review* (27 November): 11, 29, 30.

Null, G. 1987. *The vegetarian handbook: Eating right for total health*. New York: St Martin's.

Oakley, D. A. 1985a. Cognition and imagery in animals. In *Brain and mind*, ed. by D. A. Oakley, 99–131. London: Methuen.

——. 1985b. Animal awareness, consciousness and self-image. In *Brain and mind*, ed. by D. A. Oakley, 132–51. London: Methuen.

O'Brien, R. C. 1972. *Mrs. Frisby and the rats of NIMH*. New York: Atheneum. (Made into movie "The secret of NIMH".)

Oldfield, J. 1898. Vegetarian still: A reply to Sir Henry Thompson. *Nineteenth Century* 44: 246–52.

Olmsted, J. M. D. 1944. *François Magendie: Pioneer in experimental physiology and scientific medicine*. New York: Schuman's.

Orlans, B. 1980. Humaneness supersedes curiosity. In H. McGiffin and N. Brownley (1980, 106–18).

Orlans, F. B. et al., eds. 1987. *Effective animal care and use committees*. Cordova, TN: American Association for Laboratory Animal Science. (Also *Laboratory Animal Science* 37, Special Number, January 1987.)

Ost, D. E. 1986. The case against animal rights. *Southern Journal of Philosophy* 24: 365–73.

Overcast, T. D. and Sales, B. D. 1985. Regulation of animal experimentation. *Journal of American Medical Association* 254: 1944–9.

Owen, R. 1881. Vivisection. *Nineteenth Century* (December): 931–5.

——. 1882. *Experimental physiology*. London: Longmans, Green.

Paget, J. 1881. Vivisection. *Nineteenth Century* (December): 920–30.

Paget, S. 1900. *Experiments on animals*. London: T. F. Unwin.

Pains, W. 1925. *Richard Martin, 1754–1834*. London: Leonard Parsons.

Paley, W. ⟨1785⟩ 1803. *The principles of moral and political philosophy*. Vol. 1. London: R. Faulder.

Partridge, E. 1984. Three wrong leads in a search for an environmental ethic: Tom Regan on animal rights, inherent values, and "deep ecology." *Ethics and Animals* 5: 61–74.

Passmore, J. 1974. *Man's responsibility for nature: Ecological problems and Western traditions*. New York: Charles Scribner's.

——. 1975a. The treatment of animals. *Journal of the History of Ideas* 36: 195–218.

——. 1975b. Attitudes toward nature. In *Nature and conduct*, ed. by R. S. Peters, 251–64. New York: Macmillan.

Paterson, R. W. K. 1984. Animal pain, God and Professor Geach. *Philosophy* 59: 116–20.

Paton, W. 1983. Vivisection, morals, medicine: Commentary from a vivisecting professor of pharmacology. *Journal of Medical Ethics* 9: 102–4.

———. 1984. *Man and mouse: Animals in medical research.* Oxford: Oxford University Press.

Pavlov, I. 1906. Scientific study of the so-called psychical processes in the higher mammals. *Lancet* 2: 911–15.

———. ⟨1917⟩ 1962. Physiology and psychology in the study of the higher nervous activity of animals. In *Essays in psychology and psychiatry*, 67–84. New York: Citadel Press.

Perry, C. 1981. We are what we eat. *Environmental Ethics* 3: 341–50.

Perry, C. and Jones, G. E. 1982. On animal rights. *Applied Philosophy* 1: 39–57.

———. 1983. Equal consideration and animal rights. *International Journal of Applied Philosophy* 1: 87–8.

Perry, G. 1973. Can the physiologist measure stress? *New Scientist* 60: 175–7.

Philanthropos [F. Heatherly]. 1883. *Physiological cruelty: or, fact v. fancy.* London: Tinsley Bros.

Physicians Committee for Responsible Medicine. 1987. *Alternatives in medical education: Non-animal methods.* Washington, DC: PCRM.

Physiologus. ⟨between 2d and 5th cents.⟩ 1979. Trans. M. J. Curley. Austin: University of Texas Press.

Pierce, C. 1979. Can animals be liberated? *Philosophical Studies* 36: 69–75.

Place, U. T. 1966. Consciousness and perception. *Aristotelian Society Proceedings* Suppl. 40: 101–24.

Plamenatz, J. P. 1938. *Consent, freedom and obligation.* London: Oxford University Press.

Plato. ⟨5th–4th cents. BC⟩ 1961. *The collected dialogues of Plato*, ed. by E. Hamilton and H. Cairns. Princeton: Princeton University Press.

Pliny. ⟨1st cent.⟩ 1967–80. *Natural history.* 10 vols. Cambridge: Harvard University Press.

Pluhar, E. B. 1981. Must an opponent of animal rights also be an opponent of human rights? *Inquiry* 24: 229–41.

———. 1982. On replaceability. *Ethics and Animals* 3: 96–105.

———. 1983. Two conceptions of an environmental ethic and their implications. *Ethics and Animals* 4: 110–27.

———. 1984. Speciesism not justified. *Ethics and Animals* 5: 122–9.

———. 1985. On the genetic manipulation of animals. *Between the Species* 1 (Summer): 13–18.

———. 1986a. Speciesism revisited. *Between the Species* 2: 184–9.

———. 1986b. The moral justifiability of genetic manipulation. *Between the Species* 2: 136–8.

———. 1987. The personhood view and the argument from marginal cases. *Philosophica* 39: 23–38.

———. 1988a forthcoming. Speciesism: A form of bigotry or a justified view? *Between the Species.*

———. 1988b forthcoming. On the relevance of marginal humans: A reply to Sapontzis. *Between the Species.*

Poole, T. B., ed. 1987. *The UFAW handbook on the care and management of laboratory animals.* 6th ed. Harlow, Essex: Longman Group UK Limited.

Powys, J. C. 1937. *Morwyn or the vengeance of God.* London: Cassell.

Pratt, D. 1980. *Alternatives to pain in experiments on animals.* New York: Argus Archives.

———. 1986. *Animal films for humane education.* New York: Argus Archives.

Preus, A. 1983. Biological theory in Porphyry's *De abstinentia. Ancient Philosophy* 3: 149–59.

Pritchard, M. S. and Robinson, W. L. 1981. Justice and the treatment of animals: A critique of Rawls. *Environmental Ethics* 3: 55–61.

Pumphrey, R. J. 1954. The evolution of thinking. *British Journal of the Philosophy of Science* 4: 315–27.

Pybus, E. M. and Broadie, A. 1978. Kant and the maltreatment of animals. *Philosophy* 53: 560–1.

Quaker Concern for Animal Welfare. 1985. *Regarding animals: Some Quakers consider our treatment of animals in the modern world.* Braintree, Essex: QCAW.

Rachels, J. 1986. *The end of life: Euthanasia and morality.* Oxford: Oxford University Press.
Rawls, J. 1963. The sense of justice. *Philosophical Review* 72: 281-305.
———. 1971. *A theory of Justice.* Cambridge: Harvard University Press.
Ray, P. M., ed. 1987. *The teaching of animal welfare.* Potters Bar, Herts: Universities Federation for Animal Welfare.
Ray, P. M. and Scott, W. N. 1976. U. K. legislation relevant to the keeping of laboratory animals. In *The UFAW handbook on the care and management of laboratory animals,* ed. by UFAW, 5th ed., 1-6. Edinburgh: Churchill Livingstone.
Redman, C. 1986-87. The meateaters. *Between the Species* 2: 139-47, 197-200; 3: 25-33, 86-93.
Reece, K. A. 1988/89. *Animal organization & Services Directory.* Huntington Beach, CA: Animal Stories.
Reed, T. J. 1978. Nietzche's animals: Idea, image and influence. In *Nietzsche: Imagery and thought,* ed. by M. Pasley, 159-219. Berkeley: University of California Press.
Regan, D. H. 1986. Duties of preservation. In *The preservation of species,* ed. by B. G. Norton, 195-220. Princeton, NJ: Princeton University Press.
Regan, T. 1976a. Broadie and Pybus on Kant. *Philosophy* 51: 471-2.
———. 1976b. McCloskey on why animals cannot have rights. *Philosophical Quarterly* 26: 251-7.
———. 1977a. Frey on interests and animal rights. *Philosophical Quarterly* 27: 335-7.
———. 1977b. Narveson on egoism and the rights of animals. *Canadian Journal of Philosophy* 7: 179-86.
———. 1978. Fox's critique of animal liberation. *Ethics* 88: 126-33.
———. 1980a. Utilitarianism, vegetarianism, and animal rights. *Philosophy and Public Affairs* 9: 305-24.
———. 1980b. On the right not to be made to suffer gratuitously. *Canadian Journal of Philosophy* 10: 473-8.
———. 1981a. Utilitarianism and vegetarianism again. *Ethics and Animals* 2 (March): 2-7.
———. 1981b. Duties to animals: Rawls' dilemma. *Ethics and Animals* 2: 76-82.
———. 1981c. The nature and possibility of an environmental ethic. *Environmental Ethics* 3: 19-34.
———. 1982. Frey on why animals cannot have simple desires. *Mind* 91: 277-80.
———. 1983. Veterinary ethics: Between a rock and a hard place. *Journal of Veterinary Medical Education* 9: 113-15.
———. 1984. Honey dribbles down your fur: Remarks on environmental ethics. In *Social policy and conflict resolution,* ed. by T. Attig et al., 138-55. Bowling Green, OH: Bowling Green State University.
———. 1985. Letter: The dog in the lifeboat. *New York Review of Books* (25 April): 56-7.
———. 1987. When thinkers collide. *Animals' Agenda* 7 (November): 3, 54.
Regan, T. and Jamieson, D. 1978. Animal rights: A reply to Frey's "Animal rights." *Analysis* 38: 32-6.
Reines, B. 1986. *Cancer research on animals: Impact and alternatives.* Chicago: National Anti-Vivisection Society.
———. 1987? *The truth behind the discovery of insulin.* Jenkintown, PA: American Anti-Vivisection Society.
Research Defence Society. 1927-85. Stephen Paget memorial lectures. London: RDS. (54 lectures related to and generally defending animal experiments. Nine most recent: S. Shuster, "Science, safety, sentiment and the skin: A topical debate on biomedical research," 1977; W. D. M. Paton, "The evolution of animal experiment," 1978; G. R. Dunstan, "A limited dominion," 1979; G. J. Carter, "The law of the matter,

viewed in relation to ethics," 1980; J. Butterfield, "The Medicines Commission, its work and responsibilities," 1981; E. Bárány, "The Swedish system of ethical committees in the laboratory animals field," 1982; R. Calne, "Can medicine advance without experiments on animals?" 1983; J. Vane, "How animals discover drugs," 1984; M. Warnock, "Law and the pursuit of knowledge," 1985.)

———. 1979. *Notes on the law relating to experiments on animals in Great Britain*. London: RDS.

Richet, C. 1908. *The pros and cons of vivisection*. London: Duckworth.

Rickaby, J. J. ⟨1888⟩ 1918. *Moral philosophy*. 4th ed. London: Longmans, Green.

———. 1902. *Political and moral essays*. New York: Benziger Brothers.

Rimbach, J. A. 1982. The Judeo-Christian tradition and the human/animal bond. *International Journal for the Study of Animal Problems* 3: 198–207.

Ristau, C. A. 1983. Language cognition and awareness in animals. *Annals of the New York Academy of Sciences* 406: 170–86.

Ristau, C. A. and Robbins, D. 1982. Language in the great apes: A critical review. *Advances in the Study of Behavior* 12: 141–260.

Ritchie, A. M. 1963–64. Can animals see? A Cartesian query. *Proceedings of the Aristotelian Society* 64: 221–42.

Ritchie, D. G. ⟨1894⟩ 1952. *Natural rights*. London: George Allen and Unwin.

———. 1900. The rights of animals. *Ethics* 10: 387–9.

Ritson, J. 1802. *An essay on abstinence from animal food as a moral duty*. London: Richard Phillips.

Ritvo, H. 1984. *Plus ça change*: Anti-vivisection then and now. *Science, Technology, and Human Values* 9 (Spring): 57–66.

———. 1987. *The animal estate: The English and other creatures in the Victorian age*. Cambridge: Harvard University Press.

Roberts, C. 1971. Animal experimentation and evolution. *American Scholar* 40: 497–503.

———. 1974. *The scientific conscience*. London: Centaur Press.

———. 1980. *Science, animals and evolution*. Westport, CT: Greenwood Press.

Roberts, W. G. 1979. Man before beast: The response of organized medicine to the American anti-vivisection movement. Undergraduate thesis, BA degree, Harvard College. Boston, MA: HUA.

Robinson, E. 1906. *Crowleigh Hall*. London: The Animals' Guardian.

Rodman, J. 1977. The liberation of nature? *Inquiry* 20: 83–131.

———. 1979. Animal justice: The counter-revolution in natural light and law. *Inquiry* 22: 3–22.

Roitblat, H. L. 1982. The meaning of representation in animal memory. *Behavioral and Brain Sciences* 5: 353–72.

Rollin, B. E. 1977. Moral philosophy and veterinary medical education. *Journal of Veterinary Medical Education* 4: 180–2.

———. 1979. On the nature of illness. *Man and Medicine* 4: 157–72.

———. 1983. Veterinary ethics and animal rights. *California Veterinarian* 37: 9.

———. 1986a. On *telos* and genetic manipulation. *Between the Species* 2 (Spring): 88–9.

———. 1986b. Moral, social and scientific aspects of the use of swine in research. In *Swine in biomedical research*, ed. by M. E. Tumbleson, vol. 1, 29–37. New York: Plenum Press.

———. 1986c. "The Frankenstein thing" – The moral impact of genetic engineering of agricultural animals on society and future science. In *Genetic engineering of animals*, ed. by A. Hollaender and J. W. Evans, 285–97. New York: Plenum Press.

———. 1986d. Letter on animal rights and veterinarians. *Journal of the American Veterinary Medical Association* 189: 602–3, 638.

Rolston, H. III. 1986. *Philosophy gone wild: Essays in environmental ethics*. Buffalo, NY: Prometheus Books.

———. 1988. *Environmental ethics: Duties to and values in the natural world*. Philadelphia, PA: Temple University Press.

Rorty, R. 1979. *Philosophy and the mirror of nature*. Princeton: Princeton University Press.

Rosenfield, L. C. ⟨1941⟩ 1968. *From beast-machine to man-machine: Animal soul in French letters from Descartes to LaMettrie*. Rev. enlarged ed. New York: Octagon Books.

Ross, M. W. 1981. The ethics of experiments on higher animals. *Social Science and Medicine* 15F: 51–60.

Ross, W. D. 1930. *The right and the good*. London: Oxford University Press.

Rothschild, M. 1986. *Animals and man*. Oxford: Clarendon Press. (The Romanes Lecture for 1984–85.)

Rousseau, J. J. ⟨1772⟩ 1973. *The social contract and discourses*. Trans. G. D. H. Cole. London: J. M. Dent.

———. ⟨1762⟩ 1979. *Émile: or, On education*. Trans. A. Bloom. New York: Basic Books.

Routley, R. 1981. Alleged problems in attributing beliefs, and intentionality, to animals. *Inquiry* 24: 385–418.

Routley, R. and V. 1979. Against the inevitability of human chauvinism. In *Ethics and problems of the 21st century*, ed. by K. E. Goodpaster and K. M. Sayre, 36–59. Notre Dame, IN: University of Notre Dame Press.

———. 1980. Human chauvinism and environmental ethics. In *Environmental philosophy*, ed. by D. S. Mannison et al., 96–189. Canberra: Australian National University.

Rowan, A. N. 1977. Alternatives to laboratory animals in biomedical programmes. *Animal Regulation Studies* 1: 103–28.

———. 1979. *Alternatives to laboratory animals: Definition and discussion*. Washington, DC: Institute for the Study of Animal Problems.

———. 1980. The concept of the three R's: An introduction. *Developments in Biological Standardization* 45: 175–80.

———. 1981a. Alternatives to laboratory animals: Scientific, fiscal and philosophical considerations. In *Nonanimal research methodologies*, ed. by A. Posner, 5–13. Washington, DC: George Washington University Ethics and Animal Society.

———. 1981b. Animals in education. *American Biology Teacher* 43: 280–2.

———. 1983. Alternatives: Interaction between science and animal welfare. In *Product safety evaluation*, ed. by A. M. Goldberg, 113–33. New York: Mary Ann Liebert.

———. 1987. Scientific perspectives in the development of alternatives in toxicology. *Comments Toxicology* 1: 275–88.

Rowan, A. N. and Goldberg, A. M. 1985. Perspectives and alternatives to current animal testing techniques in preclinical toxicology. *Annual Review of Pharmacology and Toxicology* 25: 225–47.

Rowan, A. N. and Tannenbaum, J. 1986. Animal rights. *National Forum* 66 (Winter): 30–3.

Rowsell, H. C. 1977. The ethics of biomedical experimentation. In (Institute of Laboratory Animal Resources 1977, 267–85).

———. 1978–79. The right animal for the right reason. In *Proceedings of 1978/79 CALAS convention*. Edmonton: Canadian Association for Laboratory Animal Science.

———. 1980. High school science fairs: Evaluation of live animal experimentation – The Canadian experience. In (H. McGiffin and N. Brownley 1980, 85–98).

Roy, R. 1985. *The chimpanzee kid*. Boston: Houghton Mifflin.

Rupke, N. A., ed. 1987. *Vivisection in historical perspective*. London: Croom Helm.

Russell, B. 1956. *The analysis of mind*. London: George Allen and Unwin.

Russell, G. K. 1978. *Laboratory investigations in human physiology*. New York: Macmillan.

Russell, W. M. S. and Burch, R. L. 1959. *The principles of humane experimental technique*. London: Methuen.

Russow, L-M. 1982. It's not like that to be a bat. *Behaviorism* 10: 55–63.

———. 1988. Regan on inherent value. *Between the Species* 4 (1988): 46–54.

Ryder, R. D. 1976. Speciesism. *Journal of Medical Ethics* 2: 124–5.

———. 1978. Professor Shuster: A reply. *New Scientist* 77: 82–3.

Sagan, C. 1977. The abstractions of beasts. In *The dragons of Eden*, 105–24. New York: Random House.

Sagoff, M. 1984. Animal liberation and environmental ethics: Bad marriage, quick divorce. *Osgoode Hall Law Journal* 22: 297–307.

Sainsbury, D. 1986. *Farm animal welfare: Cattle, pigs and poultry*. London: Collins.

Salt, H. S. 1900. A reply to Professor Ritchie. *Ethics* 10: 389–90.

———. 1930. Two anti-vegetarian sages. In *Company I have kept*, chap. 15. London: G. Allen and Unwin.

Sapontzis, S. F. 1982a. On being morally expendable. *Ethics and Animals* 3: 58–72.

———. 1982b. Response to Regan's "The nature and possibility of an environmental ethic." *Ethics and Animals* 3: 33–9.

———. 1983. Interests and animals, needs and language. *Ethics and Animals* 4: 38–49.

———. 1984. Review of J. B. Callicott's "Animal liberation: A triangular affair." *Ethics and Animals* 5: 113–23.

———. 1987. The moral significance of the "innocence" of animals. *Between the Species* 3 (Winter): 12–15.

———. 1988 forthcoming. Speciesism. *Between the Species*.

Savage-Rumbaugh, E. S. 1986. *Ape language: From conditioned response to symbol*. New York: Columbia University Press.

Scharfenberg, J. A. 1982. *Problems with meat*. Santa Barbara, CA: Woodbridge Press.

Schochet, E. J. 1984. *Animal life in Jewish tradition*. New York: Ktav.

Schopenhauer, A. 〈1813〉 1974. *On the fourfold root of the principle of sufficient reason*. Trans. E. F. J. Payne. LaSalle, IL: Open Court.

———. 〈1819〉 1958. *The world as will and representation*. 2 vols. Trans. E. F. J. Payne. Indian Hills, CO: Falcon's Wing Press.

———. 〈1839〉 1985. *On the freedom of the will*. Trans. K. Kolenda. Oxford: Basil Blackwell.

———. 〈1841〉 1965. *On the basis of morality*. Trans. E. F. J. Payne. Indianapolis, IN: Bobbs-Merrill.

———. 〈1850〉 1974. *Parerga and Paralipomena: Short philosophical essays*. 2 vols. Trans. E. F. J. Payne. Oxford: Clarendon Press.

Schwantje, M. 〈early 20th cent.〉 1976. *Gesammelte werke*. Bd. 1: *Vegetarismus – Schriften und notizen zur ethischen begründung der vegetarischen lehre*. Bd. 2: *Tierschutz – Schriften und notizen zum tierschutz*. München: F. Hirthammer Verlag. (Not cited.)

Schwartz, B. W. 1974. Estate planning for animals. *Trusts and Estates* 113: 376–9, 411.

Schweitzer, A. 1949. *Out of my life and thought*. Trans. C. T. Campion. New York: Henry Holt.

———. 〈1875–1950〉 1950. *The animal world of Albert Schweitzer*. Trans. C. R. Joy. Boston: Beacon Press.

———. 〈1875–1961〉 1961. *Pilgrimage to humanity*. Trans. W. E. Stuermann. New York: Philosophical Library.

———. 〈1875–1965〉 1965. *The teaching of reverence for life*. Trans. R. and C. Winston. New York: Holt, Rinehart and Winston.

———. 〈1875–1965〉 1980. *Reverence for life*. Trans. R. H. Fuller. New York: Irvington.

———. 〈1875–1965〉 1982. *Animals, nature and Albert Schweitzer*, ed. by A. C. Free. New York: Albert Schweitzer Fellowship.

Sechzer, J. A. 1983. The ethical dilemma of some classical animal experiments. *Annals of the New York Academy of Sciences* 406: 5–12.

Seidler, M. J. 1977. Hume and the animals. *Southern Journal of Philosophy* 15: 361–72.

Sessions, G. and Naess, A. 1986. The basic principles of deep ecology. *The Trumpeter* (Canadian Ecophilosophy Network) 3 (Fall):14.

Seton, E. T. 〈1898〉 1987. *Wild animals I have known*. Berkeley, CA: Creative Arts.

Shaw, G. B. 1898. Interview with Shaw. *Vegetarian* (15 January).
——. 1911. Preface on doctors. In *The doctor's dilemma: A tragedy*, v–xcii. New York: Brentano.
——. 1927. Against vivisection. *Sunday Express* (7 August).
——. 1933. *The adventures of the black girl in her search for God*. London: Constable.
Shelley, P. B. 1813. *A vindication of the natural diet*. London: J. Callow.
Shepard, P. 1974. Animal rights and human rites. *North American Review* 259 (Winter): 35–42.
Shugg, W. 1968. The Cartesian beast-machine in English literature, 1663–1750. *Journal of the History of Ideas* 29: 279–292.
Shuster, S. 1978. The anti-vivisectionists: A critique. *New Scientist* 77: 80–2.
Silverman, P. S. 1983. Attributing mind to animals: The role of intuition. *Journal of Social and Biological Structure* 6: 231–47.
Silverstein, H. S. 1974. Universality and treating persons as persons. *Journal of Philosophy* 71: 57–71.
Singer, B. J. 1986. Having rights. *Philosophy and Social Criticism* 11: 391–412.
Singer, I. B. 1968. The letter writer. In *The seance and other stories*. New York: Farrar, Straus and Giroux.
——. 1972. *Enemies: A love story*. New York: Farrar, Straus and Giroux.
Singer, P. 1977. A reply to Professor Levin's "Animal rights evaluated." *Humanist* 37 (July–Aug): 13, 16.
——. 1978. The fable of the fox and the unliberated animals. *Ethics* 88: 119–25.
——. 1980a. Utilitarianism and vegetarianism. *Philosophy and Public Affairs* 9: 325–37.
——. 1980b. Reply to H. L. A. Hart's review of *Practical ethics*. *New York Review of Books* (14 August): 53–4.
——. 1981. *The expanding circle: Ethics and sociobiology*. New York: Farrar, Straus and Giroux.
——. 1983. A comment on the animal rights debate. *International Journal of Applied Philosophy* 1: 89–90.
——. 1985a. Ten years of animal liberation. *New York Review of Books* (17 January): 46–52.
——. 1985b. Letter: The dog in the lifeboat. *New York Review of Books* (25 April): 57.
——. 1987. The man and the movement ten years after the rise of animal liberation (Singer interviewed by D. Macauley). *Animal's Agenda* (September): 6–9, 42–3.
Skriver, C. A. 1987. *The forgotten beginnings of creation and Christianity*. Trans. and ed. by A. Ingle, M. Skriver and K. Akers. Arlington, VA: Vegetarian Press. (Originally published in German as *Die vergessenen anfänge der schöpfung und des Christianity*, Lübeck-Travemunde, 1977.)
Slade, R. and Shultz, L. 1986. What price research? The case against certain kinds of experiments. *Barrister* 13 (Spring): 22–5, 30, 56.
Smart, B. 1981. General desires as grounds for the wrongness of killing. *Inquiry* 24: 242–51.
Smidt, D., ed. 1983. *Indicators relevant to farm animal welfare*. Boston: Martinus Nijhoff.
Smith, J. 1845. *Fruits and farinacea, the proper food of man*. London: J. Churchill.
Smith, P. 1982. On animal beliefs. *Southern Journal of Philosophy* 20: 503–12.
Smyth, D. H. 1978. *Alternatives to animal experiments*. London: Scolar Press.
Sober, E. 1986. Philosophical problems for environmentalism. In *The preservation of species*, ed. by B. G. Norton, 173–94. Princeton, NJ: Princeton University Press.
Solomon, R. C. 1982. Has not an animal organs, dimensions, senses, affections, passions? *Psychology Today* (March): 36–45.
Sperling, S. 1988 forthcoming. *Animal liberators: Research and morality*. Berkeley, CA: University of California Press. (Not cited.)
Spinoza, B. ⟨17th cent.⟩ 1910. *Spinoza's "Ethics" and "De intellectus emendatione"*. Trans. A. Boyle. London: J. M. Dent.

Spira, H. 1984. Constructive proposals from an animal activist. In (United States 1984a, 171–7).

Spitler, G. 1982. Justifying a respect for nature. *Environmental Ethics* 4: 255–60.

Spring, D. and E., eds. 1974. *Ecology and religion in history*. New York: Harper and Row.

Squadrito, K. M. 1979. Locke's view of dominion. *Environmental Ethics* 1: 255–62.

——. 1980. Descartes, Locke and the soul of animals. *Philosophy Research Archives* 6: 372–83.

——. 1981. Locke's view of property rights and the rights of animals. *Philosophia* 10: 19–22.

State Normal School of San Diego, California. 1906. *Bulletin on Humane Education*. Sacramento, CA: Superintendent State Printing.

Steinbock, B. 1978. Speciesism and the idea of equality. *Philosophy* 53: 247–56.

Stephen, L. 1896. *Social rights and duties*. 2 vols. London: Swan, Sonnenschein.

Stephens, M. L. 1986a. *Maternal deprivation experiments in psychology: A critique of animal models*. Boston: New England Anti-Vivisection Society and other societies.

——. 1986b. *Alternatives to current uses of animals in research, safety testing, and education: A layman's guide* Washington, DC: Humane Society of the US.

——. 1986c. The significance of alternative techniques in biomedical research: An analysis of Nobel Prize awards. In (M. W. Fox and L. D. Mickley, eds. 1986. 19–31).

——. 1987. *A critique of animal experiments on cocaine abuse*. Jenkintown, PA: American Anti-Vivisection Society.

Sternberg, M. and Miller, G. 1988. *Fur–Feathers–Feelers*. San Diego, CA: Brighton Press. (Published too late to be annotated in this *Keyguide*. Sternberg's perceptive poems and Miller's exquisite illustrations convey an animal rights spirit. The two-page poem "Lobster" is worth the purchase price of this elegant hand-printed, hand-bound edition.) (Not cited.)

Stevens, C. 1979. The legal rights of animals in the United States of America. *Animal Regulation Studies* 2: 93–101.

Stevenson, L. G. 1956. Religious elements in the background of the British anti-vivisection movement. *Yale Journal of Biology and Medicine* 29: 125–57.

Stewart, D. 1972. The limits of Trooghaft. *Encounter* 38 (February): 3–7. (Reprinted in [121, pp. 238–45] and [317].)

Stich, S. P. 1979. Do animals have beliefs? *Australasian Journal of Philosophy* 57: 15–28.

Stiller, H. and M. n. d. *Animal experimentation and animal experimenters*. Jenkintown, PA: American Anti-Vivisection Society.

Stone, C. D. 1976. Toward legal rights for natural systems. In *Transactions of the 41st North American Wildlife and Natural Resources Conference*, 31–8. Washington, DC: Wildlife Management Institute.

——. 1984. Legal rights for nature: The wrong answer to the right(s) question. *Osgoode Hall Law Journal* 22: 285–95.

——. 1985. Should trees have standing? revisited: How far will law reach? A pluralistic perspective. *Southern California Law Review* 59: 1–154.

——. 1987a. *Earth and other ethics: The case for moral pluralism*. New York: Harper and Row.

——. 1987b. Legal rights and moral pluralism. *Environmental Ethics* 9: 281–4.

Swift, J. ⟨1730⟩ 1979. *A modest proposal for preventing the children of poor people from being a burthen to their parents or the country*. Cambridge, MA: Friends of Harvard College Library.

Sylvan, R. 1987. Do moral matters matter – environmentally? *Between the Species* 3: 163–76.

Tait, L. 1882. *The uselessness of vivisection on animals*. Birmingham: Herald Press.

Tannenbaum, J. 1985. Ethics and human-companion animal interaction. *Veterinary Clinics of North America: Small Animal Practice* 15: 431–47.

———. 1986a. Review of M. A. Fox's *The case for animal experimentation*. *The Scientist* 1 (20 Oct.): 19, 22.

———. 1986b. Animal rights: Some guideposts for the veterinarian. *Journal of the American Veterinary Medical Association* 188: 1258–63.

———. 1986c. Letter on animal rights and veterinarians. *Journal of the American Veterinary Medical Association* 189: 638, 640.

Taylor, G. B. 1977. Animal welfare legislation in Europe. *Animal Regulation Studies* 1: 73–85.

Taylor, P. W. 1983. In defense of biocentrism. *Environmental Ethics* 5: 237–43.

———. 1984. Are humans superior to animals and plants? *Environmental Ethics* 6: 149–60.

———. 1987. Inherent value and moral rights. *Monist* 70: 15–30.

Terrace, H. S. 1982. Animal versus human minds. *Behavioral and Brain Sciences* 5: 391–2.

———. 1984. Animal cognition. In *Animal cognition*, ed. by H. L. Roitblat et al., 7–28. Hillsdale, NJ: Lawrence Erlbaum.

———. 1985. Animal cognition: Thinking without language. In *Animal intelligence*, ed. by L. Weiskrantz, 113–28. Oxford: Oxford University Press.

———. 1987. Thoughts without words. In *Mindwaves*, ed. by C. Blakemore and S. Greenfield, 123–38. Oxford: Basil Blackwell.

Thelestam, M. and Gunnarsson, A., eds. 1986. *The ethics of animal experimentation*. Proceedings of the second CFN symposium, Stockholm, Sweden, 1985. *Acta Physiologica Scandinavica* Supplementum 554: 1–269.

Thomas, R. H. 1983. *The politics of hunting*. Aldershot, Hants: Gower Publishing. (Not cited.)

Thompson, H. 1898. Why "vegetarian"? *Nineteenth Century* 43: 556–69, 966–76.

Thoreau, H. D. ⟨1854⟩ 1939. Higher laws. In *Walden*, 215–26. New York: Heritage Press.

Thorndike, E. L. 1899. A reply to W. Mill's "The nature of animal intelligence and the methods of investigating it." *Psychological Review* 6: 412–20.

———. 1911. *Animal intelligence*. London: Macmillan.

Thorpe, W. 1974. *Animal nature and human nature*. London: Methuen.

Threadingham, T. 1986. *Animals in education: Resource list*. Potters Bar, Herts: Universities Federation for Animal Welfare.

Tinbergen, N. 1953. *Social behaviour in animals, with special reference to vertebrates*. London: Methuen.

———. 1972–73. *The animal in its world: Explorations of an ethologist*. 2 vols. Cambridge: Harvard University Press.

Tiptree, J., Jr. 1977. The psychologist who wouldn't do awful things to rats. In *The best science fiction of the year #6*, ed. by T. Carr, 115–44. New York: Holt, Rinehart and Winston.

Tischler, J. S. 1977. Rights for nonhuman animals: A guardianship model for dogs and cats. *San Diego Law Review* 14: 484–506.

Tolstoy, L. ⟨1892⟩ 1968. The first step. In *The complete works of Count Tolstoy*, trans. by L. Wiener, vol. 19, 365–409. New York: AMS Press.

———. 1895. *Plaisirs cruels*. Trans. E. Halperine-Kaminsky. Paris: Bibliotheque-Charpentier.

Tondorf, F. A., ed. 1920. *A vindication of vivisection*. Washington, DC: Georgetown University of School of Medicine.

Townsend, A. 1979. Radical vegetarians. (Critical review of P. Singer's *Animal liberation* [115] and S. R. L. Clark's *The moral status of animals* [122].) *Australasian Journal of Philosophy* 57: 85–93.

Tranöy, K. E. 1959. Hume on morals, animals, and men. *Journal of Philosophy* 56: 94–103.

Tribe, L. H. 1974. Ways not to think about plastic trees: New foundations for environmental law. *Yale Law Journal* 83: 1315–48.

Trimmer, S. ⟨1786⟩ 1977. *Fabulous histories, designed for instruction of children, respecting their treatment of animals.* London: T. Longman, 1786. (Later editions under title *The history of robins.*) Reprint: New York and London: Garland Publishing, 1977.

Truett, B. 1987. Letter on use of animals in biomedical research. (Criticizing C. Cohen (1986).) *New England Journal of Medicine* 316: 551.

Trull, F. L. 1987. Animal "rights" v. animal research: A worldwide movement challenges biomedical science. *Progress in Clinical and Biological Research* 229: 327–36.

Tuan, Y-F. 1984. *Dominance and affection: The making of pets.* New Haven, CT: Yale University Press. (Not cited.)

Tudge, C. 1973. Farmers in *loco parentis. New Scientist* 60: 179–81.

Turner, P., ed. 1983. *Animals in scientific research: An effective substitute for man?* London: Macmillan.

Tuttle, M. W. 1978. *Crimson cage.* Vineyard Haven, MA: Tashmoo Press.

Twain, M. ⟨1896⟩ 1973. Man's place in the animal world. In *The Works of Mark Twain,* ed. by P. Baender, vol. 19, 80–9. Berkeley: University of California Press.

———. 1901? *Mark Twain on vivisection.* Boston: New England Anti-Vivisection Society.

———. 1904. *A dog's tale.* New York: Harper.

Tyrrell, G. 1895. Jesuit zoophily: A reply. *Contemporary Review* 68: 708–15.

United States. 1966. *Animal dealer regulation.* Hearings before the Committee on Commerce, Senate, 89th Cong., 2d sess., 25, 28 March and 25 May 1966. Washington, DC: USGPO.

———. 1966–1985. Animal Welfare Act of 1966 (Public Law 89–544), amended in 1970 (Public Law 91–579), amended in 1976 (Public Law 94–279), amended in 1985 (Public Law 99–198). *United States Code.* Washington, DC: USGPO.

———. 1970. *Care of animals used for research, experimentation, exhibition, or held for sale as pets.* Hearings before the Subcommittee on Livestock and Grains of the Committee on Agriculture, House, 91st Cong., 2d. sess., 8 and 9 June 1970. Washington, DC: USGPO.

———. 1974. *Animal Welfare Act amendments of 1974.* Hearings before the Subcommittee on Livestock and Grains of the Committee on Agriculture, House, 93rd Cong., 2d sess., 6–8, 13–15, 20 August, 30 September, 2 October 1974. Washington, DC: USGPO.

———. 1975. *Animal Welfare Act amendments of 1975.* Hearings before the Subcommittee on Livestock and Grains of the Committee on Agriculture, House, 94th Cong., lst sess., 9 and 10 September 1975. Washington, DC: USGPO.

———. 1976. *Commission on humane treatment of animals.* Hearings before the Subcommittee of Livestock and Grains of the Committee on Agriculture, House, 94th Cong., 2d sess., 30 September 1976. Washington, DC: USGPO.

———. 1978. *The Belmont report: Ethical principles and guidelines for the protection of human subjects of research.* Department of Health, Education and Welfare Publication No. (OS) 78–0012. Washington, DC: USGPO.

———. 1981. *Trends in bioassay methodology, in vivo, in vitro and mathematical approaches.* National Institutes of Health. Washington, DC: USGPO.

———. 1982. *The use of animals in medical research and testing.* Hearings before the Subcommittee on Science, Research and Technology of the Committee on Science and Technology, House, 97th Cong., lst sess., 13 and 14 October 1981. Washington, DC: USGPO.

———. 1984a. *National symposium on imperatives in research animal use: Scientific needs and animal welfare.* National Institutes of Health publication 85–2746. Washington, DC: USGPO.

———. 1984b. *Improved standards for laboratory animals.* Hearing before Committee on Agriculture, Nutrition, and Forestry, Senate, 98th Cong., lst sess., 20 July 1983. Washington, DC: USGPO.

———. 1984–1987. *Laboratory animal welfare.* Specialized bibliography series (annual). Bethesda, MD: National Library of Medicine.

———. 1985. *Guide for the care and use of laboratory animals.* National Institutes of Health.

Washington, DC: USGPO.
———. 1986a. *Alternatives to animal use in research, testing, and education*. US Congress Office of Technology Assessment. Washington, DC: USGPO.
———. 1986b. *Public Health Service policy on humane care and use of laboratory animals*. (Revised as of September 1986.) Bethesda, MD: National Institutes of Health.
———. 1987. Animal welfare: Proposed rules. Department of Agriculture, Animal and Plant Health Inspection Service. 9 CFR Pts. 1 and 2. *Federal Register* 31 March 1987, 10292–10322.
Universities Federation for Animal Welfare. 1977–1987. Potters Bar, Herts, England. Partial list of publications: (1) *The care and management of farm animals*, ed. W. N. Scott, 1978. (2) *The UFAW handbook on the care and management of laboratory animals*, ed. T. B. Poole, 1987. (3) *Guidelines on the care of laboratory animals and their use for scientific purposes*, pt. 1. Incorporating provisions of the Animals (Scientific Procedures) Act 1986. Co-publisher: The Royal Society, 1987. (4) *Feral cats: Suggestions for control*, 1985. (5) *Tissue culture investigations*, 1982. (6) *Humane killing of animals*, 1978. (7) *Alternatives to factory farming: An economic appraisal*, 1983. (8) *Man and beast*, C. W. Hume, reprinted 1982. (9) *Status of animals in the Christian religion*, C. W. Hume, reprint 1980. (10) *Laboratory animal legislation*, P. McEwen, 1986. Summaries of national laws. (11) *A summary of the statute law relating to animal welfare in England and Wales*, pts. 1–3, W. Crofts, 1987. (12) Proceedings of recent symposia and workshops: (a) *The teaching of animal welfare*, 1987. (b) *Humane slaughter and euthanasia*, 1986. (c) *Self-awareness in domesticated animals*, 1981. (d) *Standards in laboratory animal management*, 1983. (e) *The humane control of land mammals and birds*, 1984. (f) *The ecology and control of feral cats*, 1980. (g) *The welfare of the food animals*, 1978. (h) *The pharmaceutical applications of cell culture*, 1977 (i) *The rational use of living systems in biomedical research*, 1972. (13) Hume Memorial Lectures: (a) *Conflicts and inconsistencies over animal welfare*, M. Midgley, 1986. (b) *Animals in society – A veterinary viewpoint*, F. J. Lawson Soulsby, 1985. (c) *Pain in animals*, A. Iggo, 1984. (d) *The teaching of responsibility*, B. E. Rollin, 1983. (e). *Science and sensibility*, G. R. Dunstan, 1982.
Universities Federation for Animal Welfare. 1979. *The welfare of the food animals*. Potters Bar, Herts: UFAW.
———. 1981. *Alternatives to intensive husbandry systems*. Potters Bar, Herts: UFAW.
———. 1983. *Animals in scientific research: An audio-visual list for use in higher education*. Potters Bar, Herts: UFAW and British Universities Film and Video Council.
———. 1986. *Laboratory animal legislation*. Potters Bar, Herts: UFAW.

VanDeVeer, D. 1976. Defending animals by appeal to rights. In [121, pp. 224–9].
———. 1979. Of beasts, persons, and the original position. *Monist* 62: 368–77.
———. 1980. Animal suffering. *Canadian Journal of Philosophy* 10: 463–71.
Varner, G. E. 1987. Do species have standing? *Environmental Ethics* 9: 57–72.
Vaughan, J. S. 1903–04. Cruelty to animals and theology. *The Humane Review* 4: 142–54.
Vendler, Z. 1972. *"Res cogitans": An essay in rational psychology*. Ithaca: Cornell University Press.
Vetri, K. 1987. Animal research and shelter animals: An historical analysis of the pound animal controversy. *St Louis University Law Journal* 31: 551–75.
Visscher, M. B. 1967. Medical research and ethics. *Journals of American Medical Association* 199: 631–6.
———. 1972. The newer antivivisectionists. *Proceedings of the American Philosophical Society* 116: 157–62.
———. 1975. The ethics of the use of lower animals in scientific study. In *Ethical constraints and imperatives in medical research*, 74–83. Springfield, IL: Charles C. Thomas.
———. 1979. Animal rights and alternative methods: Two new twists in the antivivisection movement. *Pharos* 42 (Fall): 11–19.

———. 1982. Review of B. E. Rollin's *Animal rights and human morality*. *New England Journal of Medicine* 306: 1303–4.

Voltaire. ⟨18th cent.⟩ 1962. *Philosophical dictionary*. Trans. P. Gay. New York: Basic Books.

Wade, N. 1976. Animal rights: NIH cat sex study brings grief to New York Museum. *Science* 194: 162–7.

Wagner, R. ⟨1879⟩ 1966. Against vivisection. In *Richard Wagner's prose works*, trans. by W. A. Ellis, vol. 6, 195–210. New York: Broude Brothers.

Walker, S. 1983. *Animal thought*. London: Routledge and Kegan Paul.

Wall, G. B. 1983. Animal suffering. In *Is God really good?* 93–107. Lanham, MD: University Press of America.

Walters, L. and Kahn, T. J., eds. 1975–1986. *Bibliography of bioethics*, vols. 1–12. Washington, DC: Kennedy Institute of Ethics. (Many entries under "Animal experimentation" and "Human experimentation," covering English-language journal and newspaper articles, monographs, essays, court decisions, bills, etc.)

Warnock, G. J. 1971. *The object of morality*. London: Methuen.

Warren, M. A. 1983. The rights of the nonhuman world. In *Environmental philosophy*, ed. by R. Elliott and A. Gare, 109–34. University Park, PA: Pennsylvania State University Press.

———. 1986. Difficulties with the strong animal rights position. *Between the Species* 2: 163–73.

Washburn, M. F. 1908. *The animal mind*. New York: Macmillan.

Wasserman, E. A. 1981. Comparative psychology returns. *Journal of the Experimental Analysis of Behavior* 35: 243–57.

———. 1983. Is cognitive psychology behavioral? *Psychological Record* 33: 6–11.

———. 1984. Animal intelligence: Understanding the minds of animals through their behavioral "ambassadors." In *Animal cognition*, ed. by H. L. Roitblat et al., 45–60. Hillsdale, NJ: Lawrence Erlbaum.

Watson, J. B. 1913. Psychology as the behaviorist sees it. *Psychological Review* 20: 158–77.

———. 1914. *Behavior: An introduction to comparative psychology*. New York: Henry Holt.

Wayman, S. 1966. Concentration camps for dogs. *Life* 60 (4 February): 22–9.

Weber, E. von. 1880? *The torture chamber of science*. (Trans. from German, 6th ed.) London: Victoria Street Society.

Weber, H. 1986. Democratic expression of public opinion on animal experimentation. *Journal of Medical Primatology* 15: 379–89.

Weiss, D. D. 1975. Professor Malcolm on animal intelligence. *Philosophical Review* 84: 88–95.

Weiss, P. 1947. *Nature and man*. New York: Henry Holt.

Welch, W. H. 1898. Objections to the antivivisection bill now before the Senate of the United States. *Journal of the American Medical Association* 30: 285–90.

———. 1900. Argument against Senate Bill 34, fifty-sixth Congress, first session, generally known as the "antivivisection bill." *Journal of the American Medical Association* 34: 1242–4, 1322–7.

Wells, H. G. 1927. For vivisection. *Sunday Express* (24 July).

———. 1934. *The island of Dr. Moreau*. New York: Dover.

Wemelsfelder, F. 1985a. The question of animal awareness. In (M. W. Fox and L. D. Mickley, eds. 1985a, 1–18).

———. 1985b. Animal boredom: Is a scientific study of the subjective experiences of animals possible? In (M. W. Fox and L. D. Mickley, eds. 1985a, 115–54).

Wenz, P. S. 1979. Act-utilitarianism and animal liberation. *Personalist* 60: 423–8.

———. 1988. Civil liberties and cruelty to animals. *Philosophical Forum* 19(4).

Wesley, J. ⟨1782⟩ 1985. The general deliverance. In *The works of John Wesley*, ed. by A. C. Outler, vol. 2, 437–50. Nashville, TN: Abingdon Press.

Westacott, E. 1949. *A century of vivisection and anti-vivisection*. Ashingdon, Rochford, Essex: C. W. Daniel.

Westermarck, E. A. 1939. Christianity and the regard for the lower animals. In *Christianity and morals*, 379–93. New York: Macmillan.

Whewell, W. 1852. *Lectures on the history of moral philosophy in England*. London: J. W. Parker.

White, L. 1967. The historical roots of our ecological crisis. *Science* 155: 1203–7.

White, P. 1973. *The vivisector*. London: Allen Lane.

White, R. J. 1971. Antivivisection: The reluctant hydra. *American Scholar* 40: 503–7. (Reprinted in [121, pp. 163–9].)

———. 1988. The facts about animal research. *Reader's Digest* (March): 127–32.

Whittall, J. D. 1981. *People and animals*. London: National Anti-Vivisection Society.

Whorton, J. C. 1977. "Tempest in a flesh-pot": The formulation of a physiological rationale for vegetarianism. *Journal of the History of Medicine and Allied Sciences* 32: 115–39.

Wilkinson, L., ed. 1980. *Earthkeeping: Christian stewardship of natural resources*. Grand Rapids, MI: William B. Eerdmans Publishing.

Wilks, S. 1881. Vivisection. *Nineteenth Century* (December): 936–48.

Will, J. 1986. The case for the use of animals in science. In (M. W. Fox and L. D. Mickley, eds. 1986, 205–13).

Willard, L. D. 1982. About animals having rights. *Journal of Value Inquiry* 16: 177–87.

Williams, B. 1973. *Problems of the self*. Cambridge: Cambridge University Press.

Wilson, E. O. 1975. *Sociobiology: The new synthesis*. Cambridge: Belknap Press of Harvard University Press.

Wise, S. M. 1983. Lawyers in the movement: Using courts for animals. *Animals' Agenda* (July–Aug): 8–9.

———. 1986. A day in court – corporations, towns, estates and ships can have one; farm animals cannot. *Animals' Agenda* (May): 14–15, 36.

Wittgenstein, L. 1953. *Philosophical investigations*. Trans. G. E. M. Anscombe. New York: Macmillan.

Wood, F. 1916. *Suffering and wrong: The message of the new religion*. London: G. Bell.

Wood-Gush, D. G. M. 1973. Animal welfare in modern agriculture. *British Veterinary Journal* 129: 167–74.

Woolman, J. ⟨1774⟩ 1922. *The journal and essays of John Woolman*, ed. by A. M. Gummere. London: Macmillan.

Woolsey, T. A. et al. 1987. The playwright, the practitioner, the politician, the president, and the pathologist: A guide to the 1900 Senate document titled "Vivisection." *Perspectives in Biology and Medicine* 30: 235–58. (About H. Burgh, A. Leffingwell, J. H. Gallinger, W. W. Keen, W. H. Welch.)

Wreen, M. 1984. In defense of speciesism. *Ethics and animals* 5: 47–60.

———. 1986a. My kind of person. *Between the Species* 2: 23–8.

———. 1986b. If at all humanly possible. *Between the Species* 2: 189–94.

Wundt, W. 1894. *Lectures on human and animal psychology*. London: Swan Sonnenschein.

Yntema, S. K. 1987. *Vegetarian children*. Ithaca, NY: McBooks Press.

Young, T. 1984. The morality of killing animals: Four arguments. *Ethics and animals* 5: 88–101.

Zola, J. C. et al. 1984. Animal experimentation: Issues for the 1980s. *Science, Technology, and Human Values* 9 (Spring): 40–50.

Appendix A
The Rights of Animals: A Declaration against Speciesism

Inasmuch as we believe there is ample evidence that many other species are capable of feeling, we condemn totally the infliction of suffering upon our brother animals, and the curtailment of their enjoyment, unless it be necessary for their own individual benefit.

We do not accept that a difference in species alone (any more than a difference in race) can justify wanton exploitation or oppression in the name of science or sport, or for food, commercial profit or other human gain.

We believe in the evolutionary and moral kinship of all animals and we declare our belief that all sentient creatures have rights to life, liberty and the quest for happiness.

We call for the protection of these rights.

This declaration was signed by some 150 people at the time of the symposium at Trinity College, Cambridge on 19 August 1977. The signatories included the following:

Richard Adams, John Alexander-Sinclair, Rev. Jack Austin, Mary Rose Barrington, Brigid Brophy, Bill Brown, R. MacAlastair Brown, John Bryant, Susan Bryant, Dr Stephen R. L. Clark, Rev. Kevin Daley, Carol Dear, Anne Douglass, Clare Druce, Maureen Duffy, Robert Elliot, Dr Michael Fox, Ann Cottrell Free, Prof. R. G. Frey, André Gallois, Clifford Goodman, Judith Hampson, Clive Hollands, Susan Hough, Lord Houghton, Robin Howard, Helen Jones, Ronnie Lee, Rev. Andrew Linzey, Jack Lucas, Ian MacPhail, John Melville, Mary Midgley, Chris Murphy, David Paterson, Kerstin Petersson, John Pitt, Ruth Plant, Prof. Tom Regan, Jan Rennison, Richard D. Ryder (Chairman, RSPCA Council), Mike Seymour-Rouse, Prof. Peter Singer, Violet Spalding, Dr Timothy Sprigge, Margery Sutcliffe, M. E. Tait, Angela Walder,

Robert Waldie, Phyllis Walker, Barbara Walton, Caroline Wetton, Dave Wetton, Alan Whittaker, Rev. B. Wrighton, Jon Wynne-Tyson, Robert Young.

(Reproduced from *Animals' Rights – A Symposium* [143, p. viii] with kind permission of RSPCA.)

Appendix B
Universal Declaration of the Rights of Animals

1. All animals are born with an equal claim on life and the same rights to existence.
2. All animals are entitled to respect. Man as an animal species shall not arrogate to himself the right to exterminate or inhumanely exploit other species. It is his duty to use his knowledge for the welfare of animals. All animals have the right to the attention, care, and protection of man.
3. No animals shall be ill-treated or be subject to cruel acts. If an animal has to be killed, this must be instantaneous and without distress.
4. All wild animals have the right to liberty in their natural environment, whether land, air, or water, and should be allowed to procreate. Deprivation of freedom, even for educational purposes, is an infringement of this right.
5. Animals of species living traditionally in a human environment have the right to live and grow at the rhythm and under the conditions of life and freedom peculiar to their species. Any interference by man with this rhythm or these conditions for purposes of gain is infringement of this right.
6. All companion animals have the right to complete their natural life span. Abandonment of an animal is a cruel and degrading act.
7. All working animals are entitled to a reasonable limitation of the duration and intensity of their work, to necessary nourishment, and to rest.
8. Animal experimentation involving physical or psychological suffering is incompatible with the rights of animals, whether it be for scientific, medical, commercial, or any other form of research. Replacement methods must be used and developed.
9. Where animals are used in the food industry they shall be reared, transported, lairaged, and killed without the infliction of suffering.
10. No animal shall be exploited for the amusement of man. Exhibitions and spectacles involving animals are incompatible with their dignity.
11. Any act involving the wanton killing of the animals is biocide, that is, a crime against life.

12. Any act involving the mass killing of wild animals is genocide, that is, a crime against the species. Pollution or destruction of the natural environment leads to genocide.

13. Dead animals shall be treated with respect. Scenes of violence involving animals shall be banned from cinema and television, except for human education.

14. Representatives of movements that defend animal rights should have an effective voice at all levels of government. The rights of animals, like human rights, should enjoy the protection of law.

(This declaration was adopted by the International League of the Rights of Animals and the affiliated national leagues in London, 21–23 September 1977. The declaration was solemnly proclaimed in Paris, 15 October 1978, at the House of the UNESCO. Detailed information on this declaration is available from Ligue Française des Droits de l'Animal [377].)

Appendix C
Audio-visuals: Films, Videotapes, Audiocassettes, Filmstrips, Musical Recordings

D. Pratt's (1986) *Animal films for humane education* describes 136 films, including filmstrips and videotapes, under the headings: attitudes toward animals, fights, food and commercial uses, hunting, performing animals, pets, research and testing, riding, service animals, transportation, trapping, veterinary medicine, wildlife, zoos. For each film there is description, producer, distributor, evaluative opinion, audience reaction, suggested audiences, discussion questions. G. Nilsson (1986, 190–7) annotates 75 films on endangered species and conservation. Universities Federation for Animal Welfare (1983) provides a list of films for use in higher education on animals in scientific research. C. R. Magel's [176] bibliography lists 31 films (entries 2688–2718).

People and animals [177] includes many films and filmstrips in recommended resources for humane education, preschool through grade six. Focus on Animals [484], in its current catalog, annotates 16 films and videotapes which it sells and rents: *We are all Noah; Suffer the animals; Unnecessary fuss; Britches; Breaking barriers; B. L. T.; Healthy, wealthy, and wise; Vegetarian cooking for the athlete; The guns of autumn; A voice in the wilderness; Never cry wolf; Voyages to save the whale; End of the game; Skins; Charlie, the dog nobody wanted; Kiss the animals goodbye; Voices I have heard.*

Michigan Media, University of Michigan Media Resources Center, Ann Arbor, MI 48103, publishes an annotated list of films and videos which it rents: "Animal Welfare and Endangered Species." The International Society for Animal Rights [344] rents videocassettes: *The animals are crying; The animals' film; B. L. T.; Eating for life; The hunter; The other barred; The vegetarian world; Hidden crimes; Products of pain: Inside the Gillette animal lab; We are all Noah; Animal liberation from laboratories.*

People for Ethical Treatment of Animals [503] sells and rents videos: *Unnecessary fuss; Britches; We are all Noah; The Silver Spring monkeys; Breaking barriers.* The RSPCA [451] issues a film and video catalog. Athene Trust [435] makes available the video *The choice is yours: Animal suffering or cruelty-free food?* Compassion in World

Farming [442] has two videos: *Hopping madness* (frogs' legs trade) and *Screaming for change* (tethered sows).

Chickens' Lib [439] rents the video *Chicken for dinner?* *Time to care* is a videotape on trapping available from Protection of Fur-Bearing Animals, 2235 Commercial Drive, Vancouver V5N 4B6, British Columbia. Animal rights and animal experimentation are covered by the video *About animals the question is . . .* produced by Progressive Animal Welfare Society, 15305 44th Ave West, Lynnwood, WA 98046. Luke Dommer of Committee to Abolish Sport Hunting [480] is featured in the video *A voice in the wilderness* available from Animal Rights Associates, Box 801, Trumbull, CT 06611. The film *Tools for research* is available from Bullfrog Films, Oley, PA 19547.

Lifeforce [364] is the source of five videos on animal experimentation: *Broken promises; Primates – Far from home; Psych research – A shocking story; Beau & Captain: Let them live; Canada – Part of the pain. Progress without pain*, a video on alternatives to the use of animals, is available from American Fund for Alternatives to Animal Research [460] and National Anti-Vivisection Society (London) [449].

Animals Rights Information Service [468] produces and distributes weekly video programs under the series title "Animal Rights Forum." An "Animal Rights" series of interviews with major animal rights activists is available on videotapes for broadcast on public access cable TV stations; contact Mary Valette, 154 Newbury St, No. 24, Peabody, MA 01960. Voice of Nature Network [515] is planning extensive, regular television coverage of animal rights issues.

A. Linzey and T. Regan discuss animal rights on audio tapes [287]. Audiocassettes of 70 radio broadcasts in the series "Food for the Thoughtful," on vegetarianism and animal rights, are available from Cultural Media Services, P.O. Box 1598, Soquel, CA 95073. Animal Rights Network [470] offers a 20-minute filmstrip slide presentation: *Animal rights: The issues, the movement.*

Four musical recordings: (1) *Animal liberation* album or cassette or compact disc (songs by Lene Lovich and Nina Hagen, Attrition, Chris and Cosey, Colourfield, Luc Van Acker, Shriekback, Captain Sensible and Howard Jones) available from People for Ethical Treatment of Animals [503]. (2) *Their eyes don't lie* (45-rpm extended-play record) produced by Student Action Corps for Animals [511]. (3) *Meat is murder* album by The Smiths, available from Mobile Animals Shop, 2 Onslow Gardens, London E18. (4) *Animal tracks* album by Country Joe McDonald, available from Animus, 34 Marshall St, London W1V 1LL.

Appendix D
Magazines and Journals

There are few magazines or journals devoted exclusively or heavily to animal rights and related issues: (1) *Animals' Agenda: The Animal Rights Magazine* (monthly). P.O. Box 5234, Westport, CT 06881, USA. An independent magazine of the animal rights movement, published by the Animal Rights Network [470], giving news, views and articles about animal rights, welfare and protection, and about the people who are making animal rights a major issue. Lists approximately 20 animal rights books which can be ordered from the magazine's office. (2) *Between the Species: A Journal of Ethics* (quarterly). P.O. Box 254. Berkeley, CA 94701, USA. Interdisciplinary journal, published by the Schweitzer Center of the San Francisco Bay Institute/Congress of Cultures [505], emphasizing philosophy but including religion, fiction, poetry, history, psychology, social criticism, literary criticism, biography. (3) *Animal Liberation: The Magazine* (quarterly). P.O. Box 221, Mitcham, Victoria 3132, Australia. Published by the State Branches of Animal Liberation [352], investigating and reporting on all aspects of animal rights and welfare worldwide, and serving as a forum for the promotion of non-speciesist attitudes. (4) *Anthrozoös* (quarterly). University Press of New England (publishing for the Delta Society), 17½ Lebanon St, Hanover, NH 03755, USA. A new multidisciplinary journal on the interactions of people, animals, and the environment. Serves as a scholarly forum for research and commentary, embracing such disciplines as sociology, psychology, philosophy, epidemiology, medicine, anthropology, and animal behavior.

Magazines on vegetarianism: (1) *Vegetarian Times* (monthly). P.O. Box 570, Oak Park, IL 60303, USA. Popular, largest vegetarian magazine in the world, containing news, investigative reports, information on diet and nutrition, recipes, profiles of vegetarians. Includes a ''Bookshelf'' listing 26 vegetarian cookbooks purchasable from the magazine's office; also books on nutrition, health and vegetarianism. (2) *The Vegetarian* (6 issues per year). The Vegetarian Society (UK) Ltd., Parkdale, Dunham Road, Altrincham, Ches WA14 4QG, England. ''The official voice of the vegetarian movement.'' Features news, articles, recipes, reviews, travel and restaurant information, etc.

R. Friedman (1988 forthcoming) will describe ten to fifteen currently available periodicals on animal rights. K. A. Reece (1988–89) provides information on many periodicals on animals, most of them published by animal rights or protection organizations.

Several recent issues of philosophical and other academic journals have exclusively or heavily dealt with animal rights issues: (1) *Philosophic Exchange*, vol. 1, no. 5, Summer 1974; (2) *Philosophy*, vol. 53, no. 206, October 1978; (3) *Inquiry*, vol. 22, nos. 1–2, Summer 1979; (4) *Etyka* (Poland), vol. 18, 1980; (5) *Monist*, vol. 70, no. 1, January 1987; (6) *St Louis University Law Journal*, vol. 31, no. 3, 1987; (7) *Philosophica* (Belgium), vol. 39, 1987. (8) *Journal of Medicine and Philosophy*, vol. 13, no. 2, May 1988.

Ulrich's international periodicals directory 1987–88 and *Irregular serials & annuals* 1987–88, both published by R. R. Bowker, New York and London, cite magazines and journals and serials under the headings: ''Agriculture – Poultry and Livestock,'' ''Agriculture – Dairying and Dairy Products,'' ''Medical Sciences – Experimental Medicine, Laboratory Technique,'' and ''Veterinary Science.'' *The international directory of little magazines and small presses* 1987–88, published by Dustbooks, Paradise, CA, describes a small number of magazines under the heading ''Animals.''

P. Greanville (1988a) discusses thirteen journals and newsletters, published by the ''laboratory animal industry,'' promoting animal experiments and testing, and frequently containing reactions to the animal rights movement. Greanville (1988b) analyzes eleven agrijournals which promote the ''animal food industry'' and which often react to the animal rights movement.

Etica & animali is a new semi-annual journal in Italian. Address: Via Marradi, 2, 20123 Milano, Italy. Mainly translations of articles and fiction in English language. Issue No. 1, 1988, contains articles by T. Regan, S. F. Sapontzis, G. Daws, P. Singer, I. B. Singer, D. VanDeVeer, M. Midgley and P. Cavalieri.

Behavioural & political animal studies is a new bi-annual published by Animal Archives, PO Box 13–104, Hamilton, New Zealand. Emphasis on animal rights, non-exploitive animal studies, and alternatives to animal exploitation. First issue (July 1988) contains articles by G. Hewitt (computer models and animal experiments), R. Latto (animal consciousness), R. W. Loftin (hunting), E. W. Kienholz (change of heart by former experimenter; vegetarianism; human slavery and animal slavery), R. Kalechofsky (''Metaphors of nature: Vivisection and pornography – The Manichean machine''; this article also in *Between the species*, 4 (Summer 1988), 179–85).

The editors of *Vegetarian times* present the *Vegetarian Times guide to natural food restaurants in the US and Canada*, compiled by D. B. Weisenthal. Avery Publishing Group, Garden City Park, NY, 1988, 154 pp. Over 1,000 restaurants.

Appendix E
Sources of Products which have not been tested on Animals and/or which are free, or maximally free, from Animal Ingredients

Personal care with principle: A guide to choosing cruelty-free cosmetics and products from major manufacturers. 39 pp. Published by and available from National Anti-Vivisection Society (Chicago) [499]. Lists over 100 firms, worldwide, manufacturing cosmetics and personal care products which *do not* use animal ingredients and/or use animals in laboratories; also 12 firms in same category manufacturing household products. Lists 45 firms manufacturing cosmetics and personal care products which *do* use animal ingredients and/or use animals in laboratories; also 16 manufacturers of household products in the same category. Lists over 260 firms which did not respond to requests for information in regard to tests on animals and/or animal ingredients.

The Compassionate Shopper (3 issues per year). Published by Beauty Without Cruelty USA (not affiliated with the cosmetic company or animal defense societies of the same name), 175 West 12th St, New York, NY 10011, USA. Provides information on firms and brands in regard to alternatives to fashion and cosmetic items using animal ingredients or involving tests on animals.

PETA News, published by People for the Ethical Treatment of Animals [503], has a Special Edition titled "Animals Poisoned and Blinded in Product Tests." Describes the Draize Eye Test and the LD50 Test. Lists 39 manufacturers which do not test on animals. Reproduces catalog issued by Amberwood, Route 1, Box 206, Milner, GA 30257, USA, listing and describing products (household, skin care, hair care, personal care, cosmetics, fragrance) from various companies, and which can be ordered by mail, and which contain no animal ingredients and have not been tested on animals.

Choose Cruelty-Free magazine, published by British Union for the Abolition of Vivisection [437], is one of many pieces of literature used in this organization's "Choose Cruelty-Free" campaign for the use of products free of animal testing or ingredients.

The Cruelty-Free Shopper by Lis Howlett is published by and available from The

Vegan Society [455]. In its 124 pages the book lists thousands of products which contain no animal products and which have not involved animal testing. Sections include food and drink, toiletries and cosmetics, remedies and supplements, footwear and clothing, household goods and gift ideas.

Mark Gold's *Living without cruelty: Choose a cruelty-free lifestyle* (Green Print, Marshall Pickering, 3 Beggarwood Lane, Basingstoke, Hants RG23 7LP, England, 1988, 192 pp.; also available through Animal Aid [433]) makes the connections between abuse of animals and abuse of humans. Contents include: animal suffering, human health, meat and drugs, dairy produce good for you?, human hunger, vegetarianism for a greener world, living without cruelty, experiments on animals, beyond the food cupboard, parents and children, shopping guide, recipes for change by Sarah Brown, living without cruelty in action.

Index

The Index is a single alphabetical sequence of authors, titles, subjects, persons, countries and organizations. All entries are in some way related to animals. Examples: the entry "behaviorism" should be interpreted to mean "behaviorism and/on animals," the entry "poetry" to mean "poetry on animals," the entry "Christianity" to mean "Christianity and/on animals." Numbers without brackets refer to page numbers. Numbers within brackets refer to item numbers in Parts II and III.

Marine Mammal Protection Act 1972
 (US), [113], [125]
marine mammals, 29, 52, 57, [113],
 [125], [158], [207], [296], [319],
 [338], [467], [471], [482], [487],
 [508]
Markham, E., [73]
Markham, W. O., [70]
Marsh, F. H., 52
Marsh, N., 42
Martin, M., 23
Martin, P. W. D., 35
Martin, R., 53, [16], [26], [89]
Martinengo-Cesaresco, E., 4
Martin's Act (UK), 32, 53, [26]
Marx, K., 4
Mason, J., 41, 43, [163], [224], [246]
Mason, W. A., 36
Masri, Al-Hafiz B. A., 62, [269], [290]
Massachusetts Society for the Prevention
 of Cruelty to Animals, [493]
Mathiot, E., [327]
Matthews, G. B., 6, 12, [128]
Mayo, D. G., 20-1, [207]
media and animals, [178]
Medical Research Council (UK), [98]
Medical Research Modernization
 Committee (US), 40, [494]
medicine, human, 39-40, 50, [84], [231],
 [233], [272], [329], [494]
medicine, veterinary, 19, 32, 39, 44-5,
 50, 227 (UFAW), 235, [306], [473],
 [494]
medicine and animals, 26-45, 50, 233
MEDLINE database, 34
Medobcinsko Drustvo Proti Mucenju
 Zivali (Yugoslavia), [517]
Melville, J., 231
memory capacity of animals, 11, 14, 29,
 [30], [208]
Menander, 4
Mendel, L. B., 65
Mendus, S., 6
mental capacities of animals, 10, 14, 27-9,
 31, 59, [30], [41-2], [80], [117],
 [121], [317-18]
Merleau-Ponty, M., [130]
Merrill, G. F., 37
Merton, T., [296]
Metcalfe, H., [98]
Metcalfe, W., [44]
Metz, H., 55
Mexico

laws, 56
 organization, 177
mice, 12, 54-5
Michelet, J., [44]
Mickley, L. D., 44, [261]
Midgley, M., 12, 16, 21, 25, 227
 (UFAW), 231, 238, [102], [121],
 [129], [185], [206], [246-7], [262],
 [317]
military use of animals, [437], [503]
Mill, J. S., x, 8, [121], [267]
Millennium Guild (US), [495]
Miller, H. B., 25, [207]
Miller, N. E., 37-8, [234]
Mills, B., [293]
Mills, E., [293]
Mills, W., 27-8
Ministries for Animals (US), 60, [496]
misery of animals, x, [30]
Mobilization for Animals e.V. (Germany
 - Federal Republic), [383]
Monck, W. H. S., [69]
Montagu, A., [130], [198]
Montague, P., 16
Montaigne, M. de, 5, [44], [47], [121]
Montefiore, H., 59, 61, [156]
Monthly catalog of government publications
 (US), 35
Moore, J. H., x, 34, 65, [53], [65-6]
moral agents, animals as, 14
moral behavior of animals, 13, [189]
moral status of animals, 14-20, 25,
 [24-5], [65-6], [79], [83], [96-7],
 [121-2], [131], [137], [140-3], [151],
 [156], [169], [171], [176], [181],
 [184], [195], [204], [206-9], [237],
 [242], [244], [246], [274], [277],
 [283], [292], [299], [301-3], [307-8],
 [315], [317], [320], [328], [335]
Moran, V., 39, 49, [238], [291]
More, T., [44]
Moretti, D. S., 54
Morgan, C. L., 27, 29-30, [318]
Morocco, organization, 177
Morris, C., 51-2, [88]
Morris, R. K., [130]
Morrison, M., [185]
Morse, M., 216
Moseley, R. E., 17
Moss, A. W., 53
Moss, D., [330]
Moss, T. H., 35
Mugford, R. A., [187]

wisdom of animals, 202 (G. Cowley)
Wise, S. M., 52, [275]
Wittgenstein, L., 10, 12, [318]
Wolff, E., [327]
Wollstonecraft, M., [15]
Wood, D., [97]
Wood, F., 65
Wood, J. G., 59, [32]
Wood-Gush, D. G. M., 30, 43, [187]
Woodruff, G., [187]
Woodstream Corporation, [512]
Woolman, J., 58, 61
Woolsey, T. A., 33
Wordsworth, W., [61], [73], [296], [307]
working animals (*see also* service animals),
    233, 235
Working Party (UK), 44, [156]
world hunger argument for vegetarianism,
    22, 66, [124]
World League Against Vivisection, [98]
World Society for the Protection of
    Animals, [347]
World Week of Prayer for Animals, [322]
Wreen, M., 19–20
Wrighton, B., 232
Wundt, W., 27
Wynne, A., [178]

Wynne-Tyson, J., 66, 232, [143], [153],
    [249]

Xenocrates, 4
Xenophanes, 4
Xenophon, 4

Yerkes Primate Laboratories, [81]
Yntema, S. K., 66
Youatt, W., 34, 59, [25]
Young, R., 232
Young, T., 16, 18, 20, [19]
Young Vegetarians (UK), [456]
Yugoslavia, organization, 196

Zeno, 4
Zola, J. C., 35
Zoo Check (UK), [457]
zoocentrism, [53]
zoophily, 15, [39]
zoos, 50, 202 (M. Clifton), 215 (V.
    McKenna), 233, 235, [62], [158],
    [178], [182], [217], [235], [246],
    [257], [260], [281], [286], [306],
    [317], [332], [343], [457], [489]
Zoroastrianism, [300]